Other books by Jerre Mangione

Fiction

The Ship and the Flame
Night Search
Life Sentences for Everybody

Nonfiction

Mount Allegro
Reunion in Sicily
A Passion for Sicilians: The World Around Danilo Dolci
America Is Also Italian
The Dream and the Deal

THE DREAM AND THE DEAL

The Federal Writers' Project, 1935–1943

THE DREAM
AND THE DEAL

The Federal Writers' Project, 1935–1943

by Jerre Mangione

UNIVERSITY OF PENNSYLVANIA PRESS
Philadelphia
1983

The author is grateful for permission to quote from the following sources:

"The Inquiry" by Weldon Kees from *The Collected Poems of Weldon Kees* edited by Donald Justice. Copyright 1943 by Weldon Kees. Copyright © 1960 by John A. Kees. First published in *Poetry* in July, 1938. Reprinted by permission by *Poetry* and the University of Nebraska Press.

Orphans in Gethsemane by Vardis Fisher. Copyright © 1960 by Vardis Fisher. Reprinted by permission of Mrs. Vardis Fisher

"Thinking of Russia" by H. H. Lewis is reprinted by permission of B. C. Hagglund, publisher of the pamphlet, *Thinking of Russia*, in 1931.

"The Liberal" by H. H. Lewis first appeared in Jack Conroy's magazine, *Rebel Poet*, published in October–December, 1931. It is reprinted here by permission of Mr. Conroy.

Second paperback edition published in 1983 by the University of Pennsylvania Press
First published in 1972 by Little, Brown and Company
First paperback edition published in 1974 by Avon Books
Copyright © 1972 by Jerre Mangione

Library of Congress Cataloging in Publication Data

Mangione, Jerre Gerlando, 1909-
    The dream and the deal.

    "Selected publications of the WPA Federal Writers'
Project and the Writers' Program": p.
      Bibliography: p.
      Includes index.
      1. Writers' Program—History. I. Title.
E175.4W9M3 1983   973.917   83-1165
ISBN 0-8122-1141-3 (pbk.)

Printed in the United States of America

For all my friends, dead and alive,
who were part of the Federal Writers' Project

Acknowledgments

This book tells for the first time the comprehensive story of an extraordinary governmental enterprise — the Federal Writers' Project (1935–1943).* In attempting to breathe life into a saga that has almost passed into the desiccating realm of history, I interviewed some seventy former members of the Writers' Project in different parts of the country (see pages 403–404 for a list of their names), and corresponded with others. The extent to which this book succeeds in recapturing the atmosphere and drama of the Project experience should be largely attributed to the information and impressions transmitted to me by these men and women.

It was my good fortune to reach in time two men, now dead, who were key figures in the Project's history: Henry G. Alsberg, the Project's national director until 1939, on whose staff I served; and Vardis Fisher, the novelist, who directed the Writers' Project in Idaho. Alsberg died in November 1970, at the age of eighty-nine; Fisher, age seventy-three, died in July 1968, barely a month after I had interviewed him in Boise, Idaho. Unfortunately, some of the others who had played major roles in the Project story (Jacob Baker, George W. Cronyn, Joseph Gaer, Clair Laning, John Newsom, Lyle Saxon, and Richard Wright, among others) were either dead or on the verge of death by the time I began gathering material for this book.

As for the survivors, I am deeply indebted to Dora Thea Hettwer of

---

* After July 1939 the Writers' Project was conducted under state sponsorship and was known as the WPA Writers' Program.

ACKNOWLEDGMENTS

New York City, a member of the Project's Central Office from its first day to the last, who was Alsberg's executive secretary through most of his directorship. Miss Hettwer was able to provide me with many valuable records, and with personal reminiscences that helped to revive my own memories of the Project. I also owe special thanks to Katharine Kellock, the Project's tours editor, for permission to quote from her personal papers in the Library of Congress, and for helping me locate some of the basic data for this work.

Other former members of the Project who supplied me with useful records were Benjamin A. Botkin of Croton-on-Hudson, N.Y.; Jack Conroy of Moberly, Mo.; Stella B. Hanau of New York City; Reed Harris of Washington, D.C.; Marion Knoblauch Franc of Chicago; Bert James Loewenberg of Bronxville, N.Y.; Carl Malmberg of Warner, N.H.; Lisle Reese of Winter Park, Fla.; Ellen Tarry of New York City; Donald Thompson of New York City; Rudolph Umland of Prairie City, Kans.; Charles van Ravenswaay of Winterthur, Del.

The following ex-Project members were also especially helpful: Jack Balch, the late Josef Berger (Jeremiah Digges), Sterling A. Brown, John Cheever, Earl Conrad, Paul Corey, Miriam Allen deFord, Leon (Bill) Dorais, Ralph Ellison, Lawrence Estavan, Mary Lloyd, James McGraw, Vincent McHugh, Lawrence Morris, Harold Rosenberg, Harry Roskolenko, Morton W. Royse, and George F. Willison.

I also wish to express gratitude for illuminating letters that arrived during the years 1967–1970 from these former members of the Project: Conrad Aiken, Nelson Algren, Allan Angoff, Saul Bellow, Howard McKinley Corning, Harold Coy, Alexander Crosby, Edward Dahlberg, Billie S. Jensen, Leon Srabian Herald, Norman Macleod, Frank Mead, George McMillan, Sam Ross, Arthur M. Saxe, Basil Vaerlen, Marguerite Yancey. A number of friends who were not members of the Project were able to add to my knowledge of it, among them Daniel Aaron, Benjamin Appel, Whitfield Bell, Millen Brand, Nina Collier, Julius Davidson, Arthur and Elizabeth Goldschmidt, the late Josephine Herbst, Alfred Kazin, James Michener, Harvey O'Connor, Evanell Powell, Richard Powell.

By correspondence or interview, I obtained indispensable information about the Project's activities around the country from sixteen men and women who had once served as Project state directors: Ray A. Billington, Carita D. Corse, the late Vardis Fisher, John T. Frederick, Irene Fuhlbruegge, J. Harris Gable, Muriel E. Hawks, Dorris Westall Isaacson,

Curtis D. MacDougall, Harold G. Merriam, Dale Morgan, Ethel Schlasinger Overby, Lisle Reese, Harry Shaw, Charles van Ravenswaay, Agnes Wright Spring.

Elsewhere in this book is a listing of the sources I consulted. Here I would like to single out four secondary sources that I found particularly valuable: Daniel Aaron's *Writers on the Left,* which helped me understand more fully the effect of the Depression on the political attitudes of American writers; William F. McDonald's *Federal Relief Administration and the Arts,* which provided me with essential information about the origins and operations of the Writers' Project; and two Ph.D. theses, Kathleen O'Connor McKinzie's "Writers on Relief, 1935–1942," which helped me unsnarl the knotty adventures of the New York City Writers' Project; and Ronald Warren Taber's "The Federal Writers' Project in the Pacific Northwest: A Case Study," which added significantly to my knowledge of how the Project operated in the states of Washington, Oregon and Idaho.

My research efforts were made easier by the kindness and diligence of librarians and archivists in Philadelphia, Washington, D.C., Chicago, New York City, Berkeley, San Francisco, Denver, Lincoln (Nebraska), Salt Lake City, Columbia (Missouri), Boston, and Seattle. My thanks to the manuscript division of the University of Washington library for permitting me to examine correspondence in the Mary Farquharson Collection. I am grateful to Robert Kvasnicka and his staff at the National Archives, and to Linda Kosmin of Drexel University, whose generous bibliographical assistance lightened my labors considerably. Special thanks are due to Arthur Scharf of Pittsburgh, who compiled the checklist of selected Project books and pamphlets that supplements my history; and who loaned me his scrapbook containing book reviews of the major Project publications.

I also want to express my appreciation for the encouragement and support I received throughout this undertaking from Kenneth Burke, Thomas C. Cochran, George W. Corner, Malcolm Cowley, Loren Eiseley, Gerald Freund, Edward P. Hutchinson, Robert M. Lumiansky, Ralph M. Sargent, Harry Sions, Robert E. Spiller, and J. Kellum Smith, Jr. Financial support came chiefly from the Rockefeller Foundation; the research grant it awarded me in 1968 enabled me to gather material for this book on a broader geographic scale than would have been possible otherwise. I am also grateful to the American Philosophical Society for a 1970 sup-

ACKNOWLEDGMENTS

plementary research grant; and to the University of Pennsylvania, which granted me a year's leave of absence, 1968–1969, for travel and research.

My most heartfelt thanks are for Patricia Mangione, an unfailing source of strength, who often took time out from her painting to counsel me and to help with the variety of chores that inevitably grow out of a project as involved as this one.

J.M.

Contents

Illustrations

ILLUSTRATIONS

THE DREAM AND THE DEAL

The Federal Writers' Project, 1935–1943

One.

The Death of a Dream

Four months before my job as coordinating editor of the Federal Writers' Project came to an end, I received the following note from the White House:

May 7, 1939

My dear Mr. Mangione:

Mrs. Roosevelt has heard through Mrs. Fayerweather that you are in Washington at present, and she hopes you can come to supper on Sunday, May 14th, at 7:30 o'clock.

She is not sure that the President will be there, but she hopes that you can come. She has asked me to say that these suppers are most informal, and that the President usually wears a business suit.

Sincerely yours,

Edith Helm
Secretary to Mrs. Roosevelt

Still at an age when exhilaration came easily, I could not help spreading the news among friends and colleagues. Henry G. Alsberg, my chief and director of the Federal Writers' Project, heard about it and summoned me to his office to find out how it happened that one of his assistants had been asked to dine at the White House and he had not. I explained that the invitation had nothing to do with my Writers' Project job; it had been issued in deference to Mrs. Roosevelt's close friendship with Mrs. Charles S. Fayerweather, a writer of juvenile books then in her sixties, who as a child had played with Eleanor Roosevelt and her cousin Franklin. Mrs. Fayerweather and I had become friends through her books; she was one of the authors assigned to my care in the publishing house where, until a few years before, I had been an editor.

Alsberg seemed relieved to learn that the invitation could not be interpreted as a slight to him, and I thought he was finished with the matter. But on considering it further, he decided there was no reason why my visit to the White House need be exclusively social; he became convinced that it offered a perfect opportunity to enlist Mrs. Roosevelt's help in saving the Federal Writers' Project from what appeared to be its imminent fate, the congressional block.

It was not the first time that the Project had been in jeopardy, but never before had it been as close to the knife. The attacks from Congress and the press began four years before when the Roosevelt administration first announced its intention to sponsor four projects that would hire needy writers, actors, artists, and musicians. To the noisy criticism that followed the announcement Harry Hopkins, overlord of the Works Progress Administration that would directly supervise the projects, had a bland retort: "Hell, they've got to eat just like other people."

That was in 1935 when the Roosevelt administration could easily afford to be nonchalant about its adversaries. With the national economy depending on New Deal efforts to rescue it from the paralysis of the Depression, the Roosevelt administration was then at the height of its powers, and its critics could do little more than groan and grumble. But now, in the spring of 1939, the opposition was far stronger, and some twenty-five thousand employees of Federal One (the common official name for the WPA's four arts projects) were in immediate danger of losing their jobs.

The hostility toward the arts projects had been concretized in the House of Representatives the previous fall by Congressman Martin Dies and his newly formed Committee to Investigate Un-American Activities. A freeswinging Texan with a passion for headlines, Dies had quickly endeared himself to the adversaries of the New Deal by selecting the Writers' and Theater projects as his prime targets. His melodramatic charges of Communist activity and propaganda put his committee on the front page of every American newspaper and gained him the support of every Republican, conservative Democrat, and philistine who had long been outraged by the New Deal's propensity for experimental ventures.

The Dies Committee had a field day pillorying the two projects. Its technique, which was to be emulated a decade later by Senator Joseph McCarthy with even more monstrous success, was simple enough: rules of evidence and due process went by the board; witnesses with personal or political axes to grind were permitted to incriminate members of the projects without being confronted by them. President Roosevelt called the Dies procedure "sordid," and a number of legislators publicly shared his disgust, but the public opinion polls indicated that most Americans considered Dies a fine patriot.

No sooner had the Dies Committee held its final hearings on the projects than a subcommittee of the House Committee on Appropriations, headed by Congressman Clifton A. Woodrum of Virginia, resumed the attack. Unfortunately for both projects, Harry Hopkins, who had fathered Federal One from its infancy, was no longer WPA administrator. Early in 1939 he had been succeeded by Colonel Francis C. Harrington, a no-nonsense army engineer, who had little patience with the vagaries of the arts projects.

The attacks by the two congressional committees encouraged other congressmen to proclaim their antagonisms. A few weeks before my White House invitation came, Congressman Keefe of Wisconsin had spent thirty minutes on the floor of the House lambasting the Writers' Project for saying in its 1937 guidebook, *Washington: City and Capital,* that George Washington Parke Custis, the step-grandson of George Washington and his son by adoption, had bequeathed a tract of land "to his colored daughter, Maria Syphax." The congressman's indignation was compounded by the discovery that the Writers' Project source of information for the statement was a black historian. Other congressmen joined in the protest, but they were finally silenced by the Project's documented proof that Mr. Custis had indeed fathered a daughter whose mother was a Negro slave in the service of Martha Washington.

However effective the enemies of the Writers' Project were in their smear campaign, they were unable to discredit the excellent quality of the state and city guidebooks that the Project had begun to produce in large numbers. Alsberg's files were stuffed with reviews and letters from the nation's literary critics, lavishly praising the books in the Project's American Guide Series. Van Wyck Brooks had recently written him: "It is grand to see that the country in general is waking up to the work you are doing. As one who has watched it from the beginning, I can't tell you how grateful I am to you. Every college in the country should give you a Ph.D. Of

5

all the impossibly difficult jobs, this one has been carried out with a skill, taste and judgment that seems to be astounding. The reviewer was certainly right who said the other day that the American Guide Series will still be going strong when most of our current books are dead and forgotten." In a postscript Brooks added, ". . . and when people have forgotten the rubbish about 'Red propaganda.' "

Despite such accolades, Alsberg realized that the enthusiasts of the American Guide Series consisted of a small minority of Americans who read the book review sections or wrote for them. The majority of Americans were inclined to believe the front-page headlines created by Dies. Sensing that the Project's troubles would worsen, on January 28, 1939, a few weeks after he had testified before the Dies Committee, Alsberg transferred his personal files to his home. When investigators from the Woodrum Committee barged into his office the following month to demand access to his safe, apparently expecting to find incriminating documents, all they found were an extra pair of suspenders and a quantity of Bisodol, the medication Alsberg's doctor prescribed for his nervous stomach. The episode caused a good deal of chortling around the office, but the prevailing mood was deep anxiety over the fate of the Project. Already the Washington newspapers were hinting that it would not live out the fiscal year.

Secretly, Alsberg was doing what he could to change the situation. He wrote personal letters to his most trusted field workers warning them that the life of the Project was in danger and suggesting they persuade leading citizens to write their congressmen and senators in its behalf. He also wrote to Benjamin Cohen, a high official in the New Deal who was said to have the ear of the President, presenting detailed reasons why it would be advisable to divorce the arts projects from the WPA relief setup and establish them as a permanent government activity within an old-line agency like the Department of the Interior. The proposal was an intelligent one, yet it must have struck Cohen, a canny New Dealer, as a pathetically naïve plea, the last-ditch effort of an overly anxious general to save himself and his troops.

Alsberg was not lacking in shrewdness but often it was vitiated by a relentless optimism streaked with naïveté. Yet to work with him was to come under the spell of his faith in the future, a kind of dogged if somewhat doleful conviction that somehow complex problems could be solved, virtue could triumph. Without this late-nineteenth-century spirit, which

Henry G. Alsberg, director of the Federal Writers' Project, and Mrs. Franklin D. Roosevelt

must have been ingrained in him as a child, he might not have been able to cope with the tumult and chaos of the Project as long as he had. Although there was an air of gloom about him as he spoke to me about my impending visit to the White House, he almost convinced me that somehow I might be able to induce Mrs. Roosevelt to exercise her responsibility as the official godmother of the arts projects, a role she had been neglecting of late, and thus prevent their demise.

In his slow and heavy drawl Alsberg recalled instances of Mrs. Roosevelt's personal involvement with the Writers' Project. At one point during its planning stage she had sent a limousine around to his office with the invitation that Alsberg and his aides join her at the White House to describe the program they had in mind. Later, at a crucial time when it appeared that the federal arts program might be placed under state control, Mrs. Roosevelt had interceded in behalf of the four angry Project directors, with the result that Jacob Baker, the administrator of Federal One, who advocated state control, was replaced by a staunch federalist, Ellen S. Woodward, a friend of Mrs. Roosevelt.

It was Alsberg's belief that Mrs. Roosevelt had not lost interest in the Writers' Project but that of late she had become too preoccupied with other matters to keep track of its accomplishments. He was confident that once I impressed her with their quality and quantity she would use her influence to rescue the Project. Not knowing Mrs. Roosevelt, except by reputation, I had no reason to dispute this happy theory. The main problem, as I told Alsberg, would be to find the right moment to introduce the subject. It was after all a social occasion, Mother's Day in fact. "You'll find it," Alsberg said with a trace of weariness, and then proceeded with the help of his chief assistant, Clair Laning, to fill me with information about the Project's achievements which they expected me to pour into Mrs. Roosevelt's good ear.

In less than four years the Project had produced some three hundred twenty publications, of which about one hundred were full-sized books. Besides state, city, small town, and highway guides, the list included works on subjects as diverse as ethnic studies, place names, folklore, and zoology. More than six hundred other books were in various stages of completion. It made quite an impressive record, especially when one considered the difficulties of conducting a project made up largely of workers with little or no writing experience, most of whom had to qualify as paupers before they could be employed. The nationwide scope of the Project added to its problems; there were offices in each of the forty-eight states as well as in New York City and Washington, D.C.

The Project had hit its peak of employment in April 1936 with 6,686 men and women on its rolls. By 1939 it was down to 3,500 employees but its goals were as big and diverse as ever, and it was operating more efficiently than it had at any other time. Only a few months before, *Pathfinder* had called the Project's program "the biggest, fastest, most original research job in the history of the world." While reminding me of all this, Alsberg and Laning stuffed me with more data than I could possibly remember about the hundreds of sponsors and publishers underwriting the cost of Project publications (a total expenditure estimated at more than a million and a half dollars) and the twelve thousand volunteer consultants (most of them college professors) who were checking or helping with the preparation of Project manuscripts.

They even quoted me excerpts from articles and book reviews, written by prominent critics, which attested to the importance and the quality of the published books. But there was no need to do that. Some of the statements were forever etched in the memories of all of us who, working for the glory of the Writers' Project, felt we had never done anything of more value in our lifetime and suspected that it would be difficult if not impossible to ever find again a method of earning a living that could involve us as wholly and selflessly. Notwithstanding the dismaying confusion that attended nearly everything we did, we had the sense of being part of a significant historical event. In a literal sense, we *were* making history, for nothing like the Writers' Project or the other three federal arts projects had ever been tried by any nation anywhere.

Alsberg's recital of achievement left me dejected, more conscious of his worry that the Project might come to an end before it could complete its main work. By the time I was ready to go to the White House in my business suit, the sense of euphoria the invitation had evoked was gone, and I was in the throes of a new fear: that once I set foot in the White House I would become hopelessly tongue-tied. Only as I was ushered into the second-floor living room of the Roosevelts did I begin to breathe more easily. The warmth of Mrs. Roosevelt's greeting, along with the friendly landscape of the room, with its sprawl of pillows, books, and Sunday newspapers, quieted my nerves.

There were only four other guests, all of them old acquaintances of the Roosevelts who were spending the weekend there. With the exception of

Marguerite LeHand, the President's private secretary, their names were unfamiliar to me. To my disappointment, there was no sign of Franklin D. Roosevelt, but while we were taking our places at the table — I found myself on Mrs. Roosevelt's left, next to her good ear — the President was rolled down the dining room ramp and steered to the head of the table. It was startling to see him for the first time, and imprisoned in a wheelchair, but only for a moment did I feel any pity; the astonishing vitality of the man at once filled the room like a burst of song.

As if the guests were responding to it, from the start of the supper there was a general hubbub around the table which smacked of a family free-for-all, with everyone competing for attention, except when F.D.R., with his dominating voice, chose to engage in a monologue. Before I was able to succumb to the conversational informality, I spoke only to Mrs. Roosevelt, chiefly about Merle Colby, a colleague on the Writers' Project, who had recently returned from an assignment in Puerto Rico with some observations about the growing fascist movement there.

Colby had brought back with him a snapshot of a San Juan bus bearing the sign: VIA ELEANOR ROOSEVELT. Then and there I presented it to her with Colby's compliments, thinking it might provide me with a cue to talk about the Writers' Project. But Mrs. Roosevelt appeared to be less impressed by the fact that a street in San Juan had been named after her than she was by the report of fascist activity there. She urged me to tell the President about it, and when I had failed to find an opening in his flow of talk, she stopped him in the middle of a sentence, announcing in a rather peremptory tone of voice: "Franklin, Mr. Mangione has something to say to you."

Later, when it was too late, I realized that with sufficient cunning I could have used Merle Colby's name to effect a rapid transition from the subject of fascism in Puerto Rico to that of the Writers' Project in jeopardy. But at the time I was so carried away with my ability to deliver to the President of the United States a two-minute discourse on the Puerto Rican situation without a single stutter that, in a moment of treacherous self-congratulation, I came to an abrupt end, relinquishing the floor to the President.

There was no other opportunity to talk about the Project during the supper. Some of the topics discussed seemed far more trivial, others so important that the fate of the Project seemed puny by comparison. The administration's foreign policy as it related to the possibility of a second world war was the topic that commanded the most sustained attention, which was not surprising considering that it was the spring of 1939, four months before the Nazi army was to march into Poland. The imminence of the war had created a turning point in the evolution of the New Deal: the end of radical social reforms, the beginning of a heavy concern with military defense problems. For the first time since he entered office, the President, in his New Year message to Congress, had proposed a national defense budget larger than the one requested for the administration's public works program, and had strongly urged that provisions be made for national defense on a wartime scale.

Throughout the supper I had been struck by the President's buoyant optimism — it seemed to generate from him as naturally as heat from fire. But as he dwelled on the necessity of alerting the American people about the dangers of clinging to an isolationist point of view, he sounded worried. Acknowledging that he had "a long way to go" before he could convince enough Americans that his administration's policy of giving all possible aid to England and France made good sense, he wondered if the tide of isolationist public opinion could be turned with a blunt presentation of the European situation, expressed in three short sentences that might provoke a realistic awareness of the pressing issues:

1. There was a fifty-fifty chance that there would be a general war.

2. There was a fifty-fifty chance that Nazi Germany and Italy would join forces and win the war.

3. What would happen then?

While he speculated on the answer to the last sentence, we finished the scrambled eggs Mrs. Roosevelt had prepared in a chafing dish. The subject of the Writers' Project seemed doomed to remain on my conscience, at least during the supper; I realized I would not be able to bring it up, partly out of deference to the monumental concerns the President had been expressing, and partly out of fear that, with his somewhat alarming propensity for generalizations, he might demolish the subject with one sharp statement, or perhaps joke about it, as he had when, on being given the Project's *Washington: City and Capital,* a five and a half pound tome, he had asked: "Where is the steamer trunk that goes with it?"

The supper suddenly came to an end, moments after the President had been talking about the current economic boom in France, and praising the French people for their confidence in the future. Comparing the French situation with our own, he wished that Americans could feel as confident about the future, for only then would the nation's economy move forward more rapidly. "Americans," he observed in a puzzled voice, "seem to be afraid of something . . ."

During the intense pause that followed, Mrs. Roosevelt rose from the table to end the supper and to display an unexpected talent for expressing the last word. Addressing herself to her husband with a mischievous smile, she said: "Darling, I know exactly what they are afraid of. They're afraid of you."

The remark, with its bull's-eye precision, produced a thunderbolt of laughter. The President joined in with a gusto far beyond the call of husbandly duty.

A little later, after he had bade his weekend guests goodnight and me goodbye, he was wheeled away to his study, and Mrs. Roosevelt led her company to a nearby sitting room whose walls were almost solidly covered with family photographs. This was obviously her private domain. She picked up some knitting needles, and while her hands moved in a steady rhythm chatted with the guests. Still determined to bring up the subject of the Writers' Project, I waited until there was an opening in the conversation, and then plunged in with the observation that she, Mrs. Roosevelt, was generally regarded as the godmother of the Project. As we discussed the Project, it became quite clear that she was as well informed about the subject as I was. She spoke admiringly about the city and state guides she had read, and was enthusiastic about the newest of the Project publications, *These Are Our Lives,* a collection of spoken autobiographies by black and white workers of North Carolina, Tennessee, and Georgia.*

When I mentioned the destructive effects of the Dies and Woodrum committees on the Project, Mrs. Roosevelt nodded sympathetically, and noted that the Theater Project had also been sharply attacked by the two committees. The affection with which she spoke of all the arts projects was reminiscent of the special kind of tenderness that people are likely to express for a dying friend. I sensed how futile, and in what bad taste, it would be for me to pursue the role of lobbyist, and now knew for certain

---

* In an advance comment on *These Are Our Lives* Charles Beard, the historian, declared that as literature the book was "more powerful than anything I have read in fiction." The New York *Times* review called it "a remarkable book" and said that it presented history "of a new and peculiarly honest kind." *Time* magazine hailed it as "something new in sociological writing," adding that it was the Writers' Project's "strongest claim to literary distinction."

what I had been suspecting for a number of weeks: the oncoming war was already taking its toll; federal control of the arts program was doomed. The bad news was implicit in the obituary style with which she recited, for the benefit of the other guests, some of the Project's accomplishments.

Tempted though I was to ask Mrs. Roosevelt if there was any hope that the arts program would continue under state sponsorship, I was suddenly overwhelmed by the classic worry of the guest who does not know when to take his leave. Fortunately, as if by telepathy, one of the guests became aware of my predicament, and turned to Mrs. Roosevelt to ask if she was still planning to be aboard the ten o'clock plane to New York. Without losing a stitch of her knitting, she replied: "Yes. But I have plenty of time. I have ten minutes."

Five minutes later I was out of the White House. I walked home all the way, thinking how disappointed Alsberg and my colleagues would be to hear that the Project's fate was beyond the power of its godmother, and hearing the cultivated voice of the President resounding above all the others as it ruminated on the next world war.

May was a grim month for everyone on the Washington staff of the Project, most of all for Henry Alsberg. Not only was he subjected to new assaults from the Woodrum Committee, which he patiently tried to refute with a detailed brief, but he also found himself under attack by some of his own staff members, a group of palace revolutionists who believed that only by deposing Alsberg could the Project and their jobs be saved. Since they worked in secret, they were more difficult to deal with than the congressmen. Their main strategy was to supply Colonel Harrington's office with documented complaints which would bolster the colonel's impression that Alsberg was too poor an administrator to continue in his position.

No one, not even Alsberg, had ever contended he was a talented administrator. His chief value as a director was his intuitive understanding of what the Project was capable of doing, within the limitations of its personnel, and his steadfast devotion to the high editorial standards that made the American Guide Series a treat instead of a bore. Among his associates Alsberg's fumbling administrative style had long been a standard subject of amusement. One editor came away from the director's office with a description of Alsberg "tangled in a maze of telephone cords, crying 'Get me Florida,' and 'Get me Ohio,' rumpling papers, fingering his long locks of hair, tossing essays and tour manuscripts toward the ceiling, and presently talking to Oregon under the impression he was in communication with South Carolina."

The anti-Alsberg feeling among staff members, which was fairly recent in origin, had not developed so much from his lack as an administrator but from his loss of standing as the respected leader of the Project. It had begun to crystallize shortly after his performance before the Dies Committee in December, an admixture of deference and candor which led the committee chairman to compliment him lavishly in public for his "cooperative attitude." The liberals on the staff were appalled that Alsberg had treated the Dies Committee as though it were deserving of the deepest respect, and predicted, quite accurately, that Dies would use Alsberg's testimony to damage the Project further.

The feeling against the director grew stronger in March when Alsberg offended some of his close friends on the staff by appointing Clair Laning to the post of assistant director. Their public objection to Laning, who had been a field supervisor for the past two years, was that he lacked experience both as an editor and as a writer. But their private reason for protesting Laning's elevation was made of baser stuff. For four years they had enjoyed Alsberg's confidence and had come to regard themselves as his brain trust. Now they were being ignored, usurped by a younger man whom Alsberg obviously favored above everyone else, and they were angry. "Trouble over Clair — plots and counterplots," wrote Dora Thea Hettwer, Alsberg's secretary, in her private diary shortly after the Laning appointment.

Meanwhile, the administration itself had quietly begun to scuttle Federal One and attempt to replace it with a sharply reduced arts program that would be under state control. Unaware of this development, the liberal press kept blasting the Dies and Woodrum committees for their destructive tactics and praising Alsberg's contribution to the Writers' Project. Within the WPA, however, Alsberg's supporters were rapidly diminishing. Harrington's office was broadly hinting that he should resign, and his own colleagues were treating him as though he had a highly infectious disease. Even those who had not plotted against him prudently refrained from doing or saying anything that might suggest past or present friendship for the director. "Economic determinism," Alsberg sadly explained to Dora Thea Hettwer.

Although he had already been virtually deposed by gossip and rumor,

Alsberg continued to fight for his job and for the continuation of the Project. For four years he had been pouring all of his energies into the mammoth task of organizing a motley crew of writers and nonwriters into a nationwide staff capable of producing publishable books. Now that the Project was finally operating with a fair amount of efficiency, Alsberg could not bear the frustration of leaving his post. He was further tormented by the possibility that, if Congress succeeded in killing the Writers' Project, hundreds of manuscripts that were either completed or on the verge of completion would never be published.

His fear was shared by the publishing industry. In a letter to the chairman of a House subcommittee investigating WPA, forty-four publishers contradicted the charges that the Project was guilty of waste, inefficiency, and Red propaganda. Declaring the work of the WPA writers to be "a genuine, valuable and objective contribution to the understanding of American life," it denied that the books were instruments of propaganda. "We believe that these books contain far less personal bias than is usually found in books dealing with the American scene." As for the charge of waste and inefficiency, it was their opinion that "it is remarkable — in view of the fact that the Project has been operating on a short-term basis — that it has been able to produce in so short a time some three hundred volumes . . . and has been able to maintain throughout a uniformly high level."

The signers made it clear that their petition was not wholly altruistic in its intent. No single publishing firm, they pointed out, had the resources to collect the extensive materials contained in the guidebooks. Moreover, their publication had provided "a most timely impetus" to all the industries related to the manufacturing and marketing of books. The publishers insisted that far from being a subversive agency hell-bent on disrupting capitalism (as various congressional committees would have had the nation believe) the Project was actually strengthening the nation's fabric.

Possibly because publishers seldom collaborate on controversial issues, the press gave the letter wide publicity. Alsberg made certain, of course, that a copy of it went to every important WPA administrative officer and to Colonel Harrington himself. Subsequent events suggested that while the publishers' statement may have improved Harrington's attitude toward the Project, it did not change his opinion of Alsberg or weaken his resolution to get rid of him as quickly as possible. Everything about Alsberg must have been an affront to Harrington's military mind. While the colonel was the essence of impeccable orderliness, Alsberg resembled some shaggy bear dressed in rumpled clothes, and when he spoke, his meandering thought sequences filled a room like a smoke screen. Yet behind the slipshod demeanor, as Harrington was to learn, was a compact powerhouse of tenacity.

When Harrington became annoyed with Alsberg for not turning in his resignation, he had a talk with him and bluntly informed Alsberg of his intention to appoint a new Project director. Alsberg, no less blunt, let him know that he had no intention of resigning until he had made certain that all of the unpublished state guides were completed. This, he explained, was an obligation he owed the Project as well as the publishers who had contracted for the books. Reluctantly, Harrington agreed to let him defer the resignation for a period of two months, until August 1.

For the colonel all four of the arts projects were an administrative nuisance; they created more problems for him than the rest of the WPA agencies put together.* Although he dutifully defended them against some of the congressional attacks, he had little sympathy for their aims and was temperamentally incapable of appreciating their worth. During the crucial month of June when the fate of the arts projects was to be determined, his testimony for Senate and House investigating committees was dry and factual and often lacking in important information. Undoubtedly acting on orders from above, he conveyed the impression that the administration was prepared to sacrifice federal control of the arts projects in exchange for a large enough WPA appropriation to keep millions of blue collar workers employed beyond July 1.

When Woodrum and his fellow committee members told him they were determined "to get the government out of the theater business," he offered no objection; nor did he see any point in warning Hallie Flanagan, the director of the Theater Project. His indifference to the danger confronting her project incensed her, but it came as no surprise. During the six months since Harrington had succeeded Hopkins as WPA administrator she had not been given a single opportunity to confer with him about the project which he was expected to defend before the congressional committees. Consequently, he was so badly informed about the Theater Project as to be unable to cope with some of the questions put to him at the hearings.

His knowledge of the Writers' Project was also scanty. Appearing before

* Before succeeding Harry Hopkins as WPA administrator, Colonel Harrington had been in charge of the WPA manual program for four years.

a Senate appropriations subcommittee on June 21, Harrington pleaded ignorance when asked what books the writers expected to produce once the state guides were completed. "Well," replied the colonel, "they have an ambitious program, Senator, and I am sorry to say that I cannot give you any details about it. I have not really had an opportunity to get very much into the Writers' Project . . ."

Earlier in the same hearing, however, the colonel had made a strong statement favoring the Project. When asked by Senator Tydings which of the four art projects had provided "the greatest percentage of return," Harrington, without any hesitation, named the Federal Writers' Project, pointing out that a large group of commercial publishers and co-sponsors had guaranteed printing and publishing costs "in considerable amounts."

Although it was generally assumed that most of the enemies of Federal One were members of the House of Representatives, this particular Senate hearing suggested that even some of the senators were thinking of killing off all of the arts projects. "Now in the event that these projects were all eliminated, would it be possible to integrate any of those in Federal One in any other line?" asked Senator Tydings.

The colonel had little or no knowledge about the personnel of Federal One, but he had a ready answer. "A certain portion of them could be put in some other line. Many of these people are not physically fit for manual labor."

Having elicited this smidgen of contempt for the members of the arts projects, the senators rapidly moved into another area of WPA activity — grasshopper and beetle control — a subject in which the colonel obviously felt much more at home.

While the Senate and the House chewed over the WPA appropriation bill that would insure jobs to two and a half million workers (of which less than twenty-five thousand were employees of Federal One), various members of the arts projects, by now certain they could expect no support for federal control from the administration, began to search for ways and means of bringing pressures on Congress. Although it was against WPA rules for employees to engage in any form of lobbying, the rules were ignored by many who, like myself, felt duty-bound to help preserve the principle of federal control of the arts program.

A Sunday afternoon cocktail party I attended in Washington during June soon became conspiratorial as the guests took turns trying to suggest some spectacular and newsworthy means of demonstrating to Congress that the nation's leading intellectuals were opposed to the abolition of Federal One. There was an imaginative assortment of wondrous schemes proposed, but the only one approved generally was that of organizing a march to Washington by the most prominent figures in the world of arts and letters. The guests unanimously decided that Heywood Broun would be the ideal person to organize and lead such a march. Despite his recent and unexpected conversion to Catholicism, this beloved columnist was still regarded as a popular spokesman for the nation's liberals. Since I was the only one present who had met Broun, I was delegated to form a committee that would visit him at his Stamford, Connecticut, home.

Hallie Flanagan, the only federal director who was openly fighting for the continuation of Federal One, was to have been part of the delegation, but at the last moment she sent word that she was unable to make the trip. That left only myself and Mildred Holtzhauer, an assistant to the director of the Art Project. At Stamford we were met at the train station by Broun and his son Woody with an ancient jalopy that looked as bedraggled as Broun himself. It was some time before we could discuss our mission. For more than an hour after we were ensconced in a big living room and served drinks, Broun sipped on a Scotch-and-cream concoction while he entertained us with his experiences as a newly converted Catholic. Suspecting perhaps that I, as a lapsed Catholic, was one of the many liberals to be shocked by the news of his conversion, he seemed intent on demonstrating that he was still the same old Broun, with his sense of humor still intact.

The story he told that evoked the loudest hilarity, even from his young Catholic-born wife, concerned the efforts of a half dozen of the nation's top magazines to solicit an article from him which would give his reasons for becoming a Catholic. Without exception, Broun recalled, each of the editors who telephoned was extremely apologetic for requesting an article of such a personal nature, each one offered a huge sum for the article, and each one graciously accepted his refusal without any argument. The last editor to telephone, however, was quite unlike them. He was the editor of a small Catholic monthly which was unknown to Broun. Without any preliminaries, he said: "Mr. Broun, we want an article from you which is to be two thousand words long, explaining why you became a Catholic, and we want it within the next two weeks. We'll pay you one hundred dollars for the piece." Broun, with a sheepish grin, confessed to us that he had accepted the assignment.

Later it occurred to me that had Mildred Holtzhauer or I spoken to Broun as authoritatively as the Catholic editor, we might have fared differently. Broun liked the idea of a march on Washington, but did not feel he was the person to lead it, having been too closely identified with leftwing causes for too many years. If the march was to make any impression on Congress, it should, in his opinion, be led by some well-known literary figure who had no political label pinned to him. The writer he proposed for the role was Alexander Woollcott, whose career spanned both the world of letters and that of the theater, and whose politics were generally unknown. Broun was certain that once we explained our plan to Woollcott, he would gladly organize and lead the march. Before I could express my doubts about Woollcott, Broun had gone to the telephone and called his friend in New York to fix an appointment for us. When he learned that Woollcott was not expected back to his hotel until later that afternoon, Broun, urging us to see Woollcott the same day, promised to telephone him again after we left.

A heavy rain was falling as we were leaving Broun's home. Our host, noting that Mildred, dressed in a thin summer dress, could not get to his car without getting soaked, removed his suit jacket and placed it around her shoulders. It was the instinctive gesture of an innately considerate man, and it was the first image of him that came to me when I read of his death a month later.

That Woollcott, who was notorious for his waspish disposition, should be a good friend of Broun puzzled me almost as much as Broun's insistence that he was our man for the march. I had never encountered Woollcott socially, but I was quite familiar with his writings and his public personality. A few years before I had written a long review of his best-known book, *While Rome Burns*. Everything I knew about him suggested a hedonistic character, a man more interested in private causes than public ones, who had a following because of his sharp wit and his marvelous flair for storytelling. Now, as I faced him in his hotel suite, I tried in vain to imagine what aspect of him had led Broun to believe that he would have any desire to help Federal One survive.

There were three of us trying to interest Woollcott in leading the march to Washington. On arriving in New York, we had been joined by a mild and middle-aged assistant of Hallie Flanagan who was an ex-playwright. Woollcott, with his squat, obese body and flamboyant vest, resembled a turkey as he strutted and performed, mainly for the entertainment of the

young homosexuals who formed his entourage. Our first few minutes with
him convinced me we were wasting our time. He denied having received a
telephone call from Broun, and when I introduced him to the ex-
playwright, he glared at him for a moment, then announced: "I remember
you. You were the perpetrator of an awful play I once had to review."

He sneered at our proposal, assuring us he did not care what happened
to the arts projects, and bragged that he was a far more liberal person
than many of the "so-called liberals" who were pumping for the continuation of the Theater Project. He then turned to our ex-playwright delegate,
and began quoting devastating comments he had written in the review of
his play. Before he finished, I rose in disgust and, taking Mildred by the
arm, headed for the door. But the ex-playwright, a monument of patience,
appeared to be undaunted by Woollcott's insults. In a last-ditch attempt to
establish some dialogue with him, he informed Woollcott that I had written an unusually long and favorable review of his last book for the New
York *Sun*. The sudden change of attitude in the man was appalling. He
said he remembered the review very well, shook my hand, apologized for
his "foul mood," which he attributed to some dentistry committed on him
earlier in the day, and promised that within a few months, when he would
have more time, he would be willing to help the arts projects in any way
we wished. That would be too late, I told him, and quickly led my companions out of the place.

There was no march on Washington, but Hallie Flanagan, fighting desperately for her project, which the House had now publicly singled out for
assassination, organized a mighty chorus of actors and writers (Heywood
Broun among them) that sang out its praise of the Theater Project and
protested the congressional charges of Red propaganda. Enough senators
listened — and were sufficiently impressed — to vote for the continuation
of the Theater Project. However, when the $17 billion WPA Relief Bill
went to the Senate-House conference committee the next day, the adversaries of the Project triumphed, and its life was snuffed out forever.

In signing the bill, President Roosevelt said he had no objection to the
provision which stipulated that henceforth the Writers', Music, and Art
projects must function through state sponsors that would furnish a share
of the operating expenses, but he sharply criticized the liquidation of the
Theater Project, calling it "discrimination of the worst type." But it was
too late for him or for anyone else to do anything about it; unless he

signed the bill then and there, the jobs of two and a half million WPA workers would expire the next day.

In New York that evening, where a Theater Project unit was staging *Pinnochio* for the last time, the actors and crew members left the theater bearing placards which read: WANTED — REPRESENTATIVE CLIFTON A. WOODRUM for the Murder of Pinnochio. Few persons realized at the time that Colonel Harrington, deliberately or not, had been an accessory to the crime.

The new law gave the three surviving arts projects only two months in which to line up sponsors in the individual states who would be willing to assume responsibility for at least 25 percent of their maintenance cost. Despite the bad press the Writers' Project had been receiving from congressional committee hearings, enough sponsorship was found — within the time limit — in forty-six of the forty-eight states. The continuation of the Project, now called the Writers' Program, was assured, but it could never be the same again. With the elimination of federal control, state sponsors, who were little experienced in editorial matters, acquired more influence than was healthy for the Project. The Washington staff, no longer able to enforce creative leadership to the extent that it had, was reduced in status to that of a technical advisory service. Fortunately for the quality of the state guidebooks that remained to be published, the Washington staff retained one of its most important prerogatives — that of giving or withholding final permission to publish manuscripts prepared in the field offices.

The reorganization of August 1939 cut the Washington staff almost in half, even though the volume of material being submitted from the field did not diminish. Clair Laning, for reasons of diplomacy best known to the federal administration, was permitted to remain on the staff, with a change of duties that was never defined. Many of Alsberg's other appointees were dismissed with a month's notice, among them an editor he had known since the days of his youth who had led the palace revolution against him. I was among those dropped, but the dismissal notice came as no surprise since my main work for the Project, finding publishers for the American Guide Series, was virtually finished by then.

During the turmoil of reorganization, little or no progress was made in completing the manuscripts for the rest of the books in the state guidebook series. Alsberg, who had been busy helping to line up state sponsors, decided that the special circumstances of the past two months gave him a legitimate reason for postponing his resignation beyond the August 1 deadline given to him by Colonel Harrington. When Harrington refused to see him, he wrote the colonel a letter, reiterating his wish to remain on the Project until all of the state guides were delivered to their publishers, and asking that Harrington cite his "specific reasons" for requesting his resignation.

Out of patience with Alsberg, the colonel did not even bother to acknowledge the letter. Instead he ordered his personnel director to fire Alsberg by mail. He also directed Alsberg's successor, John D. Newsom, an ex-army man who had been directing the Michigan Writers' Project, to come to Washington and take charge of the Writing Program.

The zeal with which Alsberg had campaigned to keep his job led the administration to expect that his dismissal would be followed by an embittered backlash of public recrimination. But Alsberg, a fatalist at heart, conducted himself with exemplary decorum. In his statement to the press, prepared with the help of Clair Laning, he explained in mild language that his dismissal had followed a disagreement with Colonel Harrington, who had insisted that the Project was not being well administered. Harrington, he pointed out, had failed to indicate any specific examples of poor administration. "Maybe," speculated Alsberg with the grace of a philosopher, "the colonel wanted to spare my feelings."

In a farewell letter to Harrington, Alsberg, as worried as a parent about to leave his children behind, asked that special care be taken to maintain the quality of the Project publications. So far they had won the unstinted praise of many literary critics and scholars, but he feared that the literary prestige of the Project would decline if the Washington staff were deprived of its key editors, "all of whom were largely responsible for the high standards set and adhered to in our publications."

The liberal press was furious over Alsberg's dismissal. The *Nation* demanded a full explanation. "Vague charges of inefficiency were rumored, but not proffered or officially admitted. A considerable public would like to have the facts and have them straight. The dismissal looks too much like a living sacrifice on the altar of Messrs. Dies and Woodrum and the Red-baiting they represent. Henry Alsberg is no Communist . . ." The *New Republic,* no less angry, called Colonel Harrington's career "a disaster" and pointed to the firing of Alsberg as "the latest item in his bad record." Characterizing the colonel's action as unjust and destructive, it declared that under Alsberg's direction the Project had "a magnificent record of achievement, all the more remarkable when one considers the fact that his rank-and-file workers were without exception drawn from the unemployed."

The indignation was echoed in the publishing trade journals and in the dozens of condoling letters sent to Alsberg. Walter White, head of the National Association for the Advancement of Colored People, asked if there was anything his friends could do, and assured him he had made "a real contribution" to American culture "which petty minds do not have the capacity to understand or appreciate." Hallie Flanagan, writing to Alsberg with the empathy of one deposed leader to another, said: "In the years to come when miles of asphalt will be broken up, and my clippings about the Theater Project will crumble, your books will survive."

During his last days on the Project Alsberg continued to be shunned by many of his remaining colleagues. Those who had not schemed against him were embarrassed that they had watched their leader of four years being ejected without a single protest on their part. At the farewell garden party given in his honor by Clinch Calkins, a poet friend of his who was not associated with the Project, the attendance was sparse, the atmosphere uneasy. The presentation of the proverbial gold watch by an official of the administration only accentuated the stiffness of the occasion.

Only two members of Alsberg's Washington staff were plainly distressed by his enforced departure: Dora Thea Hettwer, his secretary, and his friend Laning. In a letter to Reed Harris, whom he had succeeded as Alsberg's chief administrative assistant, Laning expressed some of the bitterness that Alsberg must have secretly felt. "The whole affair was handled in a pretty disreputable and disorganized fashion," he wrote. "Weeks ago Alsberg told Larry Morris that he would be glad to retire and recommended that someone who could handle the job, like John T. Frederick, be brought in to help the reorganization — and that when that was completed he would be glad to withdraw gradually from the picture.* In the meantime, a reorganization could have been accomplished and the state guides been pushed along at the same time. As it is, there is complete and utter chaos. . . .

"It is evident," continued Laning, "that Harrington didn't like Henry because of his more or less radical notions, and it is evident also that they intend to kill off the Writers' Project by silent treatment. At the present

* Lawrence Morris was the WPA's administrative supervisor for the four arts programs. John T. Frederick was state director of the Illinois Writers' Project.

moment WPA is probably the most anti–New Deal agency going." In a postscript, which referred to Alsberg's experiences as a journalist in Soviet Russia shortly after the Bolshevik revolution, Laning added: "Henry says that getting out of the WPA gave him the same feeling he had when he got out of Russia."

Miss Hettwer, Alsberg's secretary from the day the Project began, wrote her former chief a personal letter in which she addressed him by his first name for the first time in their four-year association. "Of course, the new director may try to do his best," she said, "but how can he compare with you? You were the guiding star of our project. You inspired us to do our best, to do the almost impossible by showing us the way. You were, as Hamlet said:

> *A combination and a form, indeed*
> *Where every god did seem to set his seal,*
> *To give the world assurance of a man.*
> *Look you now, what follows . . ."*

So closely was Alsberg identified with the fortunes of the Writers' Project that it was generally assumed the venture would not survive his departure. Shortly before his dismissal became official, the London *Times* Washington correspondent wrote what amounted to an obituary of the Project.* After praising its accomplishments and the writing abilities of its members as "staggeringly high," he announced: "The Federal Writers' Project is doomed to die . . . the Federal Writers, as a group or school, are no more. But they have left in print several million words of penetrating and humane documentation, possessing which some future American generation may well marvel at the civilization recorded by a small library of Government sponsored volumes in those turbulent years between 1935 and 1939."

The obituary proved to be premature. Although maimed by severe cuts and harrowing reorganization headaches, the Project did not die. The momentum of the work initiated during Alsberg's rule was strong enough to keep it alive until the nation's participation in World War II took precedence over everything else.

---

* Alistair Cooke, who wrote the unsigned article, sent a copy to Alsberg with a note saying: "I hope if you see any spare copies lying around of further State guides, you will not lose sleep wondering where to send them. I hope to buy, beg, steal, annex, or 'protect' a complete library of the guides before I die."

Dora Thea Hettwer,
Henry Alsberg's executive secretary

The drama of the Writers' Project during and after federal control has fascinated this writer for several decades. Increasingly, it has become apparent to him that the series of overlapping crises which marked its existence, reflected the dreams as well as the deals of the momentous Depression era that became fused into the nation's personality.

It was a time when all America was an Appalachia on the brink of war, when Fascism was not a page in history but a living terror, when Communism was the utopia to many American writers . . .

— Benjamin Appel, *Carleton Review,* Winter 1965

Sometimes I look back on that period and I just can't imagine how I could have been damn fool enough to support the Communist party. In other moods, I look back on that period and it seems to me that it was exactly the thing I had to do at that particular time.

— Granville Hicks, in a symposium on "The First American Writers' Congress (1935)," *American Scholar,* Summer 1966

There were certain enormous ideas working through the 1930s, and one was the idea of comradeship, that you were no longer alone, isolated, helpless, but if you took the side of the working class you were one of a large body of people marching toward something.

— Malcolm Cowley, in the same symposium

Writers are pretty stupid about politics, and that includes me, too. We're always making mistakes, we're joining the wrong movements or signing the wrong petitions, or making the wrong predictions.

— William Phillips, in the same symposium

The writers were always a problem . . .

— Arthur Goldschmidt, one of the New Deal architects of Federal One, in an interview with the author, March 1969

Two.

In the Beginning

The official birthday of the Federal Writers' Project was July 27, 1935, but its period of gestation began some five years earlier with the arrival of the nation's worst economic calamity, the Great Depression. To appreciate how so bold an enterprise as the Project could have been fathered under governmental auspices, one needs to understand the desperate circumstances of the era. More than one third of the country's labor force was thrown out of work, and millions of Americans began to worry about going hungry. Far more telling than the statistics on the sharp decline of the Gross National Product were the breadlines, the shantytowns called Hoovervilles, the thousands of homeless men and women sleeping in subway stations and public parks, the anarchistic reactions of conservative farmers to the loss of their lands. These were but a part of the gross evidence that underlined the black anxiety permeating the American people.

Contributing to the anxiety during the early years of the decade was the fear that the radical left would gain enough adherents to spark a revolution. In the burgeoning leftwing press there was more talk than ever about the urgent necessity of exterminating the capitalist system and replacing it with a socialist form of government, and all over the land were demonstrations by the jobless and the dispossessed that seemed to support the revolutionary assertions of the radicals. According to at least one historian, the threat from the left was taken seriously enough to account for the vigor with which the army dispersed the Bonus Marchers in Washington during the closing months of the Hoover administration. So widespread was the notion that the country might be revolutionary-prone that *Harper's* felt obliged to published an article by George Soule assuring its readers there would be no revolution. "Revolutions are not made by the weak, the unsuccessful, or the ignorant," wrote Soule, "but by the strong and the informed."

To what extent the possibility of revolution influenced the actions of the Roosevelt administration is, of course, a matter of speculation. However, it must have acted as something of a prod for New Dealers to initiate programs like the Federal Writers' Project, which in any other era would have been considered too radical for government sponsorship. And undoubtedly, it was not without reason that Communist party leaders, before the advent of the Popular Front, branded the early efforts of the New Deal as counterrevolutionary. Rejecting the suggestion that the Roosevelt administration was largely motivated by humanitarian considerations, they flatly declared that an enterprise like Federal One was a purely Machiavellian device for subduing the revolutionary tendencies of American intellectuals by giving them jobs that would feed their bellies and their egos.

George Soule's assurances notwithstanding, the revolutionary ardor abroad in the land was a glaring fact, especially noticeable among intellectuals. Never before in American history had so many of them been drawn into the orbit of leftwing activity. The Communist party was attracting so many members that it could afford to turn away applicants who were not considered qualified. The Marxist-Leninist doctrine, as presented by the Communist party, which was bolstered by the expectation that the Soviet Union would soon develop into a model of socialism for the rest of the world to emulate, was being embraced with a religious fervor that sometimes amounted to fanaticism. As Arthur Schlesinger, Jr., later pointed out, the doctrine, with its promise of a classless society and a collective utopia, "offered light at the end of the dark cave."

As a group, writers were among the earliest and most deeply affected converts to the new faith. They expressed their devotion with a stream of proletarian novels (eleven of them as early as 1932), short stories, poems, and manifestos. A year before Franklin D. Roosevelt was first elected to the presidency, some of the nation's foremost writers became part of a group of fifty-three intellectuals who signed a statement denouncing the Democratic and Republican parties as hopelessly corrupt, rejecting the Socialist party as a do-nothing group, and declaring their support for the Communist party on the grounds that it sought to help all dispossessed classes and establish a society of equality for all. In supplementary articles of faith published in liberal and radical magazines, the writers urged all artists to find "true fulfillment" in the socialist struggle against capitalism by accepting the workers' cause as their own.

While the emphasis on "proletarian" themes grew heavier, the "art-for-art's-sake" faith of the twenties waned into an inglorious mist. The symbol of the ivory tower was replaced by that of the barricade. An early casualty of the new literary order was James Branch Cabell, whose novelistic concoctions of ironic fantasy were quickly buried in the debris of the stock market crash; any mention of Cabell after that was greeted with the kind of embarrassment that might attend the presence of a clown at a funeral. Another casualty was F. Scott Fitzgerald's novel *Tender is the Night,* which was published at the height of the proletarian literature cult in 1934, and dismissed by the book reviewers as socially insignificant because instead of dealing with workers and the class struggle it dealt with "superficial Americans living on the Riviera."

Writing which did not reflect the class struggle or the dangers of fascism was often attacked by the radical press as escapist literature, as were authors who paid more attention to form and style than to their message. To Jack Conroy, a young novelist and editor who was to be associated with the Writers' Project, a strike bulletin or an impassioned leaflet was "of more moment than three hundred pretty and faultlessly written pages about the private woes of a gigolo or the biological ferment of a society dame as useful to society as the buck brush that infests Missouri cow pastures and takes all the sustenance out of the soil."

Conroy, the son of a coal miner killed in a mining accident, was the author of one of the few notable proletarian novels of the thirties, *The Disinherited.* A veritable Johnny Appleseed of the proletarian literary movement, he was the founder and editor of three leftwing literary magazines: *Rebel Poet,* the *Anvil,* and the *New Anvil,* all of which published the earliest writings of contemporaries who later became well-known authors.* Although Conroy and his contributors were not always in agreement with the Communist party line, they were of one mind in their repudiation of the capitalist system. H. H. Lewis, a prolific writer of doggerel whose work frequently appeared in Conroy's publications, roughly expressed the attitude of many a leftwing writer:

* Among them were Nelson Algren, Josephine Johnson, Richard Wright, Frank Yerby, Edward Newhouse, Louis Zara, Benjamin Appel, August Derleth, Paul Corey.

> *I'm always thinking of Russia;*
> *Can't get her out of my head.*
> *I don't give a damn for Uncle Sham*
> *I'm a leftwing radical red.*

Then, as now, an inevitable aspect of the radical's thinking was the contempt he felt for the average liberal, a feeling which led Lewis to write:

> *When Social tremblors rock the scene*
> *And sift us, man from man,*
> *He rides the bounding fence between*
> *As only a eunuch can.*

Not all young writers had the capacity or the inclination to react as strongly to the "social tremblors," but a surprising number of them found themselves in agreement with Mike Gold, the Communist writer, who insisted that the writer "must decide now between two worlds — cooperative or competitive, proletariat or capitalist." To the young intellectual of the period whose life had been severely affected by the collapse of a system based on competition, the desirable alternatives were clear enough. Moreover, he found that the Marxists were the only ones who seemed capable of answering the troubled questions about the present and the future that he and members of his generation were asking. No matter how little knowledge he had of Marxism, it was not difficult for him to become convinced that socialism represented the only constructive goal for society, and to feel that his place was on the Communist bandwagon.

To provide young intellectuals with easy access to the bandwagon, the Communist party in the early thirties began organizing John Reed clubs in cities across the country. Named after the American journalist whom the Communists had adopted as a revolutionary hero for his participation in the Bolshevik revolution, the clubs provided a forum for discussions of Marxist-Leninist doctrine as it applied to art and literature. They also launched literary magazines to publish the work of young radicals,*

---

* The *Partisan Review* was a 1934 offspring of the John Reed Club in New York City. Later it was published in conjunction with Jack Conroy's *Anvil*. When Philip Rahv and William Phillips, the main editors of the magazine, broke with the Com-

offered public lectures on cultural topics and, in New York, even conducted courses dealing with the craft of leftwing writing. By 1934, thirty
John Reed clubs were in operation, with a membership or attendance
(one could attend without joining) that included many future employees
of the Federal Writers' Project, among them Richard Wright, who served
as secretary of the John Reed Club in Chicago.

The meetings of the John Reed clubs often resounded with the fierce
debates of its members as they argued about the nuances of Marxist dia-
lectics. As a young man attending some of the meetings of New York's
John Reed Club, I listened to poets and critics orate with an eloquence
more characteristic of barristers than writers, which alternately impressed
and bewildered less erudite members of their audience like myself. Yet
while the general tenor of the discussions was heavily intellectual, there
was also practical talk concerning such matters as distributing leaflets,
performing on public soapboxes, taking part in picketing and antifascist
demonstrations and, inevitably, agitating for a government-sponsored
agency that would give jobs to needy artists and writers.

That the Roosevelt administration might create such a project was no
extravagant dream. It had already demonstrated its willingness to help
artists on a national scale. Less than a year after the New Deal came into
power, the Treasury Department, with funds from the Civil Works Administration and with the benediction of the White House, established the
Public Works of Art Project, which hired painters and sculptors in forty-
eight states to embellish government buildings at salaries ranging up to
$46.50 a week. The brainchild of George Biddle, an artist and a personal
friend of the Roosevelts, PWAP gave jobs to thirty-six hundred artists during its eighteen months of existence and produced sixteen thousand pieces
of art.

The project was intelligently administered in Washington by Edward
Bruce, but it was an unpopular operation. Because it employed artists on
the basis of recognized competence rather than economic need, its critics
attacked it for paying salaries to affluent artists who were not in need of
work. In large cities, like New York, Chicago, and San Francisco, where
John Reed clubs and leftwing artists' and writers' unions were most active,

---

munist party, they established the *Partisan Review* as an independent periodical in
1937.

PWAP became the target of bitter demonstrations. Within its own ranks, the project experienced some of the censorship headaches that were to plague the WPA arts projects later on. In San Francisco, for example, thirty-five artists who were working on a mural about contemporary America in the Coit Memorial Tower angered the local establishment by painting leftwing symbols into the mural. The brunt of official wrath fell on the work of Clifford Wight, who had painted three small decorative panels, one of which depicted the Soviet hammer and sickle with the slogan "Workers of the World Unite."

PWAP represented a historical breakthrough, for it was the first time the government had subsidized an art project of national dimension. But it was not the only project of a cultural nature operated by the New Deal during its early months of power. Under the auspices of the two big job-making agencies that preceded WPA, the Civil Works Administration and the Federal Emergency Relief Administration, a number of small projects for needy writers and musicians were functioning in several states, including California, Connecticut and New York. PWAP, together with these state-sponsored experiments, which were initiated by politically sensitive New Dealers like Harry Hopkins and Jacob Baker, cleared the way for a federally controlled program that would provide jobs for jobless writers, artists, musicians, and actors in every part of the country. Yet without the prolonged insistence of professional artists' and writers' organizations and leftwing activity, Federal One, as it was finally conceived, might never have come into being.

The recently formed Newspaper Guild, led by its first president, Heywood Broun, was among the first of the professional groups to demand that the administration create a job program of national scope for unemployed writers. In Los Angeles Hugh Harlan, a Grinnell College classmate of Harry Hopkins, who had set up a local project for unemployed newspapermen under the auspices of FERA, echoed the same demand. Pointing to the success of his Los Angeles project, Harlan in a letter to Hopkins asked: "Why can't this thing be established on a national scale?"

Two new leftwing groups were organized specifically for the purpose of bringing pressure to bear on Washington for the establishment of a national project that would give jobs to creative writers. These were the Writers Union and the Unemployed Writers Association, both of which drew heavily on John Reed Club membership for support. Robert Whitcomb, the aggressive secretary of the second group, used the tough lan-

The poet Leon Srabian Herald was an early member of the Project in New York City

guage of the uncompromising radical when he wrote to the CWA in February 1934 to demand prompt action:

> The unemployed writers of New York City do not intend to continue under the semi-starvation conditions meted out to them, particularly while painters of pictures, some of them, receive adequate treatment from the government . . . If the government does not intend to formulate some policy regarding the class of intellectual known as a writer, who is trained for nothing else in the present economic emergency, then the writer must organize and conduct a fight to better his condition.

In a more polite mood the Authors Guild, writing to the same New Deal agency on the same day, submitted a proposal for the employment of writers "to survey varying aspects of everyday life as it is lived in all parts of the United States." Elaborating on the proposal, it suggested that an indefinite number of writers could be assigned to write "a complete hour-to-hour account of a single day in the life of a man, woman, or child in a community in which a writer lives."

The question of who was a writer differed widely. For the Authors Guild the writer was a proven professional who had published two or more books. For the Newspaper Guild he was anyone whose work appeared in print. Among some leftwingers the definition was even broader. Speaking for the Writers Union, which was to merge with the Unemployed Writers Association, Robert Whitcomb declared a writer to be "one who has earned a living as such, been published in major periodicals or who can produce satisfactory manuscripts." Whitcomb believed that the question of what constituted a "satisfactory manuscript" could be resolved by a committee of literary judges appointed by the proposed writers' project.

Not all leftwing writers agreed with him. In a noisy argument at a Writers Union meeting, Harold Rosenberg insisted that only "real writers of high intellectual caliber" be considered eligible for the writers' project. The meeting voted in his favor but a few minutes later he and another writer, H. R. Hays, became embroiled in a ferocious quarrel with the rest of the membership over some technical detail of his proposition, and the two of them left in a huff, leaving the question of who was a writer unresolved.

While there were some "real writers" in the ranks of the Writers Union, most of the members were aspiring writers who had never published anything. As many as two hundred men and women came to the weekly meetings of the group, excited to be the first in American history to band together for the sole purpose of creating jobs for writers. To dramatize their cause the group staged picket lines all over New York. The first of them, on February 25, 1935, in front of the Port Authority Building, was led by Earl Conrad who carried a placard reading: CHILDREN NEED BOOKS. WRITERS NEED A BREAK. WE DEMAND PROJECTS. The next morning the New York *Daily Mirror* reported the event with a photograph of the picket line headed: "Our Future Walt Whitmans." Part of the caption read: "Genius, it seems, can no longer be denied bread. These folks say the CWA bought the services of artists, painters, etc. — why not those of jobless writers? However, latest reports last night were that the only work in sight was for the writing of more placards."

Watching the same picket line during my office lunch hour, I spotted a number of writers I knew. In a few months nearly all of them would be taken off the relief rolls and given jobs with the Federal Writers' Project. Behind Earl Conrad I saw Maxwell Bodenheim, who not long ago had publicly repudiated the risqué novels he turned out in the twenties and declared his allegiance to proletarian literature and communism. There was also my friend Samuel Putnam, a well-known translator and literary critic, who had recently returned from seven years of expatriation in Paris. We talked as he marched and, with a communistic fervor that matched Bodenheim's, he explained to me that he had recently joined the Communist party because of his young son. "When he grows up, I want his respect. I don't want him asking me why it was that I never became a Communist."

The picket line also included Leon Srabian Herald, the Armenian-born poet, whose mystic dark eyes haunted me from the first time I saw them at a meeting of the John Reed Club. Herald, a writer of rare grace whose devotion to the Communist cause seemed inbred in him, was one of the three Writers Union delegates elected to visit Harry Hopkins in Washington with a petition for a writers' project. Accompanying him were Robert Whitcomb and Franklin Folsom, who soon afterwards became executive secretary of the League of American Writers, the broad-front organization that succeeded the John Reed clubs. The delegates had expected to encounter routine treatment in Washington but, to their surprise, they were

The Writers Union's first picket line was led by Earl Conrad in New York City on February 25, 1935

cordially received by Aubrey Williams, one of Hopkins's administrative chiefs. Williams carefully reviewed the prospectus for a writers' project, which Herald had helped to write after a Greenwich Village party, and even offered some suggestions for improving it. Herald in a letter to a friend reported that "Harry Hopkins came in toward the end of the conference to wish us good luck. On our return to New York we held several mass meetings and made our reports. At one time there were a couple of thousand people in the audience listening to us. Enthusiasm for the writers' project was catching like fire . . ."

The mass meeting referred to by Herald was that of the Conference of Professional, Cultural and White Collar Workers, consisting of twenty-three organizations who were clamoring for government-sponsored white-collar projects. In militant language, without mentioning writers and artists specifically, the conference pointed to the plight of "the half million office and professional workers in New York still without work," and demanded a program that would create employment for all workers in their special crafts, and one which would abolish the Pauper's Oath as a basis for getting a job.

Although the New Deal favored job programs that would preserve human skills and talents, its chief concern was the three and a half million persons on the relief rolls who, in effect, were paupers. In his January 1935 message to Congress Roosevelt declared his concern for the needy:

The Federal government must and shall quit this business of relief. I am not willing that the vitality of our people be further sapped by the giving of cash, of market baskets, a few hours weekly of working cutting grass, raking leaves, or picking up papers in the public parks. We must preserve not only the bodies of the unemployed from destitution, but also their self-respect, their self-reliance, and courage and determination.

To achieve all this, Roosevelt and Hopkins realized the need for a much broader relief program than either CWA or FERA, a job program that would boost the economy while stemming unemployment. In April, a Congress attentive to the President's thinking passed the momentous Emergency Relief Act of 1935, the legislation that provided the authority for the most ambitious of all the relief programs, the Works Progress Administration.

An inconspicuous but significant clause in the act authorized "assistance to educational, professional, and clerical persons; a nation-wide program for useful employment of artists, musicians, actors, entertainers, writers . . . and others in these cultural fields." The New Dealers and the professional organizations that had been pressing for a federally sponsored arts program had finally triumphed; and suddenly the Hopkins office was faced with the Herculean task of administratively translating, within a few weeks, the words of the enabling clause into an unprecedented action involving the yet-to-be-defined services of some forty thousand men and women in every state of the union.

As created by the President's Executive Order of May 6, 1935, the Works Progress Administration sounded like an agency that would be devoting itself almost exclusively to construction activities, but one phrase in the order, cannily inserted by Roosevelt, saved the day for Hopkins and his aides: "Recommend and carry on small useful projects designed to assure a maximum employment in all agencies." Since "small useful projects" were easier and cheaper to establish than construction programs, which required expensive materials and skilled labor, they and Hopkins soon dominated the activity of WPA. Before long the grant-in-aid program of FERA, which had functioned under state administration, was abandoned, and WPA, which had originally been conceived largely as a coordinating agency for FERA and the Public Works Administration, emerged as an operating body with complete jurisdiction in the states.

The complex task of organizing white-collar WPA projects that could be manned readily was undertaken by Jacob Baker, a forty-two-year-old bald and big-boned agricultural and industrial engineer who, though born in Colorado, claimed to be a descendant of the Green Mountain Boys of Vermont. Baker had been working with Hopkins almost since the inception of the New Deal, first as director of work relief and special projects in FERA, later as Hopkins's assistant administrator of CWA. Among New Dealers he was best known as a staunch proponent of the cooperative movement. Blessed with what *Fortune* magazine described as a "vigorously theoretical and inventive turn of mind," Baker shared Hopkins's broad social vision as well as the courage to experiment within the framework of government. Inevitably, it was he who became the chief architect of Federal One.

For all of his liberal philosophy, Baker was a cautious administrator who believed that, politically and administratively, it would be wiser to have the control of the arts projects decentralized in the states, with Washington simply providing necessary funds and direction of a technical and advisory nature. Baker almost had his way. In May his assistant Bruce McClure, as administrative head of the WPA Section for Professional and Service Projects (under which the arts projects were classified), informed the WPA state administrators that all arts projects were to require the sponsorship of state agencies. But a mysterious development in July produced a sharp reversal of plans. From Baker's own office it was announced that the WPA itself would sponsor the arts projects and would shortly appoint four federal directors to operate each project from Washington.*

What caused Baker and his aides to reverse themselves is a fascinating question for speculation. In his detailed study of Federal One's administration, Professor William D. McDonald offers an explanation which, though sounding plausible, seems almost too nicely existentialist to be true.† The sudden change of policy, he suggests, resulted from an interpretation of the language in the Emergency Relief Act of 1935 made by the Comptroller General's office. The interpretation, which had been submitted to WPA at the request of Bruce McClure, held that all projects "for assistance to educational, professional and clerical persons" were necessarily federal projects entitled to a budgetary allotment of $300,000,000.

---

* Baker was never happy with federal sponsorship of the four arts programs. In the spring of 1936 his advocacy of state sponsorship cost him his job. In retrospect, it seems clear that without forceful leadership from Washington, most of the state projects could not have performed as well as they did.

† *Federal Relief Administration and the Arts* by William F. McDonald, Ohio State University Press, 1969.

Jacob Baker, WPA administrator,
one of the Project's chief architects

Professor McDonald theorizes that when faced by this unexpected bonanza, the WPA administrators had no other alternative but to make the arts projects federally controlled. That a program "as fiscally unorthodox and as administratively unprecedented" (Professor McDonald's phrase) should have been prompted by a legal interpretation from an old-line government agency as conservative as the General Accounting Office was a delightful irony that superbly set the tone for the erratic and frequently zany career that the arts projects were to experience during their four years of federal sponsorship.

At the beginning of August, Baker's office issued the official announcement that Federal One had been established as a unit of the Works Progress Administration:

> It is the intention of this administration to sponsor national projects intending to employ persons now on relief who are qualified in the fields of Arts, Music, Drama, and Writing. The following persons have been appointed by Mr. Hopkins to direct each of these nation-wide projects: Art, Holger Cahill; Music, Nikolai Sokoloff; Drama, Hallie Flanagan; and Writers, Henry G. Alsberg.
>
> Each of these directors will have a staff in Washington and in the field to insure the unified planning and execution of the programs.

So began a governmental adventure in cultural collectivism, the like of which no nation has experienced before or since.

Since writing is by nature more explicit and of more discernible intent than any other art, the question of what a government writers' project should do was not an easy one to resolve. A simple solution would have been to put the writers to work producing government manuals and reports, but even the more conservative members of the WPA administrative staff conceded that such bureaucratic tasks would only add to the depression of the writers and the nation. A more glamorous alternative, one that had been advanced by various leftwing groups, would have permitted writers to work on projects of their own selection, such as novels, short stories, poems, as well as works of nonfiction. But this possibility was fraught with too many risks, the most obvious one being that some of the publishable manuscripts that were produced might be so subversive in content as to create undue embarrassment for the administration. In 1935, when the intellectual climate of the country was heavily charged with Marxist ideology, there were ample grounds for such apprehension.

Early that year, in an opening maneuver of the Communist party's Popular Front policy, the John Reed clubs, with their parochial Marxist-Leninist stance, were dissolved and replaced with a broad-front organization designed to attract all writers of radical inclination (with the exception of people like Sidney Hook and Max Eastman, who were considered "counterrevolutionary") known as the League of American Writers. The League's first action was to call for a "congress of American revolutionary writers" who recognized "the necessity of personally helping to accelerate the destruction of capitalism and the establishment of a workers' government."

The congress, held in New York's Mecca Temple on April 26, was attended by some two hundred sixteen writers who sat on the platform while some four thousand would-be writers and leftwing sympathizers packed the auditorium. One of the organizers of the congress was Orrick Johns, who in a few months was to become director of the Federal Writers' Project in New York City. Earl Browder, executive secretary of the Communist party in the United States, told the audience that the party wanted writers to be good writers, not bad strike leaders, but that, at the same time, it hoped to increase their political awareness and provide them with "a growing audience for revolutionary writing."

Not all of the speeches were of Communist orthodox stuff. The novelist Waldo Frank, chairman of the congress, castigated leftwing writers for producing propaganda instead of "deeply revolutionary art." Frank, who was not a Communist, accused them of taking orders from political leaders and turning out fiction and poems that were riddled with Communist clichés and stereotypes. James T. Farrell, speaking on the short story, criticized them for their "over politicalized and ideologically schematized fiction." But such scoldings fell mostly on deaf ears. Their fervent convictions barred objective self-appraisal and made it easy for them to adopt mechanical literary standards based on a narrow Communist catechism. Fired with the need to change the world and, while doing so, to prevent fascism, their holy goal was the greater glory of the proletariat. Emotionally, they were of the age of a young Catholic receiving first Communion.

Not content with putting words to paper, Communist-smitten writers from all strata of society became leftwing activists. Whether they were party members or fellow travelers, they worked zealously on large and small tasks — manning mimeograph machines, distributing leaflets or copies of the *Daily Worker*, participating in strikes and antifascist demonstrations, trying to organize farm workers in the South or white collar workers in the publishing firms of Manhattan. Except for the hard-boiled functionaries on the party payroll and the literary opportunists gathering material for their next book, they were as idealistic and as eager for sacrifice as the early Christians.

Malcolm Cowley, a close observer of the thirties, wrote:

> The usual sacrifice was to walk in a local picket line, to be carried off in a paddy wagon, to sing "The International" with the other jailed pickets — Mike Gold would carry the bass — to be tried before a judge who obviously wanted to acquit the prisoners, while the Communist attorney for the defense was doing his best to get them convicted and then, after the judge had overruled the attorney, to rush home and write a turgid account of the strike as the first red glow of a revolutionary dawn. There were other writers, however, who played a part in serious strikes like the big ones in Minneapolis and San Francisco, where the pickets were likely to be slugged and given stiff sentences.

More often than their families knew, they took dangerous chances. In June 1935, just before the advent of the Writers' Project, two of its future members, Emmett Gowen and Jack Conroy, joined an expedition into Alabama to protest a Birmingham city ordinance which made it a crime to possess more than one copy of a "radical" periodical. One of the writers in the group was Polly Boyden, a wealthy Cape Cod housewife with a strong social conscience who was to publish what was perhaps the oddest of all the proletarian novels. Titled *The Pink Egg*, all of its characters were birds. The hero was a robin who had defected from his middle-class family to cast his lot with the sparrows, who were the workers. The capitalists were sparrow hawks, and the villains were the fascist bluejays who had the nasty habit of incarcerating radical sparrows in mailboxes. One of the big scenes in the novel was a mass meeting on the roof of the Metropolitan Art Museum, with the robin hero as the featured speaker.

Mrs. Boyden, herself a defected robin who had joined the sparrows of the world, was one of the writers who defied the Birmingham ordinance by distributing copies of periodicals such as the *New Republic,* the *New Masses,* the *Daily Worker,* and the *Nation.* Although not actually arrested, the writers were pushed around by detectives — fingerprinted, photographed, then ordered out of town. Conroy, Gowen and Mrs. Boyden headed for Montgomery, where they hoped to persuade the governor to veto a state antisedition bill on his desk. On their way, a speeding roadster drew up to their car, a hand emerged holding a .45 army automatic pistol, and several shots were fired into the car. As Mrs. Boyden tried to bring the car to a halt, the brakes screamed, the car skidded, then jumped ahead again as the gunmen's car whizzed by.

The Alabama governor refused to provide the writers with police protection, but promised an investigation. A few days later he dismissed the episode as a cock and bull story designed to create publicity. Although the police who investigated admitted there had been a shooting, they insisted the shots were fired by the writers themselves.

For reasons of poverty, a considerable number of leftwing writers were anxious to become associated with the Writers' Project. Their political mood and the nature of their dedication being no secret, Baker and his aides were understandably reluctant to permit them free literary expression at government expense. Although there were a few WPA planners who supported the dream of making the Writers' Project a vehicle for imaginative writing, most of them, fearing the consequences of permitting leftwing writers to write what they pleased, were opposed to it. Finally, the only employees of Federal One who were officially allowed to work on their own projects (and in the privacy of their own homes) were the painters and sculptors. Nothing they produced, reasoned the planners, could cause as much trouble as the printed word.

The dream seemed impossible for another reason: rather than try to solve the riddle of who is a writer, the planners decided that any kind of a writer, who was on relief, would be eligible to work on the Writers' Project — fiction writers, copywriters, poets, newspapermen, publicity writers, technical writers, and so on. With nonfiction writers easily outnumbering the poets and fiction writers, the planners could argue that what the Project needed was a broad nonfictional program that could utilize diverse services and skills.

FERA had conducted several projects that seemed worth continuing under WPA auspices — the gathering of folklore and the recording of autobiographical material by ex-slaves were among the most successful — but none of them was large enough in scope to keep a nationwide organization sufficiently occupied. The search for a suitable project caused serious concern. Yet an acceptable solution had been germinating under the noses of the planners for some time. A year earlier, a FERA supervisor in

Michigan, Henry S. Curtis, proposed the preparation of "a sort of public Baedeker, which would point out to the curious traveler the points of real travel value in each state and county."

Similar proposals from both private citizens and government employees had been received in Washington, filed away, and quickly forgotten. But one of the suggestions, shouted during a noisy cocktail party in Washington to Baker's righthand man, Arthur Goldschmidt, made a deep enough impression to result in prompt action. Mrs. Katharine Kellock, a writer attached to the Resettlement Administration who had traveled extensively in Europe, told Goldschmidt: "The thing you have to do for writers is to put them to work writing Baedekers." The advice came at a propitious time, when Baker's staff was vainly wrestling with various alternatives, none of them quite satisfactory.

With Alsberg's approval, Goldschmidt asked Mrs. Kellock to collaborate with Nina Collier, a member of Baker's staff, on a prospectus. The final draft of the prospectus, as written by Mrs. Collier and Clair Laning (then an FERA employee helping Alsberg plan the Writers' Project) became the chief blueprint for the American Guide Series.

Actually, the idea of producing a state guidebook had already been tried in Connecticut under the auspices of CWA and FERA. Eleven relief workers with the help of a thousand volunteers had prepared a 320-page volume, the Connecticut Guide, which was just off the presses. The guide helped to clinch the plan of preparing a series of state guides that could employ the services of researchers and all kinds of writers. Although its contents fell short of the standards that were to be established for the American Guide Series, the Connecticut Guide provided Alsberg with a model that was far more useful than Baedeker's *United States,* which was now obsolete and long out of print.

The last published comprehensive guide to the United States, the Baedeker book, had been first issued in 1893 and revised in 1909. It was written by an Englishman, Findlay Muirhead, but followed the traditional Baedeker format, with introductory information about the country comprising about a fifth of the contents, and detailed travel data, illustrated with maps, making up the rest of the book. The writing was dry and factual for the most part, but under the heading of General Hints could be found such Anglicized observations as: "The average Englishman will probably find the chief physical discomforts in the dirt of the city streets, the roughness of the country roads, the winter overheating of hotels and railway cars (70–75 degree Fahrenheit by no means unusual) and in many places the habit of spitting on the floor . . ."

Finally in agreement on a Writers' Project program, Baker's staff tried to describe it in an official announcement:

> . . . employment of writers, editors, historians, research workers, art critics, architects, archeologists, map draftsmen, geologists, and other professional workers for the preparation of an American Guide and the accumulation of new research material on matters of local, historical, art and scientific interest in the United States; preparation of a complete encyclopedia of government functions and periodical publications in Washington; and the preparation of a limited number of special studies in the arts, history, economics, sociology, etc., by qualified writers on relief.

As it turned out, this original view of what the Project would be doing was inaccurate in several respects. There never was a single-volume American Guide published under government auspices.* Shortly after the inception of the Project, it was decided that the plan of preparing five regional guides that would culminate in a one-volume comprehensive guide to the nation was not administratively feasible. In changing its orders to the field offices, the Washington editors called for guidebooks to each of the states. The encyclopedia of government functions never materialized, nor did any of the "special studies" that were to be prepared by "qualified writers on relief." On the other hand, the prospectus made no mention of two large activities, which in the early months of the Project, required the full time of nearly half of its sixty-five hundred employees. These were an informational service that reported on what the various units of WPA were doing, known as the Reporters' Project, and the Historical Records Survey project.†

The same WPA memorandum that spelled out the program of the federal writers also made it clear that almost any person on relief who could write English might be eligible to work for the Project. Its explanation

---

* A single-volume guide to the United States, *The American Guide,* edited by Henry G. Alsberg, with the assistance of ten former members of the Federal Writers' Project, was published by Hastings House in 1949.

† In 1936 the Reporters' Project was integrated into the Writers' Project and ceased to exist. Early in the same year the Historical Records Survey, under the direction of Luther Evans, became an independent nationwide unit administered as part of Federal One. While associated with the Writers' Project, the members of the Historical Records Survey contributed heavily to the early research for the American Guide Series.

that a "great variety of nonmanual workers, researcher workers" would be required to gather material for the guides was, in effect, an open invitation to the army of recent college graduates who were trying in vain to find their first jobs. As if to make sure they got the message, Alsberg issued a statement of his own in which he said that in addition to experienced writers, the Project would also employ "near writers," "occasional writers," and even would-be writers — "young college men and women who want to write, probably can write, but lack the opportunity."

With such a motley staff in the offing, it is understandable that the early WPA statements about the value of the American Guide were of a cautious nature. As far as Hopkins was concerned, the primary function of the Writers' Project was to provide jobs for the unemployed; whatever else was accomplished would be considered gravy. "The Guide," read one of the official statements, "will contain certain information about the nation never before gathered together." Alsberg tried to improve on it by predicting that American writing in general would be better as a result of "seeing what is really happening to the American people." Then, in a rather poignant effort to win supporters from the large body of middle-class Americans who were unsympathetic, if not hostile, to the notion of the government becoming an employer of writers, Alsberg added that "there is the hope that narrow propagandistic and sex attitudes may be eliminated."

In the beginning the press was generally cool and sometimes disparaging. In addition to WPA shovel leaners, the nation would now have pencil leaners, one editorial complained. The Washington *Post,* while praising the Writers' Project in its news columns, doubted the wisdom of the enterprise on its editorial page. "The noblest victories which genius has won have been accomplished under conditions of misery." To this philistine myth it added the old chestnut that "luxury and ease have been handicaps to creative effort," and predicted that "even that degree of subsidization which the WPA can provide is more apt to be a blight than a help."

Newspapers also expressed impatience with a program which, during a dire depression, should be concerned with anything as intangible as culture. Some of them grumbled that with so much poverty in the land few Americans could afford to travel, let alone spend money on guidebooks. Some of the writers who expected to work for the Project were also critical; they resented the prospect of working on anything as mundane sounding as an American Guide. The frequent references to Baedeker in the

WPA news releases convinced them that their work was bound to be dreary.

But the reaction was not all unfavorable. There were writers who rejoiced that Washington politicians were imaginative enough to put needy writers to work in a manner that was bound to enhance the national culture. And there was a sizable group of intellectuals, not as young as those boarding the Marxist-Leninist bandwagon, who shared Alsberg's belief that the gathering of material for a series of American guidebooks represented an unprecedented and rare opportunity to examine, for the first time in history, the country's peoples, resources, traditions, and accomplishments in great detail. For one of the most striking anomalies of the Great Depression was that, while the gospel of Marx and Lenin was rapidly drawing converts, there was developing a strong movement to understand and interpret the American "character," which had been almost totally ignored until now. Led by such writers as Van Wyck Brooks, Randolph Bourne, Waldo Frank, and Lewis Mumford, it achieved such momentum that the Communist party felt obliged to revise its slogans to conform with the theme of Americanism.* As Professor William McDonald has pointed out, America has always had a "character" but it was not until the Depression that it recognized it and, having done so, "Narcissus-like embraced it."

Some of the proponents of the movement to rediscover America were the same intellectuals who, out of contempt and hatred for the cultural climate of the twenties, had banded together in a devastating symposium edited by Harold Stearns (*Civilization in the United States: An Inquiry by Thirty Americans,* published by Harcourt, Brace & Company in 1922) to attack major phases of American life on the grounds that ignorance and mediocrity were prevalent throughout the land and there was no room left for individuality. Matching their words with action, some of them expatriated themselves to Paris, and did not return until the early thirties, when their American sources of income were dried up.

Without the misleading tinsel of prosperity, with the country ripped at the seams by the impact of the Depression, the variegated parts of America became more visible; and these writers understood the country as they never had before. They saw, for the first time, that the population did not live solely under the influence of the Protestant ethic, with its inhibit-

* A widely used slogan of the American Communist party in the thirties was: "Communism is Twentieth-Century Americanism."

ing bourgeois vision, but that it was a mixture of different groups — Negroes, Irish, Italian, German, Russian among others — all interacting with one another in the struggle for survival and assertion and, in the process, generating their own special kind of influence. And they began to believe that the detested values of middle-class Americans could be counteracted, and even canceled, by a class of Americans that commanded their attention as it never had before — the steelworkers, bricklayers, sharecroppers, factory workers — the so-called common people whose lives were already vividly interwoven into the fabric of the national character.

Henry Alsberg, whose life had already spanned five decades, was equipped with enough cultural experience and insight to appreciate the nature of the American dream as projected by Brooks, Mumford and Bourne, and to relate it to his own aspirations for the newly formed Writers' Project. From the start, he understood the enormous opportunities that the nationwide Project represented. Yet not even he nor the Project's most sanguine champions could have suspected in the fall of 1935, when Alsberg became director, that from a project which had been given a six-month lease on life would come a seven-year body of work that could hasten the process of native self-discovery as no other literature could.

The Arts Project of WPA was, perhaps, one of the noblest and most absurd undertakings ever attempted by any state. Noblest because no other state has ever cared whether its artists as a group lived or died . . . Yet absurd, because a state can only function bureaucratically and impersonally — it has to assume that every member of a class is equivalent or comparable to every other member — but, every artist, good or bad, is a member of a class of one . . .

> — W. H. Auden, in his intro-
> duction to *Red Ribbon on a*
> *White Horse* by Anzia
> Yezierska, 1950

Work relief costs more than direct relief, but the cost is justified. First, in the saving of morale. Second, in the preservation of human skills and talents. Third, in the material enrichment which the unemployed add to our national wealth through their labors.

> — Harry Hopkins,
> March 14, 1936

The cost was ridiculous but at the same time it was an era of depression when they were putting people to work and I think it was a magnanimous gesture on the part of the government toward a better understanding of the nation which is necessary at any time.

> — Vardis Fisher, former director
> of the Idaho Writers' Project,
> in an interview with Ronald
> W. Taber, April 12, 1967

Most striking of the new departures was the WPA's Federal Writers' Project . . . At its peak it supported over six thousand journalists, freelance writers, novelists, poets, Ph.D.s and other jobless persons experienced in putting words on paper. Hacks, bohemians and local eccentrics jostled elbows with highly trained specialists and creative artists of such past or future distinction as Conrad Aiken, Maxwell Bodenheim, Vardis Fisher, and Richard Wright.

> — Dixon Wecter, in *The Age of*
> *the Great Depression* (1929–
> 1941), 1948

We were all like people on a raft, sharing a world of common disaster.

> — Lawrence Morris, former field
> editor of the Writers' Project;
> later, assistant WPA adminis-
> trator of Federal One, in an
> interview with the author,
> July 1, 1969

Three.

A Time of Overlapping Crises

Once it was decided that Federal One would be controlled from Washington, Jacob Baker and his staff began a frantic search for qualified persons to direct the theater, art, and music projects. Eva Le Gallienne was offered the job of heading the Theater Project, but she lost interest in it as soon as she learned that its program would not provide cash subsidies for existing theatrical companies like her own. Harry Hopkins then offered the post to Hallie Flanagan, a fellow Iowan who had been a student at Grinnell College at the same time he was. Mrs. Flanagan, a member of the Vassar College faculty, had a national reputation for her work in experimental theater. Nikolai Sokoloff, who had conducted the Cleveland Symphony Orchestra from 1918 to 1933, was chosen to direct the Music Project. The job of directing the Art Project went to Holger Cahill, an expert on American folk art, who had been associated with New York's Museum of Modern Art and with the Newark Museum of New Jersey.

There was no need to look for a director of the Writers' Project. It was taken for granted that the post would be assumed by Henry Alsberg. A member of Baker's staff since 1934, he had been editing two FERA magazines, one reporting on the far-flung activities of that agency, the other dealing with Baker's pet interest, government-sponsored cooperatives. The name Alsberg struck no familiar chord through the nation when his appointment was announced. He was then fifty-seven years old, but little known outside of New York City, his birthplace, where he had been a newspaperman and an off-Broadway theater director and writer, and moved in intellectual circles, chiefly among pacifists and philosophical anarchists.

Alsberg had tried to write a novel about his life but gave it up when he went to work for the New Deal. He had no lack of material. Born of Jewish-German parents (his father was a prosperous chemist), he entered Columbia at fifteen, graduated from its law school at twenty, and abandoned the practice of law after three years for postgraduate study in literature at Harvard. Except for a brief but affecting encounter with the fathers of pragmatic philosophy, William James and his friend Charles Peirce, he found his one year at Harvard dull. He began to edge his way into journalism, and in 1913 became an editorial writer for the New York *Evening Post*. Five years later he took a leave of absence to become secretary to Abraham Elkus, the American ambassador to Turkey. Through his journalist friends in Constantinople, he was able to score a coup of sorts by alerting the ambassador to the momentous news that the British army, headed by General Allenby, had thrown the Turks out of Palestine.

The excitement of being present while history was made appealed to him so much that he became a foreign correspondent for the *Nation,* the New York *World* and the London *Daily Herald,* roving through Europe and making six forays into Russia, where the Bolsheviks had recently seized power. His experience in Russia later led him to become one of the directors of the American Joint Distribution Committee, which was trying to help the famine victims of the Revolution. He was then in his early forties.

For seven months he traveled through southern and eastern Russia, riding in boxcars, sleeping in haystacks, and mixing with Russians of all kinds. Around him was a steady eruption of violence: arson, pillage, murder, and executions. In a pocket Alsberg carried some $10,000, which he was authorized to distribute to Jews in need. He would go into a village, assemble the Jewish elders, and find out what they required in the way of supplies and money. One of these conferences was interrupted by a young man who dashed in with the warning that a group of looting soldiers were approaching; they had heard there was a rich American in the village. The elders quickly disguised Alsberg as an Orthodox Jew, with an old coat and a skullcap, and rushed him toward a ferry that crossed the river into Rumania. On the way his disguise was publicized: his cap fell off, and an old woman ran after him shouting the fact. But Alsberg and his companions were aboard the ferry and well into the river when the soldiers arrived and began to shoot at them. They could see the flashes of the rifles, and hear the whining bullets around them, but no one was hurt.

Alsberg's wanderings in Russia ended when the Moscow police decided to recall him for questioning. The police agent assigned to bring him back finally caught up with him, and the two men began the long journey back to Moscow. With trains operating erratically, there was plenty of time for the two men to become friendly. When Alsberg first offered him a drink the agent refused, explaining he hardly ever took liquor. But after a few days he changed his mind and was soon consuming the stuff as though it were water. As the drinking became heavier, Alsberg found himself obliged to play the role of nursemaid, a role that became more pronounced when the agent, on the eve of their arrival in Moscow, collapsed with pneumonia. By the time they reached the police station where the agent was to report, he was semi-conscious and had to be carried. Entering the station, Alsberg deposited the body of the agent across the desk of an official and announced: "Here is the man you sent out to find me."

Like his anarchist friend Emma Goldman, who was in Russia at the same time, Alsberg soon became disenchanted with the postrevolution conduct of the Bolsheviks. He and Emma Goldman made no effort to conceal their feelings. In 1921 when Peter Kropotkin, the celebrated anarchist, died, the Bolsheviks planned to claim him in death as one of their ideologists by giving him a state funeral. Emma Goldman, a former student of Kropotkin, together with his family, refused to allow it. She also warned the Bolshevik authorities that, unless they released all jailed anarchists in Moscow long enough to attend the funeral, she would make a speech at Kropotkin's grave denouncing the Bolsheviks to the world press. The Bolsheviks took the threat seriously and followed her instruction. Alsberg, who was present at the funeral, joined the anarchists and their friends when they convened at a nearby tavern after the burial for drinks and speeches. At midnight the anarchists dutifully marched back to their jail, singing on the way, only to find the gates of the prison locked. The warden finally appeared and shouted to them: "Not tonight. Jail closed. Come back tomorrow. . . ."

On his return to the States in 1923 Alsberg joined forces with those who were protesting the Bolsheviks' suppression of civil liberties. To document the charge that the Soviets were persecuting Russians who were opposed to their regime, he edited the book *Letters from Russian Prisoners.* Throughout his forties Alsberg continued to retain his passion for social justice. When, in 1926, he was asked to contribute to a privately printed publication issued by Columbia classmates of 1900, his message to them left no doubt as to his deep dissatisfaction with the status quo: "It's very difficult to say very much," he wrote, "as I am so completely out of touch with the point of view of the majority of them. They are leading the normal life of the average American middle-class citizen. I am more or less in revolt against everything they would hold most sacred, and advocate causes that would be abhorrent to all their habits and fixed beliefs." He added that his "incidental goal" in life was "saving the world from reactionaries."

A less incidental goal was developing a career in the theater. He made an auspicious start by writing an adaptation of the famous Yiddish play, *The Dybbuk*, which ran in an off-Broadway theater for almost two years. Later it was produced on Broadway and in Chicago and London. He also became one of the directors of the Provincetown Playhouse in New York, which made a specialty of presenting plays by Americans. He helped to produce such successes as E. E. Cummings's *Him* and Paul Green's Pulitzer Prize–winning play, *In Abraham's Bosom*, and would have continued in the theater had not the economic crisis halted the activities of the Provincetown Playhouse and other experimental drama groups in New York.

Despite his association with Emma Goldman and other leftwingers of the twenties, Alsberg was not considered particularly radical during the Depression years. Like so many of his friends who had been involved with philosophical anarchists, he had little in common with the Marxian firebrands of the thirties, regardless of whether they were Stalinists or Trotskyites. Advancing age, the true enemy of all radical movements, had softened his antagonism toward middle-class values, and enabled him to take a job with the inner core of the American Establishment, the government itself. He could no longer say to his former Columbia classmates that he was in revolt against everything they held most sacred. In his more permissive attitude toward political reality, he had become more philosophical and less anarchistic, and had even stopped crusading against the inequities of the Soviet regime.

New Deal agencies served as a convenient haven for tired radicals of the twenties like Alsberg. Baker, who had known many of them, was astute enough to realize that the New Deal with its progressive goals could make good use of these men with a social conscience whose claws had been blunted by time. Perhaps the best known of the revolutionaries of the twenties to find employment with the New Deal was Floyd Dell, who had been indicted by the federal government in 1918 for his antidraft activities.* Dell, a prolific novelist and experienced editor, first entered government service in 1935 as a Washington editor on the Federal Writers' Project payroll, but instead of doing Project work, he was assigned to ghostwriting speeches for New Deal officials, a job he performed efficiently and without fanfare for the rest of the decade.

Dell's qualifications for the directorship of the Writers' Project were superior to those of Alsberg, and he was seven years his junior. But his reputation as a radical spokesman of the twenties was too well-established; the administration did not dare appoint him. Only one or two newspapers questioned Alsberg's qualifications for the job; the main criticism came from his friends who privately marveled that someone who could barely administer himself, an assistant, and one secretary, should suddenly be placed in the position of bossing a project of some sixty-five hundred employees. They were aware of his reluctance to make decisions, and his habit of leaving projects unfinished. And although they admired his daring exploits as a roving journalist, they wondered whether at the age of fifty-seven there was still enough stamina and courage in the man to undertake a task that would tax the physical and psychic resources of anyone half his age.

Yet however much they might question his administrative capacities, they could not deny his inventive mind, his encyclopedic fund of information, and his literary taste. He had still another quality that would serve him in good stead, one which de Selincourt characterized as "the most daring of faiths" — a basic faith in people which, according to the novelist Vincent McHugh, gave him an extraordinary breadth of vision that placed him in an elite group of contemporaries similarly endowed — John Reed, E. E. Cummings and John Dos Passos among them — "men with a *public* sense, a feeling for broad human movements and how people are caught up in them."

Baker knew Alsberg's plus and minus qualities as well as anyone else.

---

* The government charged him with violating the espionage law for having written in *The Masses:* "There are some laws that the individual feels he cannot obey, and he will suffer any punishment, even that of death, rather than recognize them as having authority over him. The fundamental stubbornness of the free soul, against which all the powers of the State are helpless, constitutes a conscientious objection, whatever its sources may be in political or social opinion." Indicted with him were several other staff members of *The Masses,* including Max Eastman and John Reed. The trial ended with a hung jury.

"An anarchistic sort of a fellow incapable of administration but one with a great deal of creative talent," was the way he described him to an associate several months before selecting him for the post of director.* He wisely foresaw that in order for the Writers' Project to avoid the all-too-easy pitfalls of mediocrity and dullness, it would require a man of Alsberg's integrity and taste to be in charge. Alsberg's journalistic background was another plus in his favor, for it was evident that many of the men and women on relief who would qualify for Project jobs were unemployed newspaper people. Baker may have also been influenced by the consideration that Alsberg's experience in feeding hungry Russian Jews might in some way contribute to the job of providing for hungry American writers. At any rate, he was aware of his deep sense of compassion and of his ability to deal with persons of all social strata, from Greenwich Village freaks to proud executives, all of whom were to be represented in the Project's personnel.

Fumbling constantly for cigarettes (and sometimes for Bisodol), spilling ashes and food over his clothing, Alsberg looked more like an absent-minded patriarch than an executive. Yet the craggy landscape of his brown face (absurdly interrupted by a square moustache golden with nicotine) together with his ponderous body and the rumbling Old Testament sound of his voice somehow combined to emit a steady current of authority. Not immediately apparent to Baker was an endangering trait that is often peculiar to men who have been bachelors too long: an undue reliance on persons who had the ability to amuse him. His tendency was to classify people as either "boring" or "amusing" and treat them accordingly. More often than was good for the Project he would place his trust in people whom he found entertaining and steer clear of those whom he suspected of dullness, despite their positive qualities. One small illustrative scene comes to mind. He had summoned a group of his chief assistants to help him decide whether or not a certain staff member should be promoted to a post that would bring him almost daily into contact with the director's office. Alsberg listened to the discussion patiently until he realized we were all in favor of promoting the man, at which point he grimaced, as though he had been ordered to swallow a dose of castor oil, and drawled, "Oh, no, let's not do it, fellows. The man is such a bore."

* A former colleague of Alsberg recalled that in his early days with FERA he never bothered to make carbons of letters he wrote and was in the habit of throwing away carbons made by his secretary.

Although Alsberg was occasionally witty,* he himself was often guilty of inflicting boredom on friends and colleagues with his propensity for suffocatingly long monologues, a fact which never seemed to occur to him. In general, however, he was liked and respected by his staff. Only in the closing months of the Project did any of his colleagues turn against him with destructive intent.

In an effort to compensate for Alsberg's lack of administrative talent, Baker flanked him with two men who had impressed him with their sense of practicality. Reed Harris, a young man in his twenties who had been assisting Alsberg in his FERA job, was selected to bear the brunt of the Project's administrative labors. George W. Cronyn, who had published two novels and been an English professor at the University of Montana, was given the title of associate director and placed in charge of the Project's editorial activities.†

Cronyn was a chunky middle-aged man with a methodical turn of mind. On the theory that a novelist should accumulate diverse experiences before attempting to write, he had been an apple grower, a rancher, and a plumber. Baker was pleased to note that he had also been the business manager of *Story* magazine for a time and the editor of a magazine devoted to business called *System;* and that he had served on the editorial staffs of two encyclopedias, the Columbia and the New Standard. Cronyn's first big task was to write an encyclopedic set of instructions for Project field workers called "The American Guide Manual," which, prepared under the impression that the Project was to devote itself to the preparation of six regional guides, became obsolete almost as soon as it was received in the state Project offices.

Like most triumvirates, this one proved to be a fiasco. Within the next year Cronyn and Alsberg were to find that they were temperamentally incompatible, a situation that was to contribute heavily to the initial inefficiency of the Washington office. Harris, on the other hand, was a wise choice for the job, even though his record made him sound like a dangerous nonconformist. At the age of twenty-one he had been thrown out of Columbia University for writing an exposé of commercialism in college

---

* A sample witticism of Alsberg, who was fond of paraphrasing Shakespeare: "Ah, farting is such sweet sorrow."

† George W. Cronyn's two novels were *The Fool of Venus,* a best seller of 1934 published by Covici Friede, and *Fortune and Men's Eyes* issued the following year by the same publisher. He also edited an anthology of North American Indian songs and chants, *The Path of the Rainbow* (Boni and Liveright, 1918).

football in a book called *King Football*. A tall and powerfully built figure, Harris had been a member of the Columbia football squad but turned in his uniform when the university refused to pay him for his services as a player, although it was paying some of his teammates. Harris contended that colleges should either reimburse all their football players or discontinue the practice altogether. He had also annoyed the university's administrative officials by insisting that students had the right to be taught by teachers of all political faiths, including communism.*

Before taking a job with FERA, Harris had chalked up six years of journalistic experience, first on a country weekly, then on a small city daily, and later on the New York *Journal* and the New York *Times*. Had not the Depression cut off his newspaper career, he probably would have wound up as a newspaper executive. An objective and compassionate man with a deep, slow voice that promptly commanded respect, he seemed born to the role of administrator. In an atmosphere as explosive as that of the Writers' Project, his presence suggested a veritable pillar of calm and order.

Some office wit had once spread a rumor which purported that as Alsberg's assistant on FERA Harris had done 90 percent of the work while Alsberg had done 90 percent of the talking. There may have been some figment of truth in that. But on the Writers' Project both men worked as they never had before. Alsberg had complete faith in Harris's abilities, and Harris responded with a devotion which not only spared his chief a number of onerous responsibilities but also provided a facade behind which the older man's occasional errors could go undetected. So concerned was Harris with Alsberg's welfare that at one point he pleaded with a WPA administrator that his chief be given a raise in salary since he initially had been paid less than the other arts projects directors. Alsberg made no secret of his dependence on Harris. On learning that his WPA superiors had designs on Harris's services, he told them that if he were deprived of Harris he would resign.

---

* In the early fifties, during the notorious era of Senator Joseph McCarthy's investigations of subversives in government service, Harris, then an employee of the State Department, emerged as a hero of sorts. Pilloried by McCarthy for his youthful "radical" background, Harris, according to one columnist, "stood up like a man and gave one of the most intuitive and devastating analyses ever made of the McCarthy method of character assassination." Harris then resigned from his State Department post, but was reinstated in government service eight years later by Edward R. Murrow who, in his first official act as director of the United States Information Service, appointed him a special assistant.

At first, in addition to his administrative duties for the Writers' Project, Harris had the task of supervising, almost single-handedly, the Project's WPA reporting services in thirty-six states. These units, collectively known as the Reporters' Project, consisted of former newspaper writers who prepared detailed reports on WPA activities in their areas. Harris's job was to extract from their reports material which the WPA could use to publicize its blessings.* Later, when the Reporters' Project was abolished, Alsberg burdened him with some of the Project's editorial responsibilities that could have been entrusted to George Cronyn.

Government work tends to bureaucratize human beings rapidly, particularly when they are in supervisory positions, but this did not happen to Harris, despite the entangling red tape surrounding him. His natural sympathy for the underdog characterized almost everything he did, and helped to prevent his Washington colleagues from slipping into arrogance. In one memorandum he chided them for the "school teacherish" language they used in their letters to state editors; it gave the impression that "we were posing as tin gods." Particularly offensive to him were such phrases as:

"We told you on January 11 . . ."

"This must be rewritten immediately."

"You will have to do this right away."

Harris reminded the Washington editors that often they were dealing with men and women who had had considerable experience as writers and editors and who resented being treated like children. From now on, he announced, he would review all outgoing communications so as to stop any that might create antagonism. In a second memorandum he again pleaded for more tact, and told of a staff member whose criticism of a manuscript from a southern state had been nothing more than a series of "nasty cracks." Had the criticism been sent back to the state as it was written, Harris added, "there would have been another Civil War."

In his haste to assemble a Washington staff it had never occurred to Alsberg to judge applicants by their ability to be tactful. His urgent need was to surround himself with people of experience whom he could trust. Among his earliest appointments were three of his old friends, Roderick Seidenberg, Leonard Abbott, and Waldo R. Browne. Seidenberg, who was

---

* In one of his news reports Reed Harris noted that in Oregon one WPA job holder was so overjoyed at the prospect of working after months of unemployment "that he died of heart failure before he could reach the site of operations."

an architect (he had recently designed Manhattan's New Yorker hotel) and a magazine writer, was made art and architectural editor. Abbott, a friend of Emma Goldman, who had been assistant editor of the *Literary Digest* at the turn of the century and again in the late twenties, was given the title of research editor. Browne, the former editor-in-chief of the prestigious but now dead literary magazine, the *Dial*, and once literary editor of the *Nation*, became the Project's literary editor. As a further means of making certain that the Project's editorial standards would be high, Alsberg also appointed Floyd Dell as advisory editor, only to have him snatched away after a few weeks by a higher ranking WPA official.

Except for Seidenberg, who eventually was to publish two notable philosophical works,* all these were men whose best years were behind them. Abbott, who was older than the others, loomed like a specter as he sat, year after year, in a corner of the Washington office searching for errors in the material sent in from the states. His ghostly quietness, which matched the pallid texture of his skin, seemed to embarrass his younger colleagues, and they hardly ever spoke to him.

At first the key men on the Washington staff were the field supervisors, who traveled about the country acting as troubleshooters and trying to galvanize the state Project staffs into action. Two of the men Alsberg picked for these posts were men in their thirties who were to have a significant influence on the Project's early development. One was Joseph Gaer, a small and intense Russian immigrant who had come to the United States at the age of twenty, and spoke with a pronounced accent. Gaer had already gained some experience as a government literary man on a California FERA writing project, had published extensively in literary and folklore publications, and was the author of a widely circulated book, *How the Great Religions Began*. From time to time Gaer was to raise Alsberg's hackles by openly encouraging field workers to disregard instructions from Washington in the interests of getting on with their work; but he was invariably forgiven since there was no one else on the supervisory staff who could be as effective in wresting manuscripts from state offices in time to meet pressing deadlines. Yet Alsberg was reluctant to use Gaer's services as widely as he might have. Afraid that his Russian-Jewish accent could mislead strangers into thinking he might be a dangerous

---

* *Posthistoric Man: An Inquiry* (1950) and *Anatomy of the Future* (1961). Both books were published by the University of North Carolina Press.

radical, Alsberg tried to keep him out of the Midwest and the South, but made extensive use of him in the more cosmopolitan areas.

The field supervisor that Alsberg did not hesitate to send anywhere was Lawrence Morris, a former assistant editor of the *New Republic* and a translator of French novels, who was appointed at the same time as Gaer. Soft-spoken and gentle, Morris seemed more like a poet than a trouble-shooter, but he had a persuasive manner, and soon proved he could deal successfully with all types of field personnel, including tough WPA state administrators who disliked the arts projects. A man of superb finesse, Morris was frequently able to break through their hostility and engage them in constructive dialogues. Unfortunately for Alsberg, the WPA higher echelon soon became aware of Morris's talents, and nine months after he was hired by the Project he was appointed chief administrative assistant to Ellen S. Woodward (the friend of Mrs. Roosevelt who supplanted Jacob Baker as the deputy WPA administrator in charge of all white collar projects). In effect, Morris became the administrative supervisor of all the arts projects, and it was to him that Alsberg usually had to appeal for whatever administrative help the Project required from the WPA.

The job of field supervisor was fiendishly difficult, entailing the abilities of a superdiplomat, editor, and administrator. Not all of Alsberg's appointees to the post were as effective as Gaer and Morris. Darel McConkey, a young and personable ex-columnist, proved to be more effective as an editor than as a troubleshooter, and after a few months was retired to the Washington office to supervise the editing of all guidebook copy dealing with cities.* In January Alsberg appointed as field supervisor the woman who had contributed to the idea of an American Guide Series. She was Katharine Kellock, a compulsive talker and worker who was to become one of the most influential members of the editorial staff.

In her eagerness to join the Project, Mrs. Kellock had willingly relinquished a higher-paying job she had with the Resettlement Administration. She was a widely traveled woman who had written for newspapers and magazines and contributed some thirty-five biographies to the Dictionary of American Biography. Her European travels had made her an enthusiastic advocate of the Baedeker concept of guidebooks. She viewed

---

* In 1940 Darel McConkey spent almost six months in Salt Lake City helping to complete the long delayed Utah State Guide. It was published the following year.

Henry G. Alsberg with some of his executive staff in Washington, D.C.,
1937. Left to right: Jerre Mangione, Roderick Seidenberg, Joseph Gaer

the Project as if it were a new religion charged with a sacred trust and, at times, as if she were its high priestess, endowed by fate with a set of commandments decreeing that the American Guide Series should be created in the image of the Baedeker guides — an image that was to be bitterly disputed by some of her colleagues. From the start, she did not hesitate to speak her mind. Two weeks after she had been appointed field supervisor, she wrote Alsberg a confidential memorandum expressing her scorn for the stupendous "American Guide Manual" (eventually it was to include eighteen supplements) which she considered unworkable except perhaps in the large cities. The writer of the manual, she insisted, had overlooked the fact that 75 percent of the Project workers would be located in communities that had only the most elementary reference libraries. She was especially critical of the instruction in the manual which stipulated that each writer was to produce an average of fifteen hundred words per week, "a perfectly absurd standard that invites dawdling and padding."

In South Carolina she instructed the writers to forget the fifteen-hundred-word assignment and concentrate on turning in information, then wrote her husband: "What those dreamers in Washington did was to assign a wide range of topics from history to paleontology and anthropology and appraisals of local architecture, and bid all 'writers' turn in fifteen hundred words a week. That's a hell of a way to make up a guidebook." She told Alsberg that at that rate the American Guide Series would not be completed until 1990, and as if to justify her defiance of the manual, quoted one Project worker to the effect that "the manual is like the Bible. Anyone can interpret it any way." As an afterthought she added, "Please don't think I am sabotaging . . . As you know, I care very much about getting decent guidebooks."

Her reports from the field bristled with complaints — the elderly North Carolina state director was incapable of delegating responsibility and was always in a hurry to get back to Asheville and his very young wife; many of the editors she encountered were incompetent; the director in one of the states was not spending Project funds properly, etc. The reports disturbed Alsberg's duodenum but he read them carefully, knowing Katharine Kellock well enough (she was the wife of one of his oldest friends) to realize that the quality of the guidebooks was, indeed, her chief consideration.

"I care only about results and we simply are not getting them so far as I have been able to see," she wrote from Raleigh, North Carolina. "In each state I have been able to stir up some lively stuff to be forwarded to you; it is my regret that in each place I cannot stay on and stir up more . . ." Trying to diagnose the reason that so much of the material sent to Washington from the southeastern states was of poor quality, she reported that each state director she encountered felt uncertain about what the "government" really wanted. "There is a lurking fear — in spite of interpolations to the contrary in the manual — that the product on which they will be judged is the usual kind of dull government publication full of statistics. They feel they have to leave out the juices in order to cover the dry-as-dust content. I've had to make them feel that 'National Director Dr. Henry Alsberg' is not a mixture of state archivist, Chamber of Commerce director and Chicago city magistrate, and that you want initiative and imagination. . . ."

Her career as a field supervisor was abruptly cut short after a few months by a Hearst newspaper accusation that she was a Red (an accusation based largely on the fact that her husband, Harold Kellock, was then the Washington representative of the Soviet news agency, Tass). The accusation was not taken seriously in Washington but because it diminished her effectiveness in the field, Alsberg recalled her and made her tours editor, a giant responsibility which was to entail the close supervision of more than half of the total wordage in all the state guidebooks. No one on the staff, with the possible exception of Alsberg, then realized the depth of her capacity, the intensity of her determination. She may not have known herself, this small tornado of a woman whose voice seemed to alternate between the sounds of scolding and laughter. She often rubbed her colleagues the wrong way with her demands and complaints, clashing with them more often than she herself realized. But she was as honest as she was zealous and her devotion to her task emanated a pervasive aura of dedication that seeped into the bones of the rest of the staff.

"Sometimes tactless to a grating degree," recalls a former Project associate of hers, "given to encroaching on the domain of Essays, reluctant to surrender a City, but possessed of demon vitality, she added more than we liked to concede at the time to the guidebooks. Her range of interests was wide, and it was due to her insistence that thousands of sites of battles, feuds, significant events and curious happenings appear along the highways and byways. She had a healthy hunger for the economy of a region: when avocados are picked, how automobiles came to be made in Michi-

Henry G. Alsberg

*Katharine Kellock with W. K. Van
Olinda in the Washington office*

*George W. Cronyn, associate director
of the Project*

gan, why beaver hats went out of fashion, etc. She was a demon, and
rightly so, for accurate mileage and fought like a mother lion for wordage,
holding that tours, being the raison d'être of the guidebooks, deserved the
larger part of the space."

Nearly six months were to pass before Katharine Kellock and the other
editors in the Central Office were to start receiving material from the field
in sizable volume. During those early months the main effort of the Project
was largely administrative, with the brunt of it falling on the field supervisors as they traveled from one state to another trying, against heavy odds
and WPA state administrative resistance, to assist in the birth of forty-nine
writers' projects that could function within the framework of a nationally
directed project. Unable to hire as many field supervisors as he needed,
Alsberg from time to time utilized Harris, Cronyn, and Roderick Seidenberg as field men. He also increased his field staff, while at the same time
quieting the critics who found fault with the predominantly eastern orien-
tation of his Washington staff, by pressing into service some of his newly
appointed noneastern state directors, among them Maurice Howe of
Utah, Jay DuVon of Iowa, and the novelist Lyle Saxon of Louisiana.

Reed Harris proved to be as administratively astute in the field as he
was in Washington. In Nevada, where he was sent to investigate the
abrupt dismissal of an editor on a charge of drunkenness, he found that
the editor was a moderate drinker who, for reasons that had nothing to do
with his work, was disliked by the state WPA administrator. By some
Solomon-like maneuver, Harris managed to get the editor reinstated without antagonizing the administrator. In a midwestern state he quietly
checked the report that the Writers' Project director was using Project
funds to travel from one town to another for no other ostensible purpose
than to visit the ladies of his widely scattered harem. Another charge was
that the same state director was using the facilities of the Project to do research work for his novelist son. On finding both charges true, Harris with
superb adroitness managed to fire the director without causing any scandalous newspaper publicity.

Cronyn was a fine editor but seemed to have little talent as a troubleshooter. A forthright man inclined to judge situations by their face value,
he lacked Harris's insight into the devious art of public relations. Early in
December, Alsberg sent him to California to handle the Project's first
major administrative crisis, one which was to test the principle of federal
control. The crisis had been precipitated by Paul Radin, the California

state director in San Francisco, and by Hugh Harlan, the Project's district supervisor in Los Angeles. Both men were openly defying the official edict from Washington that the preparation of the state guidebook was to be given priority over all other undertakings. Radin, a noted anthropologist, and Harlan, an experienced newspaperman, insisted on concentrating all efforts of the California Project on several special studies which they had initiated under FERA auspices. To the telegrams from the Central Office ordering them to "terminate at once all projects other than the American Guide," both men replied in a manner which Alsberg interpreted as insubordinate. In his most drastic action to date, Alsberg suspended most of the California operations; then sent Cronyn to Los Angeles and San Francisco to set things right.

In Los Angeles Cronyn quickly fired Harlan and three of his assistants, and appointed an acting supervisor. Then, rushing to San Francisco where friends of the insubordinate director were threatening a strike, he removed Radin from his job and ordered a reorganization of the California staff. All of his past experience dictated this series of actions as the only possible intelligent alternative, but he had failed to realize that the dismissal of any government official, however minor, can often lead to precarious consequences. A hot barrage of public criticism followed the dismissal of Radin and Harlan, and Cronyn was loudly accused of engaging in "arbitrary and unjust action." The reaction was so sharp and clamorous that Cronyn was hastily recalled to Washington. At the same time, Maurice Howe was dispatched to California with instructions to extinguish the blaze ignited by Cronyn's actions. As a result, Harlan (he had lost no time calling on his old friend Harry Hopkins for help) was reinstated as district supervisor of Los Angeles. In San Francisco, Paul Radin was made research editor of the California Project, which meant that he could continue the work he had begun under FERA auspices, without any fear of further interference. As the new California state director, Howe chose James Hopper, a prolific short story writer and novelist, an appointment which appeared to be a happy one at the time but which two years later was to create another crisis.*

---

* The California experience taught Alsberg a lesson in governmental procedure which he never forgot. Years later he summarized the lesson as follows: "Never fire anyone if you can avoid it; he is almost certain to have friends who will raise hell in the press and cause you more trouble than you would have had if you retained him. If you want to get rid of anyone, the best tactic is to praise the man's abilities to the skies in the hope that some other agency will hire him."

As Lawrence Morris observed, there never was a time when the Project was not fraught with crises. "Everything was an emergency situation. Difficult decisions had to be made at once — often on the telephone." For an enterprise whose life was to be a series of overlapping crises its first headquarters were all too appropriate — a former theater. The Old Auditorium, as it was now called, was a gray and cavernous structure, virtually airless, with a dilapidated stage curtain and a glaring array of organ pipes to attest to its old days of glory. In recent times its status as a cultural center had sunk to the point where the building was utilized mainly for prize fights and dog shows. With the establishment of Federal One, some misguided WPA planner persuaded the administration to reconstruct it into offices that would accommodate the Washington staffs of all four arts projects.

It must have been a last-minute decision. Even as the Federal One staffs were moving in, the auditorium's once elegant theater boxes were being converted into repositories for files, and the orchestra floor was being turned into a labyrinth of office cubicles that resembled stockyard pens. During the riveting, hammering and sawing, Alsberg was installed in an office that had formerly served as a dressing room, on the third floor directly behind the stage, from which vantage point he could observe what was happening in the cubicles.

With him was Dora Thea Hettwer, who only a few months before had agreed to become his secretary. Miss Hettwer, who held degrees from Radcliffe and Harvard and spoke several languages, had taken the job reluctantly: she had learned that Alsberg had had eleven previous secretaries in a single year. Only his "great respect for words" and his knowledge of German, a language she spoke fluently, persuaded her to try her hand as his twelfth secretary. By the time they moved into the auditorium, she had decided that no one she had ever known was as knowledgeable and as human. She became his most devoted attendant, as worshipful and as eagerly helpful as a doting daughter.

The thunder of remodeling the auditorium had barely subsided when she and Alsberg, along with all of its other tenants, were dislodged from the building and ensconced in a Florentine-style mansion which had once been the residence of Evelyn Walsh McLean, the owner of the famed Hope diamond. The new headquarters were no less bizarre than the auditorium. There were elegant chandeliers dripping with the opulence of the twenties, silken walls and mahogany paneling, a veritable museum of life-

"The Auditorium," first (and last) Washington headquarters of the Writers' Project

The Project in the McLean mansion, Washington, D.C.

size statues emulating the ancient Greeks, and a mammoth fireplace supported at each side by big-muscled, stooping men of stone. The Writers' Project was assigned the handsome ballroom on the first floor which, according to rumor, was haunted by a young woman who (presumably the victim of unrequited love) had leaped to her death from the musicians' gallery while a crowded dance was in progress. The fascination of the mansion was further enhanced by the legend that a secret tunnel connected the White House with the McLean home, at whose entrance President Harding's mistress would anxiously await the arrival of her lover.

The mansion became a scene of grotesque contrasts as the staff members of Federal One moved in. The ballroom floor was covered with some fifty desks to accommodate the Project's personnel. Files were shoved into the giant fireplace. Coats and hats were hung on the arms of the life-size statues. With the invasion of office equipment and editors in shirt sleeves, the scene evoked visions of some Russian palace during the Revolution that had just been seized by the proletariat. Except for two glass-enclosed areas occupied by Alsberg and Cronyn, and a closet behind the fireplace appropriated as an office by Seidenberg, there was no private office space. Most of the staff and secretaries worked among the clamor of typewriters, the ringing of telephones, and the occasional shouts of the office drunk.

The mansion's only living connection with its sumptuous past was its doorman, who repeatedly let it be known that he had worked for the McLeans. He no longer enjoyed his job; the new occupants of the mansion lacked "class" and he had little use for them. The "big people" who used to frequent the mansion as guests of the McLeans, he complained to Hallie Flanagan, were too gentlemanly to discuss money matters in public, but the present occupants were always saying such things as "Let's take twenty thousand dollars from Ohio and give it to Kansas," or "Let's cut New York City by fifty thousand dollars." Moreover, he was certain it was all in their imagination. "Did you ever see any of this money they talk about?" he once asked Mrs. Flanagan. She had to admit she never had. "See?" he exclaimed triumphantly. "It's all in their minds. It don't exist."

Inside this profaned symbol of capitalist America, Alsberg and the other three arts project directors worked day and night during September 1935, trying to set in motion machinery for spending about $27 million to hire for six months some thirty thousand unemployed writers, actors, musicians, and artists, most of whom were to come from the relief rolls. With sixty-five hundred men and women to put to work on the Writers' Project as quickly as possible, preferably before the November elections, Alsberg's plan was to organize the national staff along the lines of a big-city newspaper, with the Washington editors functioning in the collective role of city editor, with the state directors acting as desk men, and the field workers as reporters. He envisaged a Writers' Project office in every community of ten thousand or more population and at least one reporter in each of the nation's three thousand counties. The plan was a sensible one, but its success depended to a great extent on the caliber of the forty-nine men and women who would be appointed directors in each of the states and in New York City, which was to be treated as a state.

Finding the person with the proper qualifications for each of the states was no easy task. At first, as Katharine Kellock later pointed out, no one was sure what those qualifications might be since no job of its kind had ever existed before. When it was too late to matter, it was discovered that the ideal director was "a combination of administrator, diplomat, encyclopedist, creative writer, personnel supervisor, and publicity man." Dana Doten, the state director of Vermont, described the job as "a baffling combination of midwifery and assembly line" and the role of the director as "an absorbent of worries and an occasional suggester of similes."

Yet the search for well-qualified directors was a simple one compared to the task of coping with WPA state administrators who were inclined to dislike an enterprise which, unlike all the others they administered, took its orders from Washington yet was dependent on the state administrators for all kinds of assistance, ranging from secretarial personnel to office equipment. What especially incensed many of the WPA administrators at the outset was the assumption in Washington that a state Writers' Project director could be appointed without their approval. Baker and Alsberg did their best to appease them, but insisted on making the appointments. In Idaho, where Vardis Fisher was made director of the Writers' Project, the state WPA administrator, angry that he had not been consulted, would not provide chairs and desks for Fisher's staff members, compelling them to use boxes instead. In an attempt to placate the WPA administrators in some states, Alsberg would ask them to send him a list of their recommended candidates. But since the state administrator was likely to be a hard-boiled politician whose acquaintance with persons who might qualify was limited, the list was seldom useful.

The WPA administrator in Virginia surprised Alsberg by asking him what kind of a person he wanted for the directorship. Alsberg replied: "An editor, or journalist or someone who has written novels, somebody with some reputation and somebody not entirely helpless or whom you would have to nurse along, someone who can stand on his own feet without bothering you too much. If you have someone in your WPA organization with those qualifications, that wouldn't be bad . . ."

Yet even so soft and flexible an approach sometimes met with rejection. In Pennsylvania the WPA administrator let it be known that the name of his game was patronage. When Cronyn asked him to approve of two candidates, he refused to endorse either one on the grounds that their names had been suggested by a Republican, the president of the University of Pennsylvania. Then, on learning that the job paid $2,900 per year, the administrator sneered that Cronyn could not hire a dishwasher for that salary and insisted that the position was to pay at least $4,000. Cronyn and Alsberg, intimidated by the administrator's political muscle, went along with his demands, even that of accepting his own candidate, one Logan B. Sisson, who proved to be so unsatisfactory a state director that within a year he was removed and replaced by his assistant, Paul Comly French, another one of the administrator's candidates.

Alsberg spent most of the month of October talking with potential candidates, WPA administrators, and politicians, trying to appoint all the state directors by November 1, the official date set for starting the Project's operations. Whenever he discovered a novelist who was interested in directing the Project in his home state, he would consider him his first choice, then try to get the state WPA administrator's approval without antagonizing him. In Oklahoma his searches led him to William Cunningham, a poet and novelist whose latest novel was *The Green Corn Rebellion*. On the telephone Alsberg explained to Cunningham that the supervisory job would pay only $2,300.

Cunningham: Where would the headquarters be, Oklahoma or Washington?

Alsberg: In Oklahoma. The supervisor would look after the state for us. Our main project right now is the American Guide, which is to be done by relief workers by the collection of data, et cetera. Do you think you would be interested?

Cunningham: It would interest me. I would like to be in Oklahoma as most of my material for writing is there.

Alsberg: Can you do it for that salary?

Cunningham: I believe so.

Alsberg: We can put you down as a possibility?

Cunningham: Yes.

Alsberg: How soon? In the next two weeks?

Cunningham: Yes, I can arrange that.

But as Alsberg was rapidly learning, nothing worked out that easily in government. Two days later he received a phone call from Cronyn informing him that Senator Gore was "recommending and endorsing" his own candidate for the job, one A. L. Emery.

Alsberg: Who did you say is recommending him?

Cronyn: Senator Gore. He is the blind senator from Oklahoma . . . He is that famous blind senator.

Alsberg: I think we'll have to find out who Emery is.

Cronyn: That's what I thought too.

Alsberg: I don't think we ought to allow any senator to tell us what to do.

Cunningham got the job, but later when the Oklahoma state guidebook material was held up for a variety of reasons that were beyond the Project's power to control, Alsberg may have wondered whether he had been wise in turning down the senator's candidate. His desire not to permit senators to interfere with his appointments was genuine enough, but in any direct confrontation with a senator it was apt to crumble. In Maryland his attempt to appoint his own candidate was interrupted by a telephone call from the state WPA administrator there, who reported that Senator Radcliffe was recommending a historian named Dr. Karl Singewald for the job. His only qualification as a writer was that he had edited an obscure work entitled *Maryland in the World War: Military and Naval Service Records,* which had taken him some fifteen years to complete. Alsberg protested that Singewald was obviously not qualified to be a state director but the administrator insisted that he be given first consideration. "Well, we are the ones responsible for running the Maryland Project," Alsberg replied, irked. "The senator won't take the responsibility . . . It looks like a political appointment." The administrator denied that the senator would be "party to that," then asked Alsberg to meet with Singewald.

Following the interview, Alsberg reported to the administrator that he and Cronyn considered Singewald to be a good research man but "very shy and very retiring and nearly deaf" and therefore incapable of administering the Maryland Project. When Alsberg repeated his impression of Singewald to Senator Radcliffe (at the state administrator's request), the senator sharply disagreed with him. "I feel very strongly that Dr. Singe-wald is the person best qualified to do the work for you. I know him, because I have been working with him for fifteen years." To Alsberg's objection that he lacked administrative ability, the senator replied that Singewald was perfectly capable of managing people and was, in fact, "a forceful man." The upshot of Alsberg's discussion with the senator was that Singewald became head of the Maryland Project. In a few months, however, Alsberg's appraisal of his qualifications proved to be dismally correct. Trying to make the best of the situation, Alsberg quietly relieved Singewald of his administrative duties and unofficially placed an assistant in charge of the Project.

In Missouri the political might of the Pendergast machine was so bla-tant that Alsberg was obliged to accept the machine's candidate with little or no discussion. His own choice for the job was Jack Conroy, who the year before had published a highly praised novel, *The Disinherited,* but the post went to an amateur writer and society figure, Mrs. Geraldine Parker, who incited such havoc among the Project workers that Washing-ton was compelled to shut down the Missouri office for several months.

Another disastrous appointment, also politically inspired, was that of Elizabeth Sheehan in Nebraska. Miss Sheehan, allegedly the ex-mistress of a powerful newspaper publisher in Lincoln who was a close political ally of Senator Norris, proved to be paranoid as well as incompetent. When Lawrence Morris investigated the reports of her disruptive conduct and recommended immediate dismissal, Miss Sheehan promptly alerted her publisher friend who, in turn, wrote to Senator Norris. The result was that Morris was ordered out of the state and the senator let it be known that "as long as Nebraska had a writers' project, Miss Sheehan would have her desk."

In the meantime, Miss Sheehan was paying little attention to the opera-tion of the Project. Convinced that one of her assistants, Rudolph Umland, was a dangerous radical who was plotting to get her job, she hired a pri-vate detective agency to investigate his background. The only information it could turn up was that a brother of Umland had participated in a 1933 march of the unemployed which was led by Mother Bloor, a leading Com-munist of that era. This was all the "proof" Miss Sheehan needed to write letters to the President and numerous other government officials denounc-ing her assistant as a tool of the Communist party. When it became obvi-ous that the Nebraska Project could not function under her direction and that the administration was unwilling to dismiss her for fear of offending Senator Norris, Alsberg ordered Miss Sheehan, along with her desk and secretary, transferred to her home. There she continued to receive her director's salary regularly until the close of the Nebraska Project in 1942.

The hostile attitude of the WPA state administrators, a number of whom regarded the Writers' Project as a crackpot New Deal experiment that would be dropped in a few months, took the form of obstructionist actions, political interference, or contemptuous indifference. In Wyoming the indifference of the state administrator resulted in the appointment of a well-known Republican politician as state director. The politician made the most of his opportunity to embarrass the WPA administration further by ignoring the responsibilities of his position and by turning in unsatisfactory expense accounts. When finally he was fired, he jauntily announced his candidacy for state treasurer, and was easily elected. Alsberg appointed the ablest editor on the Wyoming staff to replace him, Agnes Wright Spring. She too turned out to be a Republican but one with honorable intentions.

Some of Alsberg's worst administrative headaches occurred in the states where there were few well-known writers. When no qualified state director could be found for the state of Washington, Alsberg acted on the recommendation of the WPA state administrator, and appointed R. W. Lahr as acting director. The appointment proved to be a gross mistake. Lahr was a bureaucrat interested only in administrative routine and paid no attention to Washington's demands that work be started for the state guidebook. Within two months he was replaced by James W. Egan, a former sports editor and a prolific writer of pulp fiction, who had been recommended to Alsberg by the Authors League of America. Egan at first impressed the Washington office with his zeal. In less than six months' time he submitted some 250,000 words of the state guidebook. However, when the material was carefully examined the editors found that only a small fraction of it was any good. Egan, according to one of his assistants who talked to the press, had been encouraging his staff to write fiction instead of fact. The assistant was afraid that if the material were published as written it would make the state of Washington "the laughing-stock of the nation." She charged that most of it was "pure fiction," prepared without research, written "in the office" to save time. Egan denied the charges, even after nearly all of the material was rejected by the Washington office, and managed to keep his job for another three years, without producing a single published Project publication during that time.

Alsberg had better luck in the states where he was able to appoint prominent authors as state directors, as in Idaho where Vardis Fisher accepted the post. Fisher, a curmudgeon with little faith in the New Deal, was reluctant to take it at first, but with a wife and two children to support he decided he needed the job, even after he had received a second telegram from Washington saying that it would not pay $2600, as indicated in the original offer, but $2200. On learning of the appointment, a state director who had recommended him sent Fisher a facetious telegram, the gist of which was:

> Congratulations on your new position. Don't take it seriously. It is not intended that we should achieve anything but only that we should put the jobless to work so they will vote for Roosevelt. Take it philosophically and if they send you a telegram from Washington 150 words long, send them one 300 words long or call them long distance collect.

But Fisher saw no humor in the telegram and took his job with such herculean seriousness that, despite constant efforts of the state WPA administrative staff to hinder his work and, later on, despite the attempts of the Washington office to have him knuckle down to its instructions, he achieved the distinction of publishing the first state guidebook in the American Guide Series.

For several months Fisher had no office. Some of the state WPA officials claimed they had not heard of his appointment or of his job. Although the state WPA administrator acknowledged hearing about it, he had no idea what a Writers' Project in Idaho was expected to accomplish. Finally, after Fisher had complained to Washington about his situation, he was provided with "a dirty one-room hole," one typewriter, and two desks for his staff of ten; and he was told that "your only job is to get people off of relief." Citing some of the obstacles put in his way, Fisher sadly wrote Cronyn that "the contempt for the Writers' Project in this WPA setup in Idaho is, I am afraid, a frightful commentary on our cultural waywardness."

The absence of competent writers in Idaho was one of Fisher's most formidable obstacles, one that would have defeated a less tenacious director. At first he tried to assemble a staff that could at least handle some of the technical aspects of producing a guidebook, such as map makers and stenographers; but he discovered that most of the men and women sent to him from the relief rolls were so incompetent as to be useless. Some of them he kept busy copying unusable material from library books. The few competent workers that he hired did not stay long; with $69 per month as the top wage for WPA employees in Idaho, they left for better jobs as quickly as possible. One of his enemies on the WPA administrative staff complicated his personnel problem by trying to pack the Project staff with former inmates of mental institutions. The same official, it was later discovered, assigned a spy to the staff with instructions to "get something on Fisher." But by that time Fisher had succeeded in researching and writing the Idaho state guidebook and was fairly safe from the machinations of politicians.

Alsberg's hasty hunt for state directors resulted in a heterogeneous roster which included a half dozen novelists, a score of journalists, several college English professors as well as college historians, some amateur poets and fiction writers of local reputation, an ex-educator, an ex-physician (a woman), an ex-newspaper publisher, and an ex-college president. Harry Hopkins was one of the first to appreciate the complexity of their jobs. Aware of how easily state directors could be caught between the demands of the Washington office and the pressures of the state WPA administrators, he tried to strengthen their position by reminding the WPA administrative staffs that the state directors of writers' projects were vested with considerable jurisdiction. "These directors make all the appointments, decide what people go to work and what sort of projects they work on," he told them at a national conference in December 1935. Nevertheless, the state WPA administrators and their assistants continued to make the lot of the state directors a painful one.

Whether the state director was a success or failure often depended on his ability to get along with the state WPA administrator. But this was only one of his problems. The most constant problem was organizing his staff into an efficiently working unit that could turn out acceptable manuscripts, a difficult feat considering the incessant and sometimes contradictory instructions sent to him from Washington. For many state directors the job proved to be too much. Only a quarter of those appointed in the early months of the Project survived long enough to produce publishable state guidebooks.

Few of the state directors were actually fired for incompetence. If they could not cope with their administrative tasks, they were usually relegated to nonadministrative jobs or transferred to the Washington staff. One man was fired for drunkenness three days after his appointment; another for "frequent and unauthorized absences." One state director lost his job for using the authority of his office to hire attractive women with the understanding that they would go to bed with him. During the investigation of his case, a WPA investigator went to the state director's home for an interview. While gazing upwards from the sidewalk, after having futilely rung the doorbell, a freshly used condom thrown through an open window struck him in the eye.

In another investigation, this one conducted by Lyle Saxon in his role as regional field supervisor, it was learned that a southern state director, the aunt of an incumbent United States senator, was ignoring the goals of the Project (which she found boring) to produce reams of her favorite form of literature, poetry. Saxon found her and her staff happily established in a palatial country home resplendent with a handsome portico and pillars that evoked an antebellum romantic atmosphere. To Saxon's question of why she had not answered any of the letters sent to her from Washington, the director replied: "Oh those silly things. I just threw them away." Then, leading Saxon to the large room where her staff was at work, she asked: "Have you ever seen such an inspiring sight? Seventeen poets, all in one room, writing poetry seven hours a day."

Of all the human frailties revealed by the newly appointed supervisors, excessive drinking was the most common one. Considering the emotional stresses of the time and the fact that the Project encompassed a great many ex-newspapermen and frustrated men of letters, this came as no surprise to Alsberg. His attitude toward them was generally one of forbearance, even when they were in key positions. In Illinois he discovered, too late, that the English professor he had appointed as a top supervisor was undergoing the emotional strain of an impending breakup in his marriage and trying to find solace in the bottle. Partly because Alsberg believed the professor could mend his ways and partly because he wanted to avoid unpleasant newspaper publicity, he was reluctant to fire him.

At the end of six months he discussed the possibility of dismissing the professor with an Illinois WPA state official who, though agreeing that the Illinois Project was floundering from lack of direction, pointed out that the professor's wife had recently threatened to "make trouble" if her husband were dropped. Alsberg decided to let the matter rest, but at the end of the year when the morale of the Project workers had degenerated badly, he felt compelled to take action. Telephoning the business manager of the Illinois Project he asked if there would be a row if he requested the professor's resignation. The business manager thought there might be, but reminded him that the situation was demoralizing the whole Project.

Alsberg: Would his wife raise trouble?

McTeague: She hasn't for the past two weeks.

Alsberg: I don't see how we can keep on with a man who is a drunk. Why don't you ask him to resign? Say that we don't want to put him in a hole, but we can't have him anymore. See how he responds, then there is nothing in writing . . . Tell him frankly we don't want to hurt his reputation, but if he doesn't resign Washington will probably dismiss him, and it is better for him to resign. Do you think that's possible?

McTeague: I do.

Alsberg: Don't give him time to think, and let me know what happens.

Nothing came of McTeague's effort, but the matter was resolved shortly afterwards when the professor went on an extended binge that prevented him from reporting to the office. Finally, Alsberg felt free to communicate with him directly to let him know he was through.

A month after the Project began to operate, Alsberg found himself obliged to hire an editor who was a known dipsomaniac. The occasion was triggered by an informal note from President Roosevelt asking Alsberg whether he could find employment for a family friend who lived in Virginia. Mrs. Roosevelt followed up the note with a telephone call in which she apologetically revealed to Alsberg that although the friend in question was a good writer, he had "a bad drinking problem." Alsberg then telephoned the state director in Virginia to discuss with him the delicate question of how important a job should be given to a friend of the Roosevelts. He and the director agreed that he was to be paid $100 a month and be given the title of district supervisor as well as an assistant who could keep him in line.

On learning about the impending appointment, Mrs. Roosevelt telephoned Alsberg again to gently suggest that since her friend was inclined to "go off on a spree every now and then," he should probably be given a less important post. She added: "He certainly needs the work because if he doesn't get something to keep him I'm afraid he will do something desperate. He has no income whatever. But I shouldn't like to see him where he has too much responsibility."

"Mrs. Roosevelt," Alsberg assured her, "if we made it a rule not to hire writers given to drink, we would probably not have a Writers' Project."

Lyle Saxon,
director of the Project in Louisiana

The New York City Project, which eventually proved to be one of the major factors in Alsberg's downfall, had a greater proportion of serious drinkers than any other. One of them was the one-legged poet and ex-newspaperman Orrick Johns, who was the New York City Project's second director.* Johns, who had a penchant for girls as well as liquor, became embroiled in a lurid scandal in the fall of 1936 which produced large headlines and cost him his job.† Johns had incited the wrath of a big redheaded seaman not only by refusing him a Project job but also by having an affair with his girl friend, a Project employee.

Plotting revenge with the connivance of the girl, the seaman entered Johns's apartment while he was out and concealed himself in a closet. When Johns arrived with a bottle of brandy which he expected to share with the girl, the seaman jumped out of the closet and proceeded to beat the poet into a state of unconsciousness. The last words Johns heard were: "You wouldn't give me a job. Well, I'm going to give you one." On regaining consciousness, Johns saw some of his teeth scattered on the floor and flames rising around him. While Johns was unconscious. the seaman had doused his wooden leg with the contents of the brandy bottle, and set it on fire. He had then rushed out of the apartment, telephoned a friend of Johns and announced, "I have just set Orrick on fire." John spent several weeks in the hospital recovering from his injuries. Shortly after he was released, Alsberg asked for his resignation. Later, the police caught up with the seaman and he went to jail for a year.

It was not the heavy drinking and the scandal alone that caused Johns's downfall. His difficulties as director stemmed mainly from a sharp conflict raging within him. As an avowed leftwinger, he could not reconcile the responsibilities of his office with the harassing demands made of him by the Project's radical unions. Yet, as he subsequently revealed in his autobiography, the reason he was first hired as a Project executive was that he

---

* During the seven-year life of the New York City Project it had seven directors and two intermediary acting directors. Orrick Johns was preceded by W. K. Van Olinda. The other directors were Travis Hoke, Harry Shaw, Harold Strauss, and Frederick Clayton. The intermediary directors were Donald Thompson and Carl Malmberg.

† The Johns scandal, which became part of the Project folklore, underwent a number of versions. The most fascinating version held that Johns, on falling in love with the wife of a staff member, sent the husband to Alaska on a special assignment. When a friend informed the husband that Johns was sleeping with his wife, the husband sped back to New York, and surprised the couple in bed. As an explanation of why he had gone so far as to set Johns on fire, the husband said: "Not only did I find him fucking my wife in my own bed, but he was doing it under the same fucking blankets I had sent her from Alaska."

was able to persuade the WPA administrators that no one but a radical like himself could handle the job.

"These writers we are going to employ are all hot for unionization," he had told the WPA official interviewing him. "They mean business and will fight for employment and for the rights of collective bargaining. I think I understand, from my labor experience, the union state of mind, and can deal with it. No reactionary boss could do that, in these experimental circumstances . . ." Much to his surprise, he was hired. For a few months he functioned fairly well as head of the New York City Reporters' Project but when he was made director of the city's Writers' Project, he found that he was quite as inept in dealing with the leftwing aspirations of the Project employees as his rightwing predecessor had been.

With too many intangible factors determining the degree of success or failure of a state director, Alsberg never knew what to expect. John T. Frederick, a professor of English at Northwestern University, proved to be one of his wisest choices. Described by one of his Project writers as "a lean, warm-faced Iowan, slow and deliberate, thoughtful and sensitive, who would do anything for a writer," Frederick succeeded in instilling a sense of order into the Illinois Project and making it productive. The WPA state office was understandably suspicious of him at first but soon learned to appreciate his worth and refrained from interfering with the operation of the Project. Of all the workers assigned to him by the WPA office he found only one of "total uselessness," an elderly Egyptian who claimed to be a hundred and twenty years old and was completely illiterate. The old man's sole contribution as a writer was a series of calling cards, written in elaborate Spencerian script and gaudily decorated, which he presented to Frederick and his assistant once every three months. Frederick kept him on the Project "because he was a source of amusement (sometimes sorely needed) and because I didn't know what would become of him."

Like the New York City Project, the Illinois Project included a high percentage of leftwing writers but Frederick, unlike the New York City directors, had little trouble with them. There were demands and protests but rarely did they disrupt the work of the office, "primarily," wrote Frederick, "because a good 80 percent of the workers were so dependent on their monthly checks and so grateful for them that they would do nothing that could conceivably endanger them; also because most were sensible enough to realize that I had little power to alter things."

While serving as state director, Frederick also taught at Northwestern

Orrick Johns at home in 1938

University and conducted a nationwide radio network program, "Of Men and Books." Alsberg had no objection to state directors who divided their energies between the Project and college teaching. The second director of the Massachusetts Project was the historian Ray A. Billington, who taught a full schedule of courses at Clark University three days a week and devoted three other days to his Project duties. According to Billington, he was hired primarily because of his indisputably Anglo-Saxon name, explaining that the job should have gone to Bert Loewenberg, a historian on the Massachusetts Project who was an able administrator, "but this was in 1936 with the election not far away and anti-Semitism was strong in those days. So I was hired . . ."

For Billington the most difficult aspect of the job was coping with the political divisions within his staff. He suspected that between one half and one third of the personnel either were members of the Communist party or were fellow travelers. Their spokesman was one of his own assistants, Merle Colby, who was later transferred to the Washington staff. Although

Billington and Loewenberg considered themselves liberals (Billington almost went to Spain to fight for the Loyalist cause) both men were frequently annoyed by what they felt were "unreasonable demands" of the Communist clique.*

"Scarcely less annoying than the Communist irrationality," recalled Billington, "was the attitude of Washington officialdom. I think back on those days as a continuous battle with Alsberg and his staff. Of course they were right. We wanted to create a guide for Massachusetts that would best mirror the situation in the state . . . Washington wanted and had to have a standard pattern. How we fought each decision aimed at uniformity! I remember, too, the impatience with which we considered criticism by our inferiors. Both Loewenberg and I were recent Harvard Ph.D.'s in history, with something of the Harvard attitude toward less fortunate beings. So when the essays that we wrote on history came back butchered by checkers in Washington (who often cited out-of-date sources) our anger steamed. Here I believe we had our way."

Another professor to become a state director was Harold G. Merriam, of the University of Montana, who was also editor of the literary magazine *Frontier and Midland*. At first he declined the job, but his need for extra money finally induced him to agree that for $90 per month he would give his Saturdays and Sundays to the Montana Writers' Project, which was located on the university campus, and keep his eye on the Project office the rest of the week. But nine months later, after he had submitted the first draft of the Montana state guidebook to Washington, he resigned, discouraged by the lack of writers in the state and by the mass of red tape he had to unravel to get any work done. As a university departmental chairman, he was accustomed to considerable red tape "but not in the amount of it dealt out by the Washington office." Merriam found himself obliged to make frequent trips to the state WPA office in Helena, where he would try to get translations of the "gobbledegook of regulations." Originally the WPA officials in Helena had been dismayed that a university professor had been chosen as director, but when Merriam kept running to them for interpretations they began to feel that he was "only a human being somewhat like themselves."

Looking back on his experience with the Project, Merriam remembered

---

* Billington left the Massachusetts Project in the fall of 1937, when he accepted a teaching position at Smith College in Northampton, which was too far from the Project's Boston office for regular commuting.

how difficult it was keeping tabs on workers in the field. "Word occasionally came that some of them were warming themselves in a country store instead of hustling for facts," but added that "the store, after all, may have been a good source of information." He had trouble with a worker who openly admitted being a Communist, "but since he was one of the best workers we could not afford to lose his services." Merriam observed that most of his workers were inexperienced in gathering information from documents or people. He relied a great deal on Horace Chadbourn, one of his chief assistants, who "in an old high-off-the-ground French automobile rode hundreds of miles on Montana roads in all kinds of weather checking distances for the tour copy," sometimes on mountain passes where the snow was so deep he had to guess where the road was.* Merriam chose Chadbourn to succeed him, but his assistant left a few months later for a better job. Five other state directors, none as able as Merriam and Chadbourn, were appointed before the Montana Project folded.

The scarcity of experienced writers and editors in sparsely populated states posed a serious personnel problem for Alsberg. In North and South Dakota he was finally obliged to hire two young journalists with little experience. When Lisle Reese was offered the job of directing the South Dakota Project in October 1935, he had just turned twenty-four and was making a living running his own news bureau. He felt that he had "no literary talent" but that since the job seemed to call for "more nerve than talent," he accepted the offer. During the next seven years he surrounded himself with a congenial and hard-working staff of ex-newspapermen, country editors, printers from defunct publications, a doctor, a lawyer, a sheepherder who had published a book, some photographers and artists, and "almost anyone who could operate a typewriter."

In North Dakota the post went to an even younger news writer, Ethel Schlasinger. Within a few weeks after she had taken office, the slight twenty-year-old girl found herself in charge of some sixty men and women

---

* Dangerous roads and weather conditions were not the only hazards that the federal writers encountered. In Arizona, E. J. Kelley, a member of the Writers' Project who had been assigned to write about old-time Arizona cowpunchers, dropped in on a meeting of cattlemen in a Douglas, Arizona, hotel to find out what modern cowpunchers were like. He had expected to be bored, but when he left the meeting he submitted this report: "While I was sitting there, one cowman pulled a .45 and aimed it at the fellow who sat next to me. This fellow had evidently been shot at before, for he dropped to the floor and the bullet hit a third man. Two other bullets shot chunks out of the ceiling . . . What will happen when I go after some of those smuggling stories?"

widely scattered through the state. There was not a writer among them; some were barely literate. The only writing assistance she was to receive was from two recent college graduates who could write clear English. The research she entrusted to a group of ex-schoolteachers, clerks, a minister, and "some bright young kids who could not find jobs elsewhere."

Like Harold Merriam of Montana, Miss Schlasinger discovered that putting up with an inadequate staff was not nearly as frustrating as trying to make sense out of the mass of instructions sent from Washington. "The mimeographed material that kept pouring into the office was written by urban-minded editors with urban areas in mind," Miss Schlasinger complained. "We had to work out our own procedures." In spite of all the difficulties, the North Dakota state guidebook was issued in 1938, long before many of the more populated states published theirs.

Nearly all of the fourteen women Alsberg appointed as state directors in the formative months of the Project had been suggested to him by WPA administrators or influential politicians.* But a surprising number of them turned out to be as capable as Miss Schlasinger. Perhaps the biggest surprise was Mrs. Irene Fuhlbruegge, the wife of a young history professor, who in February 1936 was appointed as the New Jersey Project's second director. Recommended to him by a WPA administrator who was a friend of her husband, Alsberg had made the appointment reluctantly, almost certain that Mrs. Fuhlbruegge, like her predecessor, would not be able to stand up to the rapacious demands of the notorious Hague political machine. But the new director, described by one of her associates as "a brown-eyed seemingly tireless woman who liked to get things done and quickly," refused to have anyone interfere with the goals of the Project.

The Hague machine was trying to overrun the New Jersey Project with hoodlums and political hacks. Mrs. Fuhlbruegge promptly let it be known that she would have no one but qualified workers on the staff. When confronted by her indomitable earnestness, the politicians often backed down. "I love Mrs. Fuhlbruegge," one of the WPA administrators told Alsberg. "She raps on my desk and says: 'We won't have this and we won't have that.' She lays down the law and we hop to it."

Mrs. Fulhbruegge devoted little time to editing, leaving that aspect of the work to assistants with a great deal more editorial experience than herself; she concentrated her energies on organizing a productive staff and

* Approximately 40 percent of all the employees on the WPA Federal Writers' Project were women.

on initiating new book projects that seemed to her both useful and publishable. Under her direction, the New Jersey staff produced a steady stream of publications, among them a guide to Matawan, which was published less than a year after the inception of the Project.* The New Jersey state guidebook, produced under her jurisdiction with Alexander L. Crosby supervising it editorially, was one of the best in the American Guide Series. She resigned a few months before its publication, angered by the shenanigans of the state WPA officials who had compelled her to fire two competent writers to make room for two political appointees who were incompetent. When Alsberg asked her to reconsider her resignation, she refused with the declaration that she had endured New Jersey politics and "inefficiency in the Washington office" long enough.

Even more disgusted with Washington's lack of efficiency was the state director of Minnesota, Dr. Mabel S. Ulrich, a former physician and author of a book titled *The More I See of Men*. "Four times, deadlines [for the state guidebook] were set and frantically met," she complained. "We would confidently await news of imminent publication only to be told that plans had changed, new instructions and a new wordage set up, another system of punctuation, abbreviation, and cross indexing, a new form adopted. Maps were made and remade to conform with new specifications, sent, lost, and made again; photographs were approved, then disapproved, lost, and new ones ordered."

Dr. Ulrich's exasperation reached its peak in May 1939 when the state WPA administrator, Victor Christgau, whom she admired for his ability and honesty, was forced to resign during a political contretemps with Minnesota's Governor Benson. When Harry Hopkins, acceding to Benson's wishes, demanded Christgau's resignation, she was filled with a sense of personal betrayal. "From the beginning I had clung to the belief that time and Mr. Hopkins together would bring order to the WPA chaos. I still believed in the work program, but with the collapse of faith in its disinterested leadership went my last hope of a writers' project in our state that intelligence or even pity could justify." Dr. Ulrich resigned from her

---

* Arkansas won the distinction of producing in 1936 the Writers' Project's first publication, *Guide to North Little Rock: Industrial Center of Arkansas*. It wasn't much of a guide, only twenty pages long, but Alsberg was glad to receive it, and proudly showed it to Brehon Somervell, a native of Arkansas who was New York City's WPA administrator. Somervell, a tough army colonel, took one look at the title and sneered: "Who in the hell wants a guide to North Little Rock? Don't you know it's the asshole of the world?"

Dorris A. Westall, director of the Project in Maine,
at her office in Portland, 1937

post a year after the publication of the Minnesota state guidebook, on the same day that Christgau's successor took office.

Although a brainchild of the New Deal, the Project sometimes fared better in staunchly Republican states where there was no Democratic party machine exerting power. In Maine the atmosphere was heavily charged with anti–New Deal scorn, particularly for the state Writers' Project. Yet the Maine Project succeeded in publishing its state guidebook as early as 1937. The director responsible for this feat was Dorris May Westall, whom Alsberg had appointed to rescue the Project from the paralyzed state to which it had been reduced by her male predecessor. Miss Westall's experience was scant — she had worked as a reporter on her hometown newspaper at $12 a week until she was fired for smoking — but with the encouragement of a sympathetic WPA state administrator and the help of the Washington editors whose professional opinions she welcomed, she managed to fulfill the demands of her job.

The Maine staff included several newspapermen (one of whom was a hopeless alcoholic), an elderly lady poet, a cartographer, various researchers and clerks, and two recent graduates from Bowdoin College who had majored in English. The morale was surprisingly high — nearly all the workers were dedicated to the goal of producing publishable manuscripts — and was punctured only by the periodic arrival of "pink slips" from Washington, which meant dismissal for some. For the director the most painful aspect of her job was handing out the "pink slips" to staff members, especially after one of the recipients, a typist, had quietly accepted hers, then returned to her shabby rooming house and killed herself. After that, the Project workers did their best to tide over dismissed colleagues with purchases of groceries until they could find some other employment.

Aside from the fear of losing one's job and going hungry, there was the difficulty of working constantly under pressure and trying to please the Washington editors. "There was trouble with tour checks, trouble with 'form,' the alcoholic had to be extricated from the arms of the law for the last time and dismissed," Miss Westall recalled, "and everyone had to be driven to the limit." Especially harassing were the telegrams that would be sent simultaneously from Washington, one demanding ninety thousand words of final copy, the other ordering the dismissal of more staff members. On one such occasion, Miss Westall replied with a telegram of her own: "No workers, no copy."

Few of the state directors were able to meet deadlines as punctually as

the Maine director. None was able to comply with Alsberg's original instruction that "state directors should plan to have all state copy cleared by
Washington not later than May 1, 1936." Alsberg was obliged to issue this
unreasonable instruction since Congress had given no hint of extending
Federal One beyond July 1, 1936. Nevertheless, he had expected the state
projects to have most of the guidebook copy completed by then, confident
that the projects could function efficiently within a few weeks after their
establishment. This optimistic notion was shattered even before the May
deadline, as soon as the copy submitted revealed the sad fact that much of
it was of substandard quality and would have to be returned for extensive
revision.

Only five of the forty-eight state directors were able to turn in completed guidebooks in time for 1937 publication: Vardis Fisher, and four
directors of the New England states, who received intensive editorial
guidance from Joseph Gaer in his capacity as field supervisor. The failure
of the other state directors to deliver satisfactory manuscripts within a
reasonable time was sometimes due to their lack of ability or that of their
staffs but more often could be attributed to administrative factors beyond
their control. In some states, where the projects were headed by novelists
who could exert both editorial and administrative strength, there was no
accounting for some of the delays.* Lyle Saxon, one of the most talented
of the state directors and one of the four who retained his job from the
beginning of the Project to its end, produced the New Orleans Guide (one
of the literary gems in the American Guide Series) in 1938, yet the Louisiana state guidebook did not appear until 1941.

At the heart of most of the delays and inefficiency, both in the field and
on the Washington staff, was the fear that time was running out too
quickly. Nearly always the prevalent atmosphere was one of acute emergency. The frenetic attitudes of the WPA administration as much as the
unfriendly voice of Congress conditioned Alsberg and the state directors
to act as though the Project might end at any time. As a result, there was a
great deal of costly maladministration; not enough attention was paid to
problems of organization, of appointing qualified personnel, of preparing

---

* Other novelists besides Lyle Saxon and Vardis Fisher who were in the original
roster of state directors included Edwin Bjorkman of North Carolina, William Cunningham of Oklahoma, Ross Santee of Arizona, and J. Frank Davis of Texas. Davis,
who was also a playwright, died of a heart attack on the same day that the Project
closed.

instructions. The hit-or-miss technique of doing things prevailed. Considering the amount of waste spawned by so much haste, it is a tribute to the soundness of the Project's goals that it was able to bludgeon its way through seven and a half years of survival.

No house painter was ever sent to the Art Project for work, but the public and its representatives assumed that anyone who had ever managed to have his words printed was an author, in the literary sense . . .

— Katharine Kellock, in the
American Scholar,
October 1940

In order to understand the nature, achievements, and limitations of the Project one must first understand that the term "Writers' Project" is a misnomer. A good many genuine writers have got relief from it at various times. A number of young people employed on it at various times have developed into genuine writers. But these amount to only a small fraction of the whole.

This is said without any shadow of derogation. The need of those people is unquestionable, and the propriety of employing them at the jobs they were best qualified to do is clear . . .

— Bernard De Voto, in *Harper's,*
January 1942

We adored the Project, all of us. This was in the days before gratitude became obsolete. We had never expected anyone to have any use whatsoever for us. With no grand illusions about Roosevelt and Harry Hopkins, I believe they behaved decently and imaginatively for men without culture — which is what politicians necessarily are.

— Saul Bellow, in a letter to the
author, October 1, 1969

The number of workers on the Federal Writers' Project changed continually. Just after any election the quotas were all reduced and everyone fought for his life. How we produced worthwhile books is a mystery. Pink slips and attacks from Congress kept us all in jitters. We were always on the griddle.

— Dora Thea Hettwer, former
executive secretary to Henry
G. Alsberg, in an interview
with the author, July 1, 1969

Four.

Writers and
Would-Be Writers

At the start of the new year of 1936, Henry Alsberg published a long letter in the *Saturday Review of Literature* which in its first sentence trumpeted the news: "For the first time in the history of the United States writers are working for the government as writers." He explained that although such distinguished writers of the past as Nathaniel Hawthorne, Washington Irving, William Dean Howells and James Russell Lowell had held various government posts, it was not until the launching of the Federal Writers' Project in the previous month that the government had interceded "to care for the large number of destitute writers who were fighting off starvation throughout the country."

Alsberg had barely finished writing the letter when the Authors League of America, in a communication to the White House signed by its president, Marc Connelly, took furious exception to the assumption that the Project was meeting the needs of destitute writers. His attack centered on the WPA regulation which made it mandatory that 90 percent of the Project's personnel consist of persons who had been officially certified as paupers. "It is not our purpose to deny that certain writers have been put to work, but others are starving and we speak in their behalf." George Creel, the famous publicist of World War I, writing to Harry Hopkins as head of the Authors League Fund, fumed: "The means test, together with the stupid arrangement by which each state has been given a certain amount of money regardless of whether the state has writers or not, has defeated your purpose and our hope. As you know, writers are largely grouped in various centers. As a consequence, three quarters of the states are utterly unable to find writers to fill their quotas, while in a city like New York the quota is utterly inadequate to take care of the professional writers who are desperately in need of work." *

The League's bitterness was understandable. It had battled hard for the establishment of a Federal Writers' Project with the expectation that its indigent members, who had been receiving doles from the organization to keep alive, would promptly find jobs on the Project. However, it soon became evident that the League's definition of "destitute" did not conform to that of the government. The WPA regulations stipulated that only writers on public relief could be eligible for jobs, and that the writers who had been receiving financial aid from private sources, such as that provided by the League, could not be employed, except as they might be fitted into the 10 percent category allowed for nonrelief personnel. "In other words," wrote Connelly in "An Open Letter to the WPA," "we were being specifically penalized because we had made an effort to prevent the needy of our profession from becoming public charges." He added that as a result of WPA regulations "many bona fide writers in need were unable to secure WPA employment while many people who were not writers have been employed simply because they were on relief."

Connelly reported that many League authors refused to subject themselves to the "indignities" of the means test. There were some writers "of tougher fiber" who pocketed their pride and applied for relief, but their worst fears were justified. Some were rejected because they could not meet the two-year local residence requirement. Others were kept dangling for weeks or sent from one bureau to another "until their courage was exhausted and their morale completely shattered."

Connelly's eloquent protests produced no result but when George Creel, on failing to obtain a response from Hopkins, addressed himself directly to President Roosevelt, there was action within twenty-four hours. The White House issued an order which enabled the Project to employ up to 25 percent of the total personnel from applicants who were not on public relief. The victory turned out to be counterfeit, for by the time the writers could be processed through the red tape imposed on each nonrelief appointment, the President's order was supplanted by a general WPA decree

---

* Creel's indignation was shared by a delegation of the Writers Union who informed Harry Hopkins that 3,500 persons in New York City were registered as destitute writers. The Writers' Project employment quota was then only 447.

which had the effect of reducing the number of nonrelief personnel to the original 10 percent quota.

The situation of the destitute writer was worsened by what the League bitingly characterized as "the crowning achievement in the WPA's mismanagement" — an order to discharge twenty-five hundred persons from each of the four arts projects. The wholesale cut, which came a few weeks after President Roosevelt's landslide reelection in 1936, deprived the Writers' Project of 40 percent of its personnel and fomented a series of strikes in New York City, San Francisco, and Boston. It also had the effect of discouraging many unemployed writers from making any further attempts to work for the Project.

Alsberg sympathized with the complaints of the Authors League, which reflected the dissatisfaction of unemployed writers throughout the country, but as he had no voice in formulating WPA policies, there was nothing he could do to hire genuinely qualified writers in larger numbers unless they were on relief or unless jobs could be found for them within the 10 percent quota allowed for supervisory personnel. A pragmatist by nature, Alsberg put on the best front possible and issued a series of statements designed to counteract the criticism of those who held that the Writers' Project was largely a misnomer. Katharine Kellock believed that Alsberg harbored "Greenwich Village dreams of nourishing genius on the Project," but there was little evidence of those dreams in his public utterances. The purpose of the Project, he insisted, was not to act as a patron for a few literary geniuses but to provide work for writers of all kinds, "even the mediocre."

In a terse letter to the state directors he told them that their primary job was to take people from the relief rolls and set them to work. To make certain he was not misunderstood, he added: "Our projects, themselves, no matter how important and interesting, come second." Later, as if to justify the wide latitude the Project was according to the definition of "writer," a latitude which virtually conformed to the popular myth that anyone could be a writer provided he put his mind to it, he told the Second Writers' Congress: "We must get over the idea that every writer must be an artist of the first class, and that the writer of the second and third class has no function."

No one knew for certain what kinds of writers and nonwriters were on the Project until June 1938 when Alsberg, in an attempt to silence the critics who claimed that the Writers' Project had too many nonwriters, sent a questionnaire to all of his state directors to elicit background information about their personnel. The thirty-five directors who responded informed him that of the 2,317 employees under their supervision 1,722 were engaged in editorial, literary, research, or reportorial work; the rest were doing the work of clerks, stenographers, photographers and map makers. A breakdown of the 1,722 responsible for the writing of books showed that 83 were nationally recognized authors (anyone who had published one or more books with the imprint of a bona fide publishing firm was included in that category), 107 had held important editorial posts, 105 were scholars, educators, or research workers, 393 had served on a newspaper for at least one year, 339 had sold articles to newspapers or magazines but were not nationally known, 158 had done a little newspaper work, 159 were "beginning writers with promise," * 165 had engaged in some minor form of scholarship. Two hundred and thirteen of the total could not be classified. Presumably, they included the two or three ex-check forgers who managed to land jobs on the Project.

The statistics failed to quiet the critics. As presented in summary form, they also failed to reveal one of the Project's serious deficiencies — the sharply uneven distribution of literary talent throughout its forty-nine offices. As George Creel had protested earlier, no consideration was given to the fact that there was a dearth of writers in many of the states and a heavy concentration of them in a few. Theoretically, Alsberg, as the director of a federal project, could have corrected the geographical imbalance of talent by transferring writers from one state to another. But this prerogative was a difficult one to exercise. While there were writers in the midwestern and southern states who yearned to be transferred to the New York City Project, few of the New York writers had any desire to work elsewhere. One major reason for this was the WPA wage scale, which differed from region to region, ranging from a high of $103.50 per month in New York City to a low of $50 per month in some of the southeastern states.

There were a few transfers from one field office to another — Richard Wright and Lionel Abel, for example, went from the Chicago Project to the one in New York — but most of the transfers were generally from the field offices to the Washington staff, where writers invariably received a higher rate of pay. Alsberg himself instigated such transfers. In his anxiety

* The "beginning writers with promise" may have included such future literary luminaries as Saul Bellow and Ralph Ellison.

to enlarge his staff with experienced writers, Alsberg made the Washington office a haven for talented field workers who were in one difficulty or another. An expert editor on the Michigan Project, who was not getting along with her colleagues because, as one field supervisor put it, she had the temperament of a wildcat, was transferred to Washington at Alsberg's request. "We need wildcats," he explained in ordering the transfer.

From the New York City Project he acquired another female editor who, in a moment of indiscretion, had publicly admitted membership in the Communist party. Respecting her abilities, though not her political philosophy, Alsberg appointed her photographic editor of the national staff, installed her in a small, rear-office cubicle, and asked her to keep her mouth shut as often as possible. For a similar reason Alsberg also obtained the services of Merle Colby, a brilliant Harvard graduate who had already published two novels. Colby, while assistant state director of the Massachusetts Project, had embarrassed its director by becoming a spokesman for the Boston office's leftwing contingent. Aware of his literary reputation and his editorial astuteness, Alsberg was glad to take him off the director's hands.

Colby's astuteness in all matters was responsible for his rapid rise in both the Boston and Washington offices.* In a revealing anecdote about himself, he described a ruse he had used to assure himself a job on the Massachusetts Project. While standing in a long line of applicants, waiting to be interviewed and afraid there would be no jobs left by the time he reached the head of the line, his knowledge of Boston politics inspired him to scribble a note which read: "Take care of Merle Colby." He signed it with the first obviously Irish name that came to mind, and instructed a passing boy to deliver the note to the WPA interviewer. Within moments he was taken out of line, ushered into the presence of the official, and hired as soon as he had identified himself as a certified pauper and published novelist.

The Washington office also served as a political haven for Harold Rosenberg when he came under heavy attack by the Communists on the New York City Project. Rosenberg had first joined the WPA as a relief worker on the Art Project, qualifying for the job by submitting a painting for the approval of a committee of judges. Later, he transferred to the

---

* Colby joined the Washington staff in 1937. As territorial editor, he produced guidebooks to Alaska (then a territory) and Puerto Rico. He remained with the Project until it ended in 1943.

Writers' Project in the expectation that he would become the editor-in-chief of a Project magazine which Alsberg and his staff hoped to establish on a national scale under government auspices. The Communists objected to Rosenberg's choice of assistants. During the battle that ensued, Alsberg decided to make him art editor of the national staff, and I was designated to offer him the job.

The circumstances under which the offer was made provide a serio-comic sidelight on the economic situation of writers during that era. In those days Rosenberg was trying to augment his meager salary as a Project relief worker by moonlighting as a reader for various publishing houses. One morning he visited the house of Covici Friede to report on a biography of Modigliani he had been asked to review. He told the editor that the manuscript was too poorly written to be publishable. When the editor asked what could be done with it, Rosenberg suggested it either be thrown away or completely rewritten. The editor asked whether he would be willing to undertake the rewriting and, on receiving an affirmative reply, inquired how much he would charge.

Thinking aloud, Rosenberg said it would take him at least six weeks and that he would charge fifty dollars a week, a total of three hundred dollars. The editor reacted explosively, as though Rosenberg had asked for ten times the amount. While trying to persuade him to do the job for far less money, the telephone rang. Much to the editor's surprise, it was a long distance call for Rosenberg (the operator had finally located him after reaching his Brooklyn apartment first). It was I telephoning from Washington to offer him the post of art editor on the national staff of the Writers' Project at a salary of $2400 per year.

"I accept," Rosenberg proclaimed in a stentorian voice. Then, flinging the Modigliani manuscript on the editor's desk, he announced that he had accepted "a position with the United States Government," and stomped out of the office.

"Henry Alsberg enjoyed his role as a talent scout and was unabashedly proud of his name writers," wrote Harold Coy, who served as one of the national staff's executive editors. "Hamilton Basso's visit to Washington was one of his great moments, and he dreamed in vain of adding him to the staff." Alsberg's scouting was more successful with younger writers. When Nathan Asch, one of his editors, called his attention to the *New Yorker* stories of John Cheever, Alsberg promptly invited Cheever to join his national staff. The twenty-six-year-old writer, who was then broke and subsisting on the hospitality of Yaddo (the writers' and artists' retreat at Saratoga Springs), accepted the job, despite the disapproval of his anti-New Deal family who considered any WPA employment an acute form of dishonor. Cheever lived in a rooming house with a group of other Project employees, and eventually wrote a short story about the place. He disliked Washington, finding it a city without color, a shell of a place where most people dressed alike and usually talked about the same thing, their civil service classification. The most attractive feature of the city was the large number of available girls. He availed himself of some of them, played quite a bit of touch football, and did a little writing of his own. At the end of six months he was glad to be transferred to the New York City Project where, along with such writers as Richard Wright, Charlotte Wilder, William Rollins, Jr., and Anthony Netboy, he worked on the final editing of volume two of the New York City Guide. Once that job was done, he resigned, still feeling uneasy about the disgrace he had brought on his family.

Eugene Joffe, another young contributor to the *New Yorker,* was also recruited by Alsberg for the Washington staff. On one of his numerous trips to New York Alsberg had learned that Joffe was earning a paltry salary playing piano dance music in second-rate Chinese restaurants. Alsberg was delighted with the opportunity of rescuing a blossoming literary talent from so stale an existence, and rushed through the arrangements to add him to his staff. Joffe arrived in Washington in the middle of the night and, not knowing the city, took a room in the first hotel he encountered. The next morning he was horrified to discover that he was in the very heart of Washington's Chinatown. No one was ever able to determine whether this O. Henry twist of fate convinced him there was no escape from his Chinese purgatory or whether he found that editing guidebook copy was even more dreary than playing cheap piano music. Whatever the reason, Joffe quit the Project within a few weeks and went back to New York.

Alsberg's efforts as a talent scout were not always in behalf of the Washington staff. In some states, where he distrusted the state director's judgment or where he thought he could interfere without creating antagonism, he would propose his own candidates as staff members. In Missouri, where he had no faith in Geraldine B. Parker, the director that had been foisted on him by the WPA state administrator, he offered the job of editor-in-chief to J. S. Balch, a young short story writer whose work he had read

Conrad Aiken in 1937

in little magazines but whom he had never met. Balch became the mainstay of the Missouri Project until he and his colleagues, unable to cope with their director's incompetence, were plunged into a calamitous strike. Soon afterwards, Balch, focusing on the events of the strike, produced the first novel written about the Writers' Project, *Lamps at High Noon,* in which a character who is obviously based on Alsberg is presented in an unfavorable light.

Perhaps Alsberg's most rewarding coup as a talent scout was to persuade Conrad Aiken to take a relief job with the Massachusetts Project. Aiken had already developed a solid reputation as one of the nation's most talented poets and fiction writers, but he was broke at the time and glad to have a writing job that paid approximately $100 a month. Aiken left the Project after five months, fed up with most of his colleagues whom he considered "Commies" or "hopelessly incompetent, except for the photographers." Despite his brief tenure, he did a great deal of work, contributing to the literature, music, and theater sections of the Massachusetts Guide and turning in a description of Deerfield which critics have often cited as the most poetic passage in all of the American Guide Series.

Aiken did most of his Project writing at home, and would send his wife to the Boston office with the completed work. His annoyance with the Project reached its climax when he learned that the Marxist-minded editors on the staff were objecting to his essay on literature on the grounds that it stressed the theme of individualism — "that profound individualism," he wrote in the essay, "which has so deeply marked the American character ever since, and of which Massachusetts — especially in the field of letters — has been the most prodigal and brilliant source." Ray Billington, the state director, considered the essay "perfect in composition and styling," worthy of being published exactly as written. But the essay was heresy to some of the outspoken Communists and fellow travelers on the Project who insisted that whatever was commendable about the American literary past stemmed not from individualism but from collective action.

In order to avoid trouble, Billington permitted two essays on the literary history of Massachusetts to be published in the state guidebook: the one by Aiken was simply entitled "Literature"; the other, "Literary Groups and Movements," adhered to the Marxist point of view. "The volume was hardly strengthened by this compromise," observed Billington, "but given the political divisions existing, no other solution was possible."

In Boston, as in all of the large city writers' projects, there was an ideological gap between experienced writers past thirty and young left-wingers who were filled with Marxist-minded protest. There were exceptions, to be sure — youngsters who were conservative, and older writers, like Maxwell Bodenheim and Orrick Johns, who were radicals — but the gap prevailed during all of the Project's history and accounted for some of its difficulties. In the case of Conrad Aiken the gap was created as much by his aloofness as by his conservative political philosophy. "Aiken accepted his job from on-high, worked at home, and came in once in a while to report on-high," wrote Arthur M. Saxe, a young poet who was one of Aiken's colleagues.

Despite the episode of the literature essays, Saxe claimed there was little evidence of overt leftwing activity on the Massachusetts Project. "Two or three times when Congress threatened to reduce funds, almost all of us picketed the building in excellent order and with the blessings of the management. I was surprised that so many middle-aged and even elderly people came out. After what may have been an hour and a half, we went back to our desks. One policeman was heard to say, 'Those people aren't picketing. They're just walking around the building.'"

Another poet, William C. FitzGerald, who joined the Boston office as a supervisor after Saxe's departure, shared Aiken's low opinion of the personnel, though not for political reasons. "I am sure I was resented by some of the senior creeps who passed themselves off as writers when really they couldn't have conceived decently indecent graffiti. They were simply drones, misfits, happiest when engaged in some petty conspiracy and at their sourest when one ventured to note mistakes of spelling, grammar, in such copy as they turned in — if, indeed, they submitted any at all." Although acknowledging that some of his colleagues were conscientious, most of them struck him as "sullen, incompetent, or just plain nuts; the types who feed breadcrumbs to pigeons and talk to themselves in a park." FitzGerald particularly disliked the female members of the staff but had deep respect for Muriel Hawks, who succeeded Professor Billington as director. All the other women were "Mary Petty horrors gone to seed."

Mrs. Hawks's official view of the Massachusetts staff presented a much happier profile. In a 1939 report she noted that of the several hundred persons who had been hired more than half had college degrees varying from that of bachelor of arts (or science) to that of doctor of philosophy. She also cited the presence of a half dozen authors who had published one or more books. Perhaps the most revealing statistic in the report was that

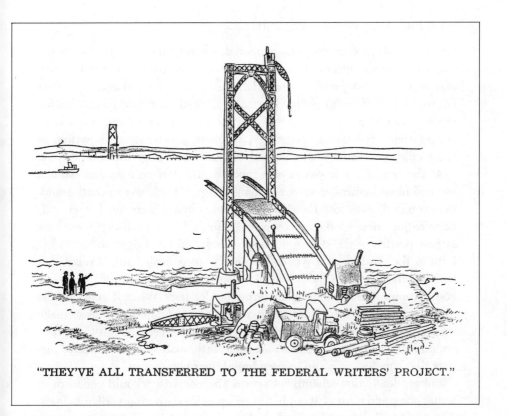

"THEY'VE ALL TRANSFERRED TO THE FEDERAL WRITERS' PROJECT."

almost one third of the employees were in the age group ranging from twenty to thirty.

The notion that lack of writing experience and youth were no deterrent to membership on the Writers' Project was publicized on a national scale in a feature story released by the WPA. The subject was an eighteen-year-old girl named Patricia Kelly, "petite, blonde and easy to look at," who had demanded a pick and shovel WPA job offered to her father which he, in sudden need of surgery, was unable to accept. The nonplussed WPA official who heard her petition turned for help to the director of the Michigan Writers' Project, who hired Miss Kelly on the grounds that she knew how to type and assigned her to the Michigan writing staff.

White collar workers who could not be fitted into any other WPA agency were likely to wind up on the Writers' Project. This was especially true in the early months of the Project, when field offices were required to hire personnel on short notice. On being ordered by Washington to hire 250 writers within ten days, Dr. Mabel Ulrich, the newly appointed director of the Minnesota Project, wondered whether there were that many "mute inglorious authors" in the state. She studied the records of the men and women on relief who were available for hire, but could find no writers beyond a handful who claimed to have worked on newspapers. Finally, she was able to choose only 120 "from the neediest and most promising," among them ex-lawyers, preachers, teachers, businessmen, a writer of vaudeville skits, and a man who had tried his hand at gentleman farming.

At the end of a few weeks, she reported, the forlorn men and women she had hired became different human beings. "Heads were raised, shoulders squared, eyes lost their haunting fear, smiles were no longer self-deprecating, new clothes were worn jauntily." Not realizing then how large a portion of the state guidebook she would be obliged to write, her faith in the wisdom of a writers' project seemed unshakable. "What if it had cost the taxpayers thousands of dollars?" she asked herself. "How can you compute human morale in terms of dollars?" What if most of the material turned in was either so "literary" or so ungrammatical as to make it seem worthless? She had confidence then that given enough time, they would learn to be writers. "At that stage little mattered," she wrote, "except that hopeless men and women found their hope again."

But gradually disenchantment set in. The nonwriters could not learn to write; nor could most of them be relied upon for gathering verifiable facts. The personnel did not improve during the rest of her three year tenure, but its character changed as more and more youngsters were added to her staff, "freshly graduated boys and girls from high schools and colleges, to whom the Writers' Project was like an easy postgraduate college course that demanded little talent or aptitude yet offered tangible rewards in dollars and cents." Their contribution was slight but they were far less jittery than their older colleagues who lived "in constant fear of being dropped back into the abyss of city relief."

One of the oldsters, who had never surrendered his gun permit, wore a pistol to the office "like a decoration"; but one morning, glowering at her, he shouted: "Fear stalks in our midst." Trying to sound casual, Dr. Ulrich asked: "Fear of what?" Like a pistol shot, the worker retorted "Fear of you." To a certain degree that was true, Dr. Ulrich wrote after she quit the Project. "I, who all my life had dreaded and resented power above everything, now found myself in a position where I had merely to sign a pink slip, a 403, and an entire family was plunged into despair again. I couldn't sign it. There were almost no other white collar projects in those days, quotas were inflexible and always filled; if I discharged a writer his only alternative was city relief."

In some states, where relief money was hard to come by, joining the Writers' Project became a matter of life and death. In Nebraska, one of the states hardest hit by the Depression, the possibility of starving to death was so imminent as to induce plans for suicide. "My husband and I seriously talked about it," one Lincoln housewife recalled. "All I could earn was three dollars a week cooking food for students. But we often went hungry, and so did our neighbors. We could no longer borrow from each other. If the Writers' Project hadn't come along when it did . . ." Another resident of Lincoln, a young writer, alarmed his friends in 1935 when he began to dispose of the books he treasured above everything else. They converged on him as a group, determined to stay in his company until his melancholia was banished. To assure them that he would do nothing desperate, he tried to buy back the books he had sold. With the help of his friends, he managed to subsist until the Project opened.

No established writers applied for jobs on the Nebraska Project, but thanks to the intercession of Lowry Charles Wimberly, a popular English professor at the University of Nebraska who was the founder of a highly regarded literary magazine, the *Prairie Schooner,* the Project acquired enough talented young writers to develop into a thriving unit. Wimberly persuaded a number of former students and contributors to the *Prairie Schooner* to apply for Project jobs, even though it meant going on relief, then used his influence to make certain they were hired.

One of Wimberly's Boys, as his protégés became known, was Loren Eiseley, the noted author and anthropologist who was to achieve national prominence with *The Immense Journey* and other books. Eiseley, who had already won recognition in Nebraska as a poet, had just acquired a master's degree at the University of Pennsylvania, where he would one day become head of the anthropology department and provost, was at loose ends when Wimberly suggested he join the newly established Writers' Project.* Weldon Kees, who was then beginning to publish the poems that would eventually win him national renown, was another Wimberly protégé.† Although neither writer remained on the Project for long —

---

* As a Project writer Loren Eiseley wrote parts of the essays on paleontology and archaeology published in the Nebraska state guidebook.

† Weldon Kees's car was found abandoned on the approach to the Golden Gate Bridge in San Francisco on July 18, 1955. He was never seen afterwards.

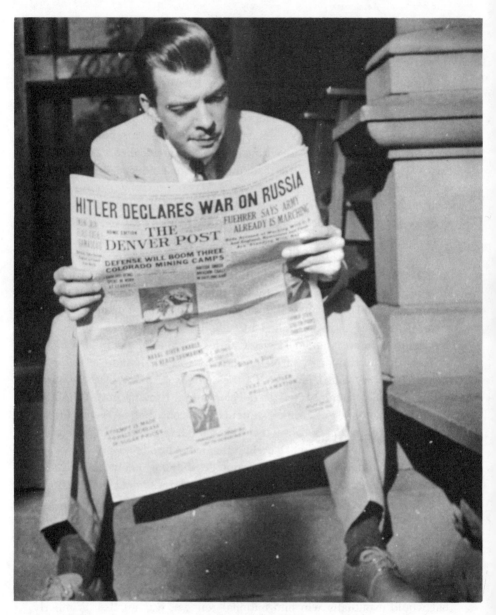

Weldon Kees in 1941, a few years after he had served on the Project in Nebraska

Eiseley for approximately four months and Kees for a year — they emerged as the Nebraska Project's most famous alumni.

The Wimberly Boy who served on the Nebraska Project almost from its beginning to its very end was Rudolph Umland, a writer whose literary career was to be prematurely cut short by illness. Umland had known Wimberly while he was a student at the University of Nebraska. He dropped out of college in his junior year and for the next three years bummed his way through forty states, Canada and Mexico, working as a janitor, farmhand, factory worker, dishwasher, logger, longshoreman, and construction laborer. The novel he wrote about these experiences, *Journal of a Floater,* never found a publisher, but parts of it were printed in the *Prairie Schooner.* During the blackest years of the Depression, 1932–35, Umland slopped hogs and plowed corn on his father's farm until, bored with it all, he decided to take to the road again; but he got no farther than Lincoln where he stopped to say goodbye to Wimberly. His friend persuaded him to apply for a job on the newly formed Nebraska Writers' Project.

Despite the annoyances of trying to work with a paranoid director — on his first day in the office Elizabeth Sheehan told him that everyone on the staff was after her job; on the second day she accused him of being one of them — Umland's wanderlust came to an end as he became involved with the work of the Project. In a short time he was made state editor and, until a way of getting rid of Miss Sheehan could be found by the Washington office, the burden of running the Project fell on him. The Project changed both his way of life and his view of himself. "I learned to be an extrovert through the necessity of working with others and having others depend on me."

When the ubiquitous Joseph Gaer asked him to recommend a successor to Miss Sheehan, Umland suggested J. Harris Gable, an unemployed librarian who had published a boys' book on exploration. He was also one of the founders of the *Prairie Schooner* and a fraternity brother of Wimberly. Gable, a Republican, had "tongue in cheek and even a chip on my shoulder" during his interview with Gaer, but on being offered more pay than he had ever received as a librarian, he accepted the job and became "loyal to the hand that fed me," even to the extent of voting for Roosevelt in 1936.

Gable, content to leave the editorial responsibilities to Umland, concentrated on administrative matters and made such a good impression on the

Washington office that he was made regional field supervisor. In that capacity he roamed through a dozen states as a trouble shooter, hiring and firing as he saw fit (in Kansas he discharged an elderly director suffering from a mental disorder and replaced him with a sane young man) and enjoying the company of celebrated artists he encountered en route, such as Grant Wood in Iowa, Thomas Hart Benton in Missouri, and John Steuart Curry in Kansas. On his visits to Washington, he would be invited to the "fabulous parties" given by Ellen S. Woodward at the Mayflower, which were sometimes attended by Harry Hopkins and by President Roosevelt. There the liquor flowed freely, though the occasions were known as tea parties, and the tables were piled high "with more canapés and hors d'oeuvres than I ever saw."

Umland got along famously with Gable, who was eight years his senior. The two men constituted the kind of a team that the Washington office tried, often vainly, to establish in all the states. Thanks to Umland's talents as an editor and writer and to Gable's bent for promotion and administration, the Nebraska Project, with not a single prominent writer to its name, exceeded, on a per capita basis, all other states in the number of books published. Umland had the assistance of a number of workers who had contributed to the *Prairie Schooner*, among them Fred Christensen, who was to help edit that magazine for forty years, Norris Getty, Arthur Bukin, Robert Carlson, and the two poets Eiseley and Kees. His chief editor was G. Gordon Dewey, who augmented his Project earnings by publishing science fiction.

But the Nebraska Project was not without its share of deadwood and nonwriters, one of whom struck Umland as being unduly "inspired." "He was inspired to such heights," wrote Umland, "that it became necessary to tie millstones to his feet." Yet even with the millstones the writer and his prose soared. One of his paragraphs read: "As we come up over the rolling hills out of Florence, what do we see to the east of us? The river, of course, the great winding river on which our forefathers traveled. To the east of the river are the high towering bluffs of Iowa. Beautiful yes, but more than beautiful, they are historic men of the ages as it were . . ."

The author of this exotic prose was removed from the Project by a simple expedient, according to Umland. "We moved the millstones from his feet and assigned him to write a description of the Nebraska State Capitol by moonlight. He soared so far that we never saw him again. It was rumored that some Republican shades caught him among the clouds."

Umland found various ways of getting rid of incompetent writers. He assigned some to doing research; the "lesser wits" he managed to transfer to other government agencies. By such stratagems the Nebraska Project achieved some degree of editorial efficiency. Most of the researchers were women, former schoolteachers, whose faith in the morality of Lincoln was shaken from time to time by scandalous material they uncovered about some of its past inhabitants. Umland and his editors made certain that none of it was discarded, and incorporated some of the juicier tidbits in the Nebraska Project's first publication, Lincoln City Guide, an eighty-seven-page illustrated pamphlet which sold for twenty-five cents. Published in 1937 on the seventieth anniversary of the city, it became a local best seller and won the praise of Republican newspapers that had expected to attack it.

One of its most entertaining features consisted of a descriptive listing of the marriageable men in Lincoln in the year 1888, which a local newspaper had published "in honor of leap year." Included was one H. W. Caldwell, an associate professor of history at the University of Nebraska, age twenty-eight, "four feet, four inches tall, weight of body 35 pounds, weight of brain 75 pounds. Would take a lady of kind disposition who would not be inclined to impose upon or terrorize her husband." Another bachelor, Frank C. Zehrung, was described as "druggist and capitalist, height a trifle short of six feet. Has smashed 14 hearts in the past 15 years. If taken, it will be a desperate struggle. When captured, will make excellent husband of refined tastes and loving disposition. Only fault is unfortunate passion for baseball."

Umland enjoyed the social life of the Project as much as the daily experience of delving into Nebraska's past. In an unpublished memoir he referred to his Project years as a happy "beer-drinking period." "I used to like to go into a tavern, order a beer, and sit and watch the other beer drinkers and speculate on them. Once or twice a week Wimberly would accompany me, sometimes at noon, sometimes at night. All this while working on writing WPA guidebooks. I became deeply conscious of local history, the drama played by Nebraska pioneers, and the passing of the generation of the old bearded men. The tavern encompassed it all. 'There's plenty of source material here,' Wimberly would say, 'right here in this Lincoln, Nebraska, tavern, enough to write a dozen books. One needn't go to New York or to California to become a writer. Think of the lives that some of these people have lived.'

Rudolph Umland gathering material for the Nebraska state guidebook

"Sometimes other Project workers would accompany me to the taverns — Weldon Kees, Art Bukin, Dale Smith, Margaret Lund, Henry Richmond, Jake Gable, and we'd sit and drink beer and talk and watch. I got to know people that way. By drinking beer with them, and got beneath their skins."

Like Dr. Ulrich, Umland suffered deep torment whenever he received orders from Washington to reduce his staff. The torment was most painful when he had to choose between a worker who was valuable to the Project because he was a competent writer and one who was not nearly as skilled but was the head of a family which depended on him for survival. The mail he received from workers who had been fired often accentuated Umland's anguish. One of the letters came from J. H. Norris, an old man who had worked in the Omaha office of the Nebraska Project until he received his dismissal notice (a 403). Only then did he reveal that although he was a widower living alone, he had been helping to support a family with three small children for the past four years. "Now I can't do anything for them and winter is coming. The other day I divided my little supply of canned stuff with them but I haven't got much of it left. I did have a pretty good stock a while ago that I was hoarding up for an emergency like this but I gave $12 worth of it to a Negro family that was destitute and it seemed that nobody wanted to help them because they were black . . ."

With the letter the old man enclosed the following verse dedicated to Umland:

THE FEDERAL WRITERS' PROJECT

What a record they carved
After coming half starved
To work on the F.W.P.
They were not much for looks
But they put out good books
While awaitin' for their Four-O-Three

They were busy as bees
Though not always at ease
When they wrote of the things they would see
For over them hung

As their pencils swung
The sword of the Four-O-Three

They worked and they moiled
And their clothing got soiled
Out researching what they could see
They got sun-burned and tanned
But they wrote things up grand
While a-waitin' for their Four-O-Three

There were shy ones and bold ones
There were hot ones and cold ones
And there was only one old one — and that's me
There were none that were lazy
Though some went nearly crazy
While a-waitin' for their Four-O-Three.

Like all other state writers' projects, Nebraska suffered its most drastic cut in 1939 during the changeover from federal to state control. Both Umland and Gable survived it; but early in 1941 Gable had some personal difficulties with the WPA administration and resigned. Umland succeeded him as state director and remained in charge until the termination of the Project.

Without the recruiting services of Lowry Wimberly and the efficient editorial-administrative team of Umland and Gable, the Nebraska Project would probably have limped along with few books to its credit and with the burden of writing falling on one or two individuals. This was the general pattern that developed in most of the states where experienced writers were either scarce or unwilling to go on relief.

Wyoming was one of these states but the director, Agnes Wright Spring, found unexpected assistance in a ranchwoman who could barely compose a sentence but who turned out to be a highly gifted interviewer; and in a Mormon mute, who had been hired out of a sense of charity, but whose reports reflected remarkable powers of observation. But this was help of a minor sort; she was obliged to do most of the writing for the Project. Besides lacking literary talent, the Wyoming Project was also handicapped by a lack of office facilities, which made it necessary for many of the employees to work at home without supervision. Some sent in their manuscripts by mail and seldom saw the Project office. One worker, who was inclined to drink heavily and raise hell, would often do his work in jail. Another member of the staff, a homesteader named Nelly Vandeveer, whose assignment it was to interview pioneers and record dance calls, would bring in her material on horseback and, during the winter, on skis.

In Wyoming, as in many other states, the hostility of the citizenry toward the WPA and the Writers' Project was often an obstacle. There was deep resentment that the government should be using taxpayers' money to pay salaries to writers. The term "writer" coupled with "WPA" connoted everything that New Deal haters considered scurrilous about the Roosevelt administration. During the fact-gathering trips the Wyoming director and her husband made around the state, she discovered that, invariably, she would be rebuffed if she identified herself as a member of the Writers' Project. Once she hit on the ruse of representing herself as a writer for the *Wyoming Stockman Farmer*, a magazine to which she had contributed, she had no further difficulty.

In some states Project workers learned from experience that since most people were unaware of the Project's existence, identification with the "Writers' Project" might not arouse any hostility, but any mention of "WPA," a household term, was bound to. In Chicago Frank Mead, who was gathering data about local fraternal groups and unions, found it expedient not to identify himself with any government agency but to represent himself as a researcher for the University of Chicago.

Many good interviews were lost because citizens, regardless of how they felt about the New Deal, became instantly uncooperative when they heard that the person at their door seeking information was "from the government." The writers on the Pennsylvania Writers' Project had several strikes against them when they visited Carlisle, which was heavily Republican, in search of information about the underground railroad that had once operated there during the days of slavery. The elderly ladies on whom they called had not been involved in helping fugitive slaves, but their fathers had been and they knew it to be an illegal (though meritorious) activity. The fathers were long since dead but the young men who would politely represent themselves as from some federal something-or-other agency to ask about these clandestine acts represented no small threat. As one of the old ladies put it, "How did I know they weren't from

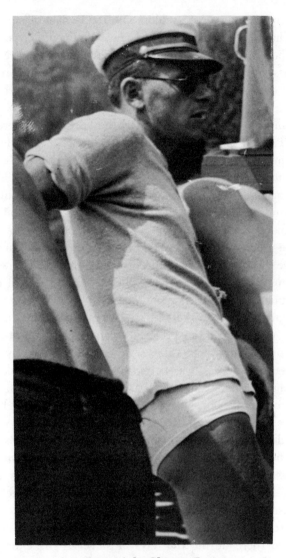

Sam Ross, of the Chicago Project,
moonlighted as a lifeguard

the government trying to find out things about Father to get us in trouble? I wouldn't put such a thing past that Roosevelt . . ."

Usually, however, it was the general feeling against WPA, which nearly every newspaper in the country persistently encouraged, that made the lot of the federal writer difficult. WPA was held in such low esteem that some of the prejudice against it was bound to rub off on many of its own employees. Among some members of the Writers' Project "WPA" connoted a stigma of the lowest order, a dark and embarrassing symbol of a time of their lives when circumstances beyond their control compelled them to admit on public record, personal defeat. For some the memory of their experience on the Project, no matter how fruitful it had been, became a secret shame, something that, if possible, should be concealed. It is a pathetic commentary on the ramifications of human insecurity that only a few of the writers who successfully nurtured their young literary talents on the Writers' Project ever made any mention of it in their published autobiographical statements.°

As might be expected, the ablest writers on the Project were to be found in New York, Boston, Chicago and San Francisco — those traditional incubating centers of literary talent. Of all the Project directors in those cities, John T. Frederick of Chicago was easily the most effective. As a professor of English deeply immersed in espousing regional writing, he regarded the Project both as an invaluable opportunity to enhance the nation's literary wealth and as a means of making writers in the region more aware of the nature and history of the world around them. Like Lowry Wimberly, who was also a staunch believer in regional literature, Frederick had a sure instinct for spotting talented young writers who could benefit by working for the Project. Once they joined it, he did everything in his power to encourage their literary aspirations.

One of the bright young writers on the Illinois Project was Sam Ross. When Frederick learned that Ross wanted to write a novel dealing with the steel strike of 1919, he allowed him to do research for the book on Project time, with the understanding that the Project would have access to whatever information he dug up but that the novel would belong to Ross.

° Several ex-Project writers who helped to provide information for this book specifically requested that no mention be made of their association with the Federal Writers' Project. A San Francisco poet, who found employment with a brokerage firm after the Project closed, never revealed her connection with the WPA in the twenty-five years she worked for the company, out of fear that her job would be jeopardized.

Nelson Algren with friends as he displays the novel he began while on the Illinois Project

"The novel was never published," Ross wrote many years later, "but writing it gave me a chance to develop whatever talent I had." *

Nelson Algren was one of the few writers on the Illinois Project who had already published a novel. Ross recalled him as "sandy-haired, looking half starved, the Madison Street Dostoievsky with *Somebody in Boots* [1935] already under his belt, striking the grimy streets of Chicago among the freaks, the drunks, the derelicts." Algren had joined the Project as a relief worker, then quickly advanced to the position of supervisor. Working alongside him was Richard Wright, who had been a post office employee until a friend suggested he apply for a Project job. Although he had published a few short things in leftwing little magazines, it was not until he became a Project writer that he began to produce the fiction that was to be the mark of his career. "The writer whom the Illinois Writers' Project helped the most was Dick Wright," according to Algren. "He was more alert to its advantages and more diligent than most of us. He used the time it gave him to write *Big Boy Leaves Home* and *Native Son*. Whether he would have been able to write *Native Son* if he had had to go on working at the post office is problematical. Surely it would have been a much harder grind."

"Everybody used the Project," Algren added, "to the extent that you could report at ten in the morning and leave at two and then you had the rest of the day to yourself." Algren too found the Project useful for improving his economic status. The salary he eventually received of $125 a month was the most money he had ever made. However, neither Frederick nor he was overly impressed with his job performance. Although he wrote most of the Galena Guide, one of the best of the small-town guidebooks in the American Guide Series, he did not become involved with the writing of the Illinois state guidebook nor with any other major book project; he developed a cynical view of his role on the Project, regarding it, in retrospect, as a training period for acquiring the "goldbricking" skills that were to serve him in good stead as a soldier in the army.

"I used to get fired every six weeks regularly by John T. Frederick," Algren recalled. "He kept assuring me I'd be happier off the Project and hand me a 403. Then I'd find I was happier on it. So I'd go down to the relief station again, register as a pauper, receive a sack of moldy potatoes;

* The best-known published novels by Sam Ross include *He Ran All the Way* (1947), *Someday, Boy* (1948), *The Sidewalks Are Free* (1950). All three novels were published by Farrar, Straus.

Saul Bellow in his twenties

and materialize the following morning in the Project office." His basic strategy (which, he claimed, was to receive the minimum check of $84 a month) worked so well that he was raised to $96 a month. "After I got fired about the sixth time it was raised to $125." Frederick's natural empathy for young writers, his reluctance to take a tough line dealing with them, is recorded in the memory of many a man and woman on the Illinois Project during his regime. One of them was Saul Bellow who, fresh out of college and unable to find a job, had qualified as a Project worker by going on relief. Bellow, whose literary talents were then unknown, was assigned a deadly boring task: compiling lists of magazines in the Newberry Library. He envied his friends and colleagues Isaac Rosenfeld and Lionel Abel because they were given far more interesting work to do. Rosenfeld, who in his brief span of life was to achieve a niche in American letters as the American Kafka, was writing an account of pigeon racing in Chicago. Abel, who was soon to transfer to the New York City Project, was helping to prepare a series of textbooks for use in vocational schools. As soon as Frederick got wind of Bellow's boredom, he put him to work at a much more congenial task, writing biographical sketches of midwestern authors.

Many Project writers of an imaginative turn of mind complained about their assignments. Although Sam Ross found his Project experience generally "exciting" he considered some of it to be "wasteful." "It was wasteful as hell when you were sent to some dusty library to excerpt columns and columns of events from old crumbly newspapers. I thought at times I'd wind up with silicosis." He was happier writing articles describing streets and places in Chicago but "the grand design was a guidebook and when all you did were a few of the articles, you had no sense of accomplishing anything, you didn't know how your material was going to be used."

A fringe Project benefit which compensated some of the young writers for the dullness of their tasks was that of associating with published authors. Although Saul Bellow struck up no friendship with the Illinois Project's two most prominent published novelists, Nelson Algren and Jack Conroy, he derived some satisfaction from being near them. "I rather looked up to them," recalled Bellow, "and they rather looked down on me." On the other hand, Margaret Walker, a good-looking black poet who was the youngest member of the Chicago office, received valuable editorial advice from Nelson Algren when she showed him her unfinished poem, *For My People,* which later became the title of a book that won the Yale Award for Young Poets.

It was Richard Wright who had first told Miss Walker that a writers' project was being organized and urged her to apply. Pretending she was twenty-one (the minimum legal age for WPA employment) she joined the Illinois Project at the age of twenty, seven months after graduating from Northwestern University. The job, which paid $85 per month and carried with it the title of junior writer, helped to support her family in New Orleans, and provided a convenient launching pad for her literary career. Shortly after she began to work on a research assignment for the state guidebook, she showed some of her own writings to her supervisor, Jack Sher. He was so impressed with its quality that he accorded her the privilege of working at home on her own material — an extraordinary bonanza granted to no other member of the Illinois staff. For the next two years she worked on a novel dealing with a Chicago ghetto entitled *Goose Island,*° and reported to the Project office only once or twice each week.

A loner who antagonized many of his leftwing colleagues by his refusal to join with them, Sher told his young protégé: "You are young and talented and have a future. Listen to the people around you but don't join them." Although Marxism was a popular magnet that attracted most of her young colleagues, her deeply ingrained Methodist upbringing made it easy for her to follow Sher's advice. As a girl with a pretty face, she received a different kind of advice from Richard Wright, who told her to beware of the lesbians on the Project. Referring to one of them by name, he warned Miss Walker, "Don't let that woman put an arm around you. And don't take candy from her."

She and Wright were close friends for three years, though never lovers. It was she who provided Wright with clippings about the Nixon murder case, which became the inspiration for parts of his most successful novel, *Native Son.* Wright, who made his first large splash in the world of letters in 1938 by winning *Story* magazine's five-hundred-dollar prize for his collection of long stories, *Uncle Tom's Children,* transferred to the New York City Project after a year in the Chicago office. In 1939, when Miss Walker visited him in Manhattan, she received the shock of her life. For reasons he never explained (though he wrote to her frequently later on) Wright abused her in foul language and ordered her out of his sight. His tongue-

° *Goose Island* was never published, but in 1966 Margaret Walker published a best-selling novel, *Jubilee* (Houghton Mifflin).

Richard Wright in 1933, two years
before he went to work for the Project
in Chicago

Jack Conroy, Nelson Algren, Emmett Dedmon (not a member of the Project) and Willard Motley, sometime after the Project ended

lashing so depressed her that she seriously considered jumping from the eleventh floor of a New York building. Only her worry about the anguish her suicide would cause her parents made her desist.

Frank Yerby, Katherine Dunham, and Willard Motley were among other black writers whose earliest literary aspirations were nurtured on the Illinois Project. Yerby, who was enrolled as an education student at the University of Chicago while working for the Project, had published an early short story in Jack Conroy's *Anvil;* but his avowed ambition was to write for money. "You intellectuals can go ahead and write your highbrow stuff," he told his colleagues. "I'm going to make a million." He more than fulfilled his boast with a string of popular historical novels of the South, an admixture of melodrama and costumery such as *The Foxes of Harrow* and *The Vixens,* which became big best sellers and were made into movies.

Willard Motley made little impression on his colleagues but went on to become famous with his first book, *Knock On Any Door,* in 1947. One of the most renowned graduates of the Illinois Project was the dancer and choreographer Katherine Dunham. On the Project she applied her University of Chicago training in anthropology to initiate several valuable black studies, one of which investigated Chicago's Negro cults (one of them later became widely known as the Black Muslim movement), another of which dealt with the storefront churches which abounded in the city's black districts. Frederick considered her one of his most capable staff members and a promising author. He was impressed with the early draft of *Journey to Accompong*, which she was then writing in her spare time. The book was published with critical acclaim a decade later.

Not all the Negro members of the Illinois Project were in the first stages of their careers. Arna Bontemps, in his early thirties when he joined the Project as a supervisor, had already published two novels, *God Sends Sundays* (1931) and *Black Thunder* (1935) and was writing his third, *Drums at Dusk* (1939). Bontemps worked chiefly with Negro materials, and was mainly responsible for *The Cavalcade of the American Negro*, issued by the Project in conjunction with Chicago's 1940 Diamond Jubilee Exposition.

One of Bontemps' best friends on the Project was Jack Conroy, a recent refugee from the Missouri Project who, along with Nelson Algren, occupied neighboring desks in the big room that held many of the Chicago office's one hundred employees.* Algren, Bontemps recalled, seldom wasted time but now and then would openly flirt with the young typists in the secretarial pool. From his desk he could also observe Fenton Johnson, an old-time poet who was then writing *WPA Poems*, a collection which was never published but which "did him a lot of good."

Two of the Project's published novelists, Stuart Engstrand and George Victor Martin, had already left the staff, but they would drop in occasionally to see how things were going.† Bontemps and his colleagues remembered Engstrand as a hypersensitive person whose life was deeply involved with his fiction writing. He published two novels while still on the Project, *The Invaders* in 1937 and *They Sought a Paradise* in 1939. When

---

* Bontemps and Conroy collaborated on a book dealing with Negro migrations within the United States, *They Seek a City* (1945), which was based largely on unpublished Project material they had helped to gather. Twenty years later the book was recast and expanded, and reissued with a new title, *Anyplace But Here* (Hill and Wang, 1966).

† Part of George Victor Martin's first and most successful novel, *For Our Vines Have Tender Grapes* (Argus, 1940), was written while he was on the staff of the Illinois Writers' Project.

he entered the manuscript of the latter book in the Harper's Prize Novel contest it evoked so much praise from the editors that he became certain he would win the prize. But his elation was premature. The prize for that year went to another Project writer, Vardis Fisher, for his *Children of God*. Although Engstrand published several other novels, he remained relatively unknown. One September day in 1955 he walked, fully clothed, into a lake in Los Angeles' MacArthur Park and kept on walking until he drowned.

Across the big room Bontemps could glimpse the separate area assigned to the Project's newly formed radio division, which had been established by Curtis MacDougall, a journalism professor at Northwestern University who succeeded Frederick in 1939. Headed by Barry Farnol, the radio division prospered and provided some of its twenty members with valuable preparation for their future literary and acting careers. Sam Ross, who later burgeoned into a television scriptwriter as well as a novelist, was one of them, as were Lou Gilbert and Studs (Louis) Terkel. For Terkel the Project represented joyous liberation from the possibility of becoming a lawyer, the profession which his parents almost imposed on him. His experience in the radio division was the beginning of his career as an actor, and later as a topflight radio interviewer.* For Gilbert the radio division provided an opportunity to keep his theatrical aspirations alive.

The radio division prepared for local broadcast such weekly programs as "Moments with Genius," "Great Artists," "Legends of Illinois," which Robert R. McCormick, publisher of the *Chicago Tribune* and one of the New Deal's bitterest foes, willingly permitted to be produced on the radio station he owned. The radio division operated with an efficiency and zeal that was often lacking in other departments of the Project. Once a week its members met around a conference table to discuss future programs and receive their assignments. "We wrote our stories, we discussed them, we got them produced," Ross recalled. "Everybody felt alive. It was about the only project at the time that had deadlines, direction, immediate production. We were linked to the community. I learned my dramatic craft there. So did the others."

Although the Illinois Project workers had plenty of time for their own writing, most of them did not take advantage of it. They spent a good deal of their leisure time bowling, shooting pool, and going to the movies. Jazz

---

* Studs Terkel also became an author: *Giants of Jazz* (Thomas Y. Crowell, 1956); *Division Street: America* (Pantheon, 1967); *Hard Times* (Pantheon, 1970).

Frank Yerby, a few years after he worked for the Project in Chicago

Studs Terkel wrote radio scripts for the Illinois Project, 1938

Katherine Dunham, of the Project's Chicago staff, in 1938

was a steady preoccupation; Chicago could offer it in abundance all during the thirties. Most of the parties they attended were usually for the purpose of raising money for some leftwing cause; for several years the main cause was that of the Spanish loyalists and their war against the forces of Franco. At all times sex was fairly free and active, according to Ross. "You'd go to the parties and dances and meet the girls. They knew you and you felt comfortable . . ."

A high percentage of the Project members, particularly the young, dreamed of writing short stories, poems, or novels; but they talked more than they wrote. "Some of us did find a way of telling stories, of writing nonfiction books and articles," observed Ross, "but very few. The Project helped those who did. Some of us became famous like Dick Wright, silver-voiced, clearheaded, who wrote about the black man like nobody before him — or like Algren, soft-voiced, moody, hardly articulate except when he wrote. Most were never heard of and went about their ways. But the Project helped a lot of people all over the country, and the talent it did help develop was immeasurable."

The California Writers' Project had its share of bright young writers but it failed to be as fertile a spawning ground for literary talent as the Chicago Project. None of its alumni achieved the kind of recognition that came to writers like Richard Wright, Saul Bellow, Nelson Algren, Frank Yerby and Willard Motley, possibly because there was no John T. Frederick in charge to spot and encourage young writers. During most of its years the California Project suffered from poor direction and excessive deadwood. Yet thanks to a small nucleus of diligent young writers led by Walter McElroy and Leon Dorais, who headed the Los Angeles office, the California Project managed to produce a larger number of major publications than any other writers' project, among them the encyclopedic California state guidebook (713 pages) and book-length guides to San Francisco, Los Angeles, San Diego, Santa Barbara, the Monterey Peninsula and Death Valley.

The most prominent writer on the California Project was James Hopper, its second director, who had already published several novels and more than four hundred short stories, many of which appeared in such magazines as *Collier's* and the *Saturday Evening Post*. Other published fiction writers on the staff included Carl Wilhelmson, an ex-sailor who had written several novels but published only one, *Midsummernight;* Nahum

Sabsay, a Russian refugee who was the author of *The Hurricane* and had contributed short stories to the *Atlantic Monthly* and *Scribner's;* and Eluard Luchell McDaniel, a Negro who was that rare species of a literary artist — a primitive writer unhindered by rules of grammar. McDaniel quit the Project in order to join the Abraham Lincoln Brigade in Spain, saying to his colleagues, "I'm going to join up and get myself one of those Moors." In Spain he cut a dashing figure as a courageous soldier and became known as El Fantastico.

There were also a number of published poets, among them Madeline Gleason, Dorothy Van Ghent, who had published under the name of Dorothy Bendon, Cornel Lengyel, and Raymond E. F. Larsson, a well-known Catholic poet. Larsson suffered a nervous breakdown while on the San Francisco Project and escaped to a retreat in the backwoods of Georgia, where Alsberg finally found him and reinstated him on the government payroll with the assurance that he need never report to any office or supervisor.

The poet who dominated the atmosphere of the San Francisco office with his volatile personality and compulsive storytelling was Kenneth Rexroth, who had been a mural painter on the San Francisco FERA art project before joining the Writers' Project. A philosopher with an inclination for experimentation, Rexroth had been a postulant in an Anglican monastery and a member of the Friends Service Committee. In the early thirties he cast himself in the role of a Marxist and helped give birth to the San Francisco Artists and Writers Union, which agitated for the creation of the Writers' Project. Rexroth's peculiar relationship with the Communists was neatly summarized in a statement he liked to show his friends which was signed by the Communist leader Earl Browder: "This man is a valuable comrade but an incorrigible anarchist."

On the San Francisco Project Rexroth delighted his colleagues with his displays of erudition and endless stories about his experiences in Chicago, which later became the substance of an autobiographical work. In the early days of the Project when the workers had little to do, Rexroth's sizable audience included Leon Dorais, who felt that "listening to Rexroth was like extending one's liberal arts education." There were times, Dorais remembered, when he and his colleagues would also listen to William Saroyan who, though not a member of the Project, would drop in between his bouts with the typewriter and talk about the success he was beginning to know; but it was Rexroth who held the floor most of the time. When at

Kenneth Rexroth joined the California Project in San Francisco at its inception in 1935

last the Project swung into action there was less time for talk as Rexroth went off on field trips to collect data on California's flora and fauna, the guidebook topic assigned to him. His last stint for the Project was to contribute to the final draft of the San Francisco Guide. He resigned from the Project in 1939, as soon as he learned of the "tragic charade" at Munich, "too politically disgusted to be on any government payroll."

Probably the most versatile writer on the California Project was Miriam Allen deFord, poet, novelist and social historian, who was then in her forties. Alsberg, who was familiar with her work, had hired her as a non-relief writer while she was passing through Washington. At the time she was earning only twenty dollars a month as the San Francisco correspondent of the Federated Press; the prospect of earning more than five times that amount delighted her. But she soon found the Project job rather dispiriting since too many of her colleagues were clearly incompetent. "When a person on relief could read and write and could not do manual labor — a shoe clerk, for example," she wrote, "he was shunted into the Writers' Project."

The most pathetic of her colleagues were the old and senile. One of them was a septuagenarian Englishman who constantly carried a brown paper bag containing clippings of news stories he had written in bygone days when he had been a distinguished journalist. Now he was incapable of writing the simplest report, but because his wife was a bedridden invalid, no one had the heart to fire him. Without his Project job, his income as a welfare recipient would have amounted to ten dollars a month, hardly enough to keep his invalid wife and himself alive. But while there was little objection to his presence on the staff, there were many complaints about the way he smelled. Enveloping him like a polluted aura, the stench he exuded belied the old man's rather neat apparel, which consisted largely of an ancient coat with a faded velvet collar. "Keep away, Caswell," one of his colleagues grumbled, exasperated by the stench. "You smell." The old man replied with considerable dignity, "Yes, I smell of Lysol." His colleague disagreed. "No, you smell of the past." The old man, who cried easily, sat down and sobbed.

The problem of excessive staff deadwood was augmented in San Francisco by the heavy infiltration of leftwing personnel who, according to Miriam Allen deFord, were more intent on functioning as missionaries for Marxism than workers for the Project. In the early months of the Project, when they were largely in command, there was a great deal of political commotion and little work done. The situation remained unresolved because it was illegal for the administrators to question the political affiliation of any WPA worker (a point insisted on by the Republicans in Congress who were afraid that the Democrats would discriminate against Republicans applying for WPA jobs), but gradually it eased as the cooperative spirit of the Communists' popular front policy began to filter down to the rank and file. Eventually the desire of leftwing leaders to make the Project a productive body was so marked that members of the party who were derelict in their Project work would be severely reprimanded.

Despite the presence of several militant leftwingers in the San Francisco office, all efforts to organize a Project union failed. The only union that prevailed was the Workers Alliance, which consisted mainly of unskilled WPA workers, but was an effective force among employees of Federal One in both San Francisco and New York. In both cities it helped men and women on relief obtain jobs in the arts projects; it also provided leadership for demonstrations that protested impending Federal One reductions in personnel. When, in July 1936, the California Writers' Project was temporarily shut down for lack of funds, one hundred members of the Project, directed by the Workers Alliance, burst into the office of the California state WPA administration to demand its continuation.

A year later, responding to massive cuts in the writers', theater, and sewing projects, twenty of the discharged WPA workers staged San Francisco's first sit-down strike. They spread blankets over the cement floor of the WPA office lobby and spent the night there. The next morning the police arrived and took them away. In the confusion, a young and pretty redhead, who had been working for the Writers' Project, was left behind. Furious, she chased the police wagon all the way to the station, then demanded that she be arrested with the rest of her comrades. The policeman to whom she directed the demand asked her name. "Angela McCann," she replied, flashing Irish blue eyes. "My name is Murphy," responded the policeman in a brogue. "Go home to your mother and stay there."

(It was not the first time that Angela McCann's Irish eyes had affected the officials she encountered, nor was it to be the last. The same Miss McCann had been hired by Robin Kinkead, a Project supervisor who, struck by her beauty, gave her a job despite her meager newspaper experience and her lack of relief status. But he could do nothing for her when a general WPA order made the dismissal of many nonrelief Project members mandatory. A determined girl, Miss McCann, who had enjoyed her

Project work almost as much as she enjoyed the presence of Mr. Kinkead [whom she later married], decided to be reinstated on the Project as a relief worker. The Workers Alliance carefully coached her on what to tell the welfare office in order to qualify as a certified pauper, but in the excitement of being interviewed by a welfare official she forgot the advice and let her imagination take over. Her parents, she told him, were both dead. Her mother had been blown up in an explosion during a Central American revolution. With the insurance money she received, she had taken a journey around the world, and now found herself destitute. After truthfully answering the official's last question, "Where did you eat dinner last night," saying she had gone without dinner, the official informed her that his office's investigation of her case revealed that her mother was quite alive and anxious to have her return home. "However," added the official, "after hearing your story, it is clear to me that with such an imagination you should be on the Writers' Project." With that, he signed the certificate she needed to get back to the Project and Mr. Kinkead.)

As in other metropolitan centers, the unrelenting newspaper attacks on the Project for "harboring" radicals and the ensuing investigations were as demoralizing as the constant threat of reductions in personnel and appropriations. One of the many Project writers falsely accused of being a Communist was Lawrence Estavan, a leader of the Project's literati and a former San Francisco newspaperman, who was dismissed in 1938, along with several other similarly accused Project supervisors. Estavan's accuser was a woman in the Communist party who did research work for the Project. Her reason for considering Estavan a Communist member was that he would permit her to leave the office in the middle of the afternoon, whenever she pleaded illness; she was certain that he knew that was the time when Communist cell meetings took place and was aware of the fact that she was attending them. Estavan was the only one of the dismissed supervisors who insisted on a full investigation of his situation, and the only one reinstated. His clearance, however, extended only to his Project job, and he had difficulty finding steady work thereafter, despite the fact that his accuser, while on her deathbed, wrote a statement confessing she had lied.

The fever of Marxist ideology that possessed some of the California Project members was a debilitating factor; it divided the personnel into quarreling political factions. The most militant of these were the Stalinists and the Trotskyites, who though ostensibly committed to the struggle against fascism and capitalism, reserved their most virulent hatred for each other. Their heated battles affected everyone else on the Project and impeded its administration. It was not uncommon for supervisors in both the San Francisco and Los Angeles offices to be accused of being Stalinists by the Trotskyites and Trotskyites by the Stalinists. In San Francisco, as in all the big city writers' projects, the Stalinists outnumbered the Trotskyites.

In addition to those who openly admitted membership in the Communist party (in the San Francisco office they constituted about 10 percent of the staff of one hundred), the Stalinists could count on the support of "fellow travelers," men and women who sympathized with the gospel of communism as expounded by Stalin, but were unwilling to become members of the party. But while the Trotskyites were fewer in number they tended to be more vocal and zealous. It was a sleuthing Trotskyite in the San Francisco office who discovered that several of his Stalinist colleagues, who were working for a friendly supervisor, would be excused from their Project assignments on the grounds that they had "party work" to do. The same persons, the sleuth also learned, would beg off doing their political chores by convincing their party leaders they had Project work to do.

Although there were not enough leftwingers on the California Project to generate the kind of disruptive political action that was to make the New York City Project an administrative inferno, their influence often prevailed. When James Hopper proved to be an ineffectual director, it was a group of leftwingers in the San Francisco office who loudly recommended to the Washington authorities that he be replaced. In the shakeup that followed his ouster, the apolitical members of the staff, who did not have the support of the leftwing element, fared badly. Ed Radenzel, an experienced newspaperman and a liberal who had been second in command during Hopper's regime, found himself without a job. Basil Vaerlen, one of the most competent supervisors in the San Francisco office, was demoted without any explanation.

Vaerlen blamed his demotion on a supervisor with leftwing sympathies by the name of Margaret Wilkins, and for a long time refused to speak to her. She, in turn, avoided him. On one occasion, however, they found themselves alone in the same elevator, and Miss Wilkins felt constrained to break the silence. "Well, well, Mr. Vaerlen, I presume," she said. "You do presume," Vaerlen replied. But his most heated encounter was with another leftwinger, Kenneth Rexroth. The young poet, enraged that Vaerlen had changed some of his copy, shouted, "Goddam you, I'll throw this typewriter in your teeth." Vaerlen promptly threatened to throw it back, but nothing more happened.

The antagonism between recognized writers on the California Project and writers who were little known seldom developed into such open hostility; yet it was always present. The published writers did not hesitate to let it be known that they considered the writing of guidebooks a form of hack work which contributed nothing to their literary development, notwithstanding statements by Henry Alsberg to the contrary. Led by Rexroth, they, "the real writers," kept demanding that they be relieved of their mundane assignments and be permitted to work on their own material. The other writers on the staff, who far outnumbered the "real writers," deeply resented this kind of snobbery. Their chief complaint was not with their guidebook assignments but with the lack of public acknowledgment for their contributions to the Project publications.

Basil Vaerlen's experience could have been cited as a case in point. For five years he worked steadfastly on a half dozen Project publications, yet his name appeared in only one — not a guidebook but the *Almanac for Thirty Niners,* a minor work, to which he had contributed the couplet "There, little doggerel don't you cry/ You'll be a classic bye and bye." Throughout the states the names of Project editors and supervisors were sometimes mentioned in prefaces to guidebooks but seldom the contributors of lesser status.* Actually, younger members of the staff sometimes turned out to be more skillful guidebook writers than their more experienced colleagues, partly because they tended to be more flexible in adjusting to the stylistic requirements set in Washington, and partly because they were eager to make their Project experience count in their training as writers.

For no member of the staff was the task of turning out acceptable guidebook copy an easy one. Even as expert a writer as Miriam Allen deFord,† who wrote or edited all the material in the California Guide dealing with the state's large cities, was sometimes lost in the maze of conflicting instructions that kept arriving from Washington periodically.

* Anonymity was the general policy, a policy formulated by WPA administrators whose names appeared unfailingly and prominently in every Project publication.

† Miriam Allen deFord left the Project in 1939 when a new director forbade her to do any of her Project work at home.

Miriam Allen deFord, of the San Francisco Project,
in the thirties

Her consternation inspired her to dash off some verse which expressed the sentiments of many a Project editor throughout the land:

> *I think that I have never tried*
> *A job as painful as the guide.*
> *A guide which changes every day*
> *Because our betters feel that way.*
> *A guide whose deadlines come so fast*
> *Yet no one lives to see the last*
> *A guide to which we give our best*
> *To hear: 'This stinks like all the rest!'*
>
> *There's no way out but suicide*
> *For only God can end the Guide.*

The two young writers on the California Project who fared best were Leon Dorais and Walter McElroy. Dorais, who had published a few stories, was placed in charge of a Los Angeles staff that included among others Carl Foreman, who later achieved fame as a Hollywood screenwriter, and two poets who had recently transferred from New York, Kenneth Patchen and Harvey Breit. McElroy proved to be the wonder boy of the California Project. With little previous experience either as an editor or writer, he performed brilliantly in both roles and ultimately became the head of the Project, providing it with a direction and stability it had not known under its previous directors. While he was an assistant state director, he and Dorais were instrumental in getting the mammoth California Guide to press in 1938. To expedite the book, Alsberg had summoned McElroy, Dorais and James Hopper to Washington, where the trio worked with the national editors for four months until the manuscript was completed.

Both McElroy and Dorais returned to California with a better impression of the Washington editors than they had had from the long and sometimes angry exchange of letters that preceded their trip. Both men became convinced that the Washington staff, though sometimes arrogant in its assumption that it knew as much about California as the California writers themselves, were generally expert in their editorial appraisals. Dorais became particularly respectful of Katharine Kellock's editorial talents. It was she, he claimed in retrospect, who taught him how to put together an effective English sentence and also how to rid a manuscript of its fatty matter.

No such endorsement for any member of the Washington staff ever came out of the Pennsylvania Project where the rank and file, led by its director, firmly believed that the Washington editors constituted an irksome obstacle that should be circumvented whenever possible. This despite the fact that the Pennsylvania Project, sadly lacking in talented writers, would have benefited from any editorial guidance offered by experienced editors.

In a state where it had long been customary for most of its promising writers to migrate to New York City, the Pennsylvania Project, which numbered some 240 persons, had only one writer of any reputation. He was Samuel Putnam, who had not lived in Pennsylvania until he joined the Project there. Putnam, a literary historian and expert translator of Pirandello and Rabelais (later of Cervantes' *Don Quixote*), had recently returned from a seven-year period of expatriation in Paris and, on his arrival, become a member of the Communist party. He was a sad-faced romantic idealist whose mild disposition was at odds with a shockingly deep crevice in his forehead, a fierce deformity which appeared to have been inflicted by a saber but which, in fact, was the result of an ineptly performed sinus operation.

As the only Project writer of any stature, Putnam automatically became the Philadelphia office's editorial mediator, the referee of all wrangles that developed between those who wrote and those who edited. His colleagues were mainly ex-newspapermen and magazine writers, teachers, and a scattering of recent college graduates who had received good grades in English. The official headquarters of the Project were technically in Harrisburg, the capital, but most of the action was in the Philadelphia office, where a hundred and fifty members of the Pennsylvania Project were stationed and where Paul Comly French, the state director, spent most of his time.

French was a former newspaperman who had become deeply involved in the affairs of the Newspaper Guild, particularly in trying to find jobs for the many unemployed newsmen in Philadelphia. He was an affable and ambitious Quaker, something of an entrepreneur, who seemed determined to make the Pennsylvania Project one of the most successful in the coun-

Portrait of Samuel Putnam by Alice Neel, 1933

try. Enterprising to a degree that at first impressed Alsberg and later depressed him, French operated on a scale which sometimes went beyond the boundaries of Pennsylvania, and occasionally beyond the bounds of official regulations.

In addition to developing a map-making department that produced work for writers' projects in other states, he was the instigator and organizer of the William Penn Association, which was intended to act as a publishing agency for Project publications produced in Pennsylvania and elsewhere. It was a bold concept, and one that appealed to Alsberg at first. Shares in the association were sold to members of the Project and whoever else would purchase them at twenty-five dollars a share, with the expectation that any profits which accrued would be divided proportionately among the shareholders. All went well until the WPA Finance Office, on discovering that members of the Project were shareholders in the association, declared that it was illegal for the association to sell material that was prepared at government expense and on government time. French and all other Project employees were ordered to disassociate themselves from the group.

When French seemed slow in conforming with the government's order, Alsberg became nervous and in a telephone conversation with him threatened to withhold a pay raise that the Pennsylvania director was to receive. "I think you have a claim to the raise," he told French in September 1937, "but I think we must settle this other matter first, I mean about the William Penn Association. The raise is all right in principle, and I think you are entitled to it, but we must settle the other matter first."

The more Alsberg dealt with French the more uneasy he became. On the surface French treated him with deference, but it became increasingly clear to Alsberg that behind the deference was an attitude of contempt. Unlike most of the Project field offices, French and his associates had never overcome the initial hostility that the Washington staff inspired in the field when it first began to impose its editorial dictates. French and nearly all of his associates remained convinced that Alsberg and his staff were Washington bureaucrats so immersed in red tape as to hinder rather than facilitate the publication of Project material; with the result that, whenever possible, French and his editors would try to bypass the Washington editors rather than accept their criticism.

The only ally French had on the Washington staff was Alsberg's field representative, Joseph Gaer, who in his eagerness to see Project manuscripts converted into printed books and pamphlets, would sometimes advise state directors to save time by disregarding Washington's editorial instructions. Not all of the state directors who received this advice from Gaer were happy with it. When James Hopper, the California Project director, heard that Washington was sending a field man to work with him, he was heard to exclaim, "My God, they'll send Gaer again and he will tell us we can do anything we want to, regardless of how cockeyed it is, and we will then go ahead in good faith and Washington won't let us do it."

French, on the other hand, had no fear of Washington, knowing that perhaps, with Gaer's help, he could do virtually as he wished; also that Alsberg would not dare fire him because of his connection with the Newspaper Guild. Alsberg, though unhappy with French and aware of his faults, defended him to his Washington editors on the grounds that he was more industrious and more aware than most other state directors of the pressing need to prove to Congress that the Writers' Project was not sitting on its hands. In his dealings with French, Alsberg treated him with all the tact he could command, even when he felt exasperated over some of French's actions. The following telephone dialogue between the two men, recorded in January 1937, more or less typified their method of responding to each other:

Alsberg: Listen, why don't you send us your introductory essays [for the Pennsylvania state guide book], then we can look them over and shoot them back to you.

French: Oh, I didn't think you wanted them separately. Mr. Gaer said we should send them all together.

Alsberg: That's funny. Mr. Gaer is just sitting at my elbow, and he told me to ask you to send them. There must be some misunderstanding. (*A long pause in which French says nothing*) You see, if you send us a part we can get right to work; otherwise, when it arrives all in one, we have to put almost the entire staff on it to get it out.

French: Yes, I get it. (*Changes the subject*) We'll have two more pamphlets for you soon.

Alsberg: What are they?

French: Harmony Society and Fishing Creek. [The latter was never published.]

Alsberg: That will be fine. Now don't forget to send us those essays.

Alsberg's associates were more explicit in expressing their resentment over French's tactics. When George Cronyn learned that, on Gaer's rec-

*Paul Comly French (center), director of the Project in Pennsylvania,
at an editorial meeting in Harrisburg, 1938*

ommendation, Alsberg had permitted French to send the manuscript of
the Philadelphia Guide to the printer without submitting it to Washington
for review, he wrote Alsberg a long and angry memorandum, which contributed to the breach growing between him and his chief. In one paragraph he scolded:

"If the responsibility for the Philadelphia Guide does not rest with us
but with the Philadelphia staff, I would like to know who will write and
answer any criticism that may come because of errors in fact, faults in
style or poor organization. Indeed, if it is not our job to see that writing
everywhere is as high in quality as possible then I can see no reason for
maintaining a central staff whatever, and we should have stopped it a year
ago and allowed all the states to do exactly what they wanted to do."

Cronyn's apprehensions about the quality of the Philadelphia Guide
were justified. When the almost three-pound, 704-page book was published early in 1938 by the newly reorganized William Penn Association, it
became one of the few major Project publications to receive an unfavor-

145

able press. The New York *Times* reviewer complained that "it lacks all too plainly the perspective, the culture and the thoroughness of knowledge which are needed to select facts and, even for a guidebook, weld them into a dependable, useful and informative whole." The Washington *Post,* devoting four columns to the book, described it as "an example of the kind of corporate literature that might be produced through the agency of an American corporate state." And although the reviewer marveled at the large number of facts the book contained and called it "useful and interesting," he found that it was "very rarely an objective account of facts about the city." On the same book page the Washington *Post* reviewed in glowing terms (but smaller space) another city guidebook produced by the Writers' Project, the New Orleans City Guide, which it said "made the city and its environs live and breathe."

The generally scornful attitude of the Pennsylvania Project toward the Washington office was one of the few things which French and his staff members all had in common with one another. On nearly all other Project matters, there were noisy grievances and sharp divisions of opinion, especially in the staff's appraisal of French's capabilities. His more friendly colleagues considered him dynamic, but to the point of often becoming impatient; independent, but to a degree that invariably created friction with his WPA superiors; and kind, but to the extent that he found it difficult to fire personnel, even when it would benefit the Project. One of his assistants recalled that in the spring of 1938, when there had been a general reduction in the staff ordered by Washington, French retreated to his Harrisburg office for the rest of his tenure rather than face the unpleasant consequences. His enemies regarded him as a self-seeking opportunist with ambitions that were beyond his abilities. Although acknowledging that French generally conducted himself as a political liberal, somewhat more to the left than most liberals, one of his staff members, a young Project supervisor who was a member of the Communist party, disliked him "because at a time of our lives when ideals seemed particularly important, French didn't seem to have an ideal to his name." * Both his friends and enemies were in agreement that French was a poor judge of people.

* During World War II French headed the National Service Board which worked in behalf of conscientious objectors. In 1946 he became the first executive secretary of CARE (a post he held until his death in 1960), and for his humanitarian endeavors received decorations from France, Austria, Italy, and The Netherlands. Contrasting his work for CARE with the job he had previously held on the Federal Writers' Project, the Philadelphia *Inquirer* noted that "his present post is closer to his Quaker ideals of humanitarian service."

French's difficulties with the Pennsylvania Project began when he first became its director. In the course of trying to win the support of the two main warring factions on the Project — the former newspapermen who belonged to the Newspaper Guild and the young radicals who were members of the Writers Union — he wound up antagonizing both groups. The leftwingers, impatient with French for not meeting all of their demands, began to scheme to overthrow him as director and replace him with their own candidate. As in a cheap scenario, the candidate was one of French's most trusted lieutenants, an administrative assistant he had entrusted with the task of establishing branch offices of the Project throughout Pennsylvania.

The assistant, a willing conspirator, had a dazzling gift of gab and a mesmerizing personality. Working with the zeal of an inspired Iago, he led the plotters in their arduous campaign to throw French out of office. Labor disputes were started that would put the director in a bad light; destructive rumors calculated to discredit him were circulated, and anonymous letters of poisonous intent were addressed to high government officials. The young "idealists" in the Writers Union stopped at nothing that would help to undermine French, even blaming him for dismissals ordered from Washington over which he had no control. The plot would have succeeded, except for a few powerful members of the group who had second thoughts about the assistant's qualifications to head the Project, and withdrew their support.

The antagonism toward French did not let up, even after members of the Newspaper Guild and the Writers Union had become friendly enough to play poker together and to organize joint delegations to Washington that protested impending personnel cuts. In 1939, when the Project was about to change nationally from federal to state sponsorship, a self-appointed committee, headed by Irving Ignatin, a Project supervisor, secretly met with French's WPA boss in Pennsylvania, Mrs. Anna M. Lebengood, and apparently convinced her that the Project would be better off without French. Shortly afterwards Mrs. Lebengood requested his resignation on the ground that his appointment as director in the reorganized setup "would be incompatible with the policies under which the proposed new Project is to be operated."

Aubrey Baldwin, one of French's chief assistants, came to his defense in a letter to Mrs. Lebengood and asked her to reconsider her decision, but many of the Project workers were not sorry to see him go. In September

1939 when Richard Powell, then a reporter for the Philadelphia *Inquirer*, talked to employees about the Project, he had no trouble garnering numerous complaints.* Their main themes were inefficient administration, favoritism, and sloppy work. One Project employee told Powell that workers were often asked to do work that had been done, and that some workers assigned to do library research would lift whole passages from standard historical volumes and submit them as original pieces. Another employee asserted that the Project executives hired men with no writing experience "as long as their ideas were sufficiently Red and as long as they had friends among the executives." One so-called writer, he added, was a former janitor who had never finished grammar school; in another case, a former sports editor of a large daily was obliged to submit his copy to a former office boy.

According to one Project worker, the supervision on the Project was a "joke." "You could check in by phone in the morning and only report once a week for a conference to tell what you'd been doing." Another Project employee disagreed. "There was a lot of supervision, and it was for the purpose of needling workers who didn't belong to the ruling clique . . ." He said that French and his top executives had a "spy system." "They would ask supervisors to check on field workers," then "the top executives would go out and spy on the spies."

* Richard Powell, who has since become a successful novelist, was one of the Republican-minded newspapermen of the thirties who at first had little use for the Writers' Project but later appreciated its merits. His first story about the Pennsylvania Project, written as a young reporter on the anti–New Deal Philadelphia *Ledger,* poked fun at the Project. In a letter to the author (November 19, 1968) Powell told what happened when he was gathering information for the story: "I collected a story, feeling quite superior to the out-of-work copy boys and drunks who comprised much of the initial personnel of the Project. In doing so I happened to see the back of somebody's paycheck. On it was printed: 'If you cannot write, mark an X.' Well, of course, this made a perfect lead for my story: a writers' project whose members might have to sign their names with an X. Management at the *Ledger* was delighted." But a year later, in 1936, when the *Ledger* merged with the Philadelphia *Inquirer* and Powell saw three of his friends summarily dismissed but rescued from unemployment by the Writers' Project, "I began to regret my nasty little feature story about the Project."

Powell added: "I had further regrets eight years ago, when I began research for an historical novel about southwest Florida [*I Take This Land*] and discovered that the Writers' Project Florida Guide was far and away the best of all the reference sources I could locate. I am sure that, as time goes on, the American Guide Series will be recognized as a uniquely valuable source of information on these United States. No commercial publisher could have subsidized such a massive undertaking. It resulted in the collection of information that could never otherwise have been gathered, and that in fact would have disappeared to a considerable extent if it had not been collected in the 1930s. So, free enterpriser though I am, this is one case in which I vote for governmental enterprise."

Despite all the complaints, an impressive number of publications were produced by the Pennsylvania Project, under French's direction and also during the period after his departure when a number of projects initiated by him were completed. One of the most unusual of them was a series of elementary science books on some twenty-eight different subjects ranging from clouds to grapes. These brief books, which were used in the Pennsylvania schools, were mainly the work of Kay Britton, who as a result of her Project experience later became an associate editor of the *Saturday Evening Post.*

While most of the Pennsylvania publications were brief pamphlets, there were at least ten substantial books among the Project's total output, among them *Pennsylvania Cavalcade,* a group of historical essays edited by Grant Sassaman which was of sufficient quality to be issued by the University of Pennsylvania Press; the aforementioned Philadelphia Guide, which despite its defects become a popular reference work, and the Project's magnus opus, the Pennsylvania Guide, which Oxford University Press published about a year after French left the Project, and which had the editorial blessings of the Washington editors to whom the manuscript was submitted for approval.

No state Project, large or small, was able to win Washington's approval for an important manuscript without a certain amount of rewriting. Yet the editorial standards set in Washington, although professional, were not unduly high; they required only those language skills that are usually developed in high school. The Project writers who had the most difficult time satisfying the Washington editors were often ex-newspapermen, particularly reporters. Trained to deal with the immediate present, they lacked the sense of historical perspective essential for the writing of guidebooks. Too often the supervisors themselves were ex-reporters who were incapable of performing as competent editors. The frustration of field workers and supervisors in not being able to satisfy Washington standards often led to even more insecurity than they had felt before joining the Project; and heavier drinking.

By and large, the novelists and poets, especially the younger ones, came out best. Their ability to recognize significant and arresting information and present it in logical sequence, together with their sensitivity for language, stood them in good stead as did their sense of rapport with the American past. One of the Project's most successful field workers was Paul

Corey, an aspiring young fiction writer who had published some short stories in little magazines and was working on a first novel, *Three Mile Square* (1939), which was to become part of a trilogy about Iowa farm life.* Corey had reluctantly left his small chicken farm in Croton-on-Hudson, where he lived with his poet wife Ruth Lechlitner, to join the New York State Project in Albany at $125 a month. Unlike the rest of his colleagues, Corey had no difficulty getting his guidebook copy approved in Washington. His amazed supervisor once exclaimed: "You're the only sonofabitch on the staff who can write the kind of shit they like in Washington."

For Corey writing guidebook copy was far more simple than working on a novel, but not as exciting, and he longed to return to his unfinished manuscript and to his farm. On one occasion, partly out of boredom and partly to test the alertness of his supervisor, he incorporated a spirited defense of Benedict Arnold in some guidebook copy; but the material was rejected. However, Corey was by nature a conscientious worker; so much so that he was openly critical of a colleague who steadily ignored his Project work in order to write political campaign speeches for a candidate friend. Resenting the criticism, his colleague initiated a poison pen campaign which held that Corey was a member of the Communist party. Corey had no difficulty clearing himself when he was officially investigated, but the experience left a bad taste in his mouth, and he decided to resign. Fearful of losing the services of a writer whose work required little or no editing, Alsberg, at Katharine Kellock's instigation, summoned Corey to Washington to ask him to reconsider. But after listening to Corey describe all of his reasons for resigning, Alsberg heaved a sigh and, turning to Katharine Kellock, said: "Let the man go back to his wife and chickens."

Corey's predecessor on the New York State Project was Robert West Howard, one of those rare newspapermen who could write intelligently in any medium.† In 1934 Howard had been one of fourteen men fired from the Depression-stricken Syracuse *Herald*. The following year, on the recommendation of New York State historian Alexander Flick, he landed a job on the Writers' Project and before long was advanced to the post of assistant state director. Although the state Project employed 370 persons,

* The other two novels in Paul Corey's trilogy are *The Road Returns* (1940) and *County Seat* (1941). The novels were published by Bobbs-Merrill Company.

† Robert West Howard subsequently became a prolific author. He has published some fifteen volumes, many of them of a historical nature.

Paul Corey and Henry Christman, of the New York State Project, on the Corey farm, 1938

he found that only a half dozen of them were capable of turning out guidebook copy. "As far as local politicians were concerned," he observed, "the Writers' Project was the place where you dumped the bastard you didn't know what to do with."

Howard's Project work consisted largely of editing essays and writing tour copy. His companion on the road while gathering material for the tours was an ex-businessman, who took notes while Howard yelled out his observations and drove. The men had been told by their director to cover an area of fifty miles each day. To warm up to their assignments, the two men would sometimes go to Canada for four or five days of "delightful drinking," then return to New York State and cover four or five hundred miles in a single day. Only once did the two men quarrel. A poker game in a Poughkeepsie hotel room incited a violent argument, which ended abruptly when the ex-businessman left the game table, checked out of the hotel, and took a train back to Albany. Howard got into his car and followed, arriving at the Albany railroad depot just as the train from Poughkeepsie was pulling in. His collaborator stepped off the train and moved toward Howard's car with his chin down, his shoulders sagging. He opened the car door, took his place next to Howard, and muttered, "You son of a bitch." They then returned to Poughkeepsie to resume their Project assignment.

When Howard left the Project in 1937 for a job on the New York *Post*, the work on the New York State Guide was seriously impaired until Paul Corey was found to replace him. The loss of competent Project men who found better paying jobs in private industry pleased the WPA administrators but added seriously to the problems of operating a productive Writers' Project. In most instances, the men and women who moved from the Project into private industry were the cream of the personnel, the ones who had benefited most from their Project training.

Harlan Hatcher, the state director of the Ohio Project during its most productive years, described the ambivalent situation in which most state directors found themselves: "The dilemma with which I was constantly confronted was that of preparing and publishing a guide with the help of relief personnel, and at the same time I was duty bound to help these people whom I had trained to find jobs in private employment. One of my best people who worked on the 'Essays' got a fine job in the midst of our labors and went off to a prosperous career."

The steady loss of some of the Project's most capable personnel, coupled with the retention of its least able workers, impeded the progress of the state writers' projects, and placed an extra burden on the Washington staff, which, in the final analysis, was responsible for the quality of the state guides. Without enough competent writers and without a director capable of doing most of the writing himself, deadlines for many of the state guides were often meaningless. In half the states the frequent delays extended over a period of five years or more. In a number of those states the guidebooks would never have been completed but for the intercession of flying editorial squads from Washington.

The mixture of art and politics is a dubious business. But we were fed and survived.

> — Lawrence Fixel, a former
> member of the New York
> Writers' Project, in a letter
> to the author, December 18,
> 1968

I'm truly grateful to the Communist activists who revealed to me, away back then, what a bastard a dedicated Communist, by definition, must be . . . The New York Project was deliberately and often successfully harassed by the Communist party. I knew the score well; our Red friends loved to plot but they weren't very adroit at it.

> — Donald Thompson, former
> acting director of the New
> York City Writers' Project,
> in a letter to the author,
> May 31, 1969

Organization and protest and demand alone held the Project together. It was all very precarious. We all had the feeling that if we didn't keep calling for the maintenance of the Project it would fold up.

> — Earl Conrad, former member
> of the New York City Writers'
> Project, in a letter to the
> author, October 26, 1967

There were Communists, conservatives, Trotskyites, Cannonites, old-time Republicans and Democrats. The Communists were supposed to be the dominant group, and there were many stories and legends about the way they operated. Anyway, both the Project and the Writers Union provided a lot of fun for many members like myself who had no political affiliation, but who found them both rich in personalities and in the kind of turbulence that suggested vitality rather than depression.

> — Allan Angoff, former member
> of the New York City Writers'
> Project, in a letter to the
> author, December 17, 1967

Five.

Manhattan Hotbed

On no other Writers' Project was the turbulence of the thirties more evident than on the New York City Project. Almost from the day it sprang into being, it became a maelstrom of conflicting personalities and ideologies which often got out of hand, a vast psychodrama with elements which Orville Prescott characterized as "quixotic good intentions, hysterical folly, pitiful bungling and general bedlam."

The cast of characters included men and women of every age bracket and of every political faith. Many of them were amateur revolutionists blindly caught up in the dream that the next American revolution was just around the corner. There was also a minority band of rightwingers — "enemies of the working class" as they were solemnly dubbed by their leftwing colleagues — whose only time of glory came when the Project was under investigation by Communist-hunting agents of the Dies and Woodrum congressional committees. There were men and women of all nationalities, among them Jews and Italians who could not write English. There were well-known authors like Maxwell Bodenheim, Claude McKay, Vincent McHugh, Harry Kemp, Anzia Yezierska, Edward Dahlberg; rising authors like Kenneth Fearing, Lionel Abel, Harry Roskolenko, Norman Macleod, John Herrmann, William Rollins, Jr., Joseph Vogel; and fledgling authors like Ralph Ellison, David Ignatow, Earl Conrad, Anthony Netboy, Ellen Tarry.

For the young the New York City Project had the lure of a mecca, and some came from long distances to become part of it, eager to rub elbows with published authors and ready to tell whatever lies were required to obtain a pauper's certificate, the official passport to the Writers' Project. For many of the ex-newspapermen and published authors the Project was a badge of poverty, a barely tolerable refuge from the Depression. Yet in the beginning, before the Project got under way, the enthusiasm of some of the older writers, such as that of Anzia Yezierska, matched that of the young.

Miss Yezierska's stories about immigrant life on Manhattan's East Side had won her acclaim and Hollywood riches in the twenties, but by the mid-thirties she was destitute and unable to find work of any kind. In her autobiographical work, *Red Ribbon on a White Horse,* she described the joyful shock she and her literary friends experienced when they first read that the government was about to launch a program for unemployed artists of all kinds. "When they were finally convinced that their dream was about to be realized," she wrote, "the discussion became a joyous shouting celebration. A new world was about to be born. A world where artists were no longer outcasts, hangers-on of the rich, but backed by the government, encouraged to do their best work. The President had said so. People who no longer hoped or believed in anything but the end of the world began to hope and believe again . . ."

But the dream was soon shattered. Miss Yezierska rushed to the headquarters of the new Writers' Project expecting to be put to work at once only to learn that to qualify for a job she would first have to be on the relief rolls. Her friends assured her there was nothing to it. "Just remember the rules," they told her. "Two years' residence in the city. No relatives. No friends. No insurance. No money. No nothing — you've got to be starving to death." To meet all these qualifications she was urged to resort to trickery, as many others were doing. One man told her he had been in the city for only a month but arranged with a friend to pretend he had lived at his address for the required period of residence. The friend gave him some envelopes he had received in the mail over the past two years and some ink eradicator with which he could rub out the friend's name and substitute his own. "It's being done by the best people," Miss Yezierska was assured.

A woman told her that to qualify for relief she had been obliged to swear that her mother was dead, that she had no home, no means of support. Actually, her mother was alive and operating a rooming house, but was going deeply into debt because most of her roomers could not pay the rent and she did not have the heart to evict them. Had she told the truth, she would have killed her chances of getting any relief job. By building a careful structure of lies to qualify as a pauper, within WPA definitions, she was able to land a job on the Writers' Project. Miss Yezierska's refusal to tell lies prolonged the investigation of her case and many weeks passed before she was deemed suitably poor to be hired by the Project.

The New York City Writers' Project, whose initial work was to write reports on WPA activities, began to operate in September 1935 with Orrick Johns in charge. As soon as the word was broadcast that there were jobs for writers who were on home relief, hundreds of men and women applied for work. Because regular office space was scarce, Johns and his assistants had to interview them in a vast armory building, at Lexington Avenue and Twenty-sixth Street, where, as Johns recalled, "our staff looked like the pygmies they felt," while the applicants filed past and "related their sorry tales." The interviewers listened to "stories of long unemployment, of jobs on vanished publications, and claims of creative talent." Only a small percentage of them had valid enough credentials to be hired. Several of them brought clippings of letters they had written to newspapers; some were former public officials whose chief writing experience had consisted of writing memoranda. An unemployed mail carrier insisted, with a straight face, that he was qualified because the social worker who investigated his case had called him "a man of letters." Many were frank in admitting that their sole qualification as "writers" was based on their ability to write an English sentence.

There was no time to check on what the applicants told the interviewers. Most of the people hired could show newspaper experience. There were one hundred jobs available, but after several days the interviewers had found only fifty qualified men and women. Writers were hired in two classes: legmen at $21.67 a week and editors at $23.86. Six weeks were to pass before the staff could be increased to its full quota. When it became apparent that many of the professional writers in New York would not apply for Project jobs because they could not or would not be certified as paupers, the Project eased its hiring requirements. Writers with little or no experience, who were on relief, could now be employed by submitting sample manuscripts that met with the approval of a board of Project judges.

Johns and his staff were housed in a vacant, cavernous floor of the building of the Port of New York Authority, on Eighth Avenue, "a Gulliver among buildings," with freight elevators large enough to carry ten-ton trucks. These were the only elevators permitted to the Project workers, whose ragged attire inspired the building guards with contempt. The floor assigned to the writers as working quarters was as large as a city block but the only equipment was one old desk and a swivel chair. When requested by Johns to "dream up an assignment" for the newly recruited staff, his assistant James McGraw ordered the workers to scrounge the neighborhood for boxes and orange crates that could be used as desks and chairs. He also asked them to bring in whatever writing equipment they could muster. Nearly all of them brought in paper and pencil. Although some of the writers had owned typewriters, all of the machines were now in hock. The writers worked on orange crates with pencil and paper until desks, chairs, and typewriters arrived several weeks later. Among the items that had been ordered was a gross of pencils. But the order was misread in Washington and the New York office received 144 gross of pencils. "There were crates and crates of pencils," recalled McGraw, "but it was easier to keep them than to deal with all the red tape it would have taken to return them to Washington. We used to say to our staff members, 'Please take a hundred pencils home.' We were lousy with pencils."

Despite all the initial difficulties of organizing a working staff, the earliest days of the New York Project were a happy time. Anzia Yezierska wrote: "I had seen these people at the relief station, waiting for the investigating machine to legalize them as paupers. Now they had work cards in their hands . . . They had risen from the scrap heap of the unemployed, from the loneliness of the unwanted, dreaming of regeneration, together. The new job look lighted the most ravaged faces."

Commenting on that period, McGraw, who had been an unemployed newspaperman until the Project came along, observed: "After being on relief for several years, or just getting handouts here and there, or small writing jobs — some of us were writing pornography to stay alive — we were all joyful at the prospect of getting a weekly salary and doing work that had some connection with our skills."

On the first payday many of the Project employees repaired to a nearby bar to celebrate. "We were as hilarious as slum children around a Christmas tree," Anzia Yezierska remembered. "Men who hadn't had a job for years fondled five- and ten-dollar bills with the tenderness of farmers rejoicing over a new crop of grain." Among the celebrants Miss Yezierska recalled a young black who had yet to publish his first book, Richard Wright.* "He had the calm smile of a young Buddha. His well-modeled head on straight-built shoulders stood out among the white-faced men drained by defeat."

"Folks," Wright shouted jubilantly. "Where I come from, they're all singing:

> *Roosevelt! You're my man!*
> *When the times come*
> *I ain't got a cent,*
> *You buy my groceries*
> *And pay my rent.*
> *Mr. Roosevelt, you're my man."*

Not everyone was jubilant. One of the leftwing radicals in the party called the WPA a form of "mass bribery," a means of keeping the "busted" capitalist system going. "We'd fight, we'd stage riots and revolutions if they didn't hush us up. We're all taking hush money . . ."

After having known idleness for many months and even years, the Project workers could not immediately adjust to the routine of steady effort. Strangers to the time sheets, "they lounged in and out, sprawled or traded wisecracks, wore their hats and hoisted their feet as journeyman reporters do," wrote Johns. "They were all from home relief rolls and it took weeks for some of them to get the habit of clean shirts and pressed trousers. They ran the gamut of mental states, the scared and the stolid, the humble and the proud, the reserved and excitable, with a scattering of plain drunks. . . ."

The drunks, plain and otherwise, provided the most immediate personnel problem. An ex-newspaperman who did his heaviest drinking before arriving at the office every morning was finally warned by his friend McGraw that if he came in drunk once more, he would be instantly discharged. The next morning he was as sozzled as ever, and McGraw carried out his threat. In a few minutes he was visited by a grievance committee of the Newspaper Guild who demanded to know what proof McGraw had that the man was drunk. McGraw conceded he had none but pro-

---

* Wright must have been visiting New York; at the time he was a member of the Illinois Writers' Project. He transferred to the New York City Project about a year later.

posed that if his friend, who had accompanied the grievance committee, would come forward and say, "Jim, I was not drunk," he would rescind the dismissal. As the man started toward McGraw, he fell flat on his face and passed out.

For a few of the hard-drinking members of the Project, the job routine sometimes acted as a deterrent to excessive imbibing. Although strongly given to tippling, Maxwell Bodenheim, the Greenwich Village Bohemian turned Communist who was probably the New York City Project's best-known author, faithfully executed his assignments in a tiny and meticulous handwriting. He was part of a staff that reported in detail on the latest achievements in the New Deal's public works program. So well did Bodenheim do his work that he was promoted to the position of supervisor. He took his new responsibilities seriously, though there were times when he enjoyed entertaining his colleagues by reading to them some of the material he had assigned to younger members of his staff. One of his assistants was David Ignatow, a future poet, who had been hired on the Project on the strength of having a published short story listed in the honor roll of Edward J. O'Brien's *Best American Short Stories for 1933*. Bodenheim, Ignatow recalled, on one occasion asked him to write a feature story about "a newly completed bandstand built on top of a shithouse, and he nearly died laughing reading it aloud to the assembled staff."

Bodenheim's career as a steady and fairly sober employee came to an abrupt end when he (along with a few other writers of established reputations) was unofficially permitted to do his own work at home. The only strings attached to this arrangement were that he report to the Project office once a week and show what writing he had done. For Bodenheim, who until then had managed to report to work punctually every day, the once-a-week trip to the office became a prodigious ordeal. He would arrive in front of the office building in a semi-inebriated state; then, unable to summon enough will power to enter, would go to a bar across the street to continue his drinking. Eventually, it would take two of his Project friends to escort him, protesting and staggering, from the bar to the office.

Although hampered by drunkenness and other variations of nonconformity, the New York City Project's most serious problems did not stem so much from the conduct of its personnel as from a marked lack of forceful leadership during the early months of its existence. Orrick Johns, though a fairly good poet, was not a talented administrator of the Writers'

Project reporters unit. But even less talented was Walter K. Van Olinda, a former editor of encyclopedias, who had been selected to head the larger Writers' Project unit, which was to compile a New York City guidebook. With Van Olinda, the Project began to experience the administrative vicissitudes that were to hasten its demise as a federally sponsored enterprise. Van Olinda's first blunder was to appoint a managing editor who was found guilty of discriminating against the blacks on the staff. At Alsberg's insistence, the editor was promptly fired.

The main trouble was that Van Olinda had little stomach for administrative duties and was all too willing to abdicate the responsibilities of his office. He committed another serious blunder when he permitted an assistant, Samuel Duff McCoy, to handle all of the administrative work. McCoy was a veteran newspaperman who had won the Pulitzer Prize for reporting in 1923 and was the author of several books of verse and a novel. But he had little administrative experience and quickly antagonized the leftwingers on the Project both by his dictatorial style and by his sponsorship of a group of self-styled patriots who tried to counter the influence of the leftwing unions on the Project with an organization known as the Federal Writers Association. A savage political battle ensued. The leftwingers, who had organized about 75 percent of the Project workers, fought with picket lines and delegations to Washington; the rightwingers used the press as their chief weapon.

With work in the New York City office at a virtual standstill, Alsberg tried to resolve the situation by transferring Van Olinda to the Washington staff as music editor and replacing him with Orrick Johns. The situation immediately became worse. McCoy, although considered a friend of Johns, reacted bitterly to his appointment as director and refused to take orders from him. When McCoy, for reasons he would not explain, summoned the police to the Project offices one morning, Johns fired him.* The New York press, avid for WPA scandalmongering, became McCoy's chief ally as he aired his grievances and demanded that he be accorded a public hearing, so that he might "expose the Reds" who, he claimed, controlled the Project.

Alsberg, backed by his WPA superiors, denied that McCoy had the right to appeal his case, insisting he had been fired for reasons of "insubor-

* The explanation offered unofficially by several Project workers was that before calling the police McCoy or one of his friends had planted a gun and a series of Communist pamphlets in Johns's desk. The alleged attempt to frame Johns failed when he discovered the gun and the pamphlets shortly before the police arrived.

Maxwell Bodenheim in 1929, at the height of his literary fame. Six years later, he joined the Writers' Project as a relief worker

dination and inefficiency." He pointed out that although McCoy had been assistant director of the Project for several months, he had not made any of his complaints public until his dismissal. He added that although a good deal of material for the New York City guidebook had been gathered under McCoy's direction, there had been a lack of competent editing and little or no progress. He also produced a letter McCoy had written him less then two weeks before his dismissal admitting a number of errors on his part and saying: "I am now wondering if you did not commit a similar error when you appointed McCoy to his present post."

During the heavy exchange of charges and countercharges, the press denounced Johns as a former editor of the *New Masses*, Alsberg as a Soviet sympathizer, and the Writers Union and the Workers Alliance, the two leftwing unions chiefly involved in the battle against McCoy, as "Red unions." Only one newspaper, the Republican New York *Herald-Tribune*, touched on McCoy's rightwing sympathies. "It was reported that Mr. McCoy had been closely associated with an individual [on the Project] who boasted that he was a member of Oswald Moseley's British fascist party, and the implication was that McCoy, too, was a fascist." The same news account reported that Alsberg and WPA officials were not interested in the politics of any Project worker as long as he did his work.

In the shakeup that accompanied McCoy's ouster, fourteen workers, who were leaders of the two opposing factions that had paralyzed the work of the Project, were transferred to the Reporters Project. James McGraw, who succeeded Johns as the head of that unit, let it be known the workers would be under close scrutiny and would be dismissed if they engaged in any further political fighting on the Project or if they failed to do their work properly. At the same time William Nunn, the WPA supervisor for the four arts projects in New York, declared that the administration would resist any attempt to make a closed shop of the Project and would deal drastically with any attempt to force out of the Project individuals who belonged to no political faction. When C. K. Coleman, a Project editor, resigned as a protest against the domination of the Project by City Project Council Local 1700 (the white collar division of the Workers Alliance) and urged the removal of Johns, Nunn replied that Johns was doing "splendid work" and bringing order out of chaos, pointing out that thirty thousand words had been written by Project employees in the past three days as contrasted with previous lack of performance.

McCoy and the newspapers finally had no more to say about the fracas, but tranquillity did not come to the New York City Project, least of all to Orrick Johns. Despite hints from Washington that personnel would be curtailed before the close of the year, the Writers Union launched a campaign for a larger employment quota. Picket lines paraded and shouted before the Project's headquarters, and delegations streamed in and out of Johns's office at all hours of the day. Johns could not help but be sympathetic to the demands of the union, but on one occasion when there was a demonstration that halted the work in the office, he lost his patience and called the police. Later, he regretted his action because the police had treated the demonstrators with sadisic roughness.

As an act of penance, perhaps, in October 1936 Johns openly supported a sit-in hunger strike staged in his office by thirty-five unemployed members of the Writers Union who were determined not to eat or budge until they were promised jobs. The strike leader, a vivid brunette, assured Johns that none of the working staff would be disturbed and there would be no violence; but she made it clear that only forceful ejection by the police could remove them. Johns, according to the New York *Times,* made the hunger strikers as comfortable as possible, letting them have as many chairs as could be spared. In return, the demonstrators politely volunteered to give up any chair when it was needed. Asked by reporters what action he intended to take, Johns said he would not call the police; the strikers could sit as long as they wished.

They sat for twenty-six hours. At that point WPA officials, perturbed by the publicity the hunger strike was receiving, agreed to increase the New York City quota of 526 jobs by fifty more. But Johns still had to contend with the strikers; they refused to vacate the premises until he promised to assign twenty of the fifty new jobs to members of their union.

By cooperating with the strikers to the extent that he did, Johns must have realized that his was an act of defiance that would surely antagonize the martinet-like Lieutenant Colonel Brehon Somervell, who had succeeded Victor Ridder as chief of WPA operations in New York City, and hasten his departure from the Project. At the same time he must have experienced one of the few satisfactions he derived from his job as director. Most of the time he was beset with a deep sense of frustration and harassment. He felt oppressed by the staggering amount of red tape — "forms, forms, forms, in sextuplicate on white, salmon, blue, pink, yellow and green paper"; in his autobiography he complained that the paperwork left him almost no time for the "primary" task of training writers and turning out copy.

The complexity of the job and the turmoil of dealing with half-starved writers for whom he had no jobs, as well as union delegations which often voiced demands which he was in no position to grant, increased Johns's drinking and absenteeism. As a result, his friend and assistant director, Travis Hoke, soon became saddled with most of the director's responsibilities. Hoke, although a brilliant writer and editor, was unfortunately no pillar of strength. He drank almost as heavily as his friend and was plagued by serious neuroses which necessitated frequent trips to a psychiatrist. Yet he managed the Project well enough during Johns's long absences, so that when Johns was asked to submit his resignation shortly after he had spent six weeks in the hospital recovering from his brawl with the revengeful sailor, Alsberg appointed Hoke as his successor, giving the New York City Project its third director in fourteen months.

Even before Hoke's appointment became official there developed a new crisis that was climaxed by the Project's second sit-in strike. This was precipitated by the ouster of William Nunn, who was considered too liberal in his attitude toward the arts projects, and the appointment of Elmer Engelhorn as his replacement. Engelhorn, at Colonel Somervell's instigation, promptly began to investigate the home life of Project employees in an effort to determine whether or not they were actually in need of their jobs. The leftwing unions rose to the occasion with picket lines, delegations, and a sit-in strike. But unlike the first strike, this one ended quickly when Engelhorn summoned the police and forty of the strikers were arrested.

A much larger and more disruptive sit-in strike took place on December 3, a few days after the New York directors of the four arts projects were ordered to drop 1,936 persons from their rolls. The layoffs were to proceed along two lines, according to Colonel Somervell: first, the elimination of "unessential nonrelief cases" and second, the dismissal of "those least useful on the project even if they are relief cases." The announcement came as a bitter blow to the Project workers who recalled that only a few weeks before, while campaigning for his second term in office, President Roosevelt had promised that he had "just begun to fight" in his effort to provide further help to the unemployed.

The layoff orders affected about 20 percent of the Writers' Project staff in New York. Almost twice as many were dismissed in other parts of the country, but nowhere else was the reaction as dramatic. Led by the Writers Union and the Workers Alliance, some two hundred strikers barricaded themselves with desks and chairs on the seventh floor of the Project headquarters at East Thirty-ninth Street. The newspapers featured the strike with big front-page stories that told how the strikers were being denied food and use of toilet facilities. But the strikers did not go hungry. Sandwiches and coffee reached them by means of ropes lowered to friends on the sidewalk below. They were also fed by two of the Project's supervisors: James McGraw, who had been transferred to the Project's administrative staff when the Reporters Project was dissolved; and Vincent McHugh, the novelist and poet who had joined the Project less than a month before as technical editor. Both men took advantage of their prerogative as supervisors to come and go freely, stuffing their coat pockets each time with sandwiches which they would slip to the strikers when the guards were not looking.

The striking writers fared better than the two hundred members of the Art Project who had participated in a strike that turned out to be the bloodiest of all the arts projects demonstrations. After marching up eight flights of stairs to the headquarters of the Art Project, the striking artists ordered the clerical workers to stop working, cut telephone wires, and held the director as their prisoner. When ordered off the premises by the police, the artists locked arms and formed a large circle around the police. The police reacted by charging the artists with raised nightsticks and clubbing them. Thirteen of the strikers (including three women) and four policemen required hospital treatment.

Mayor La Guardia, unwilling to risk a second bloody encounter, sent word to the writers that they could remain where they were indefinitely, provided they were not destructive. But the strike came to an end after eighteen hours when the mayor and Colonel Somervell, tired of hearing angry delegations, promised to discuss the impending cuts with Washington officials. Nothing came of that, and later Colonel Somervell let it be known that the sit-in would have ended much sooner had he had his own way: he would have machine-gunned the whole bunch.

Possibly influenced by the colonel's bloodthirsty language, Philip Evergood, an artist addressing a springtime protest meeting of Federal One employees, shouted: "Spring is here, and the hunting season has started in Washington. Congress is planning to shoot down more of us." It was quite

true. With leaders of the administration claiming that the nation's economy was showing marked improvement — Hopkins's assistant, Ellen S.
Woodward, went so far as to say that "WPA as an emergency program is
over" — Congress decided to cut relief appropriations for the fiscal year of
1938 by 25 percent. Actually, the plight of the unemployed cultural
worker was as desperate as ever but, although a few WPA officials understood their situation, the administration refused to give Federal One employees any special consideration, and ordered that the 25 percent cut
apply to all segments of WPA. The four national directors of Federal One
were asked to drop eleven thousand workers in all parts of the nation,
twenty-eight hundred of them in New York City. On the New York City
Writers' Project it meant a loss of approximately a hundred and fifty persons.

In a last-ditch effort to persuade Congress to increase its appropriation
from $1.5 billion to $3 billion, the Workers Alliance ordered a one-day
work stoppage on May 27. Despite warnings from Colonel Somervell
that relief workers who participated would lose a day's pay and supervisors would be dismissed, seven thousand of the nine thousand New York
employees of Federal One responded to the order. The stoppage was sup-
plemented by brief strikes on all the arts projects, and thousands of letters
and telegrams to Washington from cultural leaders and private citizens
protesting the impending cuts. None of these actions had the slightest
effect either on Congress or on the administration.

In June all hell broke loose when Harold Stein, the recently appointed
administrative chief of the New York writers', artists', and musicians' projects, received formal WPA orders for issuing the dismissals. The supervisors on the Writers' Project, who had been requested to submit lists of
workers to be dropped, refused to do so. More strikes were ordered by the
unions on each of the projects. Into the Writers' Project headquarters the
strikers brought in cots, food, and banners, established a strike strategy
committee, without whose permission no one could either come or go, and
settled down to a siege which continued for four days.

At the headquarters of the Music Project, where a hunger strike was in
progress, pickets carried signs reading "Hunger Strike Against Hunger,"
and chanted to passers-by the number of hours the strikers had gone without food. A twenty-three-year-old girl collapsed from malnutrition, and a
typist would have jumped from an open window had she not been over-
powered in time by four of her colleagues. In one of the Federal One

administrative offices several payroll clerks, who had been staging a sit-in for two days, refused to process checks either for the dismissed workers or for any other personnel. And at City Hall two hundred dismissed members of Federal One, on being told that Mayor La Guardia was out, assembled in an empty corridor to read a message from George Bernard Shaw which expressed the opinion that Congress deserved "a drastic lynching" for forcing curtailments of the arts projects. "Those who vote for barbarism should perish by it," the message added.

The next day, six hundred artists, writers and musicians banded together to storm the Central Office of the Federal Arts Projects and make Harold Stein their prisoner. Taking possession of the office and barricading the doors with desks and chairs, they warned Stein that he would be forcibly restrained if he tried to leave before the strikers had won their two demands: that all dismissals be rescinded; that a special board of appeals be established to review the case of each dismissed worker. Stein was then ordered to make these demands known to his Washington superiors by telephone. He spoke with Ellen S. Woodward and Aubrey Williams, one of Hopkins's chief assistants, but neither one could agree to the demands. "We are agents of the law and I don't know what we can do to help you," Williams explained. Despite Stein's inability to influence the Washington administrators, the strikers refused to release him. Earlier Stein had been offered safe conduct out of the building by WPA guards but, having been told by a safety engineer that the floor of the building could support the weight of six hundred persons only as long as there was no commotion, and fearing that his departure might provoke a riot, Stein declined the offer.

After fifteen hours that stretched from late afternoon to dawn Stein was able to buy his freedom by granting all of the strikers' demands "to the limits of his authority." The document which he and heads of the New York City arts projects signed was hailed as a victory for the workers by the City Projects Council, which had staged the demonstration. Michael Jaffe, one of its organizers, triumphantly climbed on a desk and warned that Congress "cannot get away with such monkeyshines and shenanigans as it tried when it refused to enact further federal relief appropriations for the fiscal year 1938." But actually there was no victory. None of the cuts were rescinded and the only appeals board available to the dismissed workers was one previously established by Stein to consider only cases of "unfairness and discrimination." Furthermore, the act of holding a government official a prisoner created a serious backlash of public and private opinion.

The executive staff of the Writers' Project was soon besieged with dismissed workers begging for a chance to be heard by Stein's three-man Joint Appeals Board. Some alleged "discrimination" on the grounds that they had belonged to a union; others claimed they had been discriminated against because they had not belonged to a union. "Every day," recalled one of the executives, "dismissed writers came to the office to plead their cases, many of them bringing along their weeping children, or their imploring mothers and fathers, or their hysterical wives." For several weeks the Project administrators did nothing but listen to their grievances. Yet only ten cases were considered valid enough to warrant the attention of the Joint Appeals Board; three of that number were "recommended" for reinstatement but remained unemployed.

For those who were fired and for those who were not it was a time of anguish and fear; for it was evident that, even though job opportunities for unemployed writers were as scarce as ever, dismissals would continue.* That there were fewer strikes on the Writers' Project after the gloomy summer of 1937 can be attributed to the administration's tough stand in dealing with the June demonstrations and to official warnings that if the arts projects continued to be a source of trouble, they would be shut down. Aubrey Williams told a union delegation that while the administration sympathized with the plight of the needy unemployed it "deplored" such occurrences as the imprisonment of Harold Stein. "A few more things like that," he said, "and you might as well kiss WPA out of the window."

Before the end of the summer Stein was transferred to Washington and replaced by Paul Edwards, a sterner administrator who found it expedient to cooperate with Colonel Somervell as often as possible. Although Edwards did not share the colonel's antipathy toward Project unions, he offered no objections when Somervell fired eighty members of the Writers Union and the Workers Alliance in October 1938, then prohibited them from demonstrating against their dismissals. At the same time the colonel ordered each of the surviving 240 members of the writers' unit to turn in a minimum of three hundred words a day.

No one bothered to inform Somervell that lack of wordage was never a problem on the New York City Project. When Vincent McHugh was in-

* In the summer of 1938 when the New York City Project was down to three hundred workers, it had eighteen hundred job applications on file.

vited to take charge of the Project's editorial work in the fall of 1936, he was informed that more than eight million words had already been produced for the manuscript of the New York City Guide.* "All that the manuscript needs is some pulling together," he was told at his first meeting with Alsberg, Travis Hoke, Orrick Johns and Donald Thompson, who had recently been hired to assist Hoke. On asking to see the manuscript, McHugh learned that the only two copies of it had been submitted to Mayor La Guardia some time ago but that, despite repeated efforts to retrieve the copies, the mayor had refused to return them. "Why not?" asked McHugh. "Because he's afraid the damn thing will be published as it stands," was the answer.

McHugh looked like a fragile poet with his tall, thin body and china-blue eyes. For reasons of health, he subsisted largely on milk shakes and seemed incapable of putting on weight. Yet he was a vigorous and quick-witted personality and, at the age of thirty-two, enough of a maverick to relish the human spectacle offered by the Project and to empathize with it. His credentials were highly respected; he had just published a widely acclaimed novel, his third, *Caleb Catlum's America,* which one critic described as "an astonishing mixture, everything from pinochle to megalomania, from Latin conjugations to Yiddish slang, all charged with a kind of outlandish humor."

He quickly became the man of action when he found the morale of the Project staff at a dangerously low ebb. Unlike the other arts projects, the writers' unit had not produced any tangible evidence of achievement and none seemed possible in the foreseeable future; the workers lacked confidence in themselves and one another. Determined to change the situation, McHugh began by barging into the mayor's office and explaining to a sympathetic aide that six hundred members of the Writers' Project would remain in a state of work paralysis as long as the mayor continued to sit on the New York City Guide material. McHugh saw the aide disappear into the inner office occupied by the mayor, and heard La Guardia screaming out his objections as the aide argued with him. Gradually, the aide was able to persuade him that the manuscript would not be published in its present state, and he emerged from the mayor's office with both copies.

* On September 5, 1936, Orrick Johns bragged to the New York *Times* that the Project's total volume to date of more than eight million words dwarfed the combined wordage of the three "jumbo" novels of the day (*Anthony Adverse, Of Time and the River,* and *Gone with the Wind*) plus all of Shakespeare and the King James version of the Bible.

Vincent McHugh, of the New York City Project, in 1937

Ralph Ellison, of the New York City Project, as photographed by his friend Richard Wright in 1939

McHugh could easily understand the mayor's forebodings as he began to review the material. Although it incorporated a massive amount of information, it was a hodgepodge of endless miscellanea that would have required a second guidebook to explicate. McHugh scrapped most of it, then drew up four alternate plans for organizing the material, each one based on his conviction that "a guidebook must be able to take people from here to there with absolute infallibility." When he submitted the plans to Alsberg and his Washington staff, everyone had his own idea as to how the guidebook should be written, but in the end accepted McHugh's basic concept of dividing New York into boroughs, then neighborhoods, then streets. To placate Alsberg, who was insistent that every major guidebook contain essays which would provide a comprehensive cultural view of its subject matter, the staff directed McHugh to devote a first volume to essays and a second to guidebook specifics.

Returning to New York, McHugh established editorial desks for boroughs, neighborhoods, streets and essays, and assigned one hundred and fifty workers to their operation. To keep the remaining members of the staff occupied he helped to initiate eighteen other book projects, which included such ambitious undertakings as a maritime history of New York City, a motion picture bibliography, studies of the major ethnic groups in the city, and a series of books dealing with wild life. Only two projects, other than the guidebook, were in operation when McHugh joined the staff. One was *Who's Who in the Zoo*, which was being supervised by Ralph De Sola, a former Communist who later became a star performer for the Congressional committees attacking the Project; the other was *Almanac for New Yorkers*, which was being edited by Frank Shay, one of the founders of the Provincetown Players who had written or edited several books about the sea, including a compilation of sea songs and chanties, and a volume entitled *My Pious Friends and Drunken Companions*. Seizing the opportunity to raise the morale of the staff with a publication that was bound to receive considerable publicity, McHugh contributed some of his own verse to the *Almanac*, then persuaded his publishers, Simon and Schuster, to issue it in 1937 as the Project's first publication. *Who's Who in the Zoo* became the only other New York City Project book to be published that year.

Like other editorial supervisors throughout the country, McHugh found that many of the young workers on his staff had never had jobs before. They had to be trained, not only as researchers, reporters, and writers, but also as disciplined members of a staff who could adhere to WPA regulations of attendance and punctuality. On one occasion he became a reformer. On learning that the only person on his staff who knew anything about Wall Street, an important subject in the guidebook, was a former bank president who was one of the Project drunks, McHugh took him in hand and converted him to a life of sobriety which extended long enough to produce the material he needed.

He also found himself playing the role of the educator. When Philip Rahv, the literary critic and editor of *Partisan Review*, balked at being assigned an essay dealing with New York's literary history because he did not believe that New York had one of any consequence, McHugh lectured him about Henry James, Stephen Crane, Walt Whitman, Melville, and Edgar Allan Poe, all of whom had close associations with New York City. Rahv accepted the assignment with a doleful sigh but worked on it diligently until it was completed.

While the manuscript was in McHugh's hands for final review, one of the Communists on his staff broke into his desk one night and stole it. The next day the *Daily Worker*, the official newspaper of the Communist party, published excerpts from the essays with large headlines attacking Rahv as a "Trotskyite wrecker of the people"; this despite the fact that there was no apparent connection between the accusation and the contents of the essay. Incensed by the theft, McHugh turned to his chief assistant, who made no secrecy of his membership in the Communist party, and told him he wanted the essay returned by that afternoon. The assistant protested that he had not taken it. "I believe that," said McHugh, "but you know who has." The essay was returned within a few hours.

McHugh, like other executives of the New York City Project, believed in cooperating with the Communist workers on the Project as long as they put in a full day's work. To make certain that the leftwing workers would take their assignments seriously, McHugh found it expedient to select assistants who, because of their positions in the Communist party, were able to exert some authority on their Project comrades. McHugh's sole objective was to produce good books as quickly as possible; his ecumenical policy of dealing with Stalinists and Trotskyites alike as though they were all conventional Democrats puzzled the leftwingers deeply until they finally learned through experience that he had no political axe of his own to grind. In a Trotskyite publication which carefully analyzed the abilities and motives of the New York City Project employees, McHugh was the

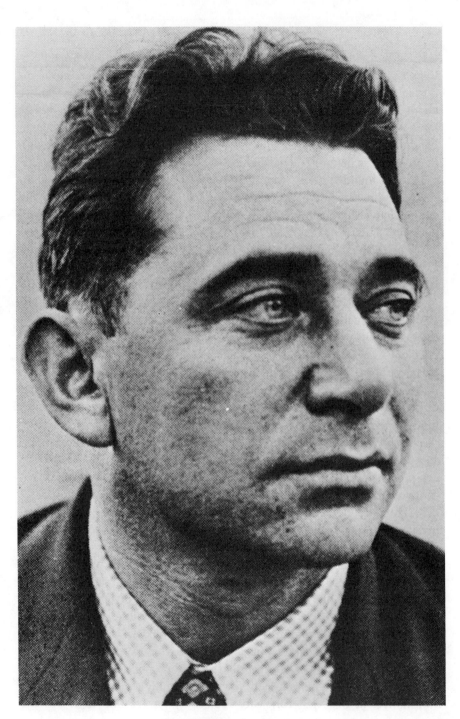

Harry Roskolenko in 1937

only supervisor who escaped unscathed. "McHugh," the report declared, "is a professional writer. He has no politics. He is only interested in doing a good job."

McHugh's policy did not, of course, ease the tension between the Stalinists and Trotskyites on the Project. They battled constantly, sometimes with their fists. Theirs were long-standing antagonisms, developed before the Project came into being, which now flared frequently as the two factions found themselves on the same premises day in and day out. The Project office became, in effect, a new battleground for an old vendetta. The Stalinists circulated a publication among Project workers called *Red Pen,* which invariably attacked as a Trotskyite anyone who opposed their policies. The "Trotskyites," who often were not so much pro-Trotsky as they were anti-Stalin, counterattacked with leaflets that lambasted the Stalinists.

In a typical issue of *Red Pen* a headline reading "Expose Trotskyite Anti-union Tactics" was followed by a denunciation of three "Trotskyites" in the local Workers Alliance union for "disrupting the democratic procedure of our unions by continually inventing petty grievances against the union leadership and by metaphysical hairsplittings." The publication warned that "they use the union floor with one aim — to carry out the counter-revolutionary program of Leon Trotsky, to denigrate the Communist party and the Soviet Union."

The leaflets produced by the opposition were no less venomous. The Communists, one leaflet charged, were trying to eliminate from the Project all workers who were not Communists, "all of its political opponents whom they label Trotskyites, whether they be Socialists, Syndicalists, former members of the Communist Party who dared leave the party, or liberals." The leaflet, which was signed by such prominent Project writers as Lionel Abel, Philip Rahv, Harry Roskolenko, Helen Neville, Henry Lee Moon and Ted Poston, declared that little fairness "can be expected of those who carry out the line of the C.P. which labels some workers as 'rats, spies and reactionaries' who must be isolated."

For anti-Stalinist vituperation few could match that of the poet Harry Roskolenko, an avowed Trotskyite who did not hesitate to tangle with the Stalinists on every possible occasion. In his book of reminiscences, written almost thirty years after his experience on the New York City Project, his disdain for the role of the Communists on the Project was as implacable as ever.* The Project, he wrote, was "more of a Leftist five-ring circus than a fertile field for thought about research and writing." He declared that the "Communists [meaning the Stalinists] who were in the vast majority had flooded the Project with half-authors who had published only in their minds," and added that "all of them used the Project to write propaganda leaflets summoning the workers of the world, at least those in New York, to various ramparts — for cultural insurrections." In his view the Communists "wanted physical domination over the the Writers' Project, to sponsor Stalin, Red picnics, proletarian literature, full-assed and half-assed proletarian dancers, and to fire all the Trotskyists and other dissenters."

The tactics of the Stalinists on the Project, according to David Ignatow, "were bound to make a Trotskyite out of any intellectual concerned with the social problems of the times." Another young writer, who was ardently antifascist, insisted he could always spot Trotskyites by "the cotton-ball substance of their ideological arguments." He called them "negative idealists: they are against anything the Stalinists are for." The intensity of the Stalinist-Trotskyite conflict, with its archetypal Cain and Abel overtones, was symbolically enacted one evening at a meeting of the Project's pro-Trotsky group. Among those present for the first time was Harold Rosenberg, an anti-Stalinist, who had come at the invitation of a Trotskyite friend. When the chairman of the meeting heard there was a Rosenberg in the audience he wrongly assumed that it was David Rosenberg, Harold's brother, a Project supervisor who was an active member of the Communist party. "There is a Stalinist wrecker in our midst," the chairman shouted. Before anyone could set matters right, the group's action squad swung into action and threw Rosenberg out.

The big political issues of the day inevitably provided additional fuel to the running battle between the two groups, strongly influenced the activities of the various Project unions, and complicated the tasks of the Project administrators, who were often accused of favoring one faction over another. Perhaps the two most incendiary themes were the Moscow Trials of 1937, and the war between the Spanish loyalists and the fascist forces of Francisco Franco.

The Spanish war directly involved four members of the New York City Project who had quit their jobs to fight in the International Brigade. An issue of the *Red Pen* proudly published on its front page a letter from one of them which began: "Greetings from war-torn romantic Spain." The

* *When I Was Last on Cherry Street* (Stein and Day, 1965).

same issue castigated the Trotskyites for demanding the overthrow of the Popular Front in Spain. Accusing them of being "counterrevolutionary allies of Franco," the editors reproduced a cartoon from an anti-Stalinist magazine showing a hand labeled "Popular Front" plunging a dagger into the back of a soldier labeled "Spanish Workers."

Only occasionally did the spirit of personal friendship transcend political ideology. The poet Kenneth Fearing, who was closely identified with the Stalinist faction, was one of the Project's most popular staff members and had friends in all camps. The same was true of Richard Wright, whose Communist party affiliation was well known. One of the most surprising friendships on the New York City Project was that of Samuel Duff McCoy, who was considered a "fascist" by many of his colleagues, and Norman Macleod, the poet, who was a contributor and editor of such Communist publications as the *New Masses* and *International Literature*. Shortly after their meeting McCoy gave Macleod a book of his own poems with the inscription "For Norman Macleod because of what he told me about an American who threw up a 1,000 rubles a month job in Moscow in order to come home, and for other reasons, purely personal."

The American in question was Macleod himself, who had thrown up another job — cleaning stencils for $25 a week — and applied for relief in order to join the Writers' Project, anxious to be part of an extraordinary cultural venture. He was soon promoted to the rank of borough editor in charge of the Bronx, an area he had visited only once in his life, and given a staff of twenty-five reporters. The first assignment he gave them was to determine the agricultural output of the Bronx. Most of the work seemed pointless and boring to him, especially during the earliest weeks of the Project when there was not enough copy submitted to keep the editors occupied all day. "At lunch some of us drank more beer than the amount of food we ate, and as the beer began to wear out during the long afternoon, some tempers became frayed, editors started gossiping, some began developing animosities, conspiracies. There was an atmosphere of nervousness and even hysteria . . ."

In poor health at the time and out of patience with the Project's frustrating atmosphere, Macleod became infected by the hysteria. One day, at the height of the clash between McCoy and Orrick Johns, he impulsively interrupted a crucial conference between the two men and their assistants. "I shot off my mouth, and then, realizing what an ass I had been, went to my desk and tore up some papers. I then left the office." He was promptly charged with having destroyed "government records" but the charge was dropped when it was found that he had torn up copies — not originals. "I was never a threat to anyone," recalled the tall, blond poet. "I was not power hungry, but I was in poor emotional shape. So I lost my job the same time McCoy lost his, and I never heard from or saw him again."

Through Orrick Johns's intercession, Macleod got a job on the New Mexico Writers' Project. As one of the few members of the staff who could write, Macleod was made state editor. The director of the Project was Mrs. Inez Cassidy, a woman of matriarchal temperament with whom he got along famously. On one occasion when he wound up in jail after a drinking spree, she came to his rescue and had him released. "The first time you go to jail," she told him, "we get you out. The next time we let you rot." Despite his love for Santa Fe, he missed his friends in the East. Quitting his job, he returned to New York and began writing a novel about his experiences on the two writers' projects titled *You Get What You Ask For*, which was published in 1939.

One of Macleod's companions on the New York City Project was the notorious eccentric Joe Gould, who despised all political activists on and off the Project and was fond of dreaming up epithets attacking Communists, which he would sometimes drop in McHugh's ear. Also known as Dr. Seagull because he liked to flap his arms up and down to simulate a flying gull, Gould was then combining his Project assignments with his Oral History of the World, a presumably vast compendium of conversations he had with everyone he encountered.* Gould attached great importance to the history, and liked to document each entry with the time and place where he had written it. "I finished this draft while sitting on the toilet of the Forty-second Street library," he wrote at the end of one section.

Between writing chores, Gould cadged drinks, slept in flophouses, attended parties where his favorite act was to see how many of his clothes he could discard before being stopped by the host, and engaged in such

---

* The question of how much material was contained in the Oral History of the World confounded Gould's friends and became a matter of speculation for many years afterwards, particularly in the *New Yorker* magazine, where Joseph Mitchell advanced the theory that Gould had perpetrated a giant hoax. The Oral History consisted of only a few thin notebooks, he claimed, not of many mammoth manuscripts stored in warehouses. Millen Brand, who was once Gould's friend, recalled reading thirty-five thousand words of the history, most of which he found "pedestrian." Norman Macleod recalled seeing Gould emerge from the offices of a publishing house with a manuscript about two feet thick, fuming about the stupidity of all publishers.

Portrait of Kenneth Fearing by Alice Neel, 1936

Norman Macleod with his second wife

memorable witticisms as "I have delusions of grandeur; I sometimes think I am Joe Gould."

He also liked to bombard the editors of newspapers and magazines with kernels of verse which long predated Ogden Nash in their frisky play with misspelled words. One of his "poems," published in the correspondence section of the *New Republic,* was titled "Song of the Glass-Conscious Intellectuals":

> *Dearly we love the working class*
> *The tovariski, the downtrodka*
> *We also love the foaming kvass*
> *The viski and the vodka.*

Gould's appearance suggested a sardonic but harmless leprechaun with his stringy goatee, thick glasses, bald pate, and skinny body. But behind this benign facade bubbled a volcano of bad temper which was apt to erupt when anyone crossed him. One of his victims, a black sculptress who had apparently spurned his advances, he attacked with a barrage of obscene phone calls and letters. When the novelist Millen Brand, a friend of the sculptress, tried to make him desist, Gould began bombarding him and his wife with obscene letters. Brand finally felt compelled to complain to the police, who issued a warrant for his arrest. As soon as the warrant was served Gould got in touch with Brand and begged him to drop the charge, confessing he had been similarly served on two other occasions; another time would mean going to jail. A kindly man, Brand agreed to withdraw the charge but not before making it clear that one more letter or phone call either to his family or to the sculptress would land him in jail.

Displays of neuroses were abundant on the New York City Project. In his book *When I Was Last on Cherry Street* Roskolenko wrote of a worker who became desperate when he was assigned the chore of copying Bronx street names which were to be used for a map of the borough. "If you don't take me off that stupid project," he threatened his supervisor, "I'm going to commit suicide. I, who have dedicated my whole life to poetry, would rather die than go on working on a street map for the Bronx." He was assigned to a less mundane chore, even though it was found that his only published work to date consisted of a brief poem eulogizing a goat in the Bronx Zoo.

In the same memoir Roskolenko tells of a writer who was on the verge of being fired because he repeatedly failed to carry out the assignment of gathering information about Staten Island. The worker told his irate supervisor that sending him to Staten Island was equivalent to sending him to his death, for he had a mortal fear of the two mile ferry journey from Manhattan to Staten Island; also he was convinced that even if he arrived there alive, he would be devoured by mad dogs, which he was certain overran the island. A letter from his physician indicated that he was speaking the truth: "This man has a one hundred percent case of hydrophobia — fear of dogs *and* water. Please assign him to some other project."

Roskolenko's gallery of grotesques also included a teetotaler on the Project who, when assigned to write a report on Bellevue's alcoholic ward, tried a few experimental drinks on the way, and arrived at the hospital so drunk that he was detained in the hospital's alcoholic ward. Eventually he became a dipsomaniac.

One of the most neurotic members of the New York City staff turned out to be the director himself, Travis Hoke who, after succeeding Orrick

Johns in the post, suffered a mental breakdown. Like Johns, he found himself overwhelmed with too many administrative details and with union problems that seemed insoluble. During his illness his Project friends were afraid he might commit suicide, and took turns spending the night with him in his Chelsea Hotel room to make certain he would not harm himself. Their fear proved to be justified. One night Vincent McHugh, who was one of his self-appointed guardsmen, saw Hoke rise from his bed and creep toward an open window. McHugh called out his name sharply and Hoke sheepishly returned to bed. Another time Hoke, in a desperate frame of mind, telephoned the Project office, pleading: "Come and get me. This time I'm really going out the window." When his friends arrived, he begged them to put him behind bars. Obligingly, they persuaded the police to lock him up, then made arrangements to admit him to a sanitarium. There he remained for three weeks (the Civil Liberties Union, of which he was a board member, paid the bill) charming his fellow inmates with his wit and warmth, and winning the confidence of the hospital staff to such a degree that he was put in charge of a contingent of male patients in their promenades outside the hospital grounds. During one of the promenades Hoke secretly led his group to and from the joys of a Broadway whorehouse without any mishap.

With Hoke totally incapacitated, Alsberg appointed Donald Thompson acting head of the New York City Project in the summer of 1937. Thompson, James McGraw and Vincent McHugh formed, in effect, a troika that tried to pull the Project out of its tangled troubles. The situation they faced would have unnerved the most experienced of administrators: a demoralized staff, traumatized with threats of firings and hopelessly fragmentized among a dozen unions, many of them struggling for power at one another's expense. In less than a year's time McHugh had managed to impose some kind of order into the editorial procedures of the office and the two-volume New York City guidebook was beginning to emerge; but the Project was still suffering severely from the failures of its first three directors — failures which provoked the WPA administrators to give serious consideration to the idea of shutting it down.

Hopkins, disturbed by the fact that the Writers' Project's largest unit had not produced a single guidebook in two years' time, assigned Robert W. Bruere to investigate the anatomy of the New York City Project and try to determine what was wrong. In his report Bruere blamed the Project's inefficiency chiefly on the psychological insecurity of the workers, who

Portrait of Joe Gould by Alice Neel, 1933

were constantly afraid of being fired. By implication, at least, he also held Alsberg partly responsible for the Project's lack of direction. The Washington office, he said, "had been singularly unfortunate in its selection of directors for the New York City enterprise, and hesitant in dealing with them when they had established their unfitness beyond a reasonable doubt." He also suggested that Alsberg's frequent visits to the New York City office tended to reduce the authority of those he had put in charge. "That the Project has not failed worse than it has," he wrote, "is due of course fundamentally to the economic cohesion of the 525 men and women on its payroll, but it is also due to the courage and initiative of a number of second-line executives in assuming the authority which the imperative demands of the Project required with or without confirmation from Washington."

The "courage and initiative" of Thompson and McGraw was repeatedly put to the test by their endless dealings with the dozen unions representing different political affiliations and ethnic interests. Thompson and McGraw spent a large portion of their office time listening to their grievances. The Jewish group alone, which was working on various Yiddish book projects, was represented by four unions. Their grievances often consisted of complaints about one another. The most aggressive of the unions were the Writers Union and the Workers Alliance City Projects Council; they conducted most of the campaigns for jobs and pay raises.

The City Projects Council prospered by playing on the fears of those who already had jobs as well as those who needed them. The employed were told that their best chance of retaining their jobs was to join the Workers Alliance; the unemployed were assured that membership in the union would result in a job. "It is not necessary to run around for jobs," read one leaflet. "It is necessary to join your union. Don't be a dope. Join now." The advice was not without foundation. In all of the union jousting with administration officials, the Workers Alliance far exceeded all other unions in exerting the kind of pressure that influenced the administrators.

Thompson, who was a writing man both by experience and inclination, did not relish his role as acting director. "It was a case of the people versus the administration," he wrote, "and I was regarded as the administration." Much of the union activity on the Project made little sense to him. "The union membership was without money, yet they were agitating in a manner that threatened the life of the Project. Every time they struck or demonstrated, they lost part of their wages. They were often desperate and

Some of the New York City Project staff. Left to right: Frances Fuchs (later Mrs. James McGraw), James McGraw, Donald Thompson, Nicholas Wirth, Harold Rosenberg, Bertha Brand

borrowing from one another. It was both maddening and heartbreaking."

His friend McHugh was occasionally called upon as an arbitrator to help settle the editorial grievances of the various unions, a responsibility which he enjoyed. Unlike his administrative colleagues, he found the drama of the Project exhilarating. When Alsberg offered him a more prestigious job on the Washington staff, McHugh quickly turned it down, explaining that the New York City office was "more fun than anywhere else because that's where the big row is." *

Despite the strife and insecurity, many of the younger Project workers shared his sense of excitement, though for different reasons. Allan Angoff, who had left his hometown (Boston) for the express purpose of joining the New York City writers' unit, was thrilled with the opportunity of

* That was in 1936. But the "big row" turned out to be bigger and rowdier than anyone could have anticipated. McHugh left after two years, thoroughly surfeited by the kind of "fun" the New York City Project offered. By contrast, the *New Yorker* magazine, his next place of employment, struck him as "a rest home."

working in the same office with some of his favorite authors. "Why, those mornings on the Project when we young guys would talk with Max Bodenheim and Edward Dahlberg and others were priceless experiences. The guidebooks are good, but the opportunity to work with these men was in some intangible way the most valuable contribution of the Project . . ."

For neophyte novelists and dramatists, such as Ralph Ellison, Saul Levitt and William Gibson, the Project provided a certain degree of literary training and enough income to enable one to observe, eat, and do one's own writing. As a member of the Project's folklore unit, Levitt's job was to go into the streets and listen to the speech of all kinds of people, an activity that was to serve him in good stead later on when he began to write dialogue for his plays. "They were times of despair but not of defeat," recalled Levitt. "We felt wonderfully alive." Yet the daily agenda of life for him and his colleagues was relatively simple. After work, they would dine at a 14th Street restaurant (Il Faro) where they could buy a good meal for sixty cents. Afterwards, they would usually visit a billiard academy called "Julian" and shoot pool until late at night. Zero Mostel, who was then a painter on the Art Project, was a regular member of the group. Sometimes, instead of playing pool, they went home to write or meet their girl friends. On the weekends, they attended political rallies and fund-raising parties and dances for leftwing causes. "We all thought then that there were political solutions to society's problems," Levitt reminisced, "and we had the optimistic view that men could improve their social and political relationships."

Off and on the Project some of this faith was engendered by the strong sense of camaraderie that men and women of similar political persuasion enjoyed. Many of them lived together without benefit of clergy.* For them legal marriage seemed out of the question, not only because of the dismal insecurity of the times but also because the institution of marriage implied a bourgeois philosophy that was incompatible with their ideals. As part of their life-style, the woman did not hesitate to support her man if he was without a job. "In a period when man's traditional role of bringing the world's resources to his woman was severely dislocated," observed Levitt,

* Some of the women working for the Writers' Project were "living in sin" (their own sardonic term for nonlegal marriage) with men employed on the same project, but keeping the fact a secret from Home Relief investigators. In other instances, legally married couples pretended not to be married in order that both of them could draw salaries from the Writers' Project.

"the female of the species demonstrated a gallantry that was unprecedented, except perhaps in pioneer days. The girls took care of us when we
were sick and in between jobs. They were the schoolteachers, the stenographers and the filing clerks of those days, who gave more than they got
with little complaining and at a time when we all needed womanly
women as we never had before. Ah, the wonderful women of the thirties!"

Unlike the Greenwich Villagers of the twenties, the unmarried couples
did not practice "free love" but generally lived the conventional life of
regularly married spouses, except in one respect: they were psychologically incapable of planning for the future. Caught in the turmoil of the
present, they lived from day to day in constant dread of losing their jobs
and in mortal fear of the growing Nazi menace in Europe. Such anxiety,
combined with their idealistic leftwing goals, strongly conditioned their
political and social lives.

As in Chicago and San Francisco, many of the fund-raising parties attended by members of the Writers' Project were to support the cause of
the Spanish loyalists. The parties were often held in the luxurious apart-
ments of wealthy radicals, and sometimes featured as guests of honor antifascist refugee writers who were German or Spanish, or some young
American who was about to journey surreptitiously to Spain to join the
Abraham Lincoln Brigade. These affairs were always well-attended; they
provided impoverished writers and artists with a first-hand view of the
opulence enjoyed by a lucky few, as well as an opportunity to meet some
of the literary celebrities of the American radical movement, such as
Granville Hicks, Isadore Schneider, Kenneth Fearing, Clifford Odets, William Rollins, Jr., John Howard Lawson, Robert Forsyth (the pseudonym
for Kyle Crichton), Edward Dahlberg, and Malcolm Cowley. The Project
workers also attended fund-raising dances in far less fancy surroundings,
at Webster Hall in downtown Manhattan and at the Savoy Ballroom in
Harlem, where the swing era was in full swing.

Now and then the Project workers would throw their own parties, usually to cheer up some colleague who was being dismissed. One such party
turned out to have disastrous consequences. The guest of honor was Edwin P. Banta, a sickly old man who had been the Project's dues collector
for the Workers Alliance and was generally considered a Communist. As an
expression of their regard for Banta, his colleagues presented him with a
copy of *The People's Front* by Earl Browder. During and after the party
the old man, who seemed deeply touched by the gift, told his colleagues

that he would appreciate having their signatures in the book. Over one hundred men and women complied enthusiastically, many of them adding to their signatures such phrases as "Yours for a Soviet America," "Revolutionary greetings," and "Comradely good wishes."

Later, the book with all the inscriptions wound up in the hands of Martin Dies, chairman of the newly formed House Un-American Activities Committee. Banta, it developed, was not a benign old Communist but a rightwing informer. It was his testimony, together with the incriminating book, that led Congressman Dies to choose the Federal Writers' Project in 1938 as a primary target for attack — an attack that proved to be the beginning of the end for federal sponsorship of all the arts projects.

Ironically, the Dies attack came in the same year that the New York City Project, after many tribulations, was finally becoming sufficiently efficient to produce books at a rapid clip. In 1938 the New York Project published the first volume of the city guide, *New York Panorama;* a second *Almanac for New Yorkers;* an ethnic study, *The Italians of New York,* which was issued both in English and Italian; an illustrated natural history, *Birds of the World;* and a tome of 397 pages in Yiddish entitled *The Jewish Landsmanschaften of New York.*

The final preparation of *New York Panorama* caused the only dissension between Alsberg and McHugh. In his determination to make the New York City guidebook "infallible," McHugh, according to Alsberg, was slowing up its progress by personally checking each fact in the manuscript over and over again. Pressed on every side to prove that the New York City Project could produce a guide, Alsberg put Joseph Gaer, his trouble-shooting editorial supervisor, in charge, and assigned McHugh the writing of the opening chapter in *New York Panorama,* "Metropolis and Her Children." Gaer, always a forceful executive, commandeered the services of the Project's most capable writers, despite the complaints of the unions, and, with the help of John Cheever, whipped both volumes of the New York City Guide into final shape within a relatively short time.

In the meantime, Alsberg was searching for a new director to take charge of the New York Project. With McHugh about to leave, he was anxious to find someone who was as expert in editorial matters. He chose as his candidate an ambitious young New York University English instructor, Harry L. Shaw, Jr., who had recently published a college textbook on writing and rewriting. At Alsberg's suggestion, Shaw agreed to go to

Washington to be interviewed by Hopkins. But it was Hopkins's deputy, Aubrey Williams, he saw instead. No sooner had he entered his office than Williams, obviously worried about the New York City Project's "Communist" reputation, asked: "When were you in Russia?" Once he was assured that Shaw had never set foot in that country, Williams hired him without any further questions.

Obtaining a leave of absence from his university, Shaw in 1938 became the New York City Project's fifth director in three years.

Like his predecessors, Shaw was soon engulfed by the demands of the job. No less than thirty book projects were then in progress; many had been contracted by publishers who were demanding that the overdue manuscripts be delivered without further delay. While trying to placate them, Shaw found himself constantly interrupted by aggressive union delegations presenting long lists of complaints. "It was a nightmare," Shaw recalled, "trying to meet publishers' deadlines while coping with the protesters. The workers seemed to be more interested in raising hell than in getting on with the business of the Project."

Nine months after taking office, Shaw resigned and returned to the relatively tranquil world of academia. As his successor, Alsberg appointed Harold Strauss, a magna cum laude Harvard graduate, who had been in the New York publishing scene as a book editor for almost a decade. But Strauss arrived too late to ameliorate the unfavorable image of the Project publicized by the Dies and Woodrum committees. During his and Shaw's tenure the New York City office suffered from these committees some of the most severe assaults it had experienced in all of its stormy history. With each assault the fear that the Project would end loomed larger and the demonstrations of the workers became correspondingly more intense.

A graphic picture of a New York Writers' Project sit-down strike in the late spring of 1939, when the death of the Project appeared imminent, was depicted by Alfred Kazin in his autobiographical work, *Starting Out in the Thirties*. Kazin, having just been offered an editor's job in the Washington office, was visiting the headquarters of the New York City Project for an exploratory interview. He entered a room "crowded with men and women lying face down on the floor, screaming that they were on strike. In order to get to the supervisor's office at the other end of the hall, I had to make my way over bodies stacked as if after a battle; and as I sat in the supervisor's office, he calmly discussed the job while shouts and screams came from the long hall outside. I made my way out again between and over the bodies."

In that demonstration were workers of varying political allegiances protesting together, among them Trotskyites and Stalinists — a sure sign that the Writers' Project was in a truly desperate situation.

The standards of the editors of the Writers' Project are virtually the same as the standards of any publisher's editor. When a new book is proposed, the first question is whether it can be published at a profit by a commercial publisher. The second question is whether the proposed book is useful to the community or to the nation.

— *Publishers' Weekly,*
March 18, 1939

By telephone and letter Alsberg told me repeatedly that for Idaho to be first [published] among the forty-eight states would be a dreadful embarrassment. I thought the national office so incompetent and cynical and political that I cared nothing about its embarrassment.

— Vardis Fisher, former state
director of the Idaho Federal
Writers' Project, in an interview with the author,
June 4, 1968

The men and women who were my associates in this work gave to their task such loyalty and enthusiasm as private industry is very seldom able to command.

— John T. Frederick, former
state director of the Illinois
Federal Writers' Project,
Chicago *Daily News,*
December 4, 1940

There is little question that a well-trained team of researchers could have produced the Massachusetts Guide with one fourth the number and less than one fourth the time. . . . But we must remember always that the three hundred or so workers who gathered those materials would have been starving if they had not done so, and that the Project rescued them for further service to humanity.

— Ray A. Billington, former
director of the Massachusetts
Federal Writers' Project, in a
letter to the author,
January 28, 1969

Six.

The Dream and the Action

In the early stages of Federal One, when some of its directors felt hamstrung by rigid WPA regulations, they demanded and obtained an audience with Harry Hopkins, their titular chief. Hopkins listened patiently to their complaints for some time; then, noting that Henry Alsberg was the only one who had not said anything, asked: "What about you, Henry? What is your gripe?" Alsberg grinned and in his slow and heavy voice replied: "I don't have any gripe, Harry. I haven't had as much fun since I had the measles."

The statement, which charmed Hopkins, may well have raised some eyebrows among the other directors who were familiar with some of the complex problems then plaguing Alsberg and his staff. Apart from the steady attacks from Congress and the press and the almost constant eruptions in the New York City Project, there was trouble in nearly all the other writers' projects. Some of it proliferated from unwise appointments of state directors, some from the general failure of the field offices to meet their deadlines for the state guidebooks; some of it was stimulated by self-appointed censors who, in the name of patriotism or civic pride, objected to New Deal attitudes expressed in some of the Project publications.

From beneath the surface of such administrative and editorial aggravations there began to emerge the harsh disparities between the dream and the reality. The dream, begot by the Project idealists who saw in the American Guide Series the hope of portraying the nation in such an honest and effective way that it would help create a more noble standard of social behavior, began to wither in the first year of the Project's existence. In Missouri, where the Pendergast political machine was powerfully entrenched, the dream and the reality came to grips in a pitched battle, with ignoble results on both sides.

The dream was more or less personified by Jack Balch, a young short story writer who had been selected by Alsberg to be assistant director of the newly formed Missouri Writers' Project. The reality was symbolized by the state director, Mrs. Geraldine Parker, who had been chosen by the Pendergast machine. Mrs. Parker had written some folk plays and stories based on her knowledge of the Ozarks, but Balch never had any inkling that she knew anything about the art of writing. During their first interview she confined her conversation to the art of preparing martinis and French onion soup, after which she informed him that he was "in the picture," a bit of political slang which Balch took to mean that he had met with her approval and was hired.

Apart from the emotional relief of no longer being unemployed, Balch was delighted to become a participant in a pioneer cultural enterprise like the Writers' Project. That such a project could have been conceived at the federal government level seemed to him little short of a miracle, an unexpected affirmation of cultural strength which, in its search for truth, could provide a sense of direction in a nation besieged with negative values. But within a few weeks it became clear to Balch that such a vision was beyond the ken of Mrs. Parker, who seemed to have no commitment to the task of producing a truthful portrait of Missouri. Her only commitment was to the political machine that had placed her in office.

Balch found himself at odds with nearly all of Mrs. Parker's policies. He was appalled by her prejudice against Negroes. Although a number of blacks with advanced academic degrees had applied for jobs, she refused to hire more than one. Her attitude toward white applicants was no less disturbing. All she needed to know about an applicant was that he was politically endorsed. She gave little or no consideration to his qualifications, with the result that the Missouri staff consisted mainly of men and women who could neither write nor do research.

Her policy on editorial matters was consistent with her allegiance to the political machine. Before reading any of the manuscripts submitted to her, she sent them to the office of the WPA administrator for censorship. Only after a manuscript was cleared was it sent on to Washington. Balch became incensed when the administrator's censor deleted from the guidebook material a large section dealing with miners in the Tiff region of the state who often died of silicosis poisoning. In another instance, the censor eliminated favorable references to Thomas Hart Benton, Missouri's most renowned painter. Neither Mrs. Parker nor Matthew Murray, the state WPA administrator, had any use for Benton's social realism. "I wouldn't hang him on my shithouse wall," Murray told a protesting delegation of Project workers. "Why don't you write about our beautiful roads instead? Now there's something really worth writing about."

Balch, despairing of turning out "meaningful work," communicated his complaints to Lawrence Morris, who was then Alsberg's chief field supervisor in the Midwest. Morris agreed that the situation was intolerable but indicated that for political reasons beyond the control of the Washington office Mrs. Parker could not be removed. However, since he shared Balch's concern about producing a "meaningful guidebook," he established a system for handling manuscripts that would completely bypass Mrs. Parker. Henceforth, Balch would be the one to decide what manuscripts were to be sent to Washington. Balch was further assured that the new arrangement would not jeopardize his job, or that of the other nonrelief writers on the staff; that none of them could be dismissed without the consent of the Washington office.

Yet, soon afterward, Mrs. Parker fired Balch's colleague Wayne Barker on charges of "lack of cooperation and constant inefficiency." Mrs. Parker was suspected of other motives for her action, one being that Wayne Barker was chiefly responsible for organizing a Writers Union in the office; another was that Barker had openly accused Mrs. Parker of mishandling funds she had solicited from Project workers to finance a dinner in honor of Alsberg. Taking up cudgels for Barker, the Writers Union protested his dismissal to Alsberg and when they got no response from him, they called for a strike, the first one in the history of the Project. Seventeen members of the union, all of them nonrelief workers, answered the strike call. Mrs. Parker retaliated by firing Balch, Jack Conroy and Edwa Moser, the Project's most experienced writers, on grounds of "absenting themselves from the office."

"We felt that we were being patriotic in going on strike," Balch recalled, "that we were acting in Washington's best interests by opposing those forces in Missouri who were trying to reduce our Project to a boondoggling and patronage activity." For Balch, a cautious man, the strike was a risky venture, one that might have been averted if Barker had been more temperate in his accusations against Mrs. Parker. For Conroy, who had been in other strikes, this one seemed hopeless from the outset, useful perhaps only as an ideological gesture. For Edwa Moser, who came from an upper middle class background, the strike was something of a lark. When the strikers were arrested for "disturbing the peace" and placed in separate cells, according to their sex, she climbed up on the prison bars and emitted a few Indian whoops. The guard was furious. "Get your ass down, girlie," he shouted. "I know what you're up to. You're gonna fall down and claim we beat you up."

Writing about the strike for the *New Masses,* Conroy reported that Alsberg had told Balch he was unwilling to order Barker reinstated because Barker had embarrassed the administration. Conroy attributed the "embarrassment" to an article Barker had written for the *New Masses,* using the pen name of Michael Hale, which exposed the murderous plans of one James True, inventor of the "kike killer," a truncheon designed to split the heads of Jews. According to Barker, True and his fascist friends intended to kill Justices Cordoza and Brandeis of the United States Supreme Court, Isidor Strauss, then ambassador to France, Secretary of the Treasury Morgenthau, and, because he had chosen a Jew for a wife, Secretary of State Cordell Hull.

Conroy's article expressed the bitter mood of the strikers. "There is involved here," he wrote, "a moral lesson for bright young men employed on the Writers' Project. Confine yourself to the dull flatulence of Chamber of Commerce puffs, and you'll never get your tail in a sling. If you unmask the enemies of all culture and progress, you'll end up wetting the soles off your feet walking the streets and pounding your ear in flophouses. Take it slow and easy, boy, get wise to yourself. Everybody's doing it." In a more serious vein, Conroy declared that the administration deserved credit for removing writers from semi-starvation on relief rolls by giving them "new purpose, hope, and direction," but he posed this question: "Does the administration intend to stimulate and foster writers, or is it its purpose to stifle and emasculate them, close their mouths, keep them in intellectual bondage and submission twenty-four hours a day? Those of us who went at the job of writing the American Guide with the determination to make it a full-bodied, rich and recognizable picture of life in the United States — the land, its people, their customs, their folklore — would like to know."

To *New Masses* readers, who knew Alsberg to be a Jew and and an antifascist, the claim that Alsberg had wanted Wayne Barker fired because of his article exposing a fanatical anti-Semite must have seemed quite far-fetched. Alsberg's lack of sympathy over Barker's dismissal was partly based on some daring methods Barker had used to obtain information for his *New Masses* article while visiting Washington, and partly on Mrs. Parker's off-the-record allegation that Barker made "improper use" of the Project's photographic facilities. "I'm glad they fired him," the director told Mrs. Florence Kerr, regional WPA administrator. What perturbed him chiefly about Barker's dismissal was that it had given Mrs. Parker the opportunity to fire the only other writers on the staff who were capable of turning out a guidebook.

He had no use for Mrs. Parker. Weeks before the strike he had realized there could be no guidebook with her in charge but, as he admitted to the WPA regional administrator, he was afraid to ask for her dismissal just before the November election. "She will surely run to the newspapers, and we can't afford that." He was also afraid of Matthew Murray, her political backer. When Murray, just before the elections, threatened to fire everyone who was on strike, Alsberg became alarmed and telephoned the regional WPA administrator in Chicago.

Alsberg: The Missouri situation is pretty disquieting. As I told you, they have been striking on account of Wayne Barker. The workers have been picketing. They called me up on their own at my house . . . I have a feeling they will go back to work, but that they were scared about their own jobs. I don't think that Murray ought to do any wholesale firing . . .

Mrs. Kerr: I think he thinks there are a few other people who should go.

Alsberg: I think he ought to wait until after Tuesday [Election day].

Mrs. Kerr: I think he will probably do that.

Alsberg: The more people he fires the stronger he makes the position of Mrs. Parker. I don't want the Project broken up. I think the firing of Wayne Barker was a good thing, between you and me, but I don't want to have a row all over the country . . . I would like Murray to go slow. On the Barker thing I said I wouldn't interfere. It is a local matter . . .

Mrs. Kerr: The whole point [of the picketing] is the dismissal of Barker?

Alsberg: The real thing is that they are worried about their own jobs. I don't think they would put up a fight on Barker, but they feel they will be next. I am telling you that if Mrs. Parker had more control of the Project and had done any kind of a job, this mess wouldn't have occurred. She's no good.

Mrs. Kerr: That's true, too.

Alsberg: When they telephoned me I said, "You are simply making things worse by striking. I don't want to talk to you on the phone about it." They are scared, and, although Mr. Murray may be indignant about it, it can be made into a national issue. They have the Newspaper Guild worked up, which is not radical, and they will get the Authors League . . .

Since Alsberg would not discuss the strike with the strikers by telephone, a delegation of them and representatives of the Writers Union, the Workers Alliance and the Newspaper Guild called on him in Washington. Wayne Barker immediately infuriated Alsberg by asserting that it was he, Alsberg, who had initially issued the order for his dismissal but had then withdrawn it, preferring to let Murray and Mrs. Parker take the responsibility for it. "That is an absolute lie," shouted Alsberg. "It came to me as a surprise. I knew nothing about it. I gave no orders."

Barker held his ground, adding that Murray and Mrs. Parker had fired him for two reasons: for his part in forming a Project union and for having published the *New Masses* article without having it approved by Mrs. Parker who, he said, had ruled that any material written on a worker's own time could not be published without her approval.

"That is contrary to any instructions we have given out here," Alsberg said. "Our people can write whatever they want as long as it isn't political . . ."

To this, Barker replied: "Many of the things that have gone on in the Missouri Project are absolutely contrary to the rules of the WPA as a whole, and if the administration allows them to act contrary to the rules, then we must be the ones to take action."

Shortly after Roosevelt was reelected, Alsberg sent Reed Harris to Missouri to investigate the situation and take whatever action seemed necessary. Harris reported that Barker was not fired for union activity nor for writing the *New Masses* article. "The charges against him have to do with illegal disposal of government property, improper use of project photographic facilities, etc. There is no frame-up involved and the man should have been fired long ago."

Having rounded up enough evidence to prove that Mrs. Parker was an incompetent administrator, who did not keep promises and who deliberately misstated facts on a number of occasions to give the impression she was doing worthwhile work, Harris was able to persuade Murray that she should be removed from her post. Her successor, Harris announced, would be a Mrs. Esther Marshall Greer, who had Murray's "complete approval." Understandably apprehensive about the qualifications of a director recommended by Murray, Harris expressed the opinion that Jack Conroy, who was one of the strikers offered reinstatement after the strike was lost, would "make an excellent state director" but, as he was "identified with the activities of the Communist party," Murray would not have approved of him. He closed the report with the news that although Conroy, Balch and four other strikers had been offered reinstatement, they had refused to return to work until all the strikers had been reinstated, a stipulation that had been rejected by Murray.

While Harris was writing his report, Mrs. Parker, by prearrangement with Murray, "resigned" from her post, explaining that the "labor troubles" in the Missouri office had been settled and that the job of compiling the Missouri guidebook was "nearly complete." The latter claim bore no resemblance to the truth. The manuscript was in a sorry condition. It did not improve with the new director in office. Mrs. Greer proved to be as unqualified as her predecessor, and after a year Alsberg was compelled to shut down the Missouri Project until an "expert editor" could be found.*

By then, the Missouri press was quick to point out, the Missouri Project had spent about $227,000 on salaries and expenses without having produced a single book. Only once, during Mrs. Parker's reign, had the Project come close to publication. The Ozark Guide, prepared by Vance Randolph, an authority on that region, was completed and in page proof when its sponsors, the local Chamber of Commerce, decided that the book "played up the delinquencies of Ozarkians to an extreme degree, saying nothing about their good traits," and withdrew its contribution of $3,000 for printing costs. Murray, supporting the Chamber's stand, declared that the criminal elements described in the manuscript consisted of villains who had come to Missouri from neighboring states.

After divorcing himself from the Project, Balch began writing his novel *Lamps at High Noon,* using the strike as the central action in the narra-

---

* Not until 1939, when Charles van Ravenswaay, a former president of the Missouri Historical Society, was appointed state director, did the material for the Missouri guidebook begin to assume final shape. The book was published in 1941.

tive. The story opened with the master plan of the Project's dream: "To produce the Story of America. Not just history, not merely the politics, the economics, the village folklore, the literature, but the whole thing." The national director in charge of this great enterprise was "the man who stood at the main switch ready to flood the land with light . . ." At first, Charlie Gest, the hero, was pleased with everything about the Project. Even the instructions made him happy because they reflected a grass-roots approach to an understanding of America, and he read them "as though they were words in a poem." Gradually, however, Charlie Gest saw his dream being pushed aside by the political claws of an authority that insisted on its own version of the New Deal — an old deal concept of business as usual which emphasized political patronage, disregarded the literary objectives of the Project, and turned the whole enterprise into "a house built on sand."

In dealing with the strike, Balch at one point turns the spotlight on a character called Hennessey (nicknamed "Four-Star") who is obviously modeled after Jack Conroy. Four-Star tells Charlie Gest that in the past he has never gone into a strike without the feeling that it could be won, but this time he is certain the strike will be lost. When his friend asks why he is so pessimistic, Four-Star replies: "Mainly because the Project is a non-profit organization . . . And you can't strike against the hand that's feeding you. You can only strike against the hand that you are feeding. You take an industrial plant. You strike a day, and the company loses in orders. It's big dough for them, and you strike until either you starve or the shareholders lose their shirts . . . But in this strike, who's going to lose the money? Only us. The government saves the money."

The novel adheres fairly closely to the actual events of the strike, but toward the end Balch reports on a purely imaginary confrontation between Alsberg and one of his field supervisors who, appealing to his chief's conscience, pleads with him to oppose the Missouri political machine and declare himself openly on the side of the strikers and their dream. The plea is rejected. The director is convinced he is in no position to fight a powerful political machine which had twice helped put Roosevelt in the presidency.

As the novel indicates, the aftermath of the strike left the strikers with the impression that they had been betrayed by the Washington office. Without Washington's opposition to the political machine, the strike was doomed from the start. Harris's report on his investigation confirmed the strikers' suspicion that all the cards were stacked against the strikers. Although no one could doubt Harris's integrity, Balch and some of his colleagues were convinced that Wayne Barker had been framed by Mrs. Parker. Moreover, they were disgusted that the Washington office would ally itself with Murray against the strikers, especially after having admitted that Mrs. Parker, who had worked with him hand in glove, was not fit to direct the Missouri Project.

The intensity of the Writers' Project's administrative headaches seriously hampered its editorial efforts and strengthened the hand of the anti–New Deal critics who attacked the enterprise as a blatant boondoggle. Not until the spring of 1937 did the Project begin to command nationwide respect as a productive and worthwhile endeavor. Published within a year were the Idaho state guidebook, the gargantuan guidebook to Washington, D.C. (1,141 pages), all six of the New England state guidebooks and, unexpectedly, a highly informal guide to Cape Cod, *Cape Cod Pilot*, which captivated most reviewers.

That the Idaho Guide, and not the Washington, D.C., Guide, should have become the Writers' Project's first major publication, came as a jolting surprise to Alsberg and his staff. For months a squad of expert editors, led by Herbert Solo, had been concentrating on the task of making the Washington book the first. Strategically, it seemed like the wisest of moves to launch the American Guide Series with a guidebook to the nation's capital, one that might quiet the congressional grumbling about the Project's failure to date to publish anything of consequence. But suddenly Vardis Fisher, who almost alone had been working on the manuscript of the Idaho guidebook, announced that the work was almost completed and that arrangements had already been made to have it published locally by Caxton Press.

A dyed-in-the-wool individualist, Fisher had been a source of irritation to the Washington staff from the start when, eschewing diplomacy for candor, he wrote in a letter to George Cronyn: "I don't like all this bewilderment of orders that rescind orders or contradict orders. The discrepancies in the various instructions we have received leave our finance administrator throwing up his hands. What I want is explicit and irrevocable orders to go ahead as I was first instructed to, or an invitation to resign." Fisher's disgust with the mass of confusing directives he received from Washington finally led him to consign them to the furnace without bothering to read them.

Vardis Fisher, director of the Project in Idaho, 1937

The question of how tour copy should be written provided one of the many conflicts between Fisher and the Washington editors. In May 1936 the Washington office announced that henceforth all tours must be described uniformly: north to south and east to west. Fisher objected on the grounds that at least eighty percent of the traffic in Idaho moved south to north. Alsberg replied that the forty-eight state guides had to be uniform in concept and that no exceptions would be permitted.* There were also skirmishes over problems of censorship. At Alsberg's insistence the remark in the Idaho Guide manuscript that Pocatello was "the ugliest of the larger Idaho cities" was deleted, as were all references to difficulties between railroads and truckers. Fisher was called to task for trying to make some of the writing "interpretative." A government-financed book, he was told, meant that there could be no "personal opinion in regard to some fact or

---

* Fisher disregarded Alsberg's order. The effort of the Washington office to establish a uniform pattern of directions for the state guidebook tours also failed in New England where Joseph Gaer, who was in charge of the final editing for the six New England state guides, reversed the directions of the tours without consulting the Washington staff.

situation in the state." His derogatory remarks about Zane Grey, the dentist who became one of the nation's most popular western novelists, were removed from the copy, as were those he made about the state of Wyoming. According to Ronald Warren Taber, who analyzed all of Fisher's dealings with the Washington editors, "the national office reminded Fisher monthly that as an employee of the Federal government he was not free to express a 'private' judgment."

Despite all his feuding with the Washington office, Fisher managed to produce a prodigious amount of work, writing single-handedly, 374 pages of the 405-page Idaho guidebook within ten months. In his own words he worked himself "half to death" to put Idaho first among the forty-eight states and "bring honor to this small segment of a nationwide boondoggle," realizing, of course, that the first state guidebook to be issued in the American Guide Series would reap the maximum amount of attention. In addition to doing most of the writing, he personally logged all of the state's roads. During that time his staff varied from fifteen to twenty but only two members, his secretary, Ruth Lyon, and his stenographer, Helen Howell, could provide him with any real assistance.

Not all of Fisher's correspondence with Alsberg and his staff was disagreeable. Early in their relationship Alsberg and George Cronyn expressed delight with the excellent quality of the essays he had submitted. In February 1936 Cronyn wrote him: "In spite of the many handicaps you have had in your organization and editorial works, yours is the only body of state editorial copy which we have retained as being suitable for Central Office editing. The materials from other states so far have not been in any condition to edit here."

Two months later Alsberg went even further in extolling the quality of Fisher's manuscripts. "To be quite frank," he wrote, "I didn't expect any real literature from our directors. Therefore, your piece (a section on the Salmon River area) came as an unexpected windfall. I want you to know that we all appreciate it. I passed it along to the higher-ups, so they could see the quality of work that is being turned out in Idaho." A few months later Cronyn informed him that he (Fisher) had succeeded in "raising Guide writing to the plane of permanent literature," and that "no one in the country has given more intense personal energy and creative thought to work than you, even though you may have experienced at times considerable irritation at editorial judgments in this office."

But Fisher's announcement in the fall of 1936 that he was about to go to press with the Idaho Guide signaled the end of all such amenity. In a tactic to delay its publication, the Washington office began demanding an extraordinary number of revisions. Fisher retaliated by threatening to write an introduction to the guidebook which would say that the Washington editors, not the Idaho office, were responsible for the edited copy. Angry with Fisher's attitude, Alsberg informed the WPA state administrator in Idaho of the director's "inability to understand the difference between his position as a private writer and a government employee." Fisher denied the charge by citing the enthusiastic praise he had received from Alsberg and Cronyn for the very same material that was now being "edited to death." Idaho Senator James P. Pope came to Fisher's assistance by asking that Alsberg not delay publication of the state guide, warning him that the Caxton Press would not publish it if Washington continued to order more corrections.

Forced to show his hand, Alsberg telephoned Fisher to appeal to his sense of propriety: it would be highly inappropriate, he said, for a small state like Idaho to be the first with a published guide. That distinction properly belonged to the Washington, D.C., Guide since it dealt with the nation's capital. After the Washington book was issued, Alsberg continued, guidebooks for some of the larger states would follow and, in due course, the Idaho Guide. Fisher's response to all this was profane, belligerent, and adamant. So abrasive was the language he used that his staff, who had gathered around the telephone for what they regarded as a showdown, were certain he had talked the Idaho Project out of existence.

But Alsberg did not give up, and dispatched a trusted aide to Idaho with instructions to delay the publication in any manner whatsoever. The aide arrived in Boise with a briefcase containing nearly two thousand more changes, corrections, and additions. Fisher was well prepared for the encounter. Knowing of the man's fondness for liquor, he and J. H. Gipson, head of Caxton Printers, had concocted a plan for getting him drunk. All evening the two men pretended to drink a prodigious number of straight whiskies — actually, their drinks consisted of whiskey-colored water — while serving the aide genuinely hard liquor. After dinner the aide asked to see the illustrations being considered for the Guide. He was presented with a pile of some two hundred photographs depicting various phases of Idaho geography and culture. What happened next is vividly described in an autobiographical novel Fisher published in 1960.*

* *Orphans in Gethsemane* (Allan Swallow, 1960) contains a long section dealing

The man didn't merely lay a rejected photograph aside. He would take one from the pile, glance at it, and saying "No!" in a voice that was loud and sounded angry he would send the photographs sailing across the room. To the second, the third, the fourth, the fifth his response was exactly the same . . . The sixth photograph was a magnificent field of potatoes, the potatoes sacked and the sacks standing row on row. Bingham [the aide] studied it a few moments and said, "No photographs of potatoes," and sent it after the others.

"No photographs of potatoes?" asked Rhode [Gipson] with deadly politeness.

"No photographs of potatoes, Mr. Rhode."

"But potatoes are Idaho's most famous agricultural product. Wouldn't it be a strange guide —"

"Every state has things it has overadvertised. We're not a chamber of commerce. There will be no hyperboles in these guides. Idaho has boasted so much of its potatoes that Idaho potatoes have become, to put it simply, a frightful bore."

"But the fact remains, Mr. Bingham —"

"I said no photographs of potatoes."

"Yes, Mr. Bingham. May I fill your glass?"

Bingham was gazing at a photograph. "What is this supposed to be?"

Rhode leaned forward to look. "Onions, Mr. Bingham. Idaho produces some of the finest onions —"

"No onions," said Bingham, and the photograph of a field of onions went sailing across the room. Then Bingham looked around for his glass. . . . He was getting drunk, and more arrogant. Hardly glancing at them at all, he would send photographs flying, one after another. He said, "We'll choose the photographs for you in Washington."

In some of the most comic passages in the novel Fisher described the wild automobile ride to the railroad station where the aide was to take a train back to Washington. Delayed on the way by a flat tire, Fisher was driving around mountain roads at a speed of eighty miles an hour, pursued by a police car blowing its siren. The aide, frightened out of his wits, kept pleading with him to slow down, even though it meant arrest, but Fisher was bent on getting his passenger to the train.

"I'd rather be arrested than die in Idaho," the aide told Fisher.

"It's a good place to die," was the reply. "We'll bury you in a potato cellar and pile onions on top of you."

The argument about the photographs persisted until a few weeks before

---

with most of Fisher's experiences on the Federal Writers' Project. All of it, he claimed, was "essentially true."

publication date, but in the end Fisher and the publisher had their own way. Their final selection included not only photographs of the potato and onion fields but also all the other photographs that had been initially rejected by the Washington office.

When the Idaho guidebook was published in January 1937, it carried no mention of Vardis Fisher's name, but his personality was visible on nearly every page. The opening paragraph was like a bursting bugle call proclaiming the start of a performance that would dazzle the reader with the author's salty style:

> After three centuries of adventurous seeking, the American continent has been explored and settled, and the last frontier is gone. The lusty and profane extremes of it still live nebulously in the gaudy imbecilities of newsstand pulp magazines and in cheap novels, wherein to appease the hunger of human beings for drama and spectacles, heroines distressingly invulnerable are fought over by villains and heroes and restored to their rich properties of mine or cattle ranch; and the villain if left unslain, passes out of the story sulking darkly; and the hero, without cracking a smile, stands up with the heroine clinging to his breast and addresses the reader with platitudes that would slay any ordinary man. But these villains with their Wild Bill moustaches, these apple-cheeked heroines agog with virtue, and these broad adolescent heroes who say "gosh ding it" and shoot with deadly accuracy from either hand are remote in both temper and character from the persons who built the West. They are shoddy sawdust counterfeits who would have been as much out of place in the Old West as Chief Nampuh with his huge feet would have been among the theatrical ineptitudes of a Victorian tea.

True to Fisher's prediction, the Idaho Guide, as the first published volume in the American Guide Series, was reviewed in all parts of the country, nearly always with enthusiasm. The historian Bruce Catton, in a widely syndicated NEA article, hailed it as a book that was "not merely a comprehensive and readable guide to the state of Idaho, its history, its resources and its scenery" but also as "a bit of literature worth reading for its own sake and reflecting vast credit on everybody concerned." He declared that the Idaho Guide abundantly justified the WPA's attempt to put unemployed writers to work, and marveled that less than $15,000 had been spent to produce the book.*

Bernard De Voto, then editor of the *Saturday Review of Literature*, devoted all of his weekly editorial page to the publication. Although he

---

* The actual cost was closer to $16,000, according to Ronald Warren Taber.

cited a number of minor faults, the most serious one being an insufficient index, he wrote that "whatever the difficulties caused by the extemporized and necessarily haphazard method of producing the guide, working with an untrained personnel, without precedent and handicapped by constantly changing regulations, the final result is an almost unalloyed triumph." He added that if the rest of the state guidebooks were up to this standard, they would "not only vindicate the Writers' Project but will heighten our national self-consciousness, preserve invaluable antiquarian material that might have perished, and facilitate our knowledge of ourselves."

A number of reviewers, including the one in the New York *Times*, observed that the word "guide" was far too modest a term for the book. The reviewer in the Salt Lake *Tribune* noted that "the quality of the writing is as far removed from what one has come to expect of this form as could well be imagined." The writer credited the merits of the book to Fisher's abilities as "one of the most powerful imaginative writers of our day," and was certain that Fisher had written most of the material. The Boston *Post* praised the book as "more than a mere guidebook of a state," and expressed the opinion that "if all the state books which follow measure up to the standard set up by the Idaho book, then critics all over the nation will acclaim the federal writers' projects."

Even before the notices began to appear, Alsberg, a philosopher at heart, softened his attitude toward Fisher, and playfully began to refer to him as "the bad boy of the Project." In a congratulatory letter he acknowledged what Fisher already knew — that "we, here, had hoped to beat out Idaho with the District of Columbia Guide" — and thanked Fisher and his staff for the excellence of the Idaho Guide. As soon as he received advance copies of the book, Alsberg sent one to Harry Hopkins with a memorandum that expressed his modified appraisal of Fisher:

> This book is not strictly in the form in which the majority of the State Books will appear. Partly, this is due to the fact that the State Director, Vardis Fisher, who is a well-known novelist, was rather obstinate in his insistence on doing things his own way — in fact, we had a constant struggle with him to make him adhere, even to the extent he has, to our prescribed forms — and partly to the fact that this is the first State Book we have produced . . . The compensation for sins of omission and commission in the text is to be found in the vivid style in which the book is written. In this respect this State Guide will be unique, since it bears throughout the stamp of Fisher's unusual personality.

Not all of Alsberg's staff shared his forgive-and-forget stance. Fisher's defiance of editorial instructions from the Washington staff were particularly irksome to Katharine Kellock, who considered him a "pain in the neck" and regarded the Idaho Guide as an exercise in literary self-indulgence, "an old-fashioned kind of travel book that wandered from subject to subject that interested the author." She was convinced that if all the "personal cracks" he had written in the guidebook copy about Idaho's citizens and institutions had been allowed to stand, the entire Project would have been torpedoed. If her colleagues shared her opinions, there was no evidence of that when "the bad boy of the Project," at Alsberg's invitation, came to Washington in April 1937 and, according to Fisher himself, was given "the red carpet treatment." There were several parties for him, one by George Cronyn at his home. Katharine Kellock was one of the invited guests. "As I came in," recalled Mrs. Kellock, "Cronyn turned to a man beside him and said, 'There she is,' and then to me, 'Here's Fisher.' Vardis dove at me, hugged and kissed me, then said, 'Now do you forgive me?' "

The success of the Idaho Guide drastically changed the working relationship between Fisher and the Washington staff. For almost a year there was no hostility on either side. When Fisher returned to Washington with the manuscript for an encyclopedia of Idaho under his arm, he was greeted like a hero. The idea for the encyclopedia had developed from Alsberg's suggestion, in 1936, that the Idaho staff prepare a state atlas. Fisher proceeded to enlarge on it. He organized a task force of four hundred Idahoans to gather data, and within ten months produced an encyclopedia of 350,000 words, with sixty maps. Fisher considered it a far more difficult and valuable work than the state guide, especially as it was based on a variety of primary sources not utilized in the guide. Alsberg's staff pored over it for several months, then returned it with a letter from the director saying: "Nobody in this office is qualified to pass judgment or check up on any of this material in this exhaustive and excellent job you have done, so we are returning the manuscript to you without criticism." The Idaho Encyclopedia was published shortly thereafter by Caxton Printers, on January 1, 1938. On the title page in big bold type was the name of Vardis Fisher, a bit of self-advertising, the likes of which no other state director ever dared.*

* In an introductory note Fisher acknowledged the assistance of several staff mem-

Washington: City and Capital, which the Washington office had struggled to bring out first, was published in April 1937, three months after the Idaho Guide. It was of alarming size. Bound in black cloth, it weighed about five and a half pounds and it contained 1,141 pages of heavy coated paper, as well as a thick pocket on the inside of the back cover which held a voluminous map. As he weighed the ponderous book in his hands, Harry Hopkins said it would make a perfect doorstop. No one, including the Superintendent of Documents who issued it under the auspices of the Government Printing Office, had given any thought to its Samson-like proportions. Perhaps it was just as well. In a nation conditioned to respect bigness, its size, if nothing else, may have made the deepest impression on the members of Congress who had been complaining about the paucity of the Project's output.

Alsberg made certain that every senator and congressman received a copy of the book, and even encouraged them to request further free copies. Copies also went to every cabinet member, governor, WPA administrator, and to all the daily newspapers. With the government footing the bill for the first printing of five thousand copies, the Project could afford to be lavish in using the book to win friends and soften adversaries.* The loudest praise came from those who were already friends. In the House of Representatives, Congressman Maury Maverick of Texas hailed the guidebook as an example of the "permanent value" that could accrue to the nation from some of its white collar WPA projects.

Addressing himself to the opponents of Federal One, Maverick said: "There are those who believe that the WPA should be confined to hard, dirty work; that anything clean, cultured or thoughtful is a Sin. The guidebook of the Capital, by that token, is a book of sin, because it is a clean, cultured, thoughtful work." He then reviewed the book at great length, and emphasized the fact that "almost unanimously" the press had wel-

---

bers, with special thanks to F. M. Tarr, the map maker of the book, who "often labored sixteen hours a day." Tarr received a salary of $69 per month. Also mentioned in the introduction are the services of Opal McCabe, who later became Fisher's third wife in a marriage lasting thirty-five years, which ended with the death of Fisher on July 9, 1969.
* The first printing, which cost $12,500, was paid out of a special publication fund set aside for the Writers' Project by the President. The second printing of eight thousand copies was intended for general sale, and issued at the expense of the Government Printing Office. The book was sold at three dollars per copy.

comed it as "more than a guide, as a splendid job of writing as well as an invaluable source of information."

As was to be expected, Mrs. Roosevelt in her syndicated column, "My Day," joined in the chorus of acclaim, describing the work as "the most comprehensive and really wonderful book on Washington." It was also praised by a number of newspapers, like the New York *Times,* which until now had been coolly disposed toward the Project. In honeyed language, the Sunday *Times* reviewed the book in its book and magazine sections. R.L. Duffus especially admired the wide scope of the contents. "Extend this method to all America," he wrote, "and it is apparent that we shall have something useful now and in time still to come. Trials of composing and editing there have been and will be, but perhaps these guides, taken together, will enable us for the first time to hold the mirror up to all America."

In the nationwide shower of praise only a few reviewers mentioned the book's stunningly honest treatment of the capital's seamier aspects. Harry Hansen, of the New York *World Telegram,* was one of them. "*Washington: City and Capital,*" he wrote, "offers no bunting, no flags to the eye or to the mind. The approach of its authors is by way of social criticism. Almost immediately the reader becomes aware that though Washington will be described as a great city and a worthy capital, he is going to get a cross-cut that includes the marbles of the Capitol and the disease-infested alley tenements, an essay on the disabilities of the Negro as well as the Folger Shakespeare Library . . ."

Just as the problems of the Negro were generally ignored throughout the nation during that era, so was the section in the book dealing with the Negro in Washington. Written by Sterling A. Brown, a poet and professor of English at Howard University, his chapter on the subject constituted the most forthright analysis of the plight of the blacks in Washington ever to be published under government auspices. Brown examined the lot of the Washington Negro from early slave years to the present. His prose, though well-tempered, enunciated a forceful indictment of the forces in White America that kept Negroes subjugated in the ghettos of the nation's capital, some in the very backyard of the Capitol itself.[*] The chapter, a literary and sociological milestone, began by quoting the Irish poet Thomas Moore who, after visiting Washington in its earliest years, wrote:

[*] When *Washington: City and Capital* was reissued by Hastings House in 1942, Brown's essay was severely bowdlerized.

Even here beside the proud Potowmac's streams
The medley mass of pride and misery
Of whips and charters, manacles and rights
Of slaving blacks and democratic whites.

Brown ended on the theme, "In this border city, Southern in so many respects, there is a denial of democracy, at times hypocritical and at times flagrant."

The enthusiastic reception accorded to *Idaho* and *Washington: City and Capital* bolstered the morale of the Writers' Project and helped to ease some of the pressures placed on the Project both by Congress and by the administration itself. The image of the Project was further improved that year with the publication of *Cape Cod Pilot*, a guide written in an unorthodox style which landed in the lap of the Project in an unorthodox manner. The product of one man, Jeremiah Digges (the pseudonym of Josef Berger), it increased the Project's literary prestige and brought to its author a certain degree of fame.

Berger, with his wife and daughter, had come to Provincetown in 1934 to eke out a living as a free-lance writer. But until the Project was established the following year, he had difficulty earning enough money to feed his family and was often dependent for food on whatever free fish he could get from his Portuguese fishermen friends. His credit at the grocery store was stretched to the breaking point when he learned that a national writers' project was being formed. He immediately applied to the Boston office, listing an impressive number of published stories and articles; but his application was turned down. Outraged, he joined forces with two other unemployed Provincetown writers whose applications for Project jobs had also been rejected.

One of them was George F. Willison, who was about to publish two books, *Why Wars Are Declared* and *Here They Dug the Gold.** The other was Carl Malmberg, who had been writing novels for a New York publisher at a salary of fifteen dollars a week. Together, the three men composed a blistering letter protesting the action of the Boston office. The letter, addressed to Alsberg, was placed in the hands of Mary Heaton

---

* George F. Willison joined the national staff of the Writers' Project in 1938 and eventually became its editor-in-chief. In 1945 he published *Saints and Strangers*, a group biography of the Pilgrims, which was a national best-seller.

Vorse, a noted Provincetown author whom they knew to be a friend of the national director. Alsberg responded with an alacrity far beyond their expectations, ordering the director of the Massachusetts Writers' Project to put the men on the payroll as professional writers at twenty-three dollars a week.

The men were assigned various sections of Cape Cod to be included in the state guidebook, and permitted to work at home. Occasionally, a representative from the Boston office would visit Provincetown to check on their activity but otherwise they worked without supervision, and with the understanding that four days a week were to be devoted to Project work; the rest of the week to their own writings. Berger found the arrangement ideal as he had contracted to write a guide to Cape Cod which Paul Smith, a local bookseller, was to issue as the first book bearing the imprint of the Modern Pilgrim Press. He finished writing the book a few months after joining the Project, and Smith, happy with the result, sent it to the printers.

One Sunday, while Berger was correcting galley proofs, he had two unexpected callers from Boston: the industrious Joseph Gaer, who was then supervising the completion of the Project's six New England state guidebooks; and Merle Colby, who was then assistant state director of the Massachusetts Project. Ostensibly, the two men had dropped in to check on Berger's Project work, but the sight of the galley proofs spread all over the Berger living room immediately engaged their attention. Gaer seemed particularly fascinated; he grabbed some of the galleys and began reading. Colby followed suit. Immersed in the material, they paid no attention to Berger's explanation that the book was one he had written on his own time. Finally, Gaer looked up from the galleys and said to Colby, "Just what we want. This is just what we want."

Berger protested that the book belonged to him; he had been collecting material for it long before the Project came into existence. And he pointed out that the entire work, unlike any of the books planned by the Project, was written in the first person. Gaer brushed aside all arguments with the declaration that the book should be published under the auspices of the Writers' Project since Berger had been supported by the United States Government while writing it. Colby added that it would be to Berger's advantage to have it issued as a Project publication because it would mean far more reviews and sales than it would receive otherwise. After consulting with Paul Smith, Berger finally capitulated but with the stipulation that the title page would carry the byline of Jeremiah Digges and that he was to receive all royalties earned by the book. Gaer, with Alsberg's prompt consent, accepted both conditions, and arranged with Smith to have the first edition issued by his Modern Pilgrim Press, the second by the Viking Press in New York.

When *Cape Cod Pilot* appeared in June 1939, Berger was shocked to find that under the name of the author was a line which read "with the editorial and research assistance of the Federal Writers' Project, Works Progress Administration for the State of Massachusetts." Also disturbing was the chilling silence that greeted its publication. Although Smith had provided the Washington office with 150 free copies for distribution to the press, there were no reviews. Apparently misunderstanding the purpose of the free copies, the Washington office had distributed them among its chief editors and WPA officials. Smith provided 150 more free copies but this time, to make certain they reached their destination, mailed them to the reviewers himself. Within a few days there was an avalanche of reviews, most of them singing the praises of *Cape Cod Pilot*, some of them expressing amazement that such delightful writing could come from anyone working for the WPA.

Time magazine called it "the boldest and best of the American Guide Series." The New York *Post* wrote that "one trouble with a brightly anecdotal book like *Cape Cod Pilot* is that every two or three pages you come upon something you want to share with somebody, and you can't go about quoting a whole book." Lewis Gannett in the New York *Herald-Tribune* began his review by stating that he had "never expected to read a guidebook through word for word." The first two editions of the book, totaling five thousand copies, sold out immediately.

Encouraged by all this, Berger continued writing about the Cape. His next book entered into the realm of fantasy. Drawing from his western-orientated subconscious (he was born in Denver, Colorado) and his love for Cape Cod, he concocted a mythical figure named Bowleg Bill, an eight-foot bronco buster from Wyoming inhabiting the Cape. Berger wrote of his astounding adventures in a series of tales which began with the episode of Bowleg Bill lassoing a delectable mermaid out of the New Bedford sea. Once more Gaer insisted that this was material that should be published by the Project, but this time Berger, now under contract to a national publisher, ignored his arguments and threats. When the tales were collected in book form, his only concession to Gaer was a line acknowledg-

Josef Berger (Jeremiah Digges) and his wife on Cape Cod in 1938

Josef Berger interviewing Portuguese fishermen as a Project worker

ing that he was indebted to the Federal Writers' Project for supporting him while writing the book.

Meanwhile, the publication of *Cape Cod Pilot* netted Berger one of the prizes most coveted by young writers: a Guggenheim Fellowship. With his livelihood assured for one year, Berger quit his Project job and began working on a book about the Portuguese fishermen of Cape Cod, a history which was published as *In Great Waters*. It was only after he left the Project that he began to think of its value as an institution. "Because we were in desperate straits our immediate situation — not that of the Project — was the center of interest. My family and I needed a means of eating, so that I could go on writing." In retrospect, Berger regarded the Project as an opportune rescue operation. "I had been trained as a writer. I had published, and wanted to continue as a writer because it was the only ability I had. If the Project had not come along, just as I was at the end of my rope, I would have had to abandon the profession I had been trained to do."

The Project, in turn, benefited deeply from *Cape Cod Pilot*. Along with Fisher's Idaho Guide, it humanized its national image. Among Project workers it also strengthened the dream that they themselves might be able to function as individual writers rather than as cogs in a big writing apparatus controlled from Washington. It was, to be sure, a spurious hope based on lack of information about the genesis of the Fisher and Berger books. But it was one which, for a time, was taken seriously by many, and nurtured to some extent by Alsberg and his cabinet with the publication of *American Stuff*, an anthology of writings by Project members done on their leisure time which was published two months after *Cape Cod Pilot*. The power of the dream also spurred the Washington staff into an attempt to establish a national magazine, under WPA auspices, which would continue to publish the off-time efforts of Project workers. This effort (as will be shown in the next chapter,) was doomed by the refusal of the leftwing forces on the New York Project to rise above their narrow political obsessions.

Nevertheless, 1937 proved to be the Writers' Project's most auspicious year in several respects. After a series of unfortunate starts, the enterprise began to function as an integrated producing unit. Although overwhelmed with work, the Washington staff, having at last agreed on a set of instructions that were more or less feasible, was on far better communication terms with the field offices than ever before. There was greater hope about the continuation of the Project, and belief in Alsberg's prediction that all of the state guidebooks would be in published form within a year.* Moreover, with the publication of the Massachusetts, Vermont, Rhode Island and Connecticut state guides in the fall of 1937, the complaints in Congress and in the national press that the Project had been sitting on its hands began to subside. The notion that the Project was performing a valuable service for the entire country began to be taken seriously, even by some anti–New Deal newspapers.

Perhaps the most eloquent appraisal of the American Guide Series was written that fall by Lewis Mumford in a *New Republic* review which examined five of the Project's most recent additions to the series. "Of all the good uses of adversity one of the best has been the conception and execution of a series of American guidebooks," he wrote, "the first attempt, on a comprehensive scale, to make the country itself worthily known to Americans . . . Future historians will turn to these guidebooks as one who would know the classic world must still turn to Pausanias' ancient guidebook to Greece."

The fervor of Mumford's encomium may have been evoked by the savage attacks directed against the Massachusetts Guide on its publication two months earlier. Unexpectedly, the guidebook had become the tinderbox of a censorship explosion that was both comic and foreboding in character. Right up until publication date not a single state official had objected to any of its contents. The letter of endorsement from Massachusetts Governor Charles F. Hurley, which prefaced the book, told how "happy" he was that "this valuable work is being made available to the citizens of Massachusetts and the Nation."

As a further expression of his happiness, the governor participated in a public ceremony on the steps of the state capitol attended by Alsberg and his WPA chief, Mrs. Ellen S. Woodward, who arrived attired in fluttering organdy. Alsberg confidently clasped a leather-bound copy of the Massachusetts Guide, which he was to present to the governor. But at the last moment Mrs. Woodward, afraid of losing the limelight, grabbed the book out of Alsberg's hands, shoved him aside, and made the presentation her-

---

* Alsberg's extravagant optimism in matters of book production, which became a topic of office humor, was part of his strategy to have the Congress and the administration believe that, given a little longer time, the Writers' Project could complete the books it had started. This strategy, which he practiced continually during his four years of office, was motivated by his understandable worry that the Project might suddenly come to an end at any time.

self — an act she was to regret the rest of her life, for the next day the Boston *Traveler* revealed that the book was loaded with political dynamite. The revelation came from an industrious reporter who found that while the 675-page book described the Boston Tea Party in fourteen lines and the Boston Massacre in five, it devoted thirty-one lines to the Sacco-Vanzetti case.

The story, printed on the front page and headlined SACCO VANZETTI PERMEATE NEW WPA GUIDE, sent Governor Hurley and Mrs. Woodward into a tailspin and became the fuse that ignited the anti–New Deal press. Although twelve years had passed since the resolution of the Sacco-Vanzetti case, it was still a painful issue that burned deeply in the public conscience. The hostile press hungrily seized on it to smear the Writers' Project (and by implication the Roosevelt administration) with charges of communism. "With the grace of a cow doing a tap dance," one editorial fumed, "they dragged in the notorious Sacco-Vanzetti case, then added a comment that would do justice to the Communist *Daily Worker*." The editorial called the guidebook an "insult" to Massachusetts. "Money paid out in taxation has been used to cast scorn on the people who paid it. And what was a sincere effort to assist jobless writers has become in a large sense a harvest of propaganda."

The headlines roared: GUIDE BOOK SEIZURE URGED ON GOVERNOR, REDS LINKED TO GUIDE BOOK, PURGE OF COMMUNIST WPA WRITERS DEMANDED. Senators Joseph Walsh and Henry Cabot Lodge, Jr., demanded that Harry Hopkins launch an investigation. Former Massachusetts Governor Joseph B. Ely expressed the opinion that "they ought to take the books to the Boston Common, pile them in a heap, set a match and have a bonfire." Although Hurley was a Democrat, he became as irate as any anti–New Dealer and denounced those "who had deliberately tried to besmirch the name of Massachusetts." He suggested that "if they don't like the United States they should go back where they came from," a piece of advice that amused the "undesirable radicals" he had in mind, nearly all of whom were native-born.

The anger mounted as it was discovered on closer scrutiny that the Massachusetts Guide contained a number of passages written from a pro-labor and anti-Establishment point of view, particularly on such matters as child labor, the Boston police strike, and the historic 1912 strike of textile workers in Lawrence. Several mayors throughout the state decided to ban the book. Governor Hurley ordered the state librarian to examine the book for all objectionable passages and asked that the writers responsible for them be identified and dismissed.

In Washington Hopkins refused to take the matter seriously. At a press conference he expressed his intention of dealing with the subject as a tempest in a teapot. He told reporters: "It sounds to me as though the publishers are in on it and I shouldn't be surprised if they started it." In Boston the reaction to this was a banner headline across the front page of the *Globe*: HOPKINS JEERS BOOK'S CRITICS. VIEWS UPROAR AS A STUNT. The only Boston newspaper that was entertained by the controversy was the *Christian Science Monitor,* which called the affair "a melodramatic comic-tragedy," and asked: "Will the drama end with a patriotic parade in gold helmets, à la Ziegfeld? Probably not. Will Houghton Mifflin sell its now well-publicized 10,000 copies of *Massachusetts: A Guide to Its People and Places?* We think so." The writer of the editorial proved to be right. Despite the threats of censors to burn the books or seize them, the publishers proceeded with a second printing, then a third.

"The whole tragicomic sequence made the dangers of censorship startlingly clear," wrote Ray Allen Billington, director of the Massachusetts Project during the fracas. Examining the passages in the guidebook which the state librarian and Governor Hurley had marked for deletion, Billington noted that "they not only requested the publishers strike out every mention of the Sacco-Vanzetti case, but all references to strikes, unions, organized labor, welfare legislation, child labor laws and virtually every progressive act in the history of the state. They even proposed dropping Labor Day from the list of official holidays!"

The Massachusetts Civil Liberties Committee in a letter to Hopkins characterized Governor Hurley's proposed censorship of the book as "either an attempt to falsify history, or a denial of the right of legitimate interpretations of historical facts." And Harold Faulkner, professor of history at Smith College, wrote Billington: "I have looked over those parts which have recently had some newspaper publicity and in my opinion the statements are conservative and accurate." Unexpected criticism of Hurley came from the governor of Georgia who, angry with him for turning down his request to extradite a Negro who had escaped from the Georgia chain gang, publicly announced that Georgia would consider purchasing the Massachusetts book as a school textbook, "so our children may be informed as to the deplorable conditions of the courts and penal systems of Massachusetts."

*Ray A. Billington (left), director of the Massachusetts Project,
with Robert Linscott (a Houghton Mifflin editor),
Henry G. Alsberg and Dudley Harwer*

Despite the enormous amount of unfavorable publicity in the Massachusetts press, the White House did not seem to be overly disturbed by the episode. A few months after the storm, the President, while touring WPA projects in Washington, visited Alsberg's office and mischievously jabbed his cane into a copy of the Massachusetts guidebook. "I understand you had quite a bit of trouble over this book," he drawled, then laughed uproariously. But if the President and Hopkins were willing to treat the episode lightly, some of their underlings were not. At Mrs. Woodward's insistence, an official censor was added to Alsberg's staff to spot and delete material in the state guidebooks that seemed politically biased. Responding to her anxieties, Alsberg also formally ordered his field offices "to curb extreme outbursts of indignation at social injustice." Hereafter, he ruled, sponsors must agree to submit to the Washington office for approval galley proofs of all Project books before publication.

There was nothing in the Massachusetts guidebook that could be characterized as an extreme outburst of indignation. No knowledgeable reader could quarrel with Professor Faulkner's judgment that the disputed passages were "conservative and accurate."* Yet the furore created by the professional patriots of Massachusetts was so intense and prolonged as to stimulate a series of repercussions that were to damage the national Project severely, and contribute to Alsberg's ouster two years later.

The gibes leveled against the Washington Guide's ponderous format were largely responsible for my job with the Writers' Project as its national coordinating editor. This sumptuous title was a euphemism that obscured my principal role in the Project's Washington office — that of literary agent, perhaps the first to be employed by any government agency. Alsberg's chief purpose in establishing the post was to encourage nationally prominent commercial publishers to issue future books in the American Guide Series, and in that way avoid any further dealings with the Government Printing Office.

Months before the GPO issued the Washington Guide, Alsberg and his staff became aware of its disadvantages as a publishing agent. The GPO — chiefly involved in printing the *Congressional Record,* sundry pamphlets, and government forms — was not geared for the complex job of

---

* No changes were made in the Massachusetts Guide while Alsberg was national director. After his departure, its publishers deleted a statement by Heywood Broun on the Sacco-Vanzetti case which read: "Though the tomb is sealed, the dry bones still rattle," and made several other changes.

book publishing. Little or no attention could be given to the niceties of designing and manufacturing as ambitious a work as the Washington Guide. Even more discouraging was the GPO's lack of marketing and distribution facilities. Copies of the book could only be purchased directly from the GPO; no discounts were offered to bookstores. Nor was there any effort made to publicize the book. The Project was obliged to send out its own review copies and to promote the publication as best as it could.

The publication of the Idaho Guide by a commercial publishing house which not only assumed its publication costs but also promoted it in the bookstores and the press inspired Alsberg to try to find commercial publishers for as many Project books as possible. The stumbling block was a federal law which stipulates that any material produced for publication by an agency of the federal government must be printed by the GPO. Vardis Fisher neatly dodged this hurdle by persuading a nonfederal government official, Idaho's secretary of state, to become the sponsor of the state guide and, in that capacity, to enter into a contract for its publication. The sponsor, in turn, also signed a pact with the Federal Writers' Project, agreeing to transfer to the United States Treasurer any royalties paid to him by the publisher. The effect of this procedure was to bypass the GPO without, apparently, infringing on the law.

Although it was a clear circumvention of the law, the procedure became the Project's standard method for having its books issued by commercial publishers. The greatest value of the system was that it transferred the heavy burden of publication expenses from the shoulders of the taxpayer to that of the publishers. This unforeseen marriage of government and private enterprise enhanced the prestige of all parties concerned and proved to be the most potent single factor in keeping the Writers' Project alive.

Most of the sponsors of Project publications who signed contracts with publishers were state or municipal officials or agencies, or nonprofit organizations, such as state historical societies. Some of the sponsoring bodies were nonprofit groups of leading citizens established for the express purpose of sponsoring Project books. Among the most active of these were the Bret Harte Associates in San Francisco, headed by Charles Caldwell Dobie; and the Guilds' Committee for Federal Writers' Publications in New York City which included the prominent lawyer Morris L. Ernst as well as such noted writers and editors as Franklin P. Adams, Lewis Gannett, Van Wyck Brooks, Henry S. Canby, Louis Kronenberger, Mark Van Doren, Clifton Fadiman, Bruce Bliven, Rockwell Kent, Alfred Kreymbourg, Malcolm Cowley. Philadelphia had a similar sponsoring group known as the William Penn Association, which sometimes published Project books; in Boston the sponsoring group of leading citizens called itself the Poor Richard Associates. Alsberg found it relatively simple to deal with such groups for, unlike some of the governmental sponsors, they were unfettered by red tape, disinclined toward censorship, and sympathetic to the aims of the Project.

My task on the Project was twofold: to line up sponsors for all publishable manuscripts, and to negotiate with publishers in behalf of the sponsors. Alsberg selected me for the post partly because I knew the New York publishing scene, having recently done a three-year stint with a Manhattan publishing firm, and partly because I happened to be close at hand when he decided to establish the job — under the very same roof, in fact. Two months before, when I arrived in Washington to work as a writer for the Resettlement Administration, my friend Wallace Krimont had invited me to move into the house he was sharing with Henry Alsberg and Clair Laning. It was a big rambling dwelling on Wisconsin Avenue; judging from the number of telephone calls received from anonymous men asking for girls by their first names, it must have once thrived as a brothel. The four of us lived there with an old black cook, who did our laundry and cooked our meals and talked nostalgically of the days when she had worked for the McLeans.

It was my initial immersion into the world of the Writers' Project, which Alsberg and Laning made the topic of incessant conversation at every evening meal. Only occasionally would Krimont or I be given the opportunity to talk, Krimont of his job as an assistant to Jacob Baker, who by now had been banished to a New Deal agency that promoted cooperatives, and I of the boredom I was suffering writing Resettlement Administration material about the problems of destitute farmers. When Alsberg invited me to join his staff, I readily consented, though it took me a full month to untangle myself from the red tape of the job I held. Once I began working for the Project, I became as obsessed with it as Alsberg and Laning, and it became virtually the only subject ever discussed at the dinner table until, in deference to Krimont, we made a rule that inflicted a one dollar fine on anyone who ever mentioned the Project during a meal. Even so, we could not keep away from the subject, and there were enough fines paid to all but finance the house's constantly ebbing gin and bourbon supplies.

For those of us close to the operations of the Project it was an exhilarating time, remote from the sour reality of the Depression. During the day we were fired with the pioneering fervor of our Project tasks; in the evening there was witty conversation, dry martinis, and good food. Often there were guests. Mary Heaton Vorse would come and stay for several days at a time, once after she had been shot at and slightly wounded while covering a strike for a magazine. Josephine Herbst, who was then writing the best of her proletarian novels, was a frequent visitor. So was Mary Lloyd, the granddaughter of Henry Demarest Lloyd and a charter member of the Project, whose radiance was so pronounced that she could make most men feel much brighter than they actually were, with the result that as many as three of our colleagues were in love with her at the same time.

Laning, whose partly American Indian ancestry gave his eyes an oriental tilt, could be crisp and efficient when the occasion warranted it and, in the presence of published authors, was as deferential as a college freshman on his first day in school; but his favorite role was that of court jester. At home he liked to report on the amusing happenings in the office and in the field, all the while half-convulsed with his own laughter. He particularly enjoyed teasing Alsberg and telling hilarious stories about him, none of which the older man seemed to mind. It is possible that if Laning had been less gregarious, more inclined toward lonely concentration, he might have developed into a published writer of Dickensian literature, for he had an unmistakable talent for caricature. Alsberg, with his frequent fits of absent-mindedness and his eccentricities, was a natural subject for his anecdotal horseplay, and the stories Laning told of him laid a secure foundation for the legend of our chief. It was a legend which all of us who had any close dealings with Alsberg were bound to contribute to with our own experiences.

One of them, which in retrospect assumed an aura of symbolism, related to Alsberg's outlandish driving. Although he drove his car to the office every morning, no one would ride with him; Washington's trolley cars seemed much safer. But one morning I left the house just as Alsberg was pulling out of the garage, and there was no escape. Nervously, I took my place next to him and, determined not to distract him, tried to give the impression I was in no mood for talk. Alsberg promptly began a lengthy monologue about some Project problem, in the midst of which, for no accountable reason, he suddenly slammed on the brakes. Seconds later the car behind us crashed into the rear of our car. In a flash Alsberg was on the street, his big body bearing down on the driver of the other car, while bellowing: "Why didn't you put out your hand?" Too flabbergasted by the question to speak, the driver could only pummel the air with his arms and emit a series of weird sounds, none of which was decipherable. "They certainly do a lot of drinking in this town," Alsberg grumbled, getting back into the car, and resuming his monologue.

Alsberg, an indefatigable talker, sometimes used talk as a weapon, much in the manner of a filibustering senator. While I was in his office one day, he received a union delegation representing the Washington staff. He listened patiently, without interrupting, while the spokesman recited a list of grievances. When the spokesman was finished, Alsberg began his monologue, enlarging on each point with a wandering essay which was replete with lengthy parentheses and footnotes; at first the union delegates listened closely, expecting to hear some resolution of their complaints. But none was forthcoming and as the monologue droned on, the delegates began to squirm and slowly back up toward the door. Alsberg continued relentlessly, speaking in grandiose circles and saying little, invading their eardrums until they could bear no more. Only a mind reader could tell whether Alsberg was simply enjoying the sound of his voice or deliberately inflicting torture. But I thought I detected a gleam of sadistic delight in his eyes when the spokesman, taking advantage of a pause in his speech, bolted out of the doorway, with all of the delegates close at his heels.

There were many complaints about Alsberg and his mannerisms, but in the spring of 1937, when I joined his staff, I found that the general attitude of most of my colleagues was an admixture of respect, fondness, and faith. By then no one had any illusions about his administrative talents, but with the appearance of the first two major books in the American Guide Series and the impending publication of the six New England guides, Project optimism was running as strongly as springtime sap, and to most of the staff Alsberg seemed peculiarly well-suited to his job. Responding to the arrival of spring and the euphoria in the atmosphere, Alsberg decided to throw a cocktail party that would celebrate the recent publication of the Washington Guide, and the Writers' Project in general.

It was a memorable bash, held in the Wisconsin Street house on a bright April afternoon, and directed by Clair Laning, who prescribed as the main libation dry martinis served out of an enormous punch bowl, whose innocent facade belied its lethal contents. Hopkins could not be present but Ellen S. Woodward, his assistant in charge of Federal One, was there, as was her predecessor, Jacob Baker, the man she had outmaneuvered in a contest for the job with the help of her friend Eleanor Roosevelt. Baker and the Hokinson-like lady from Mississippi, bedecked with her customary orchid, carefully avoided each other, but Mrs. Woodward mingled democratically with most of the other guests, including the Negro members of the Washington staff who were present. Also in attendance were Project writers and supervisors from nearby cities, among them a group from New York, headed by James McGraw, Alsberg's friend and trusted lieutenant, and Vincent McHugh, who looked almost transparent from subsisting solely on milk shakes.

The popular and potent martini punch soon put nearly everyone in a state of benumbed camaraderie. Two scenes, which took place while the guests were reluctantly departing, are forever etched in memory. One is of a Project writer on the front lawn, flat on his back with his hat intact on his head, pointing to the sky with the cane he always carried, while discoursing seriously on the moon and other heavenly bodies. The other is of Jacob Baker, hunched over the wheel of his sedan like the driver of a racer, waiting for his friends to get into the car so that he might take them to his favorite Chinese restaurant. But his friends, somewhat less intoxicated than Baker, without consulting each other but acting instinctively, filed through the back of the vehicle, going in one door and out the other, then slamming both doors simultaneously. Baker lurched forward with the empty car in a wild burst of speed, having no idea he would be dining alone.

Perhaps the most remarkable development of the party was that it became the subject of a senatorial diatribe which was reported in the *Congressional Record*. Senator Bilbo of Mississippi, in a public burst of fury over the news that Ellen S. Woodward, a lady from his own state, had attended a party where she was exposed to the presence of Negroes, attacked Alsberg and the Writers' Project. Referring to Ellen S. Woodward as "the flower of Mississippi womanhood," the senator expressed horror that the head of the Project should have invited to the same party both blacks and whites and, rising to the summit of his rage thundered: "If this had happened in Mississippi, long before the sounds of revelry had died, the perpetrator of this crime would be hanging from the highest magnolia tree."

Alsberg, who guffawed as much as anyone else at the senator's spectacular outburst, was confident that it was aimed not so much at him but at "the flower of Mississippi womanhood" for not having walked out of the integrated party in a huff. Whatever his reason for having once more proclaimed his bigotry on the Senate floor, Bilbo must have had second thoughts about it, for the tirade was expunged from the permanent edition of the *Congressional Record*.

The only other large party involving the Washington staff also created a scandal. This time the scene was the *Ida Mae*, a river schooner which the Project employees had chartered one August evening for a moonlight ride on the Potomac. Harold Rosenberg, who had recently been transferred to the Washington staff from New York, was one of the revelers. Usually Rosenberg was surrounded by a band of disciples, admiring ladies who enjoyed listening to his Marxist-Hegelian discourses on literature, art, and philosophy. But tonight he was alone with a quart of whiskey, stretched out in a lonely part of the deck with his head leaning against a mast, studying the moon while he guzzled from his bottle. Before long he became aware of a couple nearby, a young man who was in charge of the Project's map department, with one of the Project sirens.

Possibly to impress the girl, the young man, who was half the size of Rosenberg, turned on him with all the bravado of a David attacking Goliath and snarled: "Would you mind getting the hell out of here? I want to talk to this lady." At peace with the world and refusing to be disturbed, Rosenberg chose to ignore him. The young man, who later became a minor general in World War II, repeated the request several times, in terser and tougher language, finally provoking Rosenberg to reply: "Beat it, little man, let me alone." Offended by this allusion to his height, the map editor grabbed Rosenberg by the throat and began to choke him. Rosenberg tried to shove him away with his free hand (the other held the whiskey bottle) but his attacker had a good purchase on his throat and retained it until Rosenberg, after carefully corking the whiskey bottle, brought it down on his assailant's head. As soon as the hands were released from his throat, Rosenberg broke into loud laughter, shouting, "Hegel is right, Hegel is right." The laughter infuriated the young man even more and, though still reeling from the blow on his head, he flung himself at Rosenberg with murderous intent. By this time the commotion had attracted a crowd of their colleagues, and the two men were separated.

Later on when Rosenberg and the young map editor became friends,

Rosenberg was able to explain that his laughter and the reference to Hegel was based on his Marx-Hegel approach to problems. At the moment that he was being choked, Rosenberg was thinking dialectically, asking himself: "Since this man is choking me, why isn't my attempt to resist him more effective?" The question promptly suggested the Hegelian principle that the source of one's weakness should become the source of one's strength. With that inspired guidance, Rosenberg reached for the bottle of whiskey, which had rendered him weak, and brought it down on the map editor's head.

I was fortunate to join the Washington office during its happiest days, while it was located in the main ballroom of the gaudy McLean Mansion. My office occupied a corner of the big room that gave me a fine view of most of my colleagues. Alsberg's glass-enclosed office was a few yards away. On one of its walls hung the painting of a goat with a puckish grin, a loan from the Federal Art Project, which helped to expel any lingering McLean ghosts. Alsberg worked from morning to night, pausing only to eat and to sleep (occasionally in a motion picture theater where he could not be reached by telephone) and often worked at home after the rest of us had gone to bed. "Henry takes the Project home in his briefcase every night," one of his associates explained. During the day he could be seen working in his shirt sleeves and vest, dictating to his secretary with a cigarette invariably drooping from a corner of his mouth, conferring with assistants, or talking into one of the several telephones on his desk. Long distance calls took precedence over everything else, to such an extent that, sometimes when he was too busy to see me, I would wait until I got to New York and then discuss all my business with him on the telephone.

Next to Alsberg's office was the Project's only ladies' rest room. Sometimes, when most of the staff had departed for the day and Alsberg was too weary to travel downstairs to the men's rest room, he would use the ladies' while his ever-obliging secretary stood guard over the entrance. Nearby was ensconced Mary Lloyd, who assisted with both editorial and personnel matters; her secretary was a buxom girl known as Miss Hello. As a bachelor, I found the girls on the staff an agreeable source of distraction. One of them, a tall redheaded Southerner, who was Reed Harris's secretary, was openly having an affair with the estranged husband of a luscious brunette from Arkansas who was one of Katharine Kellock's editorial assistants. The two girls despised each other. The brunette, who was as bright as she was beautiful, enthralled a number of males on the staff who

227

became her lovers until the more thin-skinned ones discovered how democratically she was sharing her favors. A free spirit in politics as well as sex, she had little use for the Establishment, and delighted in expressing her contempt for the capitalist system by spitting at any Cadillac that came within target distance.

The variety of personalities on the staff was an endless source of wonder. The essays division, which was the largest of the editorial divisions, included Fred Lowenstein, who resembled an accountant with his hornrimmed glasses and efficient manner, but was an ardent trade unionist given to leftish-sounding phrases which he would try to inject into some of the essays only to have them removed by his chief. Mary Barrett, who headed the division, was a pink-faced former schoolteacher from Michigan, with silver-gray hair tightly clinging to her scalp. Her assistant was Stella Hanau, an old friend of Alsberg who had worked with him during his days with the Provincetown Playhouse. She was a small, fragile woman of angelic disposition and sly humor (she enjoyed making the point that Alsberg may have hired her because she had borrowed money from him while unemployed and wished to make certain of her ability to repay him) who had recently worked with Margaret Sanger in her crusade for birth control.

Though they may have played minor roles in the affairs of the Project, the staff members of peculiar attributes made the most lasting impression. One editor, Benjamin Guinzberg, became memorable simply because of an Alsbergian admonition. "It's all right for you to look and dress like a rabbi," he told Guinzberg, "but for God's sake don't write like one." Another was an editor who sported a celluloid collar and played the horses daily, interrupting his editing at exactly the same hour every afternoon to telephone his bookie. Two of the staff members, Louise Lazelle and Florence Shreve, seemed conventional enough though they were the staff's official censors, until they revealed themselves as informers for the Dies Committee, avid to see the Project killed.

Of all the freakish ones the most personable was an orange-haired disciple of James Joyce who frequently simply stared into space but who, when aroused to action, could demonstrate the anarchic streak that is the hallmark of any writer worth his salt. With or without alcohol, Murray Godwin expressed a freedom of spirit that put the rest of us to shame. No one else would have dared proofread the official memoranda addressed to staff members, then return the memoranda to their senders, irrespective of their high rank, with all spelling and grammatical errors carefully corrected and with the initials "M.G." affixed to each in bold script.*

More often than not he was under the influence of liquor; he drank so much whiskey that even his sweat smelled of it. In the heat of the summer, according to one of his colleagues, he could easily have been decanted. Godwin bore his addiction to alcohol with all the aplomb his staggering nervous system could summon. "What I see when I get the DT's," he once told me, "is so horrible that it scares me into a state of sobriety"; but he kept on drinking. If liquor was a necessity to him, so was his need to admit to his addiction. One morning, while he and Alsberg were conferring in the latter's office, they were interrupted by the abrupt entrance of two executive editors, Harold Coy and George Willison, who had come to complain about a staff member given to periodic drinking binges. The men explained that although the writer in question did excellent work, his absence from the office exactly every two weeks for several days at a time prevented him from meeting crucial deadlines. Alsberg, amused by the periodicity of the writer's binges, drawled: "I guess he's the only reliable drunk we've got." On hearing this, Godwin, who had receded into the background during the conversation, rose from his chair, bowed low to the three men, and announced, "Gentlemen, *I* am the only reliable drunk you have."

My Project job cast me in an unfamiliar role, forcing me to emerge from my shell as a writer and editor in order to perform, as best I could, as an extrovert. For essentially my work was that of a salesman: convincing publishers of the merits of the guidebooks, while at the same time allaying their fears that they might lose their shirts publishing such large books at the low retail price the Project imposed on them. No one but an Alsberg could have conceived of me as a salesman in those days. I was agonizingly shy with strangers, unblessed with the art of small talk, and perpetually groping for words as though English were the most foreign of tongues. (Of these deficiencies Alsberg may have been ignorant for in the relaxed atmosphere of our Wisconsin Avenue home, I could be as articulate as anyone else.) But though I lacked the personality of a salesman, I was

---

* Murray Godwin published two parts of an autobiographical work in progress while a member of the Writers' Project. The first, "Panoram," appeared in the Project anthology *American Stuff*; the second, "Fordjob" in a second collection of *American Stuff* published under the auspices of *Direction* magazine. (See page 250.) Commenting on "Panoram," a New York *Times* reviewer said that "the writer has hit upon a new and arresting way of presenting the history of an American family."

strongly motivated by my faith in the desirability of the guidebooks and in the ability of the Project to produce them at specified deadlines. As a result, my lack of glibness became advantageous as it seemed to suggest a depth of sincerity which obliterated all credibility gaps. Whatever the reason (could it have been another instance of the Marxist-Hegelian dialectic in action?), I was able to obtain more publishing contracts for the state guidebooks, at no expense whatsoever to the sponsor, than Alsberg had dreamed was possible.

Only a few weeks before my appointment Alsberg had been certain that most of the state guidebooks would need to be published at government expense, through the Government Printing Office. In an effort to make the best of the situation, he had asked Reed Harris to explore the possibility of having the printed guidebooks distributed through the facilities of the Post Office Department. "We believe that the American Guide Series might be handled through the post offices roughly in the same way that the United States Savings Bonds are handled now," Reed Harris wrote to Mrs. Woodward. "Posters would be placed in each important post office and order blanks would be furnished for the use of the postal clerks . . . If this plan were followed, we believe that all the larger city post offices should actually stock a few copies of the guide for sale."

A month later, in March, Alsberg abandoned the idea in favor of a sponsorship system of publication that would permit the Project books to be issued by commercial publishers. But he was worried about the willingness of publishers to issue all of the state guides at their own expense, pointing out that while they might be happy to publish guidebooks to such vacation states as Florida, Louisiana and California, they might refuse to publish guidebooks of less popular states, especially as the guidebooks were costly to manufacture and the retail price of $2.50 set by the Project was comparatively low — approximately half of what it ordinarily cost then to buy books as lengthy and as profusely illustrated. Alsberg believed that the only way the less desirable state guidebooks could find publishers was to offer the inducement of direct subsidy. His thinking was based on the fact that Houghton Mifflin, the Boston publishers who were about to issue the six New England state guidebooks, had required subsidies from five of their six sponsors. Only the Massachusetts Guide, the publishers felt, could be published without a subsidy at no financial risk.

Listening to Alsberg, there occurred to me a simple solution for enticing publishers to issue the less desirable guidebooks without any subsidy.

Jerre Mangione and his secretary, Frances Kendrick

George F. Willison

Why not offer such books in groups that would include at least one highly desirable guidebook, I suggested, with the stipulation that the publisher must agree to publish the entire group. The Florida Guide would be used as a magnet to attract a publisher for South Carolina and Maryland guides, which presumably would find fewer readers. This strategy proved to be so successful that within three months Alsberg became convinced that every state guidebook could be published at the expense of reputable commercial publishers. Now he began to worry about the states where, at his instigation, monies had been appropriated by state legislatures for the production of the guidebooks by local printing firms, which had no promotion and marketing facilities.

North Dakota was one of those states. Ethel Schlasinger, the Project's youngest director, had literally risked life and limb to make certain that the state legislature allocated funds for the printing of the North Dakota guidebook. When she learned that the state legislature had failed to act on the two thousand dollar appropriation she had requested, and was about to adjourn, she decided to go to the state capital and make a personal plea before the finance committee. On the day set for her hearing, North Dakota was blanketed with high snow by one of the worst blizzards in its history; all public transportation was paralyzed. Undaunted, she enlisted the services of a friend who owned a small plane equipped with skis. It was a two-seater with no heat; visibility was poor and it took an hour and a quarter to fly the seventy-five miles between Fargo and Bismark.

The landing was made in deep snow, and a wide path had to be cleared for a car to transport her from the plane. Going directly to the hearing, she arrived in the nick of time to deliver her plea. The committee and the legislature acted favorably on the appropriation bill, but when it reached Governor William Langer he informed Miss Schlasinger that no funds were available. She burst into tears and returned to Fargo, certain that the guidebook on which she had worked hard for two years would never be printed. But on the last possible day, Langer signed the bill. Later, she realized that the governor, who had known her family for some years, had used the opportunity to punish her for working for the New Deal. "He enjoyed needling me," she recalled. "Not signing the bill until the last possible moment was his way of telling me that I shouldn't be a Democrat."

Had the governor not signed the bill, the North Dakota Guide would have fared much better; it would have been issued by a national publisher

Harold Coy and Frances Kendrick

Clair Laning and Dora Thea Hettwer

*Merle Colby, Joseph Gaer, and Gaer's
secretary, Jean Lee*

Reed Harris, assistant director of the Project

who, at his own expense, would have given it a far more handsome format than the one it suffered in the hands of a Fargo printing house. But Miss Schlasinger's heroic effort to get funds took place a few weeks before the Project realized the full publishing potential of the guidebooks, when no one could have imagined that funds allotted for the printing of a book would be a liability rather than an asset.

A similar situation developed in South Dakota, where Lisle Reese, the state director of the Project, had also appealed to the state legislature for funds to print the guidebook locally. One afternoon in June 1937, when Alsberg was under the impression that there was still time to persuade the sponsor of the guide to ignore the appropriation and have the guidebook issued by a national publisher, he summoned me to his office and ordered me to fly to South Dakota that evening in order to be there the next morning. He was certain that if we acted with dispatch the guide could be saved from the fate of being handled by a local printer. Never having flown before and having no wish to do so, I tried to convince Alsberg that if I traveled by train I would get there only a day later, and nothing would be lost. But Alsberg was adamant in his fear that our cause might be lost by a matter of hours.

It was a remarkably bizarre journey, which began in the middle of a thunderstorm in a small passenger plane that made a half dozen stops during the night. In Chicago, where I was to transfer to a second plane that would take me to my destination, Pierre, the fog was too thick to permit a landing, and we came to rest on a meadow designated as an emergency landing field but populated by a herd of cows who wandered around the plane with the shy curiosity of primitives confronted by visitors from another world.

By the time we reached Chicago, it was late in the morning and the plane to South Dakota had left. There would not be another flight until the next day, I was told. Plagued with Alsberg's fears of losing valuable time, I fretted and raged until the airline officials, persuaded that I must be on some crucial governmental mission, arranged to have me flown to Minneapolis, a considerable distance out of the way, then placed on a mail plane headed for a town located some one hundred miles from Pierre. After wiring the South Dakota Project about the change in the time and place of my arrival, I boarded the plane to Minneapolis. There were no passengers, no steward, no sign of any other human being. For an hour and a half I tried to fight the nightmare conviction that either the plane

Some staff members of the South Dakota Writers' Project

was without a pilot or that I was in the process of losing my mind. But finally, as the plane approached Minneapolis, a curtain parted and, to my immense relief, I saw the hand of a co-pilot waving at me.

The mail plane to which I was transferred was only large enough for the pilot and some sacks of mail. The pilot pointed to one of the sacks, which was to serve as my seat, then lost all interest in me. Once we reached a proper elevation, he also seemed to lose all interest in the plane, and settled down to a concentrated perusal of several comic books, one of which dealt with the exploits of Superman. Only when we were about to land did he abandon them to resume his role as a pilot. On the ground I was met by two of Lisle Reese's assistants who rushed me into a car and, while speeding toward Pierre, explained that Reese had been married that very morning and was not certain he could see me before leaving for his honeymoon. The anxiety that spread over my face as I listened to all this inspired the driver to increase his speed, but when we arrived in Pierre we learned that Reese and his bride had left only an hour before for a hotel in the Black Hills.

Despite Alsberg's orders to get to Reese as quickly as possible, I decided it would be sacrilege to disturb the first phase of a man's honeymoon. I spent the night in a Pierre hotel where several hundred volunteer firemen, gathered there for a convention, caroused until dawn to the clanging of firebells. The next morning Reese's assistants returned, armed with Coca-Cola and whiskey (the favorite local stimulant) and began to whisk me across the state to the Black Hills. It was a long journey with sudden weather changes that included both snow and sandstorms, and we did not arrive until after dark. Reese had already retired with his bride, but on hearing that I had been traveling for two days to speak with him, he consented to meet me in the lobby of his hotel. There he revealed the benumbing news that my mission was in vain: more than a month before he had informed Alsberg by letter that the state legislature had appropriated funds for the publication of the South Dakota guidebook, with the stipulation that it be printed by the state publishing company. Then, politely urging me to have a good time while I was in South Dakota, he went back to his bride.

Only for a moment did Alsberg sound embarrassed when I telephoned to break the news that he had sent me on a wild goose chase. Barely acknowledging my observation that he must have forgotten receiving Reese's letter, he directed me to visit the Project offices in North Dakota, Kansas, Nebraska, Iowa and Minnesota for the purpose of making certain the guides in those states would be issued by national publishers. Everywhere I went, except in North Dakota, where Ethel Schlasinger told me about her wild flight to the state legislature, the Project directors happily received my news that their state guides could escape the fate of being published by local printers.

At the end of my ten-day journey I was cured of my fear of flying, and I had acquired a more sympathetic view of the Midwest and its people than the one conveyed to me by H.L. Mencken. I was especially struck by the valiant character of the men and women who worked for the Writers' Project. Although, like other midwesterners, they were afflicted with a feeling of separateness from the rest of the country, a spiritual isolation which sometimes gave rise to a sense of inferiority and suspicion, they were deeply dedicated to the goals of the Project. Talking with them, I could not help compare their conscientious attitude with the cynicism and chaos then rampant on the New York City Project.

At first the only office assistance I had was that of my secretary, Frances Kendrick, who was a supremely gifted administrator as well. With the

Project operating in high gear — more than fifty thousand words of material were arriving daily from the field offices — I was able to obtain the services of another assistant, Charles Edward Smith, the pioneer jazz critic who had been working as a relief employee on the New York City Project. The three of us flung ourselves into the strenuous task of lining up sponsors and publishing outlets for hundreds of publications, not only state guidebooks but also guides to historic national highways and cities, ethnic studies, maritime histories, books of folklore, books dealing with place names, nature studies. A large percentage of the completed publications, such as guides to small towns, were of pamphlet size and of no interest to large commercial publishers. They were usually issued by local printing houses. The rest of the books were placed with national publishers, often through my offices.

Acting in behalf of the sponsors, I would acquaint interested publishers with each group of state guidebooks that would soon be available and describe the Project's format requirements and terms. Later this information would be incorporated into a letter from Alsberg which would formally ask the publishers to submit their offers within a specified time. The publisher making the best offer would then sign contracts with the sponsors for each of the books in the group. Sometimes the publisher would agree to pay an advance in royalties; in other instances, where there was some reasonable doubt as to his ability to recoup his initial investment, the sponsor agreed to a forfeiture of royalties on the first edition.

Since none of the state guidebooks ever became big sellers, the royalty payments seldom involved large sums of money. The greatest monetary rewards from the books stemmed from the publishers' willingness to issue them at their own expense. By the end of 1938, the savings to the taxpayer for the publication of some three hundred titles amounted to approximately one-half million dollars. By the time Alsberg's administration ended, in the fall of 1939, approximately a million dollars worth of publication and printing costs had been incurred by publishers and sponsors. With the exception of the Washington, D.C., Guide and *Intracoastal Waterway*,* the federal government spent no money for the printing and publication of Writers' Project books, a fact which no one could have foreseen when the Project was launched, and one which spoke eloquently for the desirability of its publications.

---

* Published in the spring of 1937, *Intracoastal Waterway* described the scenery and history of the waterway between Norfolk, Va., and Key West, Florida. The 143-page pamphlet was prepared by the Washington staff of the Project and printed by the Government Printing Office to retail at twenty-five cents.

If we want to have poets in this country, we will have to keep them alive.

— Malcolm Cowley in *Poetry*,
July 1938

The Federal Writers' Project undertook to alleviate the financial unemployment of writers by providing them with paid work. To the creative writer this was but half a solution.

— Harold Rosenberg, in *American Stuff* (special issue of *Direction*), 1938

All manuscripts produced on Project time become government property. Quite naturally, very few of our writers care to risk a possible best seller as a contribution to the United States Treasury.

— Henry G. Alsberg, in *American Stuff*, 1937

The Project brought a lot of young writers down from the clouds. There was a great deal of hysteria and disorder, but, significantly, things got done and got done well.

— Vincent McHugh, in an interview with the author,
May 29, 1968

Emphasis upon folklore; the speech and mores of the common people; stress upon the contributions of minorities (like the American Negro) to the creation of a genuinely native culture; and an accent upon regional, sectional, and local characteristics . . . these were the principles that guided the thought of Henry Alsberg as he approached the creation of an American Guide.

— William F. McDonald, *Federal Relief Administration and the Arts*, 1969

Seven.

Varieties of American Stuff

"The tour form," Alsberg solemnly explained to a congressional committee which listened indifferently, "can contain as excellent material and skillful writing as any sonnet or ballade." Later on, encouraged by the enthusiasm that critics were expressing over the quality of the Project guidebooks, he also declared that the most "creative" writing of the times was being done in the field of nonfiction, adding that perhaps one of the most stimulating and imaginative of contemporary writers was "not a novelist, like Hemingway, but an economist like Veblen."

No one knows whether Alsberg actually believed such statements, but there is no doubt that they were made with the hope of appeasing those members of the Writers' Project who felt cheated because the Project failed to give them enough opportunity to develop their talents as poets, short story writers, and novelists. Nothing — certainly not Alsberg's statements — could stir them from their conviction that the writing they were doing for the guidebooks was hack work. They envied their friends on the Federal Art Project who, while receiving wages, could express their own individuality on canvas or with stone, working in the privacy of their own quarters, without anyone around to inflict changes on their output. Even the artist who was assigned the painting of a mural was better off than any Project writer, they pointed out, as he could choose his own theme, express it in his own style, and sign it with his own name.

"If the purpose of the WPA is to rehabilitate the unemployed, what more logical program for the writer than the publication of his actual literary work?" asked a disgruntled group of writers on the San Francisco Project, many of whom regarded their Project activity as "made work for hopeless hacks." When their complaints produced no result, they banded together into an editorial board and in 1936 produced a Project literary magazine, the first of its kind, to serve as an unofficial sample of what the Writers' Project could do officially all over the country. "Material Gathered," the name given to the publication by Kenneth Rexroth, consisted of more than one hundred single-spaced mimeographed pages of poems, short stories, a play in verse, two excerpts from a novel in progress, and a peppery Marxist-minded essay on "The Possibilities of an Intelligent Regionalism in California" by the only contributor who used a pseudonym.* "The social system that America has always known is in its final phase in California," he wrote. "It will cease to be an imperialist colony only when imperialism ceases."

But on the whole "Material Gathered" was surprisingly free of leftwing polemics. The introduction, written by Lawrence Estavan, called for "the establishment of federal magazines for creative writers in every locality capable of supporting them," and argued that the creative writer would have more freedom of expression in a publication produced by the government than he would in one issued under commercial auspices. Estavan maintained that manuscripts with certain themes and ideas went unpublished because of the commercial editors' "real or fancied fear that their readers would be offended, their circulation would drop, their advertisers would withdraw their support." Ignoring the might of philistine taxpayers, or being unaware of it, Estavan added: "A federal magazine need have no such qualms. It could say things that need to be said. It would be financed by the whole people and the people would make it possible to hear their writers without fear."

Surprisingly, none of the critics who reviewed "Material Gathered" commented on the touching naïveté of that statement or saw anything amiss with the notion that freedom of literary expression could best be obtained through federal sponsorship. Instead there was general agreement that the quality of the contributions was high, and that Project writ-

---

* The editorial board of "Material Gathered" consisted of Lawrence Estavan, chairman; Miriam Allen deFord, Leon Dorais, Robin Kinkead, Kenneth Rexroth, and Richard Romain. In the spring of 1937 the same board, augmented with Ben Hamilton, Dorothy Van Ghent and Margaret Wilkins, produced the first and only issue of a second "unofficial cooperative" literary magazine of the San Francisco Writers' Project, *The Coast*. This was in printed form and sold for fifty cents.

ers should be given every chance to express themselves freely. The reviewers joined the editorial board in deploring the prevalence of "false" and "vicious" writing, and urged that a San Francisco magazine be established promptly under Project auspices. "The WPA might just as logically furnish paper and printing as well as space for a fresco," wrote Joseph Henry Jackson in the San Francisco *Chronicle*.

Despite its primitive format, "Material Gathered" drew attention in several other parts of the country. In the *New Republic* Karl Schriftgiesser considered the publication as "a model for a national creative WPA magazine of merit," and praised its editors for showing "how to raise the Federal Writers' Project to a level with that of the Federal Theater Project and the Federal Art Project." Edwin Seaver, in the *Sunday Worker*, the New York official Communist publication, heartily endorsed the plea of the San Francisco writers that federal magazines be established for creative writers, and observed that there was little in "Material Gathered" that could not appear in any "good magazine" but that if young writers had to wait for them to buy their material, "we should have not a lot of promising young writers but a lot of starved young bodies."

In the same month that "Material Gathered" was issued, the Nebraska Writers' Project, "solely as recreation and practice for Project workers," published a twenty-three-page compilation of poems, articles, and stories titled "Shucks." The recreational aspect was emphasized in the opening article of the mimeographed publication, a satiric dialogue, "The Cliché Expert on Our Glorious Heritage," by Weldon Kees and Norris Getty "with a nod to Frank Sullivan." (Sullivan was then regaling *New Yorker* readers with the effusions of his own cliché expert.) The same issue included "Arkansas Hoosier," a skillfully told story by Rudolph Umland.

The appearance of "Material Gathered" and "Shucks" in the same month strengthened Alsberg's resolution to establish a national literary magazine under official Writers' Project auspices which would provide an outlet for the out-of-the-office writings of Project workers.* With the assistance of a New York sponsoring group of prominent authors, he val-

---

* The idea was not new with Alsberg. As early as June 1936, he tried to hire Susanne LaFollette, former editor of the *New Freeman*, to take charge of the projected magazine, but Miss LaFollette's appointment never materialized. The rumor that such an appointment was pending led many Project writers to mail short stories, poems, and articles to the Washington office, contributions which gathered dust, except in those instances when their writers, exasperated by the long and silent delay, demanded their return.

iantly tried to launch the publication, but, as usual, was beset with a variety of bureaucratic obstacles. Finally, "as a desperate remedy," in the spring of 1937 he began to solicit manuscripts from Project writers, with the understanding that the best of the material would be published in an anthology if and when a publisher could be found. In answer to his call, hundreds of manuscripts came in from all parts of the country but, as Alsberg pointed out later, "many of our best writers, discouraged by false alarms too often repeated, failed to take the call seriously and sent nothing or only material shopworn with rejections."

The resulting publication was one I named and helped to compile, *American Stuff*, a collection of short stories, poems, and Americana by fifty Project writers, which Viking Press issued in 1937.* In a foreword Alsberg discussed the "peculiar difficulties" the Project experienced in bringing its creative work before the public, but gave the impression that the Project workers produced only nonfiction during their office hours because no sponsors could be found to finance the publication of their fiction and poetry, in that way obscuring the two basic factors responsible for the exclusively nonfictional goals of the Project: the fear that if writers were allowed to work on their own subjective efforts, Congress and public opinion would soon put the Project out of business; and the preponderance of Project employees who, though able to function as researchers or editors, had little or no talent for imaginative writing.

Alsberg had been franker earlier that spring when he spoke at the Second Congress of American Writers. "If I had everybody working on their own manuscripts, I would be asked inside a month, What are they producing? Where is it going? What use is it to anybody? They may be writing the great American novel at home and it will not be doing the Project any good. We have to show some production in order to justify the Project at all." By then the Writers' Project had produced some sixty publications totaling more than five million words; yet Alsberg did not yet feel (nor, with his anxiety-burdened temperament, could he ever feel) there was enough public confidence in the enterprise to warrant taking any long

* The contributors to *American Stuff* included well-known writers as well as obscure ones: Lionel Abel, Nathan Asch, Salvatore Attanasio, J. S. Balch, Sterling A. Brown, Luther Clark, Merle Colby, Leon Dorais, Vardis Fisher, Murray Godwin, Harry Granick, Robert E. Hayden, Travis Hoke, Robert B. Hutchison, John A. Lomax, Margaret Lund, Jerre Mangione, Eluard Luchell McDaniel, Vincent McHugh, Claude McKay, Helen Neville, Lola Pergament, Aaron T. Rosen, Harry Roskolenko, Nahum Sabsay, Ida Faye Sachs, Donald Thompson, James Thompson, Dorothy Van Ghent, Charlotte Wilder, Carl Wilhelmson, George F. Willison, Richard Wright.

chances. But he was anxious to let the writers at the Congress know that his sympathies were with the Project members who wanted to work on their own manuscripts. "Now, if I can get a magazine," he told them, "if I can get occasional creative stuff published in a book, and if I can get out the guidebooks, I can give some writers time to do their own creative writing."

Except for the Writers Union, which was too leftwing to have much influence in Washington in such matters, none of the professional writers groups, such as the League of American Writers or the Authors Guild, seemed interested in promoting creative writing on the Project. But Alsberg, responding to the pressures of his conscience, secretly permitted ten writers on the New York City Project to work at home on their own material, with the sole stipulation that they report to the Project office once a week with evidence of their work. The beneficiaries of this arrangement were mostly writers who had already published books: Edward Dahlberg, Maxwell Bodenheim, Sol Funaroff, Harry Kemp, Willard Maas, Claude McKay, Harry Roskolenko, Charlotte Wilder, and Richard Wright.

Wright was chosen principally because he had recently published in *American Stuff* an autobiographical sketch called "The Ethics of Living Jim Crow." The sketch became part of his first published book, *Uncle Tom's Children*, a group of short fictional works which not only won him first prize in a 1938 *Story* magazine contest held for members of the Federal Writers' Project but also resulted in a Guggenheim fellowship grant.* Everything seemed to work well for Wright on the Project. As a member of Alsberg's secret creative writing unit, he made full use of his free Project time to work on his first novel, *Native Son*, which when published in 1940 put him in the forefront of American letters.

"Ethics of Jim Crow Living" was easily the most powerful piece of writing in *American Stuff*.† The other prose selections, though not as successful, emitted the same grim social atmosphere of the thirties. "There is no 'escapist' literature here," wrote Eda Lou Walton, appraising the book for the Sunday *New York Times Book Review*. Miss Walton was impressed by

---

* The judges of the *Story* magazine contest were: Harry Scherman, president of the Book-of-the-Month Club, which later chose several of Wright's books as BOMC selections; Sinclair Lewis, Nobel Prize–winning novelist, and Lewis Gannett, book critic of the New York *Herald-Tribune*. Besides awarding $500 to Wright as first prize, they gave a second prize of $100 to Meridel LeSeur, of the Minnesota Writers' Project, for a short novel, *The Horse*.

† "Ethics of Jim Crow Living" became the seed for Wright's autobiographical book, *Black Boy* (Harper, 1945).

Maxwell Bodenheim (top left), Willard Maas (top right), Sol Funaroff and Richard Wright were members of the creative writing unit on the New York City Project in 1938

the vivid picture the WPA writers presented of impoverished Americans and by "the effectiveness and precision" with which they used "exact American idiom" rather than literary English. "The WPA writers are all recording what they see," she noted. "For this reason there is almost no propaganda in this book — no dreams of Utopia and no flag-waving for a workers' world."

The lack of "literary English" bothered Alsberg. In his foreword to the anthology he wrote that "the style of the writing is sometimes crude, the technique often inexpert or diffuse, but there is sincerity in it, a solid passionate feeling for the life of less prosperous millions." Like Eda Lou Walton, most of the reviewers ignored his disparagement of the style and praised the anthology's content. But two critics, usually favorably disposed toward Project publications, did not care for the poetry and fiction in the anthology. Lewis Mumford in the *New Republic* candidly expressed the view that the work which the contributors did for the Project was more important than that which they did on their own time. He based this opinion partly on the rich Americana contained in the book, which had been collected on Project time — folk sayings, Negro convict songs and market cries, square dance calls and legends of mutiny.

Mumford saw a distinct literary advantage in diverting novelists and poets from the free play of their fantasy to Project tasks that "involved a different form of discipline." He argued that "this apprenticeship, this seeing of the American scene, this listening to the American voice may mean more for literature than any sudden forcing of stories and poems." His view was shared by Ralph Thompson in the daily New York *Times*. He found nothing of outstanding merit in the anthology, and expressed a preference for the writing being done for the American Guide Series. The WPA guides, he wrote, would be used and appreciated for generations to come, but only in this sphere of writing could the Project function effectively. "If it should invade the sphere of so-called creative writing," he warned, "it would go where it was neither welcome nor necessary."

A valid objection came from many members of the Project who complained that *American Stuff* failed to reflect a broad enough cross-section of Project writers. Almost a third of the contributors were supervisors and state directors, most of them well-established writers whose need to appear in print was far less urgent than that of the relief workers they supervised. There was a disproportionately large number of contributors from California and New York, but only one from Chicago and only two from all of the New England states. That year the Vermont Project issued a mimeographed magazine, *The Catamount,* containing five short stories, four of which were listed as "Distinctive Short Stories in American Magazines" in Edward J. O'Brien's *Best Short Stories of 1938;* yet not a single Vermont writer appeared in *American Stuff.* Conspicuous by their absence were also such talented poets and fiction writers (all hired from the relief rolls) as Kenneth Fearing, Norman Macleod, Joseph Vogel, Sol Funaroff, Edwin Rolfe, Willard Maas, Maxwell Bodenheim, Edward Dahlberg, William Rollins, Jr., Nelson Algren, Jack Conroy, Kenneth Patchen, Isaac Rosenfeld, Madeline Gleason, Weldon Kees, Howard McKinley Corning, Willard Motley, Margaret Walker, Leon Srabian Herald.

Pleased with the favorable reviews of *American Stuff* (one of them a front-page spread by Stephen Vincent Benét in the Sunday book section of the New York *Herald-Tribune*) and agreeing that more Project writers should have the opportunity to see their off-time creative efforts in print, Alsberg renewed his effort to establish a Writers' Project magazine under government auspices, and designated Harold Rosenberg, who was then a member of the New York City Art Project, to become its editor. There were immediate difficulties. No one could dispute Rosenberg's qualifications for the position — he was a published critic and poet, a man of erudition and taste — but the news of his appointment irked the leadership of the Writers Union, who demanded that Rosenberg and the two assistants he had selected, Lionel Abel and Harry Roskolenko, be ousted and replaced with three editors selected by the union. There were several objections to the three men but the Stalinist-minded leaders of the Writers Union never publicly uttered their principal objection: in their opinion, Rosenberg, Abel, and Roskolenko were Trotskyites.

Alsberg refused to drop Rosenberg as editor but permitted Roskolenko and Abel to be replaced by Fred Rothermell, a published novelist of undefined political sympathies, and George Petry, a leftwing writer who was endorsed by the union. The staff of three, aided by an advisory board consisting of Alsberg, Donald Thompson, James McGraw, Vincent McHugh, Joseph Gaer, Reed Harris and myself, proceeded to solicit material for the first issue of the magazine *American Stuff.* But when it became known that the contents were to include contributions by Roskolenko and Abel and other writers who were not of Stalinist persuasion, Petry was accused by his Stalinist colleagues of "collaborating with an enemy of the working class" (meaning Rosenberg), and the Writers Union intensified its efforts to remove Rosenberg as editor, determined that as long as he remained in that key position there would be no magazine.

In a move intended to mollify the union, Alsberg persuaded the critic Kenneth Burke, who enjoyed the respect of both Stalinists and Trotsky-ites, to serve as editor of the magazine, though he was not a member of the Project. Rosenberg was retained as managing editor. Far from being mollified, the Writers Union decided to sabotage the first issue of the mag-azine, which bore Rosenberg's name as editor, and to dissuade Kenneth Burke from associating himself with any future issues of the publication. The union succeeded in its first objective by stifling distribution of the first issue in New York City, its largest potential market. Its second objective was achieved by bombarding Burke with a series of letters which sug-gested he would be engaging in anti-union activity if he had any associa-tion with the magazine. Unwilling to become embroiled in what he later termed as "the combustion of paranoia politica," Burke temporarily with-drew as editor, explaining to Alsberg that he had agreed to teach some courses at the University of Chicago that would keep him fully occupied for three or four months, and offering to discuss the matter with him then.

The Writers Union also wrote to Alsberg, demanding the removal of Rosenberg from the staff of *American Stuff* on the grounds that the first issue of the magazine was "not the type of magazine the union could re-gard with approval." The letter characterized its contents as "vague, dated, and ineffectual," and attributed these "weaknesses" to Alsberg's failure to provide an editor who could give the magazine "the progressive positive direction requisite to its success." In order that the magazine be consistent with the union's "literary standards" and "trade union position," it also insisted on the establishment of an editorial board in which "full participation by the workers is permitted."

To Alsberg the letter, with its non-negotiable demands, represented nothing less than the Writers Union's insistence on injecting its own brand of leftwing politics into the operation of the magazine. Yet he did not give up hope, and wrote to Kenneth Burke urging him to take up the editorship of *American Stuff* as soon as he was through with his teaching chores. He assured Burke that, contrary to the impression given by the Writers Union, the selections for the first number of the magazine were not the exclusive choice of Rosenberg, but had been carefully reviewed by all members of the editorial board, including himself. He promised that in the future the method for selecting material would become even more democratic as he planned to add to the editorial board Project representatives from all major regions of the country.

Since Alsberg was unable to get government funds for the first number of the magazine, it was published as a special issue of *Direction,* a monthly literary periodical, at its expense. The selections were of a finer grain than those in the anthology, less sociological and more poetic in their sensibility; but, by the same token, they lacked the vigor that the anthology had exuded by its intense feeling for the plight of the poor and by its heavier emphasis on Americana and folklore. The title "American Stuff," though appropriate for the anthology, seemed too crude for the contents of the magazine, despite the fact that nearly half of the contributors were writers who had appeared in the anthology.

Yet it was the magazine's prefatory editorial by Rosenberg, "Literature Without Money," rather than any of its selections, that antagonized the Writers Union and caused its leaders to declare that Rosenberg's literary standards were "inconsistent" with their own. It was evident from the editorial that Rosenberg, unlike the union, had no intention of breaking with the traditional role of little magazines. The editorial stressed the close connection between the vitality of such independent literary enterprises and the development of American letters. In better times, Rosenberg noted, the writer could earn his living with odd jobs while perfecting his art as a contributor to little magazines, which as a rule could not afford to pay for material. But with the coming of the Depression and the shrinkage of literary patronage, the writer found himself in a dilemma that was both economic and literary. Not only were there no jobs to be had but also his manuscripts became "unemployed." By providing him with paid work the Federal Writers' Project had solved half of his problem. Now with the establishment of a magazine, where his manuscripts could be printed, it was contributing to his development as a writer.

While emphasizing *American Stuff's* ties with the literary past, Rosenberg did not ignore the nonliterary circumstances which produced the Project and the magazine. He wrote: "The present selection differs from earlier magazine issues in that it came into being not as a result of a theoretical or esthetic grouping, but through an economic predicament. But if the employment of all its contributors on Federal Project No. 1 does not confer upon them an esthetic unity, it does immerse them in a common social experience from which a special literary emphasis may well arise."

The implication that in the beginning the magazine could not be anything more than a miscellany was disputed by his opponents who argued that the anthology, though assembled with far less deliberation, achieved homogeneity and "a special literary emphasis" by publishing stories of a more proletarian character and interspersing them generously with Project-recorded Americana and folklore. The magazine, it is true, had made scanty use of Americana. There were only two such pieces: a composite ex-slave narrative compiled by Elizabeth Lomax, and a listing of "Phrases of the People" recorded by Harrison Dickson of Missouri which, judging from its tail-end position in the magazine and its absence from the table of contents listing, may have been included as a filler. One of the more arrest-ing selections in the magazine, Dickson's listing began with the phrase "in low water, mud turtles charges de catfishes fo' bits to shove 'em over de sandbars," and ended with:

> *Naught's a naught*
> *Figger's a figger*
> *All for de white man*
> *None for de nigger.*

The magazine relied heavily on previous *American Stuff* contributors from California and New York City, but published a number of writers from diverse parts of the country who had not appeared before, among them Weldon Kees, of Nebraska, with four brief prose sketches about fe-male librarians; Howard McKinley Corning, of Oregon, with the poem "Chant of the Cattle Breeds"; Jeremiah Digges, of Cape Cod, with an invented folktale, "Bowhead Pete and the Mermaid"; Guy H. Rader, of Montana, with a memoir, "Homestead Days"; and two poets, Opal Shan-non of Iowa and William Pillin of Illinois, the only representative of that state in the magazine. There were also two New York City writers new to *American Stuff*, Ruth Widen, with her first published short story, and B. Rivkin, the pen name of Baruch A. Weinrebe, a Yiddish writer, who contributed "The Distinguishing Characteristics of Yiddish Literature."

Notwithstanding the disruptive actions of the Writers Union, Alsberg would have persisted in his effort to continue the magazine had not the Dies Committee made it clear in September 1938 that one of its first tar-gets would be the Federal Writers' Project. Not wishing to complicate the pending defense of the Project with a precarious problem that was unre-lated to its stated goals and operation, Alsberg quietly abandoned his plans for the magazine and at the same time disbanded the secret creative writing unit he had established in New York City. When Rosenberg was summoned to the Washington office in the fall of 1938, it was not to work on the magazine but to edit guidebook copy dealing with the subject of art in America, an activity he was to pursue for the next four years.

Although *American Stuff* was nipped in the bud as a magazine, it inspired other magazines to follow the lead of *Direction* and publish special compilations of off-time material written by Project workers. The May 11, 1938, issue of the *New Republic* carried a miniature anthology of federal poets, selected by Sol Funaroff, himself a contributor. The group of poems included several writers who had not appeared in either of the *American Stuff* publications: Maxwell Bodenheim, whose poem was entitled "Dear Noel Coward," Kenneth Fearing, whose books *Angel Arms* and *Poems*, had established him as one of the outstanding poets of the period, and Eli Siegel, winner of the *Nation* poetry prize, who was well-known to Greenwich Village denizens for his histrionic renditions of Vachel Lindsay's "The Congo."

Almost simultaneously, an issue of the *New Masses* devoted thirty of its pages to Project contributors, a compilation that was led by Richard Wright's "Bright and Morning Star," one of the four novelle that were to be included in *Uncle Tom's Children*. The preponderance of contributors were poets, seventeen of them, young ones like Weldon Kees, A. T. Rosen, and Sol Funaroff, and recognized ones like Bodenheim, Fearing, and Raymond E. F. Larsson. The compilation, which was largely reminiscent of the *American Stuff* anthology in tone and content, introduced several young Project fiction writers, among them Saul Levitt, of the New York City Project, and Arnold Manoff of the Chicago Project. There was only one piece of folklore, "Street Songs of Children," collected by Fred Rolland. In a note prefacing the songs Rolland sounded like a member of the Writers Union officially expressing the group's non–Harold Rosenberg stance on ways and means of selecting literary materials: "These jingles are a product of group fraternization, amended, adopted, and accepted with collective approval." Yet most of the *New Masses* selections were singularly free of the leftwing clichés and stereotypes then prevalent in so-called proletariat writing, despite the magazine's close identification with the Communist party.

The magazine *Poetry* devoted its entire July 1938 issue to some thirty WPA poets, more than had previously been assembled in any single publication. They represented all sections of the country. For the first time there was the opportunity to examine the broad spectrum of themes engaging their attention. The majority were concerned with the anxieties of war, hunger, deprivation, "capitalistic greed," and the need for revolution. In "Summons at Night" Virgil Geddes concluded: *

> Rise we must
> Our future cannot come too soon.

A number of poems reflected the deep involvement of the American intellectual with the gory war in Spain. "1200 killed in a new raid on Barcelona/And not a quiver in this lazy air" were the opening lines of "Defenseless Spring" by H. R. Hays. Margaret Walker and Sterling A. Brown evoked the silent despair of the American Negroes. Kenneth Fearing, with the most striking voice in the anthology, contributed two poems, "Hold the Wire," and "A Dollar's Worth of Blood, Please," both replete with the sting of his forebodings. Harold Rosenberg's poem was titled "The End of the World," and Helen Neville in "Time's Embrace" asked:

> Is all reckoned? Is the world here?
> is Time now? shall we die?

There were also poems that bore no relationship to the events of the thirties but were obsessed with themes of love, loneliness, and metaphysics — some by Project poets who were already familiar to readers of *Poetry*, Mark Turbyfill, Kenneth Rexroth, James Daly, Lola Pergament, Charlotte Wilder. Lesser known was Weldon Kees, whose poem "The Inquiry" expressed the mordantly apprehensive atmosphere that was to dominate his main work:

> The streets are full of broken glass
> sparkling in this frenzied noon.
> With naked feet and bandaged eyes
> you'll walk them — not just now, but soon.

---

* In addition to being a poet, Virgil Geddes was the author of several produced plays. *The Earth Between* (1929) and *Native Ground* (1932) aroused considerable controversy because they deal with the theme of incest.

Along with the poems, *Poetry* published commentaries by Willard Maas, the editor of the compilation, Malcolm Cowley and Alfred Kreymborg, all of whom deplored the demeaning position of the American poet in the nation's culture. Maas was shocked to discover that most of the poets represented had been forced to qualify for relief in order to get a job on the Writers' Project. "It seems a little ironic," he wrote, "that the poet, the most over-romanticized of all the artists, must be reduced to destitution before being allowed a modicum of financial security in order to practice his profession."

Malcolm Cowley put the case even more strongly: "The Federal Writers' Project has not been ideal for the poets it employed. Their task has not been writing poetry but describing towns in guidebook fashion or doing historical research. They have never been sure of their pay from one week to the next; some whim of Congress or some administrative ruling might abolish their job. This situation has led to sitdowns, picket lines, telegrams to senators, and, in general, a host of distractions that have prevented them from planning their lives or their work in advance."

Kreymborg, Cowley, and Maas were in agreement that — in Kreymborg's words — "the time has arrived for the creation of an art movement supported by the people through its government, and divorced from the 'relief' and 'charity' associated with the WPA. No self-respecting individual can accept such terms, nor can any of his democratic brethren ask him to accept them." Cowley and Maas expressed the hope that the best of the Project poets could be helped through the establishment of a Federal Bureau of Fine Arts, which, according to the terms of a bill then in the House of Representatives, would be lodged in the Department of the Interior and would provide artists, within and without the arts projects of the WPA, a salary of no less than thirty dollars a week.*

The last periodical to feature a compilation of Project material was *Frontier and Midland*, the Montana-based literary magazine edited by Harold G. Merriam. Its winter 1938 issue contained forty-four pages of poems and stories by a dozen Project writers. True to its established policy of publishing regional writers, the magazine confined itself almost exclusively to contributors west of the Mississippi. For the first time in any

---

* Fathered by Congressman William I. Sirovich of New York City, H.J. Res. 671 was literally laughed out of existence when presented for a vote. Grace Overmyer, in *Government and the Arts* (1939), reported: "With a lack of dignity unworthy of a legislative body, the proposal was dismissed without due regard for its merits or its faults."

Writers' Project compilation appeared the work of Oregon-born Norman Macleod, one of the more prominent younger poets in the thirties. Because of the conservative character of the magazine's sponsor (The State University of Montana) its compilation of Project material was easily the most conventional one of all. Only one of the selections, "My Father Has Brown Eyes" by Charles Hayes, who was appearing in print for the first time, reflected any awareness of the Depression. The leading story in the magazine was "Good Christmas," a memoir of a Swedish American childhood on a farm by John Stahlberg, who played a key role in helping to complete the Montana state guidebook. Some of the liveliest pieces in the compilation consisted of folklore that had been gathered for the Project: "Webfoot Whoppers," tall tales from Oregon, and "Loup Garou," an account of the secret lives of werewolves in Louisiana.

By the time *Frontier and Midland* was off the press, the Writers' Project had been attacked by the Dies Committee, and the dream of making the Project a vehicle for imaginative writing had been murdered in the fray. By the time the Project ceased to be a federally controlled enterprise, in the summer of 1939, the remnants of the dream were deeply buried, and hardly anyone ever spoke of it, not even in New York. Only in retrospect grew the realization that although the Project had asked its writers to produce guidebook copy instead of poems and stories, it had succeeded in generating an impressive amount of creative energy. The simple act of providing writers and would-be writers with jobs that gave them a livelihood without unduly taxing their energies turned out to be the most effective measure that could have been taken to nurture the future of American letters.

Perhaps the greatest beneficiaries of the Project were its black employees. As a result of pressures brought on the New Deal administration by a self-appointed "black cabinet" of Negro leaders, which included Robert Weaver, John P. David and William Hasty, the WPA was structured to provide hundreds of American Negroes with their first opportunity to exercise skills they already had or to acquire new skills. What was an economic disaster for the country became a liberating experience for many of them. This was especially true in the WPA arts program where, as Ralph Ellison noted, "writers and would-be writers, newspaper people, dancers, actors — they all got their chance."

The emergence of Richard Wright as a top rank novelist, while still a member of the Project, was the clearest testimony of how the Project could provide a young writer with the economic means and the psychic stamina he needed to test his talent. Less known was the Project's contribution to the literary development of Ralph Ellison, who was a friend of Wright. Later on, with the publication of *The Invisible Man*, Ellison achieved a greater degree of prestige and fame than most Project writers and, like many of them, he served his literary apprenticeship on the Project.

When Ellison came to New York in 1936, after receiving musical training at Tuskegee Institute, his main interest continued to be music. But he was fascinated with literature; he had done well at Tuskegee in English department courses, and had published in the campus literary magazine his first writing, a poem about a student friend who had died of pneumonia. Through Langston Hughes he met Richard Wright. Ellison was only nineteen then, six years younger than Wright, but their friendship blossomed quickly. Wright persuaded him to write a book review, which he accepted for the *New Challenge*, a short-lived magazine Wright was then editing; then in the spring of 1938 he helped Ellison land a relief job on the New York City Project.

With Wright as his literary mentor, Ellison approached the art of writing in the same methodical fashion he had studied music. He also produced some short stories and started a novel. One of the stories, "Heine's Bull," was overly influenced by Hemingway; another was so much like Wright's own fiction that when his friend read it, he exclaimed somewhat resentfully, "Hey, that's my stuff." Ellison was not surprised that as a beginner he had imitated too closely a friend whose writing style was already crystalized. Prudently, he stopped showing Wright any more of his manuscripts, and continued the quest to find his own literary personality.*

Ellison's Project job entailed considerable drudgery but left him with enough time and energy to do his own writing. Many of his Project days were spent in the public library digging up information about Negro history. "The drudgery was good for me," he recalled. "When you start researching the history of Negroes you plunge into European history and that goes in all directions." His work assignments also included research on famous New York trials, which provided him with information about the law that proved to be extremely useful to him as a fiction writer. Later

---

* Ralph Ellison told the author that it was while writing the short story "King of the Bingo Game" that he found the "touch" he was searching for: "It had the realism that goes beyond and becomes surrealism." The short story was published in November 1944 by *Tomorrow* and has appeared in several anthologies since.

on, he was assigned to the New York City folklore project and studied the lore of black children, their games and their rhymes.

To gather such material, he talked with hundreds of black families in Harlem. Ellison was happy to be on the Project, and had little patience with his leftwing colleagues who either did not take their work seriously or ignored it. Although he sympathized with some of the Communist party goals and occasionally wrote book reviews and reportage for the *New Masses,* he could not condone the party's failure to concern itself suffi-ciently with the Project's welfare. He worked steadily on his assignments, five days a week for nearly four years, and was one of the last writers to leave the Project.

Black or white, young writers like Ellison were the most likely to profit from their Project association. Besides rescuing them from the despair of unemployment, it stocked them with information and insights about their country during a highly formative period of their literary lives. The older black writers, unlike many of the older white writers, also profited psycho-logically as well as economically. For most of them the Project was a di-rect source of creative strength. While on the Florida Project, Zora Neale Hurston published three books in rapid succession, *Their Eyes Were Watching God* (1937), *Tell My Horse* (1938), and *Moses, Man of the Mountain* (1939). Arna Bontemps published his third novel, *Drums at Dusk* (1939), while a supervisor on the Illinois Project. Claude McKay, the noted Jamaica-born poet and novelist (his 1928 novel, *Home to Harlem,* was the first best-selling novel by an American Negro), based part of his last book, *Harlem: Negro Metropolis* (1940), on information gathered by the New York City Project's Negro unit.

The Writers' Project also helped to promote the first Negro studies to be conducted in the United States on an extensive scale. The most significant, gathering ex-slave narratives, began a year before the Project came into being, in 1934, under the auspices of the Federal Emergency Relief Ad-ministration, and chiefly at the instigation of Lawrence D. Reddick, a Negro history professor at Kentucky State Industrial College. Reddick, along with other historians, held that the story of slavery and Reconstruc-tion could not be complete "until we get the view as presented through the slave himself." By the time the Writers' Project inherited the undertaking, it had been extended to eighteen states and involved the services of a number of Negro researchers.

Alert and sympathetic to the desire of the New Deal administration to make WPA jobs available to Negroes, Alsberg encouraged Negro studies and tried to persuade his state directors to hire as many qualified black writers and researchers as possible, though a number of state directors, swayed by local prejudices, showed no inclination to comply with his directives. As a way of emphasizing the Project's intentions, Alsberg, in the spring of 1936, appointed Sterling A. Brown, of the English department at Howard University, national editor of Negro affairs. The thirty-five year old Brown was well qualified for his post. He was the author of a much-praised book of poetry, *Southern Road,* and of two books of literary history about to be published that would establish him as an authority on Negro literature, *The Negro in American Fiction* and *Negro Poetry and Drama.* A man of congenial disposition, he knew many of the contemporary black writers in America personally. Although sometimes mistaken for a Caucasian because of his light pigmentation, no one could ever doubt his staunch allegiance to Negro interests.* He had been appointed to serve the Project in an advisory and editorial capacity, but before long he became an itinerant troubleshooter as well, traveling to a number of states to establish black study programs and to help resolve personnel problems affecting blacks. These varied in scope from dealing with state directors who were reluctant to employ Negroes, to coping with discriminatory practices, such as in the Project offices in Oklahoma where white Project workers refused to share a water fountain with their black colleagues.

With two young assistants from Howard University, Eugene Holmes and Ulysses Lee, Brown outlined an ambitious editorial program whose general intent was to produce a portrait of the Negro as an American through a comprehensive survey that would depict his past and present cultural and sociological situation. In instructing state directors about Brown's program, the Washington office pointed out that although a good deal had been written about the Negro in America, he had invariably been dealt with as a problem, not as a participant. "The Negro has too seldom been revealed as an integral part of American life. Many Negro historians have attempted to counter the neglect, but the result has been overemphasis and 'separateness.' Where white historians find few or no Negroes and too little important participation, Negro historians find many and too

---

* Professor Brown remained on the faculty of Howard University until his retirement in 1970. During the sixties there was a student movement to change the name of Howard University to Sterling A. Brown University, which did not succeed.

much. This racial bias is understandable but it does not produce the accurate picture of the Negro in American social history . . ."

It took Brown and his staff almost a year before they could make their editorial weight felt in the Project's field offices. Brown arrived too late to prevent the gross neglect of the American Negro in the six New England state guidebooks. And he was not always successful in persuading state editors to include Negro material in the guidebooks or in correcting material that had been distorted. Yet by and large he and his staff achieved their goal of including honest and accurate material about the Negro in most of the state guidebooks. The coverage given to the subject in these books represented, in effect, the first objective description of the Negro's participation in American life.

To compensate for the necessarily sketchy treatment of the Negro in the individual guidebooks, Brown instigated a series of field projects conducted by black writers and researchers who, working under his direction, investigated the story of the American blacks in depth. One such project resulted in the publication of *The Negro of Virginia*, a gold mine of black history and folklore which is widely regarded as a classic of its kind. The preparation of the book was supervised by Roscoe E. Lewis, a black scholar who wrote well and who had excellent rapport with all the whites and blacks involved in the study. Fortunately for the project, the state director of the Virginia Writers' Project was then Eudora Ramsay Richardson, a southern lady of keen literary sensibility who, unencumbered by any racial bigotry, shared Brown's and Alsberg's resolve to make it a model for the Negro studies that would follow. Supported by the Hampton Institute, where the Project made its headquarters, an all-Negro unit worked for several years conducting hundreds of interviews and digging up, from musty records, books and newspaper files, forgotten information about the story of the Negro dating back to 1619.

When *The Negro in Virginia* appeared in 1940, several prominent critics recognized its quality and its importance. Reviewing the book for the *Saturday Review*, Jonathan Daniels hailed it as "one of the most valuable contributions yet made to the American Negro's history, which has been left in darkness even when it was not presented in distortion." Daniels found it "free from both bitterness and prejudice and equally free of sentimentality and pretentiousness," adding that "the method of this book should be a model for the other histories that need to be written." H. L. Mencken's *American Mercury* commented: "The product of many hands,

Negro and white, it is so brilliantly edited that it reads as though it might be the individual work of a singularly competent historian." None of the reviews mentioned one of the book's most dramatic chapters, "Thirty and Nine," which discussed the inhuman treatment of Negro slaves by their owners; but one noted that the practice of slavery "gave to the sadist opportunities for the perpetration of crimes Krafft-Ebing has collected from a later day."

As Roscoe Lewis indicated in his preface, it was appropriate that the first Writers' Project book on the Negro deal with Virginia, since it was there that the first African natives were brought and held in slavery. No single volume dealing with the story of the American Negro was ever produced by the Project, but *The Negro in Virginia* came as close to the theme as any book had. "In a real sense," wrote Lewis, "the story of *The Negro in Virginia* is also the story of the American Negro, for the roots of more Negro families were nurtured in Virginia than in any other state." By its impartial treatment of "the springs that water those roots and the droughts that withered them," and its use of spoken recollections by blacks remembering their past and that of their fathers and grandfathers, the book attained the vibrancy of literature.

Two other ambitious Negro studies were conducted by the Project, in Illinois and New York, but neither one was as fruitful. In Chicago the only Project book on the Negro was a hastily concocted ninety-five-page pamphlet, *Cavalcade of the American Negro,* which was produced to coincide with the American Negro Exposition held in Chicago in 1940. In the mid-forties Horace R. Cayton and St. Clair Drake, neither of whom had any connection with the Project, drew heavily from the Illinois Project Negro material in writing their book, *Black Metropolis.* But most of the material has gathered dust in the archives of Chicago's Hall Branch public library.

In New York, where thirty Project writers and researchers helped to develop Negro material, some of the findings were used in *New York Panorama* and the New York City Guide, but no single volume dealing with the Negro in New York was produced during the actual life of the Project. In 1943 Roi Ottley, who had supervised the Negro unit in the New York office, published *New World A-Coming,* which utilized manuscripts that had been prepared under his supervision. Its bibliography credits: "NYC Writers' Program, Roi Ottley, Editor, *Negroes of NY,* unpublished." The book, which won the Houghton Mifflin Life in America annual award, examines the Negro's search for democracy, with Harlem used "as a sort of test tube in which the germs of Negro thought and action are isolated, examined, and held up to full glare to reflect Black America." Written in a sprightly journalistic style (Ottley had once been a sports writer), the book was highly informative but lacked the documentation and historical perspective that made *The Negro in Virginia* a classic of its kind. The most valuable result of the work performed by the Negro unit in New York was *The Negro in New York,* an informal social history that begins in 1626 and ends in 1930, which was published more than a quarter of a century after the death of the Writers' Project.

Ottley's relationship to the thirty-five manuscript boxes that constituted the New York Project's effort in black studies is a curious one, which began with his election as head of the Negro unit. In an assertion of black power, the Negroes on the Project had demanded and obtained the right to elect their own supervisor and deal with the study of their people in their own way. Ottley created some discontent among his workers by his failure to discuss with them the overall design he had in mind for the work. "We all knew eventually that we were writing a history of the Negro in New York," recalled Ellen Tarry. "But I do not remember that anyone showed us the overall plan or told us what anybody else was doing."

Ottley exerted considerable power on the Project. When a young black woman in his unit complained to two of her white colleagues that he had made unwelcome advances, the two men suddenly found themselves transferred to another unit, and when the matter came up before the Project's grievance committee, the young woman denied ever having complained about Ottley. But Ottley's boldest assertion of authority came in 1939, when he and many other Project supervisors were dismissed following the end of the Project as a federally sponsored enterprise. Figuring perhaps that the Negro material that had been accumulated might be wasted if left in the files, Ottley decided to take it all home with him. At least one of the Project administrators realized what Ottley was up to but, being under the erroneous impression that the New York City Project was finished (actually it was to continue for nearly three more years under other auspices), he did nothing to stop Ottley, though he was, in effect, breaking the law by taking government property.

Ottley kept the material only long enough to draw from it the information he needed for his book, *New World A-Coming.* In 1940, about a year after he had left the Project, he delivered all the Project papers in his possession to the keepers of the Schomburg Collection of Negro Literature and History in the New York City Public Library. The curators accepted the material for safekeeping without asking any questions that might embarrass Ottley, apparently aware that, with the firing of Henry Alsberg from the Project in 1939 and the resignation of Sterling Brown in the following year, the Writers' Program, as it was now called, had no further interest in Negro studies.

Two librarians, Kathleen Hill and Jean Blackwell Hutson, spent about a week arranging the Negro unit materials in thirty-five manuscript boxes. Several writers utilized some of these materials in books they wrote, notably Gilbert Osofsky, author of *Harlem: The Making of a Ghetto* (1965); but not until 1967, seven years after Ottley's death and twenty-seven years after he had given the Project papers to the Schomburg Collection, was *The Negro in New York* published. In a foreword to the book, Roi Ottley took the main credit for its pre-final editing but, as pointed out by Mrs. Hutson in a prefatory note, other names appear as editors in earlier records, among them Ralph Ellison, Claude McKay, Lawrence Gellert, Bella Gross, Ellen Tarry, Ted Yates, Richard Nugent, Carlton Moss, Ted Poston, Everett Beanne, Waring Cuney, J. A. Rogers, Harry Robinson, Floyd Snelson, Abraham Hill, Simon Williamson, Carl Offord.*

In his introduction James Baldwin found the book "unavoidably sketchy and unevenly documented," but declared that "it strips the Americans of their fig leaves, as it were, and proves that Eden, if it ever existed, certainly never existed here. It proves that anyone who contends that the Northern racial attitudes have not always been, essentially, indistinguishable from those of the South is either lying, or is deluded." As a foreshadowing of the scapegoat role that the black was to play in American life, Baldwin cited from the book Peter Stuyvesant's alibi for not being able to withstand the British siege: three hundred slaves arriving just before the British entered the harbor, he explained, had eaten all the surplus food in the city. With the same eloquent bitterness that flavored the entire introduction, Baldwin commented: "Scarcely any American politician has since improved on this extraordinarily convincing way of explaining American reverses." In his appraisal of the book Professor Osofsky, a specialist in

---

* The names of Roi Ottley and William J. Weatherby appear as editors on the title page of *The Negro in New York: An Informal Social History*, published by the New York Public Library and Oceana Publications, Inc. in 1967. Weatherby was selected by the New York Public Library to do the final editing.

American Negro history, found that it suffered from having been edited by Ottley, who, with his journalistic turn of mind, "shaped his material for a popular audience." Yet he conceded that the book was a significant one, notable for its "frank handling of truths."

The first Negro study undertaken by the Writers' Project, the gathering of ex-slave narratives, was undoubtedly the most valuable contribution the Project made to the literature of American minorities. The program, which preceded the appointment of Sterling Brown, was first directed by John A. Lomax, who in 1936 became the Project's first folklore editor. Lomax extended the scope of the research initiated by the Federal Emergency Relief Administration, and issued to Project field workers a set of "detailed and homely questions" designed to "get the Negro thinking and talking about the days of slavery." There were then an estimated 100,000 former slaves still alive. Lomax's suggested questions covered nearly every conceivable aspect of a slave's life: the clothes he wore, the food he ate, the games he played as a child, the treatment he received from his owners, the manner in which he was informed of his freedom, etc. Later, to help Project interviewers cope with the difficult problem of recording dialects, Sterling Brown issued instructions which urged that "truth to idiom be paramount and exact truth to pronunciation secondary."

Lomax in 1938 was succeeded by Benjamin A. Botkin as the Project's folklore editor, but Botkin had little to do with the ex-slave narrative program until he joined the staff of the Library of Congress in 1939, when he spent two years supervising the organization of the huge mass of ex-slave material developed by Project field workers. The manuscripts, encompassing more than two thousand slave narratives and several hundred photographs of former slaves, were collated in seventeen volumes of thirty-three parts, and made available to scholars.*

Although uneven in quality, the narratives vividly recapture the wide range of experience that befell the slaves from the time they were kidnapped in Africa to the period after the Civil War when they were freed. There are detailed accounts of kindly and mean masters, descriptions of humorous episodes and superstitions, stories of runaway slaves that are as

---

* Not all of the ex-slave narratives recorded by the Federal Writers' Project are in the Library of Congress collection. Many additional narratives came in after 1939 and were relegated to the WPA storage collection of the Library of Congress. Some of the states involved in the Project retained the narratives (Louisiana and Virginia among them) in specially designated depositories.

violent and dramatic as anything found in fiction. Many of the reminiscences reflecting the sadistic horrors inflicted on the slaves by their owners have a searing authenticity.

Brandings (on the forehead, breast or back), ear clippings and beatings were common. An ex-slave of Petersburgh, Virginia, saw her mother stripped of all her clothes, then hung up by the hands, with her feet off the ground, and whipped until she bled. She was then bathed in brine. The reason for this punishment was that she had displeased her master by refusing to have sex with his overseer. Another black woman remembered: "He hanged me by the wrists and spraddled my legs around the tree trunk and tied my feet together. Then he beat me . . . Massa says I'll git well, but I'm ruint for having children."

One ex-slave told the interviewer: "Many the time a nigger git blistered and cut up so that we have to git a sheet and grease it with lard and wrap 'em up in it, and they have to wear a greasy cloth wrapped around they body under the shirt for three four days . . . I lays in the bunk two days, getting over that whipping, gitting over it in the body but not the heart. No sir, I has that in the heart to this day."

A former slave had been owned by a master who, after committing a crime, chained all his slaves together and forced them to walk barefooted all the way from Georgia to Texas, sometimes through snow. "Massa have a great, long whip platted out of rawhide, and when one of the niggers fall behind or give out, he hit him with that whip. Mother, she give out and bleeding, and her legs swoll plumb out of shape. Then Massa, he just take out he gun and shot her, and whilst she lay dying he kicks her two-three times and say, 'Damn a nigger that can't stand nothing.' Boss, you know that man, he wouldn't bury mother, just leave her laying where he shot her. You know, then there wasn't no law 'gainst killing nigger slaves."

Badly treated slaves often longed for the release of death. Many of them reported being poorly fed and going hungry. Some of them were put to work as early as the age of five. Since slaves were regarded as commodities, the practice of using plantation studs to breed more slaves was not uncommon. "If Marse have a big comely wench," a Texan ex-slave explained, "he puts her with de stud and no other man to mess with her. But supposing a nigger buck loves her and she loves him. Marse sees dat and get rid of dat buck."

Frequently, wives and husbands, brothers and sisters were sold to different owners, and suckling babes were separated from their mothers.

Whatever the age of the slave, the price he could command was a basic consideration. One former slave told that when she was placed on the auction block as a young woman, "they pulled my dress down on my back to my waist to show I ain't gashed or slashed up. That's to show you ain't a mean nigger."

Struck with the potency of the ex-slave material, Botkin excerpted from ten thousand pages of manuscript enough selections for an anthology he published in 1945 with the title: *Lay My Burden Down: A Folk History of Slavery*. A literary and commercial success (by 1969 it had gone into eight printings), Botkin's book served to make the public aware that, thanks to the Writers' Project, a significant facet of the American story had been faithfully recorded in detail and saved from oblivion. As Botkin indicated in his preface, the narratives constitute, in effect, a collective saga of slavery. "They have the forthrightness, tang and tone of people talking, the immediacy and concreteness of the participant and the eyewitness, and the salty irony and mother wit which, like the gift of memory, are kept alive by the bookless."

Like the slave narrative project, the Writers' Project's investigation of folklore materials had its original roots in the FERA. Alsberg, quick to appreciate the Project's capacity to gather folklore on a larger scale than ever attempted in the United States, as early as 1935 began instructing field offices (Katharine Kellock wrote the first set of instructions) on the art of reporting local customs and lore. When more material than anticipated began arriving, he enlisted the services of John A. Lomax, who was then on the payroll of the Historical Records Survey. Lomax, an unreconstructed Southerner from Texas, was an expert ballad hunter (he was responsible for the discovery of the great Leadbelly, whom he found in a jail) and had been made honorary curator of the Library of Congress's folk song collection.

Lomax was delighted with Alsberg's interest in using the Project to collect folklore, and together they drafted a letter to the state directors pointing out that while the immediate consideration was to provide folklore material for the state guidebooks, their staffs were in an ideal position to collect a great deal of other valuable folklore. "Such an opportunity to collect this material may never recur." Their instructions called for a wide variety of materials, including information about wishing seats, wishing wells, swamps or quicksands with sinister properties, "proposal rocks" and "localities with beneficent qualities"; stories of animals and of relations between animals and people, peculiarities of table service or dining routine, special religious customs, such as public denunciation of wrongdoing, blessings of crops or of rivers, tall tales, drinking toasts peculiar to a locality, unusual epitaphs in old graveyards, stories of persons with psychic or supernatural powers.

In some states the instructions were received with derision. "We simply could not believe our eyes," recalled Agnes Wright Spring, the former director of the Wyoming Project. "None of us had ever thought much about folklore and when we received an index to folklore subjects listing 'Animal behavior and meanings, such as a rooster crowing, dog barking, cattle lowing, etc.,' we thought it was the biggest piece of malarkey we'd ever seen." One of her former colleagues, Cal Williams, who had resigned from the Project to work for the Republican party, happened to see the folklore instructions and used them to sneer at the New Deal. An editorial he wrote for the Wyoming *Tribune* began: "The Roosevelt administration is doing things no other administration has ever thought of," and continued: "Animal behavior is being studied intensely and before long our people will know why a rooster crows and a dog barks . . . Briefly the big idea is this: 'There is no end to the work to be done — there is no limit to the money it will cost. Boondoggling must go on and you must pay the bill.' "

In Nebraska, on the other hand, the folklore project evoked a great deal of enthusiasm both on the part of the Project workers and the community. The Nebraska Project produced a series of thirty folklore pamphlets, each about fifteen pages long, for free distribution to the public schools throughout the state. Individual pamphlets were devoted to such topics as songs, ballads, dance calls, Indian ghost legends, Nebraska cattle brands. Pamphlet Number 25, titled "Pioneer Recollections," received a lengthy write-up in the New York *Times* over the headline, "Life on Frontier Vividly Recalled." The violence noted in some of the recollections — in one instance an old settler remembered how his nearest neighbors and their three children were killed and scalped by a raiding party of 120 Rosebud Indians — may have been the inspiration for a lamentation by a Nebraska Project writer which began:

> *Once I was happy, but now I'm forlorn*
> *Writing of Redskins from early morn . . .*

In Idaho the indefatigable Vardis Fisher not only wrote extensively of Idaho Indians in the state guidebook but also produced an illustrated 256 page volume, *Idaho Lore*. Fisher had collected the basic material by appealing to college students throughout the state to solicit pioneer stories from old-timers they knew. He had then rewritten the stories sent to him in order to "improve" them.

A group of tales, *Hoosier Tall Stories*, was collected by the Indiana Writers' Project and distributed free in mimeograph form. The thirty pages of whoppers included one which was prefaced by the whopping brag that no other tall story was repeated more frequently. It concerned Jeff Dawson, the laziest man in Indiana, who was finally given the choice by his fellow citizens of getting down to work or being buried alive. He chose to be buried. When a stranger encountered the coffin being taken to the cemetery, he was flabbergasted by the sight of the "corpse" calmly puffing on a corncob pipe, and asked for an explanation. On hearing it, he offered to help Jeff get a fresh start on life by giving him a bushel of corn. Jeff thought about this for a moment, then asked, "Is the corn shelled?" "Why, no!" replied the Good Samaritan. Jeff resignedly lay back again in his coffin. "Drive on, boys," said he. "Drive on."

A great mass of folk material gleaned from conversations with black and white residents of New Orleans was produced by the Louisiana Writers' Project but not published until three years after the Project's demise. Rewritten by Lyle Saxon, its ex-director, with the help of Edward Dryer and Robert Tallant, former Project editors, the 581-page book *Gumbo Ya-Ya* (Cajun for "Everybody talks at once") reflects the lore of a heterogeneous people — French, Spanish, Italian, Negro, Cajun, and Creole. "Every night is like Saturday night in Perdido Street, wild and fast and hot with sin." So begins the book, and is followed by chapters on such topics as crapshooting and playing the lottery, decaying plantations, slaves and slave tortures, buried treasure, Mississippi riverfront roustabouts and their jargon, New Orleans cemeteries (to which during rainy spells coffins are brought in on boats) and wakes, and ghost stories.

One of the ghost stories is so gruesome as to nearly defeat the lusty and amiable mood that pervades most of the pages: the unemployed father of twenty-five children eats more than half his children unknowingly in the form of roasts served by his desperate wife, then one day hears the voices of the children's ghosts singing:

> *Our mother kills us,*
> *Our father eats us,*
> *We have no coffins,*
> *We are not on holy ground.*

When the father finds a pile of small human bones under some steps, he chokes his wife to death, then has the bones of his children buried in a cemetery. The story ends with the laconic comment "and he was never able to eat meat again."

The South provided some of the Project's best collections of tall tales. James Aswell, of the Tennessee Project, who had assisted W. T. Couch in editing the highly acclaimed collection of oral histories, *These Are Our Lives,* also edited a collection of "Liars' Bench Tales" titled *God Bless the Devil!* published in 1940. In its last year the North Carolina Project, which had been chiefly responsible for *These Are Our Lives,* published *Bundle of Troubles, and Other Tarheel Tales.* South Carolina produced *South Carolina Folk Tales* (1941). The Georgia Project's effort to collect lore resulted in a book which was closer to anthropology than to folklore, *Drums and Shadows: Survival Studies among the Georgia Coastal Negroes* (1940). Based on interviews with old inhabitants, many of whom discuss relatives and acquaintances born in Africa, the book documents various parallels between African culture and the culture of Georgia coastal Negroes.

The Project's nationwide search for folklore unearthed, just in time, a vast amount of almost forgotten materials. The search ended with the arrival of World War II and the death of the Project. While it existed, the Project was able to salvage for posterity a rich and significant part of the American past that was in imminent danger of being lost through the decline of the early settlers and the accelerated development of mechanical means of communication. Yet although a great deal of material was saved and made available, much of it remained unpublished and unknown.

Despite the presence of a gifted folklore writer, Zora Neale Hurston, on the Florida Project, most of its material remained dormant, unknown except to a few scholars and occasional newspaper feature writers. Not long ago an Orlando columnist quoted some tales collected by the Florida Project forty years before, one of them by Mrs. Hurston about a mythical place called Diddy-Wah-Diddy, where there is no work and no worry and where the food is already cooked. "If he gets hungry, a traveler sits down and pretty soon a big baked chicken and sweet potato pie comes along. But as much as you eat, there's always some left. Everyone would like to live in Diddy-Wah-Diddy if they could, but it's hard to find even if you know the way, and the road leading to it has such big curves that a mule pulling a wagonload of fodder can eat off the back of the wagon as he goes."

One of the largest (and least known) collections of folklore material was assembled by the same Writers' Project staff that produced *The Negro in Virginia*. In a Washington *Star* Sunday feature story entitled "Neglected Treasure," Donald Smith described it as "the richest collection of unpublished folklore in the state and, perhaps, the nation." It reposes in thirty cardboard boxes (each one large enough to contain four volumes of an encyclopedia) in the subbasement manuscript room of the University of Virginia's Alderman Library, "right next to the John Dos Passos papers." The collection lay virtually untouched, reported Mr. Smith, until a few years ago when some graduate students began looking through it for folksongs. In 1968 Bruce A. Rosenberg, a professor at the University of Virginia, published an index (*The Folksongs of Virginia: A Checklist of WPA Holdings*) listing some twenty-six hundred folk songs and ballads alphabetically. The larger part of the collection, consisting of ghost stories, superstitions, herbal lore, and so on, gathered from the Appalachian Plateau, one of the most isolated spots in eastern United States, remains unclassified.

Until the advent of the Writers' Project, American folklore had been the almost private preserve of scholars who, with few exceptions, dealt with it formally as part of a remote past. Without any deliberate intent to be revolutionary, the Project, in its determination to produce books that would provide an introduction to American culture, broke down the barriers of academic formalism by stressing the contemporary aspects of American folklore. This happened almost from the beginning, with its development of the life history oral form, which resulted in such valuable works as the Slave Narrative Collection and the collection of oral histories titled *These Are Our Lives*. With the appointment of Benjamin A. Botkin as its folklore consultant and editor, the Project's view of folklore became broader and even more contemporary, and there was a noticeable shift from rural to urban material.

Botkin, who was born in Boston of Lithuanian immigrant parents and educated at Harvard, Columbia and the University of Nebraska, had already established a national reputation as a folklorist when he joined the Project. His interest in American folkways dated back to 1921, when he became an English instructor at the University of Oklahoma. From 1929 to 1932 he had edited four volumes of a regional miscellany entitled *Folk-Say* — a term he invented. The proletarian emphasis on American writing generated by Marxist philosophy had strongly influenced his own thinking.

"The folk movement must come from below upward rather than of above downward," Botkin wrote in the early thirties. "Otherwise it may be dismissed as a patronizing gesture, a nostalgic wish, an elegiac complaint, a sporadic and abortive revival — on the part of paternalistic aristocrats going slumming, dilettantish provincials going native, defeated sectionalists going back to the soil, and anybody and everybody who cares to go collecting." He saw the United States as a pluralistic culture rich with the dynamic life and fantasy of its cultural minorities. At the same time he understood the need to utilize folklore informants of the lower middle classes because, as he put it, "they are, in outlook and sympathy if not in actual circumstances, closer to the bottom and the bottom dog."

The Project, with its large membership of "bottom dogs" scattered throughout the country, together with a national director who sympathized with his aims, provided Botkin with an ideal opportunity to put his ideas to work. Stressing human values rather than antiquarian ones, he called for a national volume of "American Folk Stuff" told with "all the flavor of art and all the native art of casual narrative belonging to the natural storyteller." With Alsberg's consent, he associated himself with the recently established social-ethnic unit on the Washington staff, and urged that folklore and social-ethnic studies be correlated since "ways of living — ways of earning a living and looking at life" were a basic part of both studies. "All types and forms of folk storytelling and all minority groups — ethnic, regional, and occupational — are to be represented," he wrote, in order to give "a comprehensive picture of the composite America — how it lives and works and plays."

Traditional rural lore was not ignored, but more and more the emphasis was on urban and industrial material. In New York City a "Living Lore Unit" of twenty-seven Project writers was formed. Headed by Nicholas Wirth, one of the most enterprising supervisors on the New York Project, it included among others Ralph Ellison, John Herrmann, Saul Levitt, Arnold Manoff, Hyde Partnow, Herman Spector, May Swenson, Joseph

Benjamin A. Botkin and Agnes Martin, a Project assistant,
Washington, D.C.

Vogel. By paying particular attention to ethnic groups, they gathered Jamaican proverbs, Irish songs and stories, Serbian, Croatian and Jugoslav songs, Jewish tales from the Café Royal, stories of Father Divine and Daddy Grace, children's street cries and games, one of which, "Chase the White Horse," became the title of the book that was being assembled. Some of the most striking materials gathered by the unit were interviews with workers of diverse occupations: construction workers, taxi drivers, longshoremen, needle trades employees, etc.

As Botkin pointed out, "living lore" was responsive to the mood of the moment but behind it was the accumulated wisdom of generations. The following excerpt, quoting in part a Jewish garment worker recalling his experience with a boss, is indicative of what he meant:

> "When is pay day?"
> He says next week. I come Thursday. He says Friday. Friday, is Saturday. Saturday I say: "Make out my name and give me the pay."
> You know how it is Saturday. A little different. I am wearing the same suit, but my shoes, I have a shine. I walk into the place. I never seen the boss before. I am dealing with the foreman, so I don't know him. You see so many dogs running around, you don't know which is the right dog.
> I wait a couple of minutes. Till the door is opening up. A man walks out. I walk in there.
> "My name is So-and-So. I came for my pay. Thursday, is Friday. Friday, is Saturday. So here I am."
> He looks me up and down. "Oh," he says, "some workers look very prosperous."
> "Sure," I answer. "Some workers look prosperous and some bosses look like rotten cockroaches."

Since "folk fantasy rather than folk knowledge" was one of Botkin's primary aims, the quality of the "living lore" material was largely dependent on skills which were more characteristic of the writer than of the scholar. The knack of asking the right questions at the right time, of intuitively providing leads that would encourage the informant to talk freely, more than compensated for the Project writers' lack of folklore training. As a result of the wide leeway they were given, fresh techniques were developed which were highly effective. Hyde Partnow, of the New York City Project, found that his best material resulted from "creative listening," foregoing the use of pad and pencil to concentrate on (and record) what he had heard. "You give them [the informants] plenty of time, you never laugh at the wrong time . . . They may talk for hours. All the time you feel that tomorrow you may not see them again, or tomorrow they may die — that's the way you listen."

One of Partnow's most successful transcriptions was the rambling monologue of a man without a job, titled "I'm a Might-Have-Been." The opening paragraph reads:

> I admit it, I'm a hog. In other words human. I enjoy women and a pair of doughnuts like anybody else. Say tomorrow I wake up I'm covered in communism, say I can go and get what I want by asking — I want six wives. You maybe want twenty-four suits and him, they gotta give him twelve yachts — otherwise, he's miserable. We're nuts, we're all deprived so long we went nuts. Plain hogs. It's chemical, you can't do nothing . . . At the same time in this kinda world, two plus two makes five. Now. Look at me. I look like a dirt monkey. True? I'm among the world of missing men. I'm so insignificant if they sent out a radio call for me a hundred years nobody would find me. Economically I'm collapsed, I could write my whole will on a postage stamp, not a single coin of the realm will you find in my pocket, I ain't got enough real estate to put in a flower pot. Tell me, then, why should I sing my country tis of thee or welcome sweet springtime I greet you in song? And *yet*, my friend, you can never tell the way you stand by the way you're sitting down. Listen to what I'm gonna say to you now, carefully — the bacteriologist of today was himself a bacteria in primeval times. Sh! Don't talk. Think it over . . .

More than any other official Project undertaking, the search for lore gave the writers engaged in it a sense of literary creativity and the satisfaction of being directly involved with the current scene. The younger writers on the Project, who were most likely to be under the influence of the proletariat literary movement of the period, tackled their assignments with particular relish. In New England, writers investigated the lives of Connecticut clock makers and munition workers, Maine clam diggers, Vermont slate workers from Wales and granite workers from Italy. From Oklahoma came stories told by oilfield workers; from Montana and Arizona tales of copper mines. In Chicago, Project workers recorded tales of railroad workers, sign painters, bricklayers, and steelworkers.

The tall story continued to be one of the most popular forms of folksaying, but the tales collected for the Project by such proletariat-minded writers as Jack Conroy and Nelson Algren assumed a distinctly twentieth-century flavor in their sociological and technological awareness, without sacrificing humor or neglecting the traditionally prodigious qualities of

Jack Conroy of the Illinois and Missouri projects, with Joe Jones,
WPA artist

their protagonists. Jack Conroy, who contributed heavily to the Illinois
Project's unpublished manuscript, "Chicago Industrial Folklore," helped
to endow the modern tall story with its special personality. In "The Demon Bricksetter from Williamson County" we learn that the hero was "the
doin'est man that ever hit this burg, and that ain't no lie nor whore's
dream"; we are also told about the hard lot of the bricksetter. "There's a
sand hard as diamonds that sticks to the bricks closer'n a brother and eats
through a rawhide mitt damned nigh as quick as hell could scorch a
feather. If you kneel down to save your poor old back, the little grains of
sand eat in your prayerbones same as a rat would gnaw a hunk of cheese."

One of Conroy's most ingenious tales concerned "Slappy Hooper,
World's Bestest Sign Painter," who gave up skywriting to paint billboards,
only to find that they were so true to life as to make trouble for everyone.
The loaf of bread he painted for a bakery enticed so many birds, who kept
pecking at it and breaking their bills, that the humane societies complained. The stove he painted for a manufacturer poured off heat in every

direction, causing dandelions and other weeds to pop out of the ground during the coldest winter recorded by the Weather Bureau. This disturbed no one, until the hoboes of the city began to hang kettles against the stove to cook their food, and soon the area around the billboard was so packed with homeless men using it as a flophouse as to create mammoth traffic jams.

Not all of the industrial folk tales dealt with the proletariat. The chief protagonist of Nelson Algren's "Hank, the Free Wheeler," was the owner of an automobile factory who wanted everything on wheels. Obviously based on the Henry Ford saga, the story tells how Hank, deciding that iron cost too much and lasted too long, scoured back alleys for every piece of tin he could lay his hands on and made "flivvers" of them. All he cared about was that his cars held together long enough to leave the factory gates. When finally his own bearings wore out, he died, despite ten thousand doctors and fifty thousand nurses. They put him in a glass-covered coffin and, after sending him down the assembly line, six pallbearers — "all drawing a six dollar a day minimum" — began carrying his coffin toward the hearse. But suddenly Hank reared up and smashed the coffin's glass and yelled: "What the hell is this? You call this efficiency? Put the thing on wheels! Lay five of these birds off, and cut the other one's wages 'cause the work is easy and the hours ain't long and the pace is slow."

The best of the industrial tall tales were intended for a national Project collection titled "A Tall Chance to Work." It was never published as a book but in 1944 some of the stories became part of Benjamin A. Botkin's anthology, A Treasury of American Folklore, the first of a series of folklore anthologies he edited in which he combined Project-gathered material with material from other sources. More than anyone else in the country, Botkin was in a strategic position to utilize the Project's treasure trove of folklore. Although he had served as the Project's folklore editor for only one year, for the next two years (1939–41) he was chief editor of the Library of Congress Writers' Unit which sifted through thousands of folklore and ex-slave manuscripts prepared by the Project throughout the nation, and organized them for deposit in the library.

A Treasury of American Folklore was a sensational success, selling more than a half million copies during its first three years of publication. He followed it with nearly a score of other folklore anthologies, among them such regional compilations as A Treasury of New England Folklore in 1947 and A Treasury of Southern Folklore in 1949. Both as a member of the Writers' Project and as a private citizen, Botkin performed a singular cultural service for the nation. On the Project he broadened and contemporized the scope of its folklore program. Later, as an anthologist, he popularized American folklore as a viable aspect of the nation's sense of identity.

Botkin also brought respectability to the Project's folklore program. Until he took charge of it in 1938, the program had been jeopardized by the snobbery of orthodox folklore scholars who considered John A. Lomax, his predecessor, unqualified because he lacked proper academic credentials. At its annual 1937 conference the American Folklore Society had formally rejected the Writers' Project as a legitimate instrument for gathering folklore with a resolution declaring that only a scientifically trained folklorist was qualified to collect "dependable folklore." Lomax shrugged off this slap in the face with the wry observation that "presumably, the collector must go out among the people dressed in cap and gown," but Alsberg took the resolution seriously enough. The following year he replaced Lomax with Botkin, whose credentials were impeccable.

Botkin's appointment produced a favorable change of attitude on the part of the American Folklore Society, one which he carefully nurtured. In a surprisingly short time the Writers' Project, thanks to his efforts and his prestige, won the endorsement of the folklore scholars as a valuable facility for gathering material. The Project's position in the folklore field was further enhanced by the election of Botkin as president of the Joint Committee on Folk Arts of the WPA, a group organized to coordinate, utilize, and distribute all folklore materials collected by all WPA agencies. As the Committee's guiding spirit, Botkin initiated a series of recording expeditions which involved, for the first time, close association between all of the government arts projects, and which brought to the archives of the Library of Congress a wealth of material.

Botkin's lively concept of folklore was belied by a quiet and studious demeanor which would have made him inconspicuous in a library but which in the frenetic atmosphere of the Ouray Building (where the Project was located after it quit the McLean Mansion) gave him the aspect of a bright banner. Although we shared nearby office space, my sharpest memory of him was in a Chicago dive, to which we had repaired one night during a three-day regional Writers' Project conference. There we watched the gyrations of a mulatto belly dancer called Lovey. During the performance I glanced at Botkin and saw him hunched over a notebook busily recording his observations of the writhing mulatto, presumably under the heading of living lore. The catholicity of his approach to folklore eventually incurred the wrath of conservative folklore scholars, especially after they examined the contents of *A Treasury of American Folklore;* but at the same time it became a liberating force, rescuing folklore from the academically embalmed atmosphere in which it had long been contained and bringing it to a large audience that was hungry for the kind of Americana which reflected the nation's varied personality.

As more and more books in the American Guide Series rolled off the presses, Alsberg became increasingly concerned with the task of presenting a more comprehensive portrait of the country than could be suggested by the guidebooks. He realized that unless the guides could be augmented with books depicting the peoples of America there would be noticeable gaps in the portrait. It was with this in mind that he encouraged ethnic studies as well as Negro and folklore research programs. By 1938 the Project had published or was about to publish a number of ethnic studies, among them the commercially successful *The Italians of New York* (both in English and Italian), the *Jewish Landsmanschaften of New York* (in Yiddish), *The Armenians of Massachusetts, The Swedes and Finns of New Jersey.* These books were well received but, being based largely on secondary sources, they contributed little information that was either new or significant, nor was the writing up to the literary standards set for the state guidebooks.

In order to improve the content and quality of future ethnic studies, Alsberg decided that the program required the supervision of an expert, and in 1938 appointed Morton W. Royse as national consultant for social-ethnic studies. When Botkin joined the Project a month later, the two men agreed to work in close collaboration, convinced that social-ethnic studies should include folklore material. The prospect of gathering material on a nationwide scale from firsthand sources in order to tell the story of how Americans lived was an exciting one to Alsberg. In a speech explaining the Royse-Botkin program, he said: "We are studying not only the migrations to this country from abroad, but also the migrations within the country, changes of habits of living and social attitudes, and conditions of living. We are not attempting this in the way trained sociologists and economists would since we are not equipped to make that kind of study. We are studying the ethnic groups from the human angle, and much of the field

277

work will be done by those of our workers who belong to the respective groups that are being studied, who know the language and the traditions and can get ready access to the human information we want to make our publications colorful and interesting to the great American public."

For all of their proper academic credentials, Royse and Botkin shared Alsberg's viewpoint that the Project's lack of trained experts could be an asset rather than a liability. They suspected that as amateur sociologists and folklore collectors, Project workers might turn up data that would be far more interesting and revealing than the dry analyses and statistics of conventional scholars. There was nothing conventional about Royse, either in his thinking or his appearance. With his bald head and aquiline nose, he resembled an eagle. The possessor of two doctoral degrees from Columbia, one in law, the other in philosophy, he had written a dissertation on "Aerial Bombardment," which became a textbook for students of military affairs, and a dissertation on European minority groups, which was hailed by a Princeton University professor of international affairs as one of the most authoritative treatments of the subject ever undertaken by an American. He came to the Project recommended by prominent scholars who were lavish in praising his talents. Royse's previous place of employment had been a workers education training center in Puerto Rico; one of its officials described him as "a man with a definite and well-defined social philosophy and unlimited courage and energy," and added that the only criticism of him was that he was "somewhat outspoken."

Royse's initial letter to the Project's state directors was a model of clarity and optimism. "We are preparing an unusual nationwide study which will require the cooperation of all state Projects," he began. "In this ethnic study, provisionally called *Composite America*, we shall try to reconstruct the building of our country, from colonial days to the present, and present the contemporary scene with all its variety and richness, with particular stress placed on human relationships and values. The building up of our country knows no parallel in historical times — in the influx of peoples from all ends of the earth, and in the freedom and opportunity which beckoned to the impoverished and oppressed of all lands. How a social and cultural unity was achieved by these people, without stamping cultural differences into one mold, producing the unique American civilization, and how this fabric of American democracy was progressively enlarged, is the crux of our story."

Royse threw himself into his new job with demonic vitality, traveling

Morton W. Royse in Italy, a few years after he left the Project

throughout the country to establish new projects and discard those he considered insignificant or unfeasible; trying to indoctrinate Project supervisors with his point of view and methodology, and talking with scores of college professors in their capacity as volunteer consultants for the Project. He even went down into mine shafts to explore the possibility of instigating new labor studies. Everywhere he went he demonstrated his remarkable talent for speedily making friends and enemies. Some Project supervisors felt he was usurping their powers. Others were delighted with his erudition and powers of perception. One of his admirers was Frank Manuel, the newly appointed regional director of New England.* Manuel was impressed with Royse's grand design to establish nationwide studies deal-

---

* Frank Manuel had been recommended to Alsberg by Felix Frankfurter, who described him as a genius. A few days after Manuel's appointment as regional director of New England, a WPA strike was called, and the entrance to his office was blocked by a picket line. Remembering his father, a baker and a strong union man who had taught his family to respect all picket lines, Manuel wept as he walked through this one. His job created another difficult conflict when it became necessary to fire a number of Project workers. Should workers be fired on the basis of need or ability, was the question that confronted him. After much agonizing, he decided that if the Writers' Project was to survive, ability was the only possible criterion.

ing with nationalities and occupations and even with entire communities, 160 studies altogether that would provide data for *Composite America*. For Manuel these studies represented the Project's "most important and interesting work."

In the South, however, Royse's efforts met with open resistance. W. T. Couch, the Project's regional director there, regarded the social-ethnic research program as an infringement on his own oral life-history project, and instructed the directors in the southern states to "concentrate on the life histories." In New York City Royse aroused the hostility of James Mc-Graw, one of the Project's chief executives, by dealing directly with the workers in the racial study unit rather than with the heads of the Project. Complaining to Alsberg, McGraw wrote: "It is all right for Royse, who only comes in here once or twice a month, to give the impression to our people that they are to take orders only from himself or from you, but we have to be here every day and are, in the last analysis, responsible. If our workers are given the impression that what they are doing is none of our business, it will be difficult for us to guide them in the writing of their respective books. We already have had a case of a worker who, on being admonished for tardiness, told the timekeeper that he was responsible to Dr. Royse alone for all of his actions on the Project."

McGraw's complaint was typical of several others that reached Alsberg's desk, but by then the director was too deeply in the throes of preparing for his impending confrontation with the Dies Committee to investigate them. A month later, however, he scolded Royse on what was a more serious matter — his methodology. Commenting on a field report Royse had sent him from Chicago, Alsberg voiced the objection that some of the social-ethnic studies smacked too much of the academic approach. "For instance," he wrote, "under the Greek studies you have one of a 'professional nature.' What does that mean? Does that mean something the University of Chicago will like? In that case, it will probably be a dull affair. I hope you are impressing on the workers everywhere that these studies must really be human documents, otherwise they will become dry, academic pamphlets which nobody will read . . . I don't want to be discouraging but I am very much worried by the probability of getting a lot of research material which will be no good to the American public, and which will get no publisher . . ."

He also complained about an oral report by Katherine Dunham on the Negro cults of Chicago, which Alsberg had heard during a Chicago Project conference. Her extensive use of "current psychological patter" disturbed him. "For heaven's sake," he urged Royse, "get these people loosened up and get them to write about how people in these various groups live and half live. One example of an interesting family and its development from immigrant through first and second generations is worth a whole volume of generalizations based on statistical data." Afraid he had been too harsh, Alsberg concluded the letter with one of his characteristically philosophic musings: "I have a feeling that you don't entirely agree with me, since you are interested more in the scientific side of the subject. Of course, when one of these studies is completed, perhaps I shall be proved wrong."

The insinuation that he, Royse, was more of a scientist than a humanist triggered an indignant rebuttal. "Nothing really is farther from the stark truth, as many well-meaning folks at Harvard, Columbia, etc., will gladly tell you. I wish you had time to read some of the chapters of my "Minority Peoples of Europe." Nor it is out of place to repeat that my 'scientific' career has been considerably punctuated with journalistic labor, including two solid years as a reporter on the old *World* . . . I have felt that you distrust our method of collecting data, but it is difficult for me to see why a systematic method of gathering difficult material should affect the form of writing, even creative writing."

In the same letter Royse took swipes at some of the various state directors who had been complaining about him, mentioning in particular Harlan Hatcher, the director of the Ohio Project, who had found fault with the amount of "statistical data" gathered for a study of "The Rubber Town of Akron." * Royse promised there would be no trace of statistics in the study but "plenty of good reading, based on statistical material," and added: "The main reason Hatcher is dubious of the work is that Hatcher is a teacher of English, schooled in the Tarkington manner, somewhat timid of the world we live in. I've read two of his books, and think them *nice,* even praiseworthy, but certainly not a Farrell etc., let alone the more plunging writers. I know you like his local guidebooks, and agree that they

---

* Harlan Hatcher had published several novels and a critical work on the American novel before he joined the Project in 1937. In 1940, a year after he left the Project, he published a historical work, *The Buckeye Country: A Pageant of Ohio,* which became a best seller. He became president of the University of Michigan in 1951, and held that post until his retirement. The Writers' Project he directed was one of the most productive in the country. By 1941 it had published some fifty books and pamphlets, chiefly of a historical nature.

are well written, but I can't reconcile myself to the thought that we must limit ourselves to such stuff."

As for Katherine Dunham, Royse conceded that she had used "current psychological patter" in her conference report but only because she thought it was expected of her. He described her as "a very human person" and assured Alsberg that "if she writes up the stuff being collected, there will be some hot stuff for your enjoyment." Then, unable to conceal his resentment of John T. Frederick, the Illinois director who, he suspected, did not approve of him, he said that under Frederick's direction Miss Dunham "was being warped — against her own savage instincts, and they are savage, as Botkin can testify to, if he can be made to talk."

Unlike Botkin, Royse was rarely afflicted with any need for reticence. In the concluding paragraphs of his letter, he completely unburdened himself: "You ask whether I am impressing workers everywhere that these studies must be human documents. In reply I can say, with hand on heart, that I've grown haggard, spending day and night, doing what nobody previously has done. My job, it seems, has turned out to be courses of training for the staffs — as nobody has really been in personal contact with them except state directors too busy with routine work to spend days in the study groups. The workers are so bogged down with guidebooks, compiling stuff that no one can make much use of, and doing just the sort of 'academic accumulating' that you think we are doing, that it takes repeated sessions getting them to look at the world around them and writing in a natural way. I can also promise you that if my weary sessions have sunk in, there won't be any masses of 'accumulated research material.' The stuff we want is contemporary and human, although you may not believe it."

Alsberg replied with a conciliatory letter two weeks later in which he admitted that he may have been unfair. "My letter was not so much a criticism of what was being done as an expression of apprehension that, despite your efforts and mine in emphasizing the human aspects of our books, the local people might slip into the easy path of chewing over secondhand material and spewing out statistical and economic data. I am sure that if you keep on hammering at them, you will eventually get what you want."

But time was getting short for both Alsberg and Royse; virtually none of the studies they initiated and argued about were to reach a point of fruition. As Alsberg feared, the mass of material accumulated would remain unknown to the reading public. One of the chief difficulties was that both men operated as though the Writers' Project would continue indefinitely. If the thought that the Project might be drastically reduced or eliminated in the near future occurred to either of them, it did not influence their long-range plans. Royse's studies were further hindered by the numerous ethnic studies that had been initiated before his arrival, studies which claimed a great deal of his time and energies. There was also a serious lack of help; not enough Project workers could be spared from what most state directors considered their primary objective: the production of a state guide-book. Aside from all these factors, there was Royse's voracious appetite for establishing new projects and contacts and his reluctance to spend enough time in the Washington office reviewing the mass of social-ethnic material arriving that required his personal attention.

In his first year on the Writers' Project, Royse launched enough labor and ethnic studies to keep its personnel engaged for a full decade. Yet his mood was not always expansive. After initiating a study of Montana copper workers, he decided to drop it, explaining to Alsberg that "copper is so bitterly controversial, and the interests so powerful, that we would likely get into hot water no matter how hard we tried to steer clear of problems." Alsberg went along with Royse's proposal that the copper study be replaced by a study of Montana's livestock resources, material which could be incorporated into the history of grazing that the Project was undertaking in most of its western state offices.*

But the Montana Project had no intention of dropping the copper study, and resumed it soon after Alsberg's departure, when individual states were given greater jurisdiction over their choice of projects. Written chiefly by William Burke, *Copper Camp: Stories of the World's Greatest Mining Town, Butte,* was published in 1943 and proved to be one of the Project's most entertaining publications. Although the book does not ignore the labor-management problems that had worried Royse, its emphasis is on the juicy personalities involved in the rough-and-tumble story of the copper industry. They range from ruthless copper magnates to sporting girls who, after any evening's work, would have so many silver dollars tucked into their stockings "that it was all they could do to navigate." Royse's influence is visible in one of the most readable chapters in the

---

* A large amount of material on the history of grazing was gathered in Washington from various western states, but the manuscript, which was ready for final editing, disappeared during the last month of the Writers' Project.

book, "Men of the Mines," which deals with copper workers from all points of the country, as well as with Finns, Irish, Serbs, Cornishmen, Swedes, Norwegians, Welshmen, Canadians, Scots, Italians, Poles and Austrians.

The only published Project book in which Royse could claim some degree of participation was *The Albanian Struggle in the Old World and the New,* a product of the Massachusetts Project published in the summer of 1939, when Alsberg was being edged out of his post. Royse and Frank Manuel had worked hard to make the book a valid ethnic study, free of the defensive attitudes flawing the Project's previously published ethnic studies. Alsberg proved to be one of the most serious stumbling blocks in the final preparations of the manuscript. Worried that it might create trouble between our State Department and the Albanian government, he kept deleting some of the book's most interesting passages and requesting further rewriting. Shortly before the book was to go to press, Manuel, almost out of patience, wrote Alsberg: "I cannot hide my misgivings that with each revision much of the zest of the original manuscript is being squeezed out." Despite such fears, the book received favorable reviews, one from the *Saturday Review of Literature,* saying: "The effect of American industrial life upon the uprooted immigrants is analyzed with sympathy and skill, for the Project's field workers talked with the Albanians, read their newspapers and records, and understood their hopes and fears amidst a rapidly changing environment. Such an extraordinarily interesting study of one small element of our heterogeneous population makes it seem all the more regrettable that Congress should have curtailed the useful activity of the Federal Writers' Project."

The failure of the social-ethnic program to produce published books robbed our heritage of what undoubtedly would have been a series of profoundly enlightening studies conducted at an ideal time — while most of the nation's twentieth-century immigrants were still alive — by a nationwide agency with fact-gathering facilities that could not be duplicated by any private group or foundation. The few ethnic studies published in the final years of the Project would not have met with Royse's approval. One of them, *The Italians of Omaha* (1941), sponsored by the Order of the Sons of Italy of Omaha, Nebraska, was a grossly superficial account. *Bohemian Flats,* produced in the same year by the Minnesota Project, contained some fascinating material about a settlement of Bohemian, Irish, Lithuanian and Danish immigrants which the city of Minneapolis wiped out in 1923 to make room for wharves and railroad yards; although better written than most of the Project's ethnic studies, it suffered from undue brevity.

Royse outlasted Alsberg on the Project by one year, but there was little he could do within the framework of a drastically reduced Writers' Project now headed by a director who was more intent on completing the state guidebook series than in encouraging long-range investigations of how America lives. His policy was understandable but unfortunate, for it is quite possible that the series of books envisioned by Royse and Alsberg would have revealed the nation's soul more tellingly than the guidebooks.

For his unmitigated gall, for his long-winded yammerings that seemingly go "babbling" on forever, and for the strange power that he appears to have over Congress, I christen him "Bubble Dancer" Dies who cavorts lumberingly on the Congressional stage with nothing but a toy balloon with which to hide his intellectual nudity. To my mind, the most contemptible human being in public life is the one who will recklessly smear another's character and then wrap himself tightly in his Congressional immunity.

— Harold L. Ickes, *The Secret Diary of Harold L. Ickes,* 1954

Mr. Henry G. Alsberg, who was very frank with the Committee, admitted that some of this material which had been received from state offices was calculated to promote class hatred and he assured the Committee that before the final publication of the state guidebooks all material of this kind would be deleted and that state guidebooks would present a fair and impartial picture.

— Martin Dies, *The Martin Dies Story,* 1963

We were then in a transition period, without yet fully recognizing it, from the Great Depression to a defense economy. The fire had gone out of the New Deal, the WPA was undergoing liquidation, and the administration was not sticking out its neck on behalf of culture. So when the Dies Committee threw a custard pie at us, and Mrs. Woodward uttered a cry of injured innocence, we got a dozen more pies, not only thrown at us but thrust into us.

— Harold Coy, former chief editor of the Federal Writers' Project, in a letter to the author, February 7, 1968

I must express my deep concern and disappointment over the very un-American way in which the Committee has handled charges made against this project under my jurisdiction.

— Ellen S. Woodward, Assistant WPA administrator, to Congressman Dies at a hearing of the House Committee to Investigate Un-American Activities, December 5, 1938

Eight.

Congress Sees Red

For Alsberg and his aides the summer of 1938 was an especially anxious one. Although guidebooks were being published at a rapid and accelerating rate and receiving critical acclaim, the first shadows foretelling the extinction of the Federal Writers' Project began to be visible.

One of the portents of that painful summer was the unexpected resignation of Reed Harris, Alsberg's right-hand man. Harris's decision to quit shocked his boss. Although not yet thirty, he had developed the sagacity of a seasoned executive during his three years on the Washington staff. Alsberg trusted him above everyone else in the office — and with good reason. No one else was as consistently loyal to him, or as able to appreciate his worth as a creative force while ignoring his ineptitude as an administrator. No one else had done more to protect both Alsberg and the Writers' Project from a long series of threatening crises.

In the summer of 1938, however, Harris sensed the approach of a new crisis that would prove more formidable than any of the previous ones, and decided he wanted no part of it. His premonition was largely based on the disruptive activities of the leftwing radicals on the New York City Project. Although these activities had subsided in recent months to the point where the New York office was beginning to function productively, Harris believed that as long as the militant leftwingers responsible for past troubles continued to be on the staff, the entire Writers' Project would remain in a dangerously vulnerable position. A WPA rule, which clearly specified that no WPA employee could be dismissed on grounds of politi-

289

cal affiliation, prevented Alsberg from firing the troublemakers, Harris realized; but he strongly felt that Alsberg should insist on a tighter administration of the New York office, one that could eliminate its worst troublemakers.

Alsberg agreed with him in principle but, except for scolding some of the radical union leaders and warning them that their tactics might precipitate the closing of the Writers' Project, he took no other steps. The supervisors of the New York Project continued to operate as they had, without any undue interference from Washington. Part of this hands-off policy stemmed from Alsberg's belief that day-by-day labor relations matters in the field offices were not his responsibility; part of it from his reluctance to interfere with the authority of some of the men operating the New York City Project who were his personal friends.

Harris's resignation became effective July 1, 1938, just a month before the newly formed Dies Committee fired an opening salvo at the theater and writers' projects. In selecting them as its initial targets, the Committee was acting on the valid assumption that, despite the praise lavished on the work of the two projects, most Americans were either indifferent or unsympathetic to the problems of unemployed actors and writers, generally regarding them as loafers and troublemakers. When Congressman J. Parnell Thomas, a member of the Dies Committee, demanded at the end of July an investigation of the two projects on the basis of "startling evidence" in his possession and declared the projects to be "a hotbed of Communists" and "one more link in the vast and unparalleled New Deal propaganda machine," only a few protesting voices were heard. It was evident that the impending attack on the two projects would be used by the Dies Committee as a means of trying to discredit the entire New Deal; but most members of the press saw nothing wrong with that and were content to sit back and wait for the show to begin.

Congressman Thomas's blast was hardly the first of its kind to be directed at the Writers' Project. Two years before, the Eastern Division of the Republican National Committee had called the Federal Writers' Project "a festering sore of Communism" and accused it of serving as a vehicle for Communist propaganda. In the same audacious, smearing style that was to characterize the actions of the Dies Committee, the Republican National Committee had branded as "well-known Communists" several anti-Communist members of the Washington staff, among them Alsberg himself. Uninhibited by any regard for truth, it had also charged that the *Red Pen,* the Communist party publication issued by Communists on the New York City Writers' Project, was "published by the Project at government expense."

There was also the censorship furore created by the publication of the Massachusetts Guide the year before, whose repercussions were felt throughout the land. Quick to enter that fray was a New York City group known as the National Civic Federation, which in a letter to President Roosevelt had charged that the entire Federal Writers' Project was dominated by Communist sympathizers whose principal interest was political agitation. In an earlier letter, Ralph M. Easley, chairman of the group, had alleged that among the supervisors of the Writers' Project were "men repeatedly convicted for the sale of obscene literature, habitual drunkards, former bootleggers and commission salesmen of questionable goods, and similiar types." In his long letter, to which the New York *Times* devoted almost two columns of space, Easley had cited statistics of a survey which purported that 81 percent of the Writers' Project employees were members of the leftwing Workers Alliance and that members of the Communist party or avowed supporters of the party numbered 42 percent. The same survey, Easley claimed, indicated that 79 percent of the Project jobs were filled by "people who have never made a living through writing and have no record of ever publishing a line." What had made Easley's charges immediately suspect was his further charge that to date (July 19, 1937) the Project had spent twenty million dollars without producing a single publication. Not only had he grossly exaggerated the cost of the Project but he also revealed his ignorance of the fact that the Project had already produced some one hundred books and pamphlets and scores of others were on the presses.*

In his letter Easley had presented himself as a friend of the New Deal. He told the President that his organization had "definite proof" of numerous cases where Mrs. Roosevelt, "in the kindness of her heart," had recommended the retention on the Project of certain individuals who had convinced her of their eligibility and need but that "her kindness had been of no avail." He had added: "It has come to the point where the impartial recommendations of the First Lady of the land are thrown into the waste basket by these communistic racketeers." While commending the Presi-

* See page 369 for the cost of the Writers' Project.

dent's purpose in establishing the Writers' and Theater Projects, Easley declared that "your principles have been perverted, your great ideals have been prostituted."

A director with fewer anxieties than Alsberg might have dismissed the Easley letter with a single contemptuous phrase, but because it had been directed to the President and received considerable attention in the press, Alsberg felt compelled to issue a rebuttal, which was even longer than the Easley statement. In it he ignored Easley's charges of radicalism and concentrated on the quantity and quality of the Project publications and on the competence of its staff. Citing the books published and on the press, Alsberg indicated that within three months there would be over two hundred books, aggregating more than twenty million words, "a series of publications twice the size of the American Dictionary of Biography, which required fifteen years to complete." He also pointed to the "almost universal praise" Project publications had received from critics and to the widespread demand for the guidebooks, as evinced by the popularity of the Lincoln City Guide, which sold sixteen thousand copies in six weeks, *Washington: City and Capital* which had almost sold out its first edition of eight thousand copies, the Galena City Guide, which sold fifteen hundred copies on the first day of publication, *Cape Cod Pilot,* which seemed headed for the best-seller lists, and others. To emphasize the growing acceptance of the Writers' Project by members of the Establishment, Alsberg listed some of the high-ranking public officials who were sponsoring Project publications, the prestigious credentials of some of the Project's state directors, the whole-hearted support of the publishing industry, and some of the literary honors garnered by writers during their association with the Project, which included three Guggenheim Fellowships.

Alsberg's statement, although published in a number of newspapers, did not deter the Dies Committee from regarding the Writers' Project (together with the Theater Project) as the soft underbelly of the WPA. The committee planned to accuse the Writers' Projects in Chicago, San Francisco and Boston of having known Communists on their staffs, but the target it had chiefly in mind was New York City. There it could reap the biggest headlines — headlines that were certain to be repeated throughout the nation to give the impression that the Federal Writers' Project was rife with Red activists. That the personnel on the New York City Project represented only 10 percent of the Writers' Project total staff was a significant detail but not one that the Dies Committee intended to explain or one that the nation's prevalently anti–New Deal press was likely to mention.

In its opening attack against the New York City Writers' Project the committee immediately grabbed front-page space and headlines by concentrating on the sensational testimony of Edwin P. Banta, a former member of the Writers' Project who, until two weeks before, had been a member of the Communist party. Banta, who was proud of his Colonial ancestry and belonged to the Sons of the American Revolution, was then a feeble old man of seventy with a paranoid personality, but all of his statements were accepted as gospel truth and went unchallenged.* The gist of his testimony was that the Communist party controlled 40 percent of the workers on the Writers' Project (no distinction was made between the New York City Project and the national Project) and that the Workers Alliance, under leftwing leadership, provided a clearinghouse for Project job applications which invariably favored Communists.

To buttress his charges, Banta turned over to the Dies Committee the prize exhibit of the hearing: a copy of *The People's Front* by Earl Browder, secretary of the American Communist Party, which had been presented to "Comrade Banta" by the Project's Communist party unit at a birthday party tendered to him by his colleagues. Banta, an indefatigable informer, had managed to persuade 106 of his fellow workers to sign the book.† A number of them added revolutionary-sounding sentiments to

* Following Banta's appearance before the Dies Committee, the Federal Writers' Project issued a brief which disputed many of his allegations about the New York Project's personnel. The brief contained a number of documents showing that Banta on several occasions had taken liberties with the truth.

† Recalling the episode in December 1950, while testifying before the Senate Armed Services Committee, James McGraw, who had been Banta's supervisor on the New York City Project, reported: "Mr. Banta told me at the time that he was a member of the Communist party, which I immediately said was none of my affair, in view of the fact that Congress had set up under WPA rules that no supervisor may at any time inquire into the political beliefs of employees . . . and I asked Mr. Banta to get to the point.

"He opened a book, which had been written by Earl Browder and signed by numerous members of the Federal Writers' Project and said: 'This is my birthday and the Project people have given me this book as a present. I would be greatly honored if you would sign it and I would be more honored if you would sign this card.' Whereupon, he produced a membership card of the Communist party. He said, 'This would be the biggest birthday present I have ever had,' and I said, 'Mr. Banta, you are going to have the biggest birthday present you ever had at this moment, because if you don't get out of this office immediately I'm going to throw you out bodily.'

"It was a bit ludicrous. Mr. Banta at the time was some seventy years old, doddering, and had been dismissed by me three times previously for incompetence and their signatures; but no one ever knew how many of the signers had read the incriminating inscription that headed the list of names: "Presented to Comrade Edwin Banta by the members of the Federal Writers' Project Unit No. 36-S, Communist party of the U.S.A., and in recognition of his devotion to and untiring efforts in behalf of our party and communism. March 2, 1938." Without giving any of the signers the opportunity to be heard, the Dies Committee branded all of them as Communists; and, again without explaining that it was speaking only of the New York City Project, categorically charged that one third of all the members of the Federal Writers' Project were also members of the Communist party.

A month before his committee began its hearings, Congressman Dies had issued a press statement brimming with noble sentiments and resolution, in which he announced his determination to conduct the investigations on "a dignified plane" and "to adopt and maintain throughout the course of the hearings a judicial attitude." He had added that his committee would "not permit any character assassination or any smearing of innocent people . . . The chair is more concerned with facts than with opinions, and with specific proof than with generalities."

Once the committee began its hearings, these angelic intentions went out the window. Providing the press with spicy copy became the foremost consideration. Reckless charges were permitted to go unchallenged; there was no semblance of judicial procedure. Undisturbed by any of this, the newspapers had a headline feast. During the Dies Committee's first six weeks of hearings, the New York *Times* gave it more than five hundred column inches of space. Other newspapers were even more generous. Except for a few leftwing periodicals, no newspaper criticized the tactics of the committee. Most readers of the daily press were given the impression that the Dies Committee was performing a distinctly patriotic service. Eventually, the committee was to win the support of three quarters of the newspaper reading public, a distinction seldom achieved by any congressional committee.

Following Banta's testimony, Ellen S. Woodward wrote Congressman Dies a respectful letter expressing surprise that Dies had not as yet called on any of the responsible administrative officials in charge of the projects, despite their offer to cooperate with his committee. "I believe that it is the

---

crackpotism; for interfering with matters that were in no way any concern of his; and I took the thing as a huge joke, and at the time told the story around with some glee."

*Edwin P. Banta testifying before the Dies Congressional Committee
on Un-American Activities*

American practice that all parties should be given an opportunity to be
heard when an investigation of this character is under way." There followed a defense of the Writers' Project employment policies, which
pointed out that political convictions could not, by congressional decree,
be the basis for hiring or firing personnel. "Persons are employed on the
Project for two reasons only. First, because of need and eligibility for relief, and, secondly, because of qualifications as writers, journalists, or research workers, to do the job that is to be done."

The letter was ignored as the Dies Committee kept capturing front-
page space by summoning one anti-Project witness after another. The witness that followed Banta was Ralph De Sola, a young Project supervisor
who had originally recruited Banta into the Communist party. De Sola,
who was to become the Dies Committee's star witness against the Writers'
Project, had, like Banta, broken with the Communists and been featured

on the front page of the *Daily Worker* as "an enemy of the working class." Like Banta, De Sola began his testimony by trying to impress the Dies Committee with the American character of his genealogical tree. "My antecedents on my mother's side were Pennsylvania Germans and Huguenots, who came here in 1732 . . . My father and a number of cousins came in 1896. We have been American citizens ever since."

Although Banta and De Sola had much in common, they were of a different stripe. Banta had joined the Communist party in his sixties for the express purpose of acting as an informer. De Sola, who was considerably younger, more idealistic and talented, had become a Communist out of his disenchantment with capitalism. After taking some courses at Swarthmore College and Columbia University, he had become part owner of a zoological garden in Miami, but the venture failed and left him deeply in debt. Unable to find a steady job, he had become a counselor in a summer camp at Ripton, New York, which was operated for a group of leftwing trade union organizations. At the Pioneer Youth Camp, as it was called, De Sola had "immediately come into an atmosphere where everything connected with the crisis, and particularly with my own predicament, was explained in terms of Marxian economics." He had joined the Communist party soon afterwards and, about a year later, had become a relief worker in the New York City office of the recently formed Federal Writers' Project. Although inclined to quarrel with his party and Project superiors, he had worked assiduously both as a Communist and as a Project employee.*

De Sola claimed that he had severed his connection with the Communist party because "the idealistic ends that I hoped could be achieved through communism were nonexistent . . . the program of the party and its actions and tactics bore no relation whatsoever to the welfare of this country." A less high-minded explanation was provided by Helen Winner, who had been his wife and a fellow Communist while they were both on the Project. De Sola, she told a congressional committee, "was always at loggerheads with the people who were running things, in one way or an-

---

* As a Writers' Project employee, De Sola's knowledge of zoology stood him in good stead. Promoted to the rank of supervisor, he and a group of assistants produced the New York Project's first substantial publication, *Who's Who in the Zoo* (1937). In the next three years De Sola and his unit were responsible for three more popular zoological publications, *The Birds of the World* (1938), *Reptiles and Amphibians* (1939) and, the biggest seller of the series, *American Wild Life* (1940).

other," and was constantly "being summoned for disciplinary action of one sort or another . . . By degrees, he began to get very disaffected."

De Sola's long career as an informer indicates that he had his own subjective, and often opportunistic concept of truth, which sometimes smacked of pure fantasy. But at no time during his Dies Committee testimony did anyone question his integrity. He spoke with an intimate knowledge of the Communist activities in the New York City office of the Project, and he identified a number of his Project colleagues as Communists. Throughout his testimony he exuded an aura of impeccable fairness. At one point he remarked that the Project Communists were quite justified in attacking Edwin Banta for addressing a meeting of the Nazi-minded German-American Bund. And at the close of his initial appearance before the Dies Committee, he expressed the pious hope that "in any recommendation that you gentlemen make to Congress you will not put in anything restricting the legal activity of these people [Communists] because, while I am against everything they stand for, if these people are maltreated as they have maltreated other people when they have held power, it is quite evident that the liberty of ourselves may be threatened at some future date. If we set a precedent of that nature, I feel that the liberty of America is at stake."

De Sola even defended the Writers' Project against Congressman Dies's accusation that the Project guides were serving as vehicles of leftwing propaganda; that the Washington office was guilty of inserting into the manuscripts from the states "material along the line of class struggle and class hatred," and was instructing the field offices to expand their material to that effect. De Sola firmly disagreed. "I question that very much," he told Dies. "In the early days of my editorship, we received quite contrary instructions, which very much alarmed me as a loyal Communist, that we were not to class-angle anything."

As a result of the high marks he won for his performance before the Dies Committee, De Sola became a favorite source of information for various federal agencies and congressional committees concerned with the subversive activities of government employees. For the next twelve years he had a busy time providing government investigators with names of persons whom he claimed to be members of the Communist party. By his own testimony, he had hundreds of conferences "with investigators from all kinds of government agencies," 125 of them with representatives of the

Federal Bureau of Investigation. In his eagerness to supply them with leads, he became increasingly careless in branding as Communists government employees who had never been Communists.

In one instance, he informed the FBI that the then public relations director of the Department of Justice, James Allen, was a prominent Communist. It would have been an easy matter to ascertain that the James Allen he had in mind, a Communist author living in New York City, was not the same Allen employed by the Department of Justice. But De Sola, emboldened by the frequency with which government investigators were consulting him, did not bother to check; nor did the FBI, on learning of his carelessness, cease to consult with him.

In 1950, however, he perpetrated his most sensational lie, and his career as a public informer came to an end. Before the Senate Armed Services Committee, which was then conducting hearings on the nomination of Anna M. Rosenberg for the post of Assistant Secretary of Defense, De Sola repeatedly insisted that at a meeting of the John Reed Club Mrs. Rosenberg had been pointed out to him as a member of the Communist party. He also claimed that James McGraw, Chief Project Supervisor in the New York office and "also a Communist Party member," had told him that Mrs. Rosenberg was responsible for passing on the appointments of Jacob Baker, Henry Alsberg, Aubrey Williams "and others who were notoriously liberal in their hiring of well-known Communists."

In one of the most dramatic confrontations reported in the *Congressional Record,* De Sola and Mrs. Rosenberg were brought face to face by the Armed Services Committee which included such prominent senators as Wayne Morse, Lyndon Johnson, William Knowland, and Leverett Saltonstall. Before the confrontation took place Mrs. Rosenberg, testifying under oath, called De Sola "a liar," saying, "It is inhuman what has been done to me in the past few days . . . I have never been a member of the John Reed Club; I have never been a Communist; I have never sympathized with the Communists . . . I tried to think: Where do I know this man? How do I know him from some place? How can a human being do this to someone? What can he have against me? I don't know him."

Mrs. Rosenberg was understandably distraught. She had held important posts with the National Recovery Administration, the Social Security Board, and the War Manpower Commission. As a personal representative of Presidents Roosevelt and Truman, she had visited Europe to report on the problems of returning veterans. Now, as a result of De Sola's accusation, the press was broadly suggesting that she, who had been one of the most trusted officials of the New Deal, had been a Communist all along.

When De Sola was brought into the same room with Mrs. Rosenberg, Senator Knowland, repeating a point that other members of the committee had put to De Sola previously, raised the possibility of mistaken identity. He asked De Sola how he could definitely identify Mrs. Rosenberg who, according to his testimony, he had talked with only once fifteen years before. "That was a long time ago, and I think I would have great difficulty remembering people whom I had casually met fifteen years ago . . ."

But De Sola was positive Mrs. Rosenberg was the same person he had seen several times and spoken to briefly at John Reed Club meetings, "the very woman . . . that I kept hearing about, and leading comrades at Communist headquarters kept telling about doing such a valuable job."

In their confrontation Mrs. Rosenberg asked De Sola where and when he had seen her in the John Reed Club.

De Sola: At the various meetings they had in the summer, the late summer and fall of 1934 and 1935. They were along Sixth Avenue between Eighth Street and Fourteenth Street . . .

Mrs. Rosenberg: And I spoke with you?

De Sola: Yes, you spoke about the growth of the John Reed Club and what an excellent device it had been for a sounding board for Communist propaganda and as a recruiting ground.

Mrs. Rosenberg: Mr. De Sola, I don't believe that any human being wants to do what you are doing purposely. Please come and look at me carefully and see whether you know me from my pictures or you actually know me. You came into the room and you said, "This is the woman." You never looked at me. Do you know what you are doing to me?

De Sola: I am looking at you and I am looking at you now.

Mrs. Rosenberg: And am I the woman that you sat next to or talked to in the John Reed Club?

De Sola: We stood up when we talked. Would you mind standing up?

Mrs. Rosenberg: I will stand up. Now tell me, am I the woman in the John Reed Club?

De Sola: Yes, ma'am, you are; I am sorry to say so.

Mrs. Rosenberg: And all these years you never found that out and you never told it to the Dies Committee? What made you tell it now, please tell me?

De Sola: Because I am sorry to see that we have a Secretary of Defense who has to be assisted by a Communist. I am sorry for our country. If you had been put in a social-security agency where it was just a question of some sort of social work, social-welfare work, I could have said cynically to myself, "Well, those people get there anyway, and she can't do too much harm," and the defense agency is . . .

Chairman: Just a moment. We will proceed in an orderly way.

Mrs. Rosenberg: I have no questions to ask this man. I would like to get on the record, Mr. Chairman, that I have never seen this man in my life . . . I have no recollection of ever seeing his face.

In a subsequent session the committee heard James McGraw testify that he had never been a member of the Communist party, had never attended any meetings of the John Reed Club, and had never met or seen Mrs. Rosenberg. In an affidavit he presented to the committee, McGraw declared that as De Sola's superior on the Writers' Project for several years, he had found him to be "a person of extreme dishonesty and one who would stop at nothing for bits of notoriety in which he could stand out. He has shown time and again his love for personal publicity and went to ridiculous means to obtain such on many occasions." Questioned by the senators, McGraw cited several instances of De Sola's propensity for telling lies.

The final witness, who left no doubt in the committee's mind that De Sola was not telling the truth about Mrs. Rosenberg, was George J. Starr, a retired FBI agent, who had dealt with De Sola on numerous occasions in his capacity as an agent. Ironically, it was De Sola himself who had suggested to the committee that Starr be summoned as a witness. He was confident that Starr would confirm his testimony that in 1937 he had told him of his meeting with Mrs. Rosenberg at the John Reed Club. But Starr did nothing of the kind. Although he seemed kindly disposed toward De Sola, he was quite certain that De Sola had never mentioned the name of Anna M. Rosenberg to him; nor could he recall that anything pertaining to the John Reed Club had come up during their discussions.

After listening to Starr, the committee quickly approved Mrs. Rosenberg's nomination. The Senate then confirmed it, and she held the post of Assistant Secretary of Defense during the next three years of President Truman's term of office. For Mrs. Rosenberg the experience with De Sola had been a searing nightmare but one which, thanks to a patient and fair-minded committee that had sat through 332 printed pages of testimony, she had managed to survive. For her accuser the resolution of the episode may have ended a dream of glory.

In De Sola's fantasy, he may well have cast Mrs. Rosenberg in the role of another Alger Hiss and himself in the role of a second Whittaker Chambers who would win fame and fortune for exposing a Communist about to occupy a high-level government post.* In one of his most revealing statements before the committee, he had said: "Can our defenses — military, social, and economic — withstand an attack from within by Anna Rosenberg and her minions? Is America really so great and strong that she can survive with such personnel within the Pentagon? The very brilliance of Mrs. Rosenberg, her record of achievement, as fine if not finer than that of Alger Hiss, is in itself a threat because of the many good connections she will use in defending her position and in subverting the work of any agency into which she or her appointees enter, be it in the field of public welfare, social security, or national defense."

By insisting that Mrs. Rosenberg was a Communist, De Sola had aimed high and lost. For although his testimony brought him a great deal of newspaper publicity and the undivided attention of some of the nation's outstanding senators, including a future President of the United States, his avocation as an informer appeared to be finished. Not even that direct descendant of the Dies Committee, the McCarthy Committee, for all of its brazen maneuvers, dared make public use of De Sola's services.

In 1938 De Sola's motivation in being a witness was of a somewhat purer strain. Understandably, he felt hostile toward the men and women on the Project who had once called him comrade but who, once he left the Communist party, described him as a stool pigeon, rat, fascist, and enemy of the working class. He welcomed the opportunity offered by the Dies Committee to get back at them and, at the same time, protect the future of his Project job by officially establishing his position as an anti-Communist. He accomplished both aims with consummate skill, impressing both members of the Dies Committee and the press with his articulate and objective-sounding statements about the Project and the Communist party.

Other witnesses who testified before the Dies Committee during its early sessions were more obvious about their antagonism toward the Writers' Project, especially Project employees who were invited to meet with members of the committee in secret session. As part of his strategy to initiate his attack on the Writers' Project with a hard offensive, Dies and Congressman Noah Mason, a member of his committee, met in executive

---

* Alger Hiss had been sentenced to prison in January 1950. De Sola testified before the Senate Armed Services Committee in December of the same year.

session with two women and a young man who were members of the Washington staff. The secret session took place four days before De Sola's initial public appearance before the Dies Committee.

One of the women, Mrs. Louise Lazelle, had been hired by Mrs. Woodward fourteen months earlier as the Project's "policy editor," presumably to make certain that nothing "subversive" crept into the guidebook copy edited in the Washington office. The appointment had been precipitated by the attacks on the Massachusetts Guide for containing passages favorable to labor and to the Sacco-Vanzetti case. But Mrs. Lazelle's role on the Project was more complicated than it first appeared to be. According to Drew Pearson and Robert S. Allen, she was a "stooge" of Mrs. Woodward, "who had taken the amazing course of sending Mrs. Lazelle to testify before the Dies Committee in executive session against the WPA project which she herself was administering." A more logical interpretation of Mrs. Lazelle's relationship with Mrs. Woodward was offered by Harold Coy, then chief editor of the Project's Washington staff. "What Mrs. Woodward apparently did not know, wrote Coy, was that her spy was a double agent, also working with Dies to undermine the whole Project, including Mrs. Woodward herself."

The other Project woman who gave secret testimony to the Dies Committee was Mrs. Florence D. Shreve, a former agent for the McCormick Committee on Un-American Activities, who was in charge of copyreading and proofreading all galley proofs of the guidebooks supervised by the Washington office.

Mrs. Lazelle, the first to testify, charged that Alsberg was responsible for inserting in the state guides "Communist teachings or phraseology," which she had no authority to delete. She found particular fault with "Communistic" statements present in the manuscripts for the New Jersey and Montana state guides.

Dies: These statements were appeals to class hatred?

Mrs. Lazelle: Yes.

Dies: Inflammatory statements?

Mrs. Lazelle: Inflammatory statements.

Dies: Did any of them go so far as to advocate revolution?

Mrs. Lazelle: No.

Dies: Did any of them go so far as to advocate complete changes in our system of government?

Mrs. Lazelle: No; only criticism. No, they would not go that far . . .

Dies: Would you say that any of the material as finally approved by the Washington office or by Mr. Alsberg constituted appeals to class hatred?

Mrs. Lazelle: Yes; definitely.

As the interview progressed, Mrs. Lazelle's charges became more sweeping. When Dies asked her whether Alsberg had revealed himself as a Communist sympathizer in his statements to her, she replied "not directly," but added as her "personal comment" that Alsberg and Joseph Gaer, "who is his right-hand man in many things," were "working now toward a Communist organization" in which key positions throughout the country "will be given to Communists."

Dies: Did Mr. Gaer ever make any statement to you to lead you to believe he was a member of the Communist party?

Mrs. Lazelle: No. He only fights me on every point in which I endeavor to smooth things out.

Dies: Has he ever made any radical or revolutionary statements to you?

Mrs. Lazelle: No, indeed. The only statement that I understood he made was that I was a dangerous Nazi. I happen to be a niece of General Zachary Taylor, once President of the United States, and I am about as much of a Nazi as he was.

Dies: Do you think Mr. Alsberg is deliberately bringing into the department as many radicals as he can?

Mrs. Lazelle: I don't know whether he is doing it under orders or voluntarily.

Dies: But is he doing it?

Mrs. Lazelle: It has seemed to us for a long while that he was bringing in such persons.

Toward the end of the session, Congressman Mason asked her: "Would you say that the Federal Writers' Project is being used by a group of radicals to propagandize the states through the use of these guides?"

Mrs. Lazelle: I do; and that is just the beginning.

Mason: And that unless we get rid of those who have the control of the Federal Writers' Project, that is exactly what will be accomplished by the issuing of these guides?

Mrs. Lazelle: Very soon.

When it came her turn to testify, Mrs. Shreve said she had tried to do her best as the Washington staff's copyreader but that "suddenly one day all that work was taken away from me, with not a particle of warning, and I was told that I was a Fascist and must not be allowed to handle copy because I would attempt to write terrible things in it. I had been taking out the little subtle things . . ."

Dies: What had you been taking out? Just characterize it.

Mrs. Shreve: Oh, the struggle between capital and labor; that the Negro had been downtrodden; and always — there was a word that they used . . .

Mrs. Lazelle: Underprivileged.

Mrs. Shreve: That is it — underprivileged; the underprivileged Negro. Those subtle little things were coming in quietly at the time. They were just creeping in. At first I was thinking that there were just certain stray writers that were a little bit prejudiced . . .

Dies: What do you mean by "things creeping in"?

Mrs. Shreve: Propaganda.

Dies: What kind of propaganda?

Mrs. Shreve: Radical labor propaganda, subtle propaganda which the Communists now use to promote prejudice between capital and labor . . .

Mrs. Shreve told Dies that "very often" the original manuscripts, as approved by Mrs. Lazelle, "had been altered somewhere along the line, and the proofs [of the manuscripts] would be a little different." She also described a contretemps she had with Alsberg after she had objected to some of the guidebook copy for Montana. Alsberg told her, in effect, that it was none of her business. The upshot of her complaints to the director was that a week before her committee appearance she was notified that her services on the Project would be terminated. "I asked Mr. Alsberg what his reason was, and he said, 'Constantly exceeding your authority.'

"I do not know how my family will eat," Mrs. Shreve continued, "but it does not make any difference. He [Alsberg] has taken my job away from me because I have been fighting for a principle."

"You have been fighting to keep communistic influences from getting into the publications of the government," Dies said.

Encouraged by the congressman's sympathetic attitude, Mrs. Shreve played her trump card, asserting that the copy for the New Jersey Guide was "the most flagrant of all." She said that it had been seized from her office by the Project's managing editor and returned after a week with "pages of notations to be inserted . . . and every one of those new notations is inflammatory."

The insertions Mrs. Shreve considered inflammatory were the following statements:

> Five months of strike in 1935 meant higher wages and the 36-hour week for members of the industrial union of the merchant shipbuilding workers of America.
>
> The entire structure is 8,536 feet long; it took 4½ years to build and cost $40,000,000. Thirteen workmen were killed in a series of accidents typical of those that occur on any large construction job.
>
> Settlement was made by agreement for an election, through which the union won exclusive bargaining rights. The LaFollette Civil Liberties Committee reported the expenditure of large sums for strikebreaking and espionage in the strike and pre-strike period. Since that time the company has signed with the union a contract providing for a scale of pay that is one of the highest in the industry . . .

Dies: Have you any more excerpts?

Mrs. Shreve: Those are all.

Dies: I think you have given us a pretty good idea of what is going on down there . . . From your experience and contacts and observations, do you feel that the Federal Writers' Project is being converted into an agency to spread communism?

Mrs. Shreve: Yes.

Emboldened by Dies's eagerness to damn the Writers' Project as a vehicle of subversive propaganda, Mrs. Shreve then presented some testimony based on hearsay to the effect that in a telephone conversation an applicant for a Project job had been recommended to Alsberg "for meritorious service to the party." Mrs. Shreve had no indication of what "party" was meant, though she was quite willing to assume that it was the Communist party. But this was going too far, even for Dies, who said to her: "Let us not have testimony based on hearsay."

Mrs. Shreve's concluding contribution was the suggestion that Dies subpoena the galley proofs of the New Jersey Guide, which were at the Viking Press. She promised that they would provide him with "the grandest evidence you can ever want." Mrs. Lazelle agreed with her, pointing out that, contrary to the usual procedure, the galley proofs had not been sent to her for checking the new material; nor had they been sent to Mrs. Woodward for her approval.

Four days later Dies announced to the press that in a secret session with "public officials" his committee had obtained evidence that "Communist phraseology had been inserted in guides from the states and in the office here in Washington," adding that the inserted material was "along lines of class struggle and class hatred." Following this announcement, he somehow came into possession of the galley proofs of the labor essays for the New Jersey and Montana guidebooks (presumably they were taken from the Washington office by one of the three witnesses who had given secret testimony) and ordered them inserted into the committee's record.*

When this action did not produce as much publicity as he had expected, Dies went one step further and issued a subpoena ordering that all the galley proofs of the New Jersey and Montana guidebooks be seized from the publishers. Although he must have realized that the paragraphs Mrs. Shreve had quoted were hardly "inflammatory," he was shrewd enough to know that the mere act of ordering the galley proofs seized would automatically suggest to the public that the Writers' Project must be guilty of using the guidebooks as instruments of propaganda.†

The publicity given to Dies's charges may have hastened the departure of Mrs. Irene Fuhlbruegge as director of the New Jersey Writers' Project. Shortly after the charges were made public, Mrs. Fuhlbruegge, who had distinguished herself as one of the Project's most efficient and productive state directors, informed Alsberg that the resignation she had submitted two months earlier, which she had been persuaded to postpone, was to take effect immediately. "Inefficiency in the Washington office," rather than the charges made by Dies, was the reason she gave for refusing to continue in office any longer.

There were other repercussions. The attack on the New Jersey and

---

* The third witness who secretly testified, along with Mrs. Louise Lazelle and Mrs. Florence D. Shreve, was Jeremiah Tax, a twenty-three year old proofreader on the Project's Washington staff, an assistant to Mrs. Shreve. During his testimony Tax declared himself to be "rabid" on the subject of Communist subversion, and offered to obtain from the Project office whatever galley proofs the committee required. Dies, speaking for the record, turned down the offer.

† The Dies Committee also subpoenaed manuscripts from the Project's Washington office, according to Harold Coy, its former chief editor. "I had the privilege, in response to a subpoena, of riding in Mrs. Woodward's limousine with her chauffeur to Dies's office," he wrote the author. "The files of the suspect material were so voluminous that they must have overawed the congressman, for the material was eventually returned with no visible signs of having been screened."

Montana guides caused Alsberg and his staff to reexamine the material for the two books and delete anything that smacked of bias. For the most part, the passages cited by Dies as examples of leftwing bias were permitted to stand. The few deletions made, over the protests of the New Jersey Guild Associates (the official sponsoring body for the guidebook) were ordered on the grounds that they might be libelous.*

The Dies Committee's reckless charges against the Theater and Writers' Projects, along with its flagrant disregard of the judicial process, had a demoralizing effect on the employees of both projects and anguished their directors. The committee was obviously attacking the two projects as a means of discrediting the New Deal; yet at the White House the main reaction was simply one of contempt.† Perhaps in the belief that given enough rope the committee would soon hang itself, neither Hopkins nor Roosevelt would take it seriously during its early months. Their attitude permeated the ranks of the WPA hierarchy and ruled out the possibility of launching a counterattack. Although their superiors gave Alsberg and Hallie Flanagan permission to require a hearing before the Dies Committee, they would not permit them to issue statements refuting the specific charges made against their projects. Emmet Lavery, a playwright friend of Mrs. Flanagan, complained in a letter to her: "Day after day hearsay testimony floods the newspapers of our country, so that slander and libel thrive on the simple fact of their constant repetition and our administrative control does nothing; does nothing so consistently that any impartial lawyer might think we were all getting ready to plead guilty and throw ourselves to the mercy of the courts!"

In the hope that Dies would soon honor their requests for a hearing, Alsberg and Mrs. Flanagan worked frantically preparing briefs that refuted the charges being made in the press. Alsberg was aided by George McMillan, one of his young staff members, who acted as a liaison between

---

* The New Jersey Guide, published by the Viking Press in June 1939, was praised by literary critics and sold five thousand copies. The second edition, published in 1946 by Hastings House, included a statement by the New Jersey Guild Associates praising the book but calling attention to facts that were "stricken from the original manuscript in 1938 at the instigation of the Dies Committee."

† Except for two Democrats (John J. Dempsey of New Mexico and Arthur D. Healey of Massachusetts), the Dies Committee consisted of congressmen who were openly antagonistic to the New Deal. The most aggressive of them was J. Parnell Thomas, a Republican of New Jersey who later went to jail for defrauding the United States Government. Thomas was credited with the classic comment that the labor essay in the New Jersey state guide "is written as if there had been trouble between labor and capital."

the Writers' Project and David Niles, an administrative assistant to Harry Hopkins who helped to formulate WPA public relations policies. At one of his meetings with Niles, Hopkins was quoted as saying that as far as he was concerned, Alsberg and Mrs. Flanagan had his permission "to go up and spit in the faces of the Dies Committee."

Dies ignored the requests for a hearing until the middle of October when he had just landed on the front pages of the nation's press with the dramatic proclamation that the workers in the Federal Theater and Writers' Project were "doing more to spread Communist propaganda than the Communist party itself." At that point the two directors were promised that they would receive hearings, but were not told when they would occur. Not until President Roosevelt launched a blistering attack on the committee's tactics during the November election campaign (the White House had finally begun to note the destructive political influence of the committee on New Deal candidates) did Dies fix a specific date in early December for the hearings.

For reasons never explained, Hopkins at the last moment ruled that the briefs prepared for the Writers' and Theater projects were not to be presented by their directors but by his assistant, Mrs. Woodward, in her capacity as director of the Women's and Professional projects, the parent agency of the four arts projects. It was not a happy decision for anyone, except for Martin Dies and his committee who ripped into the lady from Mississippi.

Parnell Thomas began the onslaught by questioning Mrs. Woodward's ability to speak for Mrs. Flanagan and Alsberg. She told the committee that while the two directors would be glad to answer any questions its members wished to put to them, she was the responsible officer in charge of their projects and would refute the charges that had been made against them. At the start of her testimony she tried to take the offensive by reminding the committee that under the law no test of political affiliation could be applied to workers hired from relief rolls. And throughout the session she kept questioning the committee's assumption that Project workers were members of the Communist party simply because they had been so identified by committee witnesses. She emphatically denied that there had been any communistic activity on either of the projects.

A valiant and sometimes tenacious witness, at one point Mrs. Woodward amazed the committee by declaring it "un-American" and criticizing it for listening to many witnesses who "were disqualified by their background to testify on the subject matter under investigation." However, the points she scored were smothered under a heavy barrage of cross-examination by Dies, Thomas, Starnes, and Mosier, the likes of which had never before been heard in Dies Committee sessions. The committee proved that, when it wished to do so, it could effectively challenge statements made by witnesses. As an observer in the audience later noted, if the same methods of thorough cross-examination had been used on witnesses such as De Sola and Banta, the charges made by the two men might have been reduced to feeble accusations.

The committee demonstrated that Mrs. Woodward was in no position to refute the charges made against the two projects, chiefly because she was not sufficiently informed. Although George McMillan was by her side to provide whatever information she did not know, it became evident that she was too unfamiliar with the operations of the projects to cope with the questions asked of her.

When Congressman Starnes asked her "about this book called *American Stuff* which Morris Ernst edited," she could not correct him by pointing out that Ernst was not an editor but a prominent New York lawyer who was one of the book's sponsors. And when the committee heard her read glowing reviews of a Theater Project play, they questioned her knowledge of the play until she was forced to admit that she had not read it.

Making much ado about *American Stuff*, the committee asked if she had read one of the selections, Richard Wright's "Ethics of Living Jim Crow." Again the answer was no. Mrs. Woodward tried to explain that *American Stuff* was not typical of the Writers' Project publications; it represented off-time work encouraged by the Project administration as a means of furthering the rehabilitation of writers hit by the Depression. But Congressman Starnes insisted that the anthology had been prepared during office hours and that there was nothing "rehabilitating" about it. He proceeded to read passages from Wright's contribution which included such words as "son of a bitch" and "fu — kin" (spelled in that manner). Starnes refused to read the latter word aloud. "I will supply that word for the stenographer because I don't like to use such a word." Dies's comment was: "That is the most filthy thing I have seen." Starnes asked Mrs. Woodward: "Do you find anything rehabilitating in that, I ask you?" To which she replied, "I think it is filthy and disgusting . . ."

The temper of the committee members rose perceptibly when Mrs. Woodward, reading from a prepared text, began discrediting Edwin P.

Banta as a reliable witness. She first quoted from a letter he had written the publisher William Randolph Hearst, Jr., which protested the *Journal American*'s failure to report a speech Banta had made at a meeting of the American Patriots, and implied that the rightwing Hearst papers must be controlled by the Communists. She then tried to introduce into the record a letter from the Vanderbilt Clinic of New York reporting on Banta's physical and mental condition, which stated that "a tentative diagnosis of a paranoid condition was made."

Determined to defend the credibility of one of his star witnesses, Dies lashed into Mrs. Woodward's contention that the letter from the Vanderbilt Clinic implied there was anything wrong with Banta's mental condition. He challenged her to explain why, if he were mentally deranged, the Writers' Project continued to keep him on its rolls.

Mrs. Woodward: He was greatly in need according to his own statement and according to the records at the Home Relief Bureau of the municipality of New York. Therefore, we wanted to aid him if we possibly could. He was in the mentally handicapped section of the hospital.

Dies: Don't you think that the people who wrote this *American Stuff* were somewhat mentally handicapped, anybody that would bring such filth in a publication of this kind?

Mrs. Woodward: Well, Mr. Chairman, I don't think that is a question that should be brought in at this particular time.

Dies: All right. Pardon me.

Mrs. Woodward: It has nothing to do with Mr. Banta . . .

Dies: We want to be absolutely fair with you, Mrs. Woodward. But here you have made a statement that this man is mentally deranged. Naturally, I think we are entitled to know if you employ people on the Writers' Project and keep them there after you have had knowledge of their mental derangement.

Mrs. Woodward: Mr. Chairman, I said he had been treated for a mental disorder at the Vanderbilt Clinic according to their statement; and I only brought that out after you had insisted on it because I have merely the letter . . . I have other letters here that I don't know whether you want introduced or not. I have no idea . . .

Dies: You may introduce any letters that you want. Let us not have any implications that we don't want you to submit full proof, even though it goes far afield from the question of communism. But the point is this: You said "mental condition." Do you mean that you consider this man incompetent to testify before a committee? Is that what you mean?

Mrs. Ellen S. Woodward, assistant administrator of the Works Progress Administration

Congressman Martin Dies of Texas, chairman of the House Committee on Un-American Activities

Mrs. Woodward: Well, I think he was not qualified.

Dies: On account of his mental condition?

Mrs. Woodward: Well, on account of his lack of qualifications technically.

Dies: But you thought these people were sufficiently qualified, didn't you, to employ them?

Mrs. Woodward: We didn't put him in a policy-making job. We didn't put him in a high position. You must realize, Mr. Chairman and members of the Committee, that we are dealing with thousands upon thousands of people who are pretty well licked by this Depression.

Dies: We are not arguing that. We don't question that. But the point is you have made that intimation. You have used the words "mental condition." Now, do you mean that you consider this man mentally unfit to tell about his experiences and actual facts that he knew to be true on the Federal Writers' Project?

Mrs. Woodward: Well, I think that any testimony of his under the circumstances, Mr. Chairman and members of the Committee, should be very carefully checked after a person has been treated for some kind of mental disorder. Now, I think any fair person would say that.

Dies: Do you think we should receive documentary proof wherein some 106 persons out of 300 on your project signed their original names attesting membership and belief in communism? Do you think that type of testimony should be received from Mr. Banta?

Mrs. Woodward: Do I think that that should be received by Mr. Banta?

Dies: From Mr. Banta.

Mrs. Woodward: Do I think you should receive that fact from him?

Dies: Yes.

Mrs. Woodward: Well, I don't see how you could expect me to answer that question, because I don't quite understand what you are trying to get at.

Dies: What I am trying to get at is this: I am asking you this question: You say that this man in your opinion was not qualified to testify, or that his testimony should be received with . . .

Mrs. Woodward: Should be checked by going to the files and by talking with the responsible officials, none of which was done.

Dies: Don't you think that the best way to check it, when the witness is presented with a book by Earl Browder signed by 106 of the 300 employees? Don't you think that is a very definite check upon the accuracy of the witness' statement?

Mrs. Woodward: I don't think because their names are in that book means definitely they were Communists.

When Dies disputed her statement by reading the inscription in the Browder book, Mrs. Woodward replied: "I think it is all right for you to make that part of your record, Mr. Chairman. But I also think that I have a right to say to you that under the law we cannot inquire into the political affiliations of the people that receive benefits under this [WPA] act."

The repetition of this point had no effect on the committee members; they kept returning to the subject of Writers' Project Communists and Banta. Gradually, they elicited from her a reading of the letter from the Vanderbilt Clinic which established the point that "the tentative diagnosis of a paranoid condition" had been made of Banta in 1933 when it was noted that "it might be only a temporary state." Only then was the letter admitted into the record. During the rest of the questioning, Dies and his colleagues became even more acerbic and sometimes seemed intent on badgering the witness. Although Mrs. Woodward clung to her basic assertions, it became increasingly clear that she did not have a sufficient amount of firsthand information about the projects to fight anything but a losing battle.

During the luncheon recess Mrs. Woodward obtained permission from Hopkins's office to let Alsberg and Mrs. Flanagan appear before the committee. "While I would like the privilege of presenting this case because, after all, whatever has happened reflects on my administration of these Projects," she told the committee, "I have with me this afternoon Hallie Flanagan and Henry Alsberg, and they are here in person and if you, Mr. Thomas, or Mr. Anybody Else on the committee want to hear them, they are here."

But having tasted so much blood in the morning session the committee members could not resist keeping her on the stand the rest of the afternoon. Not until the next morning did they get to Alsberg and Mrs. Flanagan.

If the committee expected they could bamboozle Hallie Flanagan as they had Mrs. Woodward, they were in for a surprise. The "small, red-haired lady with the firm mouth and the ferocity of a roused lion," as John Houseman once described her, was more than a match for any of its members. She set the tone for her testimony when, asked by Dies what the duties of her position were, she replied that since August 29, 1935, she had been concerned with "combating un-American inactivity" by heading a project which provided jobs for inactive professional men and women who were on relief rolls.

Congressman Starnes tried to attack her on the grounds that after a visit to Russia she had praised the Russian theater as "live and vital"; but nothing came of that except a quarrel between himself and Congressman Dempsey, who objected to his tactic of interrupting the witness before she could reply to his questions. Starnes then cited an article she had published in *Theater Arts* titled "A Theater is Born," in which she spoke of the "theater of workers" that was taking hold in the United States. Mrs. Flanagan pointed out that the article was a report, not an expression of opinion. Starnes persisted by quoting a passage from the article which included the phrase "Marlowesque madness." He wanted to know about "this Marlowe," and asked: "Is he a Communist?" Kindly giving him the benefit of the doubt, Mrs. Flanagan explained she meant Christopher Marlowe. Starnes had obviously never heard of him and ordered her to "tell us who Marlowe is." To this, Mrs. Flanagan responded, "Put it in the record that he was the greatest dramatist in the period of Shakespeare, immediately preceding Shakespeare." Her statement evoked a shout of laughter from the audience and had the effect of silencing Starnes during the rest of that session.

Dies, who conducted most of the questioning, tried some of the same tough techniques he had used on Mrs. Woodward, but this time with little or no effect. Mrs. Flanagan fought him point by point, and when Dies tried to elicit answers from her based on hypothetical premises, she told him so. Unlike the witness, Dies found it difficult to keep his wits about him, so much so that at one point he confused the Writers' Project with the Theater Project, citing testimony by De Sola and Banta who had never been on the Theater Project. Mrs. Flanagan's performance as a witness was aggressive and knowledgeable without being disrespectful. It heartened the audience at the hearing, many of whom were employees of the WPA arts program; but actually nothing substantial was gained. When Mrs. Flanagan asked that her prepared brief be entered into the record, Dies was noncommittal; and when she asked for permission to make a closing statement, Dies said he would decide after lunch. But when that time came, Alsberg was introduced as the next witness, and Mrs. Flanagan's request was ignored.

Alsberg took the stand accompanied by George McMillan, who helped to wheel in a library truck packed with Writers' Project publications. The director appeared nervous and anxious, understandably so considering the committee's attitude toward the two previous witnesses. McMillan had reminded him what Hopkins had said about spitting in the faces of the committee members, but from the outset of his testimony it was apparent that Alsberg was determined to be friendly and cooperative. He succeeded beyond the expectations of everyone concerned, including Dies himself, who twice complimented him for his helpful attitude. Alsberg's strategy was a simple one: he established himself as an anti-Communist by attacking the Soviet Union as a dictatorship, and he frankly admitted experiencing considerable difficulties with the Communists on the New York City Project during the first two years of its existence.

At first Alsberg could barely be heard and Dies had to ask him to raise his voice, but as the committee began asking questions about his background, his voice grew stronger and his poise improved. After outlining his career as a journalist and literary man, he suggested that the committee permit him to describe his personal history in relation to the Communists, in order to make it "quite clear than I am the very opposite of a Communist." With considerable pride he told of editing a book of letters written by political prisoners in Russian prisons, "which, at the time, was considered the most devastating attack on the tyrannical Russian situation, and which ran in the Sunday papers all over the country." He added that as a result of the publication he lost most of his liberal friends because they now considered him to be "the arch anti-Communist in America." He explained that this was in 1925 when many liberals "felt there should be nothing said about Russia that was not completely favorable."

"That is true today, is it not?" asked Dies.

"I don't know," Alsberg said, "but a great many of them have changed their minds. I suffered. I was blacklisted; I could not get my articles printed."

Alsberg's reference to the liberals who had turned on him for speaking out against the Russians struck a responsive chord in Starnes, who was finally vocal again after his blunder about Christopher Marlowe in the morning session. Starnes asked whether Alsberg could give any reason for the "astounding phenomenon" that a committee which was investigating subversive activities in the United States "is attacked and caricatured and called un-American because it seeks to find out the facts about Communism."

Alsberg: I hold no brief for the people who have attacked this committee. I have never uttered a word attacking this committee.

Dies: You have had the same experience yourself?

Alsberg: I had this experience which I am telling you. I cannot tell what you experience here. To this day I am considered a reactionary, a liberal who is slipping.

Dies: Do they call you profascist?

Alsberg: No; they have not done that, but they call me a poor liberal who has slipped, and that is the term that is applied to a great many liberals who do not go the full way.

Dies: They want you to go the full way or else some of the radical elements denounce you as a reactionary?

Alsberg: That is more or less what has happened.

Dies: Of course, the full way would be communism?

Alsberg: Well, I don't know. I do not think I am asked to be a Communist, but I am asked — I think the attitude is to sign a blank check on things that are done, that you do not approve of. I have always tried to maintain my independence of judgment as to what people and governments do.

Dies: In other words, you are not going to be forced; you reserve the right to oppose the Soviet Union and communism?

Alsberg: Yes, sir.

Dies: And regardless of what your friends or so-called liberals say or anything else, still you maintain the right of every American to oppose a dictatorial form of government?

Alsberg: Yes, sir.

The entente cordiale achieved between the two men on this point remained intact throughout the entire testimony, to such an extent that Dies would occasionally command Starnes to let Alsberg talk without interrupting him. Starnes tried to make something of Alsberg's friendship with Emma Goldman, but Alsberg neatly turned every insinuation to his own advantage. "Do you know whether or not your views coincided, as a rule, on international politics?" asked Starnes. "No," replied Alsberg. "We quarreled all the time, bitterly, because I do not believe in violent revolution — a quarrel that has been going on between Emma and me for years." *
And when Starnes began questioning him about Orrick Johns, the former New York City director who had admitted membership in the Communist party, Alsberg used the opportunity to point out that Johns had been dis-

* While answering Congressman Starnes's questions about leading Communists he had met when he was in the Soviet Union as a journalist, Alsberg revealed he had been introduced to Lenin and spoken with him for three minutes.

missed as a director and had been succeeded by Donald Thompson, Harry Shaw, and Harold Strauss, none of whom had any connection with the Communist party.

Alsberg also told how he had demoted or transferred all the people who were making trouble, citing, in passing, the fact that Ralph De Sola had been "moved out" to Staten Island. When the last sitdown strike occurred in New York, he continued, he had issued an order which still held: "If there is any more disturbance on the Project in New York City, the Project will close down and those people will lose their jobs." He assured Starnes: "That is flat. We will not tolerate another rumpus in New York City like that . . ."

Alsberg conceded there was still "constant pressure" in New York from union delegations. "Every time we drop a man there are delegations, there are protests . . . They have had street picketing. They have not done it in the past six months, but they had street picketing with banners, 'Alsberg unfair to Writers' Project' — wanting to expand the Writers' Project, wanting to do this and wanting to do that . . ."

Dies's benign attitude toward the witness, which grew more pronounced as the testimony continued, may have surprised some of the spectators but Alsberg seemed to take it as a matter of course; he spoke with Dies as one confides his family troubles to a friend.

Dies: You, as an administrator, are absolutely opposed to communistic activities, or any other subversive activities — fascist, communistic, or whatever it is — on the Project.

Alsberg: Yes, decidedly . . . We have given orders repeatedly there must not be any . . . I even object to their having their literature downstairs on the street, at the door. I said the last time I was up there, around election — will you pardon my strong language — I said, "For Christ's sake, cannot they peddle their literature somewhere else except the entrance to the Project door?"

In a manner verging on delicacy, Dies then moved into the subject of the 106 persons who had signed the Browder book. Alsberg said he had seen the list of names but not read them carefully. Without expressing any skepticism over this reply, Dies said of the Communists on the Project, "They are not content with working; they want to carry on their activities and their propaganda on the Project, don't they?" Alsberg assured him that "we don't let them." In the same friendly voice Dies asked: "When a

317

writer is certified to you on relief, under the law, of course, you cannot go into his political affiliations; that is true, is it not?"

Alsberg confirmed the point.

Dies: However, with reference to the supervisors and those in supervisory control, you will not permit Communists to hold those positions when you know it?

Alsberg: No. The people [the supervisors who signed the book] will have to have a trial; they will be questioned and that is being gone into now . . . There are fifty supervisors on that project, six of whom seem to have signed that book. Their signatures have to be verified and it has to be found out what their attitude is about subversive activities. . . .

An observer experienced in the tactics of trial lawyers might have suspected that Dies was carefully softening up Alsberg, preparing him for the kill. And the kill, it was assumed by some of us listening to the proceedings, would come toward the close of the testimony when Dies began to question the director about the galley sheets of the New Jersey and Montana guidebooks which, according to the committee, promoted class hatred. But here again Dies was unexpectedly gentle; he seemed almost eager to accept Alsberg's statements at their face value.

Deliberately or not, Alsberg appeared to misunderstand Dies's intent when he asked whether he had any trouble with material written "from a partisan angle." Alsberg replied: "We find statements of all kinds that are unwarranted, or overstatements — claims that 'This is the biggest something or other that ever was,' that "This is the most beautiful piece of scenery.' We have millions of 'Indian leaps,' and that sort of thing . . . There is no question about it, that we have to watch out on that continually."

When Dies told him those were not the sort of statements he had in mind, Alsberg immediately understood him and offered to make a general comment about the New Jersey book, "which perhaps will help you." Alsberg proceeded to inundate Dies with details about galley proofs which were bound to confuse anyone, and also to make the New Jersey staff the chief scapegoat of the issue. "We have struggled with the New Jersey book because of the tendency of the New Jersey State staff, frankly, to overstate and to sharpen statements about labor," he told Dies, and he assured him that the Washington office had worked consistently to tone down controversial statements.

At one point Dies asked Alsberg if he knew who was responsible for inserting statements of a partisan nature into the New Jersey galleys. Alsberg replied he did not know since the personnel of the New Jersey staff had changed considerably. "But there has been a very definite attempt from New Jersey to put this kind of thing in the guide?" Dies persisted.

"There has been some attempt," Alsberg agreed. "I would say it has not been violent propaganda, but has had a little tart flavor all of the time. Very often any one statement was not bad, but when you read fifty pages you begin to feel those people were knocking New Jersey . . ." There would be nothing "inimical" in the New Jersey Guide or in any other Project book, he promised Dies. "We are not going to muckrake the Congress of the United States," he added, possibly bearing in mind that the beleaguered Theater Project had been accused of doing just that with some of their stage productions.

Alsberg told the committee that the New Jersey galley proofs had become an issue only because uncorrected galley proofs had been sent to the publisher by mistake, but that the error was being rectified; he assured the congressmen there would be "plenty of conferences" on every paragraph in the book.[*] In his final statement he agreed with Dies that it was "wrong" to put into the guidebooks "things which seem offensive, unfair, prejudiced, or partisan, or from a class angle . . ."

The session ended with both men figuratively patting each other on the back. For the second time during the hearing Dies complimented Alsberg for his performance as a witness. "The Chair wants to commend you for your frankness, for your desire to give the committee the facts and for the attitude you have assumed, rather than to come here in a belligerent way, in an effort to cover up anything, or to assume an attitude that nothing is wrong, everything is right. I think you are to be complimented for that sort of attitude. And if we can have that attitude generally by all of us, we can be of considerable help in clearing the situation up." To which Alsberg

---

[*] Recalling the episode, Harold Coy told the author that on one of his field trips he had spent a day in the New Jersey office arriving at an acceptable version of some "pungent passages" in the guidebook manuscript which, though well written, showed "a lack of respect for the status quo." On his return to the Washington office, the approved version was duly typed up and prepared for publication. "Unfortunately, while I was on another field trip, the publisher asked for the copy and Henry had it pulled from the files and sent off — though naturally he sent the wrong version, the one with all the naughty bits. I did not learn of all this until the book was in galleys, and then, because author's corrections run high, only the spiciest of them were removed, which in a way was a triumph for the free press of New Jersey. The blame for the mistake, so I was told, Henry put on me!"

replied, "I want to thank the committee for being fair in questioning me, and I am at their disposition at any time to furnish anything they want."

George McMillan reported to David Niles that Alsberg "came off much easier than any of us thought he would." But except for the committee chairman, no one complimented him for his conduct on the witness stand. Bearing in mind Hallie Flanagan's tough-minded treatment of the committee, the liberals on Alsberg's staff felt he had been too deferential, too willing to admit to error. On the other hand, the conservatives believed that the Dies Committee had treated him too kindly.

Later on, some of his liberal colleagues, who analyzed the published testimony, changed their minds as they realized that Alsberg, while appearing to be candid, had engaged in a form of shrewdness protective of himself and the Project. Except for making a scapegoat of the New Jersey staff, a strategy that could be justified by the fact that the New Jersey director and her assistant, Alexander Crosby, had already resigned and could not therefore be seriously hurt, Alsberg had not let the Dies Committee use him as a tool. Although Dies had encouraged him to do so, he had not implicated any of his leftwing associates; and although he had promised there would be nothing "unfair" or "partisan" in the guidebooks, a study of the New Jersey Guide and other guides published during Alsberg's reign would suggest a wide difference of opinion between himself and Dies on the question of what was "partisan" and "unfair."

The immediate effect of Alsberg's testimony, however, was to alienate him from those New Dealers who viewed the Dies Committee with both contempt and alarm. They realized that Alsberg was no reactionary, that at worst he was "a liberal who had slipped" in order to protect his skin. But when they measured his performance against that of Hallie Flanagan and even that of Ellen Woodward, who had dared call the committee un-American; and when they remembered the compliments that Dies had bestowed on Alsberg, their initial reaction to his testimony was harsh. Some of them knew what Alsberg was soon to discover: that the Dies Committee, by its very nature, could not be appeased by acts of cooperation. A juggernaut bent on destroying the New Deal, it had not crushed Alsberg simply because, after the hostility displayed on the stand by the two previous witnesses, its purposes were better served by a witness who, on the surface at least, seemed to be in accord with the committee's policies. As subsequent events were to demonstrate, Alsberg's ordeal had merely been postponed.

The Dies Committee attacks on the Writers' and Theater projects undoubtedly helped to put it on the nation's political map. A Gallup Poll taken a few days after the Alsberg hearing indicated that three out of five voters in the nation were familiar with the work of the committee; of those, 75 percent were in favor of having the committee continue its investigations. When Dies issued his first report shortly after the New Year, his colleagues in the House of Representatives were impressed not so much by its contents as by the Gallup Poll report and by the mass of newspaper clippings the committee had garnered. During the four months of its existence, the committee had received more newspaper space than any other single institution in the nation. Swayed by these considerations, the House appropriated $100,000 for continuing the work of the committee for a second year. Although the liberals in Congress loudly decried the headline-grabbing tactics of the committee, they could muster only a few votes against it.

The briefs prepared by Mrs. Flanagan and Alsberg, which refuted point by point the charges aired against the projects by hostile witnesses, were not included in the official record of the Dies Committee. Nor did they receive much circulation. David Niles had promised to distribute mimeographed copies of the Theater Project brief to every member of the Congress, but the five hundred copies Mrs. Flanagan sent to his office were never distributed. The Writers' Project brief suffered a similar fate, with the result that the general public got a one-sided account of the hearings.

Only one paragraph in the Dies Committee report cast any doubt on the quality of the testimony dealing with the two projects. The brief paragraph was inserted in the Dies report after the New Deal members of the committee, Dempsey and Healey, threatened to submit a minority report if Dies did not qualify his charges to some extent. The paragraph, which received no attention in the press, disavowed responsibility for the credibility of the committee's witnesses and admitted that much of their testimony had been "exaggerated" and "biased."

Dies's sensational success in getting front-page coverage inspired one of his congressional colleagues to ape his methods. He was Clifton Woodrum of Virginia, leader of the House's conservative coalition and chairman of the House Appropriations Committee. Woodrum, who later became known as the chief executioner of the Theater Project, was not as talented a demagogue as Dies, but what he lacked in brilliance he made up for in perseverance. He announced his determination "to get the government out of the theater business" and he succeeded. He would have liked to have done the same with the Writers' Project.

As chairman of the House Appropriations Committee, Woodrum had the authority to explore the administration of the Project, the area in which it was most vulnerable, but that would have taken more investigation than there was time for. Moreover, Alsberg's superiors had made it clear to him that the director's days on the Project were numbered; that if the Writers' Project survived beyond the fiscal year, it would be administered by new personnel. Faced by these considerations, Woodrum resorted to the strategy introduced by Dies: to hit the Project at its weakest point, the New York office, using as ammunition the statements of WPA workers who had private grievances against the Project.

Once again Ralph De Sola was summoned and given the spotlight. Encouraged to identify the Communists on the Project and do what he could to lend credence to Woodrum's premise that it was "a nest of Reds," De Sola repeated the testimony he had given the Dies Committee. He had little to add in the way of new information beyond the allegation that Alsberg had reprimanded him for what he had told the Dies Committee, and that, "from almost the very hour I finished testifying," his Project colleagues began referring to his department as "the reptile corner." *

On being asked what was meant by the phrase, De Sola explained: "My particular office is in a corner of the Project, and those workers who work under me and who still remain friendly to me are considered as reptiles."

"As snakes in the grass?" one congressman asked sympathetically.

"Yes, sir," responded De Sola.

Despite the contempt for him in the office, De Sola appeared to be more sure of himself than he had been before the Dies Committee, and more willing to make general charges which he could not substantiate. Although he acknowledged having no personal knowledge of Communist party activity in states outside of New York, he did not hesitate to claim that various locals of the Workers Alliance throughout the country "cooperated" with the Communist party to create strikes, establish picket lines, and "send people to Washington to put pressure on Congress." In his Dies

---

* *Reptiles and Amphibians,* a product of the New York City Project which was prepared under Ralph De Sola's supervision, was published in 1939, the same year that De Sola testified before the Woodrum Committee.

Committee testimony he had represented himself modestly as an ordinary functionary in the Communist party, as the secretary of a local fraction, but now he gave the impression that he had been an important cog in the Communist party machinery. His most radical change of perspective was disclosed when he was asked whether Project books were "tinctured with Communism." He had previously questioned Congressman Dies's allegation that the material in the guidebooks was "class-angled," but now he blithely told the Woodrum Committee that "a good many of the state guidebooks show evidence of what the Communists call 'class-angling.'"

The sparkplug of the Woodrum Committee was its official investigator, H. Ralph Burton. His original instructions had been to investigate all aspects of the New York Project, its accomplishments as well as its shortcomings. But it soon became evident his chief goal and Woodrum's was to discredit it by whatever means could be used. Manuscripts were seized from the files of the New York office and scrutinized for Red propaganda. An attempt was made to produce photographs showing Communist periodicals scattered throughout the Project offices — periodicals which Burton's assistants had brought in during the lunch hour, when the office was almost empty, and planted on various desks. But the scheme was frustrated in time by James McGraw who, discovering what was taking place, ordered the photographers out of the building along with the periodicals they had brought. It was Burton who lined up the witnesses for the committee hearings. Disgruntled former employees, persons with political axes to grind, and plainly irresponsible witnesses became his grist for the committee's mill.

The most wanton statements were those made by Joseph T. Barrett, a former Project supervisor, who claimed that Alsberg had demoted him because of his Dies Committee testimony. Describing a sit-down strike that had occurred on the New York City Project in 1937, he said that one of the workers who was now dead (he failed to identify him) was kicked down a flight of stairs and was injured. "And I put the responsibility of that man's death on the shoulders of Henry Alsberg," he pronounced.

Instead of pressing Barrett for further details about the episode, the committee's chief counsel asked him whether Alsberg was present at the sit-down strike. Barrett then made another sensational charge: "Yes sir; he was the instigator of it." Later, when one of the congressmen asked him for details, Barrett elaborated. "Mr. Alsberg sat down with all the supervisors that went into his office, and with a grievance committee of the Workers Alliance who represented the rank and file of the Project, and he mapped out a plan as to how to fight the pending cuts and how to increase the personnel of the Writers' Project, which was at that time approximately six hundred people. This plan was mapped out by Henry Alsberg."

Congressman Ditter: Did that include instructions as to how you were to take physical possession of Government property?

Barrett: No; he did not mention anything about taking over the Project by force or by marching in. However, he did intimate that it could be a possibility.

No witnesses were called before the committee to corroborate this charge, nor was it again discussed during the hearing. Instead the witness was encouraged to make further charges. At one point Barrett alleged that in two of the books under his supervision, "class angles and class hatred had been inserted by Red writers, giving a Moscow flavor to all the literature," but he was not asked to document the statement. At another point he declared that Richard Wright, the Mississippi-born writer, was an "alien" who was "kept on the Project while veterans were being fired." No one questioned that statement, nor did any member of the committee offer any comment when, after saying that he had never read *American Stuff*, Barrett expressed the opinion that "it is reeking with Communism."

Only one member of the Woodrum Committee was outraged by such proceedings. He was Clarence Cannon, a Democrat from Missouri, who in a moment of exasperation exclaimed, "The remarkable thing about this testimony is that it is from people who either have been fired or are going to be." Burton, in particular, angered him while presenting testimony about Edwin A. Banta. After Burton retold the episode of the Browder book, Cannon asked: "Is there anything in the WPA rules and regulations or the authority creating it which provides that a man who receives relief and who goes on a project shall belong to or not belong to any party, Democratic, Republican, or Socialist, or to any organization, labor, social, or otherwise? The mere fact that the man who gets relief happens to belong to the Democratic party and happens to sign a book, would that be anything to bring to this committee or the fact that a man who got relief happened to belong to the Republican party and signed a book? Now, it is incredible that evidence, that ridiculous evidence like this should be submitted to this committee."

Woodrum: There are some people who make a distinction between what the Democratic party and the Republican party stand for and the Communist party.

Cannon: But the Constitution of the United States provides that no distinction shall be made between any party or because of a man's political or sectarian belief.

Cannon's argument was ignored as the other members of the committee resumed their discussion of Banta. Burton reported that Banta had been threatened so many times that he was afraid to return to the Project without a guard. When the guard was withdrawn and Banta did not return, he was dropped from the Project payroll. Cannon asked Burton: "You did not expect them to keep him on when he did not go back, did you?" To which Burton replied stiffly, "I have not indulged in any thought on the subject."

When it became apparent to Alsberg that neither he nor any of his aides would be given the opportunity to answer the charges made before the committee, he prepared a detailed brief rebutting them point by point. In answer to the charge that he, Alsberg, had instigated a sit-down strike on the New York Project, the brief presented a statement signed by the twenty-seven supervisors of the Project that Alsberg never discussed the strike with any of them, either individually or collectively. In the same statement Donald Thompson, former acting director of the New York City Project, asserted that the meeting described by Barrett in his testimony had never taken place. The brief also indicated that Barrett was demoted not, as he claimed, because he had appeared before the Dies Committee (a fact that was unknown to the Project at the time) but simply because "he had no ability as a writer."

In concluding the brief, Alsberg recalled that a few months earlier he had told the Dies Committee that the New York City Project "had not been functioning as smoothly as it might" but that it was "gradually rounding into shape." He now wished to bring that statement up to date by asserting that the New York Project "*had* rounded into shape" and "is functioning efficiently and without disturbance." To buttress this point, James McGraw, the chief Project supervisor in New York, declared that the charges brought against the New York City Project belonged to "ancient history," most of them dating back to 1936 and 1937.

"The picture is exactly the opposite of what it was in those days," Mc-

Graw added. "Delegations are received in a very orderly manner and are limited as to number. We have had practically no picket lines or other types of demonstrations, and differences of opinion between the unions and the administration have been ironed out in an orderly and intelligent manner." As an example of the order that now prevailed, McGraw pointed out that when, in January 1939, it became necessary to dismiss 25 percent of the Project workers, "the cut was carried out in a most efficient manner and no disorder of any kind ensued before, during, or after the dismissals."

It is doubtful that the Woodrum Committee, or anyone else controlling the fate of the Writers' Project and its director, ever read the brief. Even while it was being prepared, Colonel Harrington, who had succeeded Hopkins as WPA administrator, was honing a knife for Alsberg's beheading; and Congress had more or less decided that under no circumstances would any of the arts projects be permitted to continue under federal management.

After the few months of mix-up in 1939–40, in which a handful of us just worked any place and anyhow to meet schedules, we settled into an orderly routine in the Old Auditorium. The most amusing thing was the way the people in the states who had formerly evaded Washington direction turned humbly to Washington to strengthen their own positions. The staff was considerably reduced but that was a relief. We had had too many incompetents on before and the group had been poorly organized. John Newsom [Alsberg's successor] was an orderly person and not given to Greenwich Village dreams of sponsoring genius . . .

We did start several new things. What I most regret is the army's killing of *Blackout at the Golden Gate,* a honey of a book on the beginning of the war that Walter McElroy pulled together.

> — Katharine Kellock, former
> tours editor of the Federal
> Writers' Project, in a letter
> to the author, October 29,
> 1969

Congress did not, as some enthusiasts desperately tried to believe, view the cultural projects as the first step resulting from a commitment to subsidize American culture. While those who served on the Writers' Program thought that cultural improvement was as important as relief, members of Congress were not concerned with this extension of the Program's benefits.

> — "Writers on Relief: 1935–1942"
> by Kathleen O'Connor
> McKinzie, 1970

Conversion to War Basis: On May 1, 1942, the Writers' Projects will be on a full war basis. Six weeks before that date — March 15 — 40 state Projects reported 180 units of work for the military and civilian defense services . . .

> — John D. Newsom, director of
> Writers' Program, in a memo-
> randum dated March 15,
> 1942

Nine.

The Last Years

Although the Dies and Woodrum committees hastened the demise of Federal One, they were only partly responsible. For all the disfavor the two committees managed to generate toward the arts projects, their effort became a secondary factor in the changing political atmosphere of 1939 that was to alter the course of the New Deal. The change was largely created by the anxieties (and opportunities) attending the menace of Hitlerism and the imminence of a second world war.

Responding to new pressures, the Roosevelt administration began to deemphasize its Depression-orientated programs. On April 3, 1939, the President sent to Congress a reorganization plan which relieved the Works Progress Administration of its independent status, changed its name to Works Projects Administration, and made it a subsidiary of a parent agency known as the Federal Works Administration. In all likelihood, it was during the planning of the reorganization that the New Deal administration decided to scrap Federal One.

There was no one in a position of power to dispute that decision. Hopkins, who had made the federal administration of the arts program possible, was no longer the fervent social worker of the early New Deal era. He had become a canny politician, the new Secretary of Commerce, and his eye was on the presidency. And the man who succeeded him as WPA overlord, Colonel Harrington, a military being to the core, regarded the four arts programs as a nuisance, an impediment in the efficient operation of WPA.

It was Colonel Harrington who pronounced the administration's death sentence on Federal One. On May 23, 1939, he told the Woodrum Committee that he was prepared to take measures to reduce employment on the projects and, at the same time, "eliminate their operation as federally sponsored projects." The congressional death sentence came five weeks later with the enactment of the Emergency Relief Act of 1939. The bill singled out the Theater Project for immediate extermination, and forbade federal sponsorship of the surviving projects. The writers', music, art, and historical records programs were given permission to continue under state sponsorship, provided that sponsors could be found to contribute at least 25 percent of the total cost of each state program.

Colonel Harrington had requested Congress to allow a transition period of six months for lining up sponsors, but the law made it mandatory that the transition be effected within two months, by September 30. As a further expression of its inclement mood, Congress also stipulated that henceforth all WPA workers who had been employed for eighteen months or more must be removed from their jobs and could not be eligible for WPA reemployment until thirty days or more had passed. This ruthless provision, which worked a hardship on older persons in the arts program who could not find private employment, enabled WPA state administrators to cut employment rolls to the bone without incurring much of a union backlash.

Despite the upheaval in the personnel of the Washington staff — the imminent departure of Alsberg and some of his top aides — the Writers' Program (as it was now called), with the help of WPA state administrators, managed to line up enough sponsors before the two-month deadline to keep the Project productive in all the states but Idaho and North Dakota. Coming in the wake of the Dies and Woodrum attacks, this unexpected show of strength throughout the country must have disappointed those congressional enemies who had given the Project the short deadline in the hope of killing it, or at least crippling it so that it could not continue for long. For Alsberg, who had just been fired by Harrington, the final result of the frantic search for state sponsors amounted to a vote of confidence from the field, one that his ego badly needed after the beating it had been taking.

For the survivors of the Washington staff the summer of 1939 was one of depressing confusion. Writing to his old friend Reed Harris, Clair Laning reported: "We were moved out of our quarters in the Ouray Building without notice, and separated. The administrative staff was housed in the Old Auditorium, the editorial staff in condemned quarters in Tempo 2, and the files put in the Walker-Johnson Building. It was then announced that no leave would be granted to the staff after August 31, and anyone wanting his leave would have to take it before that date." Into this muddled situation stepped Alsberg's successor, John Dimmock Newsom, who for the past year had been directing the Writers' Project in Michigan.

Newsom, age forty-six, had been born in Shanghai, the son of an American businessman temporarily stationed there. As a youngster, he was reared and educated near Paris; as a young man, he did graduate work in England at Cambridge University. At the start of World War I he was the first American to enlist with the British army. After the war he worked in the United States as a newspaperman and freelance writer. He published a number of short stories and one novel, *Garde à vous*. At the time he was appointed director of the Michigan Writers' Project he had been trying to write another book while living on a Maryland farm.

It was through the recommendation of his friend Paul de Kruif, a best-selling author of that era, that Newsom first landed on the Project. The suggestion that he be promoted to head the Writers' Program in Washington came from Howard Hunter, a WPA assistant administrator who, in the following year, was to succeed Colonel Harrington as WPA Commissioner.* Hunter, according to Clair Laning, had been trying to get de Kruif to write a book about WPA and hoped that the elevation of his friend Newsom might persuade him to undertake the project.†

Reporting on Newsom's early activity in his new job, *Time* described him as speaking "with an efficient snap in his voice," and quoted him as saying: "This is a production unit, and it's work that counts. I've never been for art for art's sake alone." Newsom was certainly unlike Alsberg, being more of an administrator, less of a creative editor. Although he had been a good manager of the Michigan Project, he had not made much headway with the preparation of the Michigan state guide, which was not published until 1941. However, in several respects he was the ideal person to take charge of the national program when Alsberg left. He knew the art of delegating responsibility; unlike Alsberg, he was more impersonal in his dealings with his associates, yet more inclined to trust them.

Newsom's job, of course, was much simpler than that of his predecessor.

* Colonel Harrington died in October 1940.
† Paul de Kruif never undertook the project.

John Newsom with Clair Laning and Lyle Saxon in Washington, D.C.

There were not as many serious administrative problems to harass him. The chief work of his Washington staff was technical in nature — to provide editorial assistance and guidance. The immediate task was clearly defined: to complete the state guide series as quickly as possible. Although other writing projects were undertaken, most of them were extensions of what had been initiated during Alsberg's regime. With state sponsors in a position to exercise considerable authority in the new setup, the general tendency throughout the Writers' Program was to take as few chances as possible.

Several months were to pass before the new Program could function smoothly. The sharp reduction in personnel, together with the harsh stipulations of the Emergency Relief Act, accentuated the problems of reorganization, particularly in the larger field offices. A personal letter to Katharine Kellock from Walter McElroy, supervisor of the Program in San Francisco, which was written a few days after Newsom assumed office, suggests some of the difficulties plaguing them:

"We too have been moved, physically and literally twice and psychologically so many times that I've lost count. And all the other horrors you mention I can match: union meetings, gossip, tears, rages, pity, despair, violent quarrels, personal recriminations, and jealous jockeying for position. To say nothing of strikes, of which I've already survived three . . . We're still at the storm center: trying frantically to dam the rising wave of hysteria among our eighteen-monthers, begging for enough charity from sponsors to keep body and soul together, wondering desperately what goes on three thousand miles away where you are — and besides all that working night and day . . ."

As usual, the greatest degree of turmoil took place in the New York City office, which was now reduced to a staff of one hundred fifty. When Frederick Clayton was appointed director, Carl Malmberg, who had been in charge of the New York City office, was invited to stay on as his chief aide. But Malmberg, disgusted by the machinations of the Woodrum Committee and the local WPA administration (once again headed by Brehon Somervell, now an army lieutenant general) and by the provisions of the new relief act, decided to resign. Informing Newsom of his decision, he wrote that he had not been able to "stomach what so obviously is a deal between the new local administration and the Woodrum Committee." He also took exception to two new appointments that had been made on the New York City staff: "Nothing could be better calculated to ruin the Proj-

333

ect than the appointment to responsible positions of Mr. Van Olinda and Mr. Goll."

W. K. Van Olinda, Malmberg reminded Newsom, was the first director of the New York City Project, but within three months he had shown he was unqualified for the job and was transferred to the Washington staff "where he won distinction as the Project's 'comma man.'" Malmberg did not believe that a man whose chief forte was punctuation could be anything but a liability on the newly organized New York City staff. He had an even lower opinion of Oscar K. Goll, who had formerly served as managing editor of the New York staff but had been dismissed.

Goll was best known to Malmberg for his testimony before the Woodrum Committee in which he had attacked the New York City Project for its lack of qualified personnel, alleging that most of the staff members were former "fish peddlers and dishwashers" and persons who had never had any previous writing or editorial experience. In the latter category he had specifically included Frank Shay, a Project supervisor, who was the author and editor of more than thirty published books. Goll had stressed that he found conditions on the Project "intolerable"; yet, as Alsberg was to attest in his brief on the Woodrum Committee testimony, Goll had written him a number of enthusiastic reports while a member of the Project. In one report he wrote: "I can in all sincerity most genuinely attest that each and every worker on this project now recognizes that we have a genuine commitment to fulfill. They are now happy in their work."

An editorial in *Direction,* written shortly after the New York City Project's reorganization, confirmed Malmberg's premonitions:

> The results of the first six weeks of operation of the Project under local administration have amply justified the fears of those who said it would not work. Much of the best work which was in the process of completion has been unceremoniously scrapped. Today the Project is hopelessly snarled in red tape and groaning under the weight of eighteen-pound manuals of procedure . . . Worst of all, broken-down political wheelhorses are finding their way into responsible positions. Those whose testimony before the Woodrum Committee was instrumental in smearing the Project are also being rewarded. Naturally, the workers remaining on the Project resent this obvious payoff for what they regard as a very dirty piece of business.

A few Project workers (among them Ralph Ellison) were able to ignore the new developments and continue working as they had before the reorganization. But most of those who survived the changing of the guard were demoralized by the situation and clung to their jobs only because they could not find other employment. The charge of boondoggling often leveled against the Project in the past could now legitimately be made against those in charge of the New York City office. At a time when many manuscripts were close to completion, forty Project workers were assigned to Ellis Island to copy immigration records.

Only three books by the New York City staff were published during the next three years of the Writers' Program existence: *American Wild Life,* which was completed in 1939 and published in 1940; *The Film Index,* a bibliographical tome of 780 pages issued in 1941, which had been started in 1938; and *A Maritime History of New York,* a work of 341 pages on which some forty or fifty workers had collaborated, which was published in December 1941.

Among the manuscripts that were near completion but never published were "Famous New York Trials," on which Ellison had worked; a collection of folklore, "Chase the White Horse"; a bibliography of bibliographies on the subject of labor which a Woodrum Committee investigator regarded as a coded history of the American Communist party; a history of housing, which was to be published in time for the 1940 World's Fair; ethnic studies of the Jews, Irish, and Poles of New York City, and a manuscript recounting the experiences of New Yorkers who had helped to construct the Woolworth Building and the George Washington Bridge.

The twin shadows of the Dies and Woodrum committees kept menacing the New York City office. When the Dies Committee learned that the staff was preparing a manuscript called "Underneath New York," it could not resist the opportunity to let the country know that it was on the alert to protect it from the scheming of dangerous radicals. Two of the committee's investigators testified that Communists had obtained enough information from the manuscript to enable them to paralyze all of New York City within two hours. The information, they said, consisted of maps and photostats of underground water mains and of every industry essential to the city's transportation and communication systems.

The story received nationwide publicity but it was rejected by no less an anti-Communist than General Brehon Somervell. "This story is highly sensational and exaggerated and also premature," he said in a statement to the press. He assured the public there was no cause for alarm. "As far as we know, no confidential information was given to the project, but only such information as is readily available to anyone interested."

Nevertheless, *Underneath New York* was never published under the auspices of the Project. Nor was a completed bibliography of the Arctic, prepared in the New York Office, which to this day is considered a valuable work among students of geography. In 1939, when General Somervell first heard of the manuscript, he saw no reason why the New York staff should spend any time on such a work and commented that "they ought to shove it in the furnace." Taking Somervell at his word, a clerk in the office proceeded to do just that, but was stopped in time by one of the editors.

Under the new regulations, there was little that Newsom and his Washington staff could do to improve matters in the field offices. The Washington office was no longer a powerhouse; the Writers' Program was being run by the state WPA administrators and the local state sponsors. However, the Washington office still retained the right of approving or rejecting manuscripts submitted for publication, and could make certain that the major books which remained to be completed complied with the high literary standards that had been developed during Alsberg's regime.

The Washington staff, though reduced, was in a stronger editorial position than ever before. The eighteen-month ruling, however cruel, had made a fresh start possible; editors that Alsberg had found to be unproductive but had not had the heart to fire could be eliminated without any fanfare. The reorganization of the staff began in July when all staff members were notified that the Washington office would be temporarily disbanded until a local sponsor could be found for it. The editors who were to be dropped received their termination notices shortly afterwards. The rest were told that they would be recalled after the thirty-day waiting period prescribed by the new law.

Among the latter was Harold Rosenberg, who decided to spend his waiting period on Cape Cod. While sunning himself on a Truro beach, his friend Mary Barrett (a member of the Washington staff) arrived to inform him that his name had been removed from the list of editors who were to be rehired. Miss Barrett had learned that the decision to drop Rosenberg had been made by Archibald MacLeish, head of the Library of Congress, the official body that had agreed to sponsor the Washington Writers' Program. On hearing all this, Rosenberg sped back to Washington to talk with Gorham Munson, the newly appointed editorial chief of the Washington office. Rosenberg told him his explanation for MacLeish's action: he (Rosenberg) had once written an unfavorable review of a book by MacLeish for *Poetry* magazine. Despite the long trip from Truro,

Rosenberg's temper had not yet cooled. He directed Munson to tell Mac-Leish that "I won't stand for that kind of crap."

At his next conference with MacLeish, Munson conveyed Rosenberg's message as gently as he could. It was not received gently; the poet was outraged that Rosenberg had been told that he, MacLeish, did not want him on the staff. "But I had to let him know why he wasn't hired," Munson demurred. This made MacLeish even more furious. "Put anyone you want on the damn project," he yelled, "and get out of this office." Munson, describing the encounter to Rosenberg, concluded, "I guess that means you're on the Project."

Rosenberg, who had been the Project's art editor, now became a general field editor on the new staff. He and several of his colleagues constituted a flying squadron of troubleshooters whose chief task was to complete the state guidebook series. Twenty-three of the major books in the American Guide Series had already been published before Alsberg left; about a dozen more were either on the presses or in such an advanced editorial state that they could be published within the following year.* The most difficult job that remained to be done was completing the rest of the state guides: Alabama, Arkansas, Colorado, Indiana, Louisiana, Michigan, Missouri, Oklahoma, Utah, Washington, West Virginia, Wisconsin and Wyoming.†

With only eleven editors on the new staff, nearly everyone was required to spend some time in the field. In the state offices, they rewrote copy, advised, and carried on diplomatic relations with the local sponsors. Newsom never hesitated to give them full responsibility. "I am not going to burden you with gratuitous advice," he wrote Katharine Kellock in Nevada on February 2, 1940. "You know what you're doing and I am satisfied to leave the details in your hands with the complacent certainty that we're going to have a good book after you have half killed yourself ridding the manuscript of some of that quite dreadful stuff I saw when I was out there."

One of Newsom's most peripatetic field editors was Stella Block Hanau who, as the only member of the new staff of southern heritage (her parents were born in Alabama), was assigned to several southern states.

---

* As anyone familiar with publishing procedure knows, it usually takes a publisher from eight months to a year to produce a book from a manuscript.

† Except for Oklahoma, all these state guidebooks were isued in 1941. The Oklahoma Guide was published in January 1942.

In Alabama, where she spent two months, she found herself at a disadvantage for not having retained her southern accent. Her problem of communication was also complicated by a strict office rule which prevented employees from speaking to one another on government time. Her main work was "eliminating platitudes, correcting facts, and maintaining tone," but sometimes she encountered editoral problems of a purely indigenous nature. In one passage describing the Alabama city of Florence, she read:

> We must follow Florence through the terrible reconstruction; those evil days when in bitter poverty, her best and bravest of them sleep in Virginia battlefields, her civilization destroyed, the iron entered her soul. And now, when the darkest hour had struck, came a flash of light, the forerunners of the dawn. It was the Ku Klux Klan . . .

George F. Willison, who had been dispatched to his native state of Colorado to do major rewriting on the manuscript of the state guide, became involved with a local editorial problem that almost ruined his lifelong friendship with the poet Thomas Hornsby Ferrill, who was then public relations director for the Western Beet Company. When Willison had completed his work on the Colorado Guide, Ferrill objected to the picture he presented of his company's exploitation of Mexican-American field workers; he argued that such material had no place in a guidebook. But Willison would not delete the material; nor would he accept the company's figures for wages paid to sugar beet workers without checking them with the Department of Agriculture, who provided him with a correct set of figures that were more shocking than the company's. Ferrill got back at Willison by attacking the book in a review he wrote for the New York *Herald-Tribune*.* Willison protested the unfairness of the review in a letter to the newspaper, but it was never printed. A number of years were to pass before the two men could be friends again.

Harold Rosenberg's main contribution as a traveling troubleshooter was to assist with the birth of the Missouri and Washington state guides. In both states the progress of the manuscripts had been badly impeded by a series of political crises and change of directors. In Missouri the Pendergast machine's insistence on asserting its power had brought the Project to a complete standstill. In the spring of 1938 Alsberg tried to revive the

---

* In his book *Inside U.S.A.* (1951 edition) John Gunther referred to the Colorado Guide as "one of the two or three best of all the volumes in the American Guide Series."

338

Missouri Project with the help of his Kentucky state director, Dr. U. R. Bell, whose judgment he trusted. Bell solved the problem of Missouri by recruiting the services of Charles van Ravenswaay as director. He was a young man of twenty-nine with a master's degree in literature and an intense interest in Missouri history and folklore. Given a free hand, the new director discarded much of the material accumulated by his two predecessors, and traveled through the state collecting his own data and checking roads and tours. It was an exhilarating experience for him. "Suddenly I was discovering the state in a way that had not been discovered before. I found the kind of material that has since become such an integral part of the public interest that it is hard to believe it was then unknown."

Assisting van Ravenswaay at first was Gene Holcomb, an editor from the Mississippi Project. Although highly capable, Holcomb was not familiar enough with Missouri to be of much help. After his departure, van Ravenswaay's only assistant was the wife of an English professor, Mrs. Dana Jensen, a perky young woman who could help him with the writing. The rest of his staff consisted of four office girls, one of whom was a former attendant in an insane asylum. It was she, recalled Mrs. Jensen, who provided a suitable motto for the Project when she quoted a patient who had said to her: "Them doctors say I lost my mind; but, you know, I don't miss it a bit."

"The quotation was a comfort to the staff, especially in times of stress when the danger of losing one's mind seemed all too present," wrote Mrs. Jensen. Less comforting was the dreadful condition of their work quarters. They were on the seventh floor of a former factory building that had been condemned and abandoned. The only elevator in the building was intended for freight and was often out of order. Their office was a dingy expanse lighted by naked electric bulbs dangling from long cords. Van Ravenswaay and his one assistant made surprisingly rapid progress in such a dismal atmosphere, but when it became apparent that they could not meet the publisher's deadline without some expert help, Newsom sent Harold Rosenberg to St. Louis.

To the young intellectual who had spent most of his life in New York City, Missouri seemed like a new world with a strange breed of Americans; the honesty and forthrightness of the Missourians Rosenberg encountered were a revelation to him. He and the young midwestern director quickly became good friends and close collaborators. Rosenberg's job was mainly that of trimming, but he also did some of the writing. Van

Ravenswaay, while respectful of his talents, would sometimes feel compelled to edit Rosenberg's editing. "Personally, I think you're about the best revisionist I know," he wrote after Rosenberg had returned to Washington, "but some of those long sentences you love to create have to be unstrung." The two men disagreed when Rosenberg wanted to delete details from the manuscript which van Ravenswaay treasured. Yet somehow the guide was completed to their mutual satisfaction.

The state that created the most complex difficulties for Newsom and his staff was Washington. Along with Missouri, it had long been the least productive Writers' Project office in the country. As in Missouri, the Washington Project had been victimized by political shenanigans and crippled by incompetent direction. To add to its troubles, State Senator Mary Farquharson had been conducting a vendetta against the Project, objecting to its new director, Anne Windhusen, and claiming the office was "a hotbed of Communists." In February 1939 Colonel Harrington's office had investigated the senator's charges and found them baseless. But the attacks continued, generating so much heat and publicity that in August 1939, when most of the Project offices in the nation had been able to obtain state sponsors to ensure their continuation, no sponsor could be found for the Washington office, and it was forced to close down.

Six weeks later, after the State Planning Commission agreed to act as sponsor, the Washington Project reopened. In the meantime, Newsom, who had been reviewing the manuscript for the Washington guidebook, declared a state of emergency and sent both Harold Rosenberg and Mary Barrett to Seattle to assist Miss Windhusen and her newly assembled staff. The staff, together with Rosenberg and Miss Barrett, worked on the manuscript steadily from January to March 1940, at which point the State Planning Commission, chiefly as a result of Senator Farquharson's relentless campaign against Miss Windhusen, withdrew its sponsorship.* Suddenly, the two editors from Washington found themselves with no other assistance than that of a borrowed WPA typist, and orders from Newsom to continue editing the state guide manuscript until it was finished.

A month later, when the editors left, the Writers' Program in Seattle still showed no signs of life. The state WPA administration claimed it could

---

* Writing to a constituent on June 26, 1940, State Senator Farquharson said: "It took a tremendous amount of energy to finally get the thing blasted out of existence — and, of course, that was not what I really had intended to do. But with the Communist hold as strong as it was, getting the whole thing washed up seemed about the only possibility under the circumstances."

find neither a sponsor for the Program nor one for the state guidebook, despite the expressed willingness of Binfords and Mort, Oregon publishers, to issue the book at their expense. Six months were to pass before the Washington State Historical Society half-heartedly agreed to sponsor the book, and signed a publishing contract. The Historical Society then spent seven months scrutinizing and revising the manuscript before permitting it to go to the publishers. There was another long delay when the head of the Historical Society kept the galley proofs for two months, then announced that they contained hundreds of factual errors which had to be corrected. The book did not appear until late in 1941, just a few weeks before the publication of the final guide in the series, the Oklahoma Guide.

One of the most flagrant examples of calculated procrastination occurred in the state of Wisconsin, where the Wisconsin state guide would have been published in 1939 except for the election that year of a Republican governor. On discovering that the galley proofs of the book included a fifteen-page section on government which spoke admiringly of the late Senator Robert M. LaFollette, Sr., for having successfully battled right-wing elements in the state, Governor Heil introduced a delaying resolution in the Wisconsin state legislature calling for an investigation of the reasons why the guidebook had not been published in 1937, as originally planned. After the resolution passed, an investigating committee packed with a coalition of conservative Republicans and Democrats found the guidebook inaccurate, untruthful, politically biased, and badly written. The legislature then tried to put an end to the book by canceling the appropriation of $1,750 it had previously allocated for its publication costs.

But the legislators were not to have their way. A new sponsor was found for the guide, the Wisconsin Library Association, which found no traces of bias or incompetence in the manuscript. After the state Writers' Program revised it slightly to bring it up to date, the manuscript was approved, with the LaFollette material left intact, and the guidebook was issued by the New York publishing firm Duell, Sloan & Pearce, at its own expense.*

---

* A similar situation developed with the West Virginia state guidebook. When the incumbent governor, Homer A. Holt, objected to virtually all of the section dealing with labor, the state Writers' Program bided its time until he was succeeded by a more liberal governor, M. M. Neely, who approved of the labor section as submitted to him. The West Virginia Guide was one of the last three books to be published in the state guidebook series.

In Washington, Newsom and his aides generally succeeded in maintaining an editorial stance that was markedly New Deal. But there were times when their fear of the Dies Committee led them to engage in acts of extreme caution. One noteworthy example was its handling of a manuscript on the history of civil liberties in Illinois, an undertaking which Alsberg's office had certified after the Chicago Civil Liberties Union had agreed to sponsor its publication. Marion Knoblauch, an experienced journalist on the Chicago Project, supervised the research for the history and devoted much of her own time to the task of writing the final copy. When the manuscript was completed in 1940, the sponsor expected that Newsom's office would promptly approve it for publication, especially as it had the enthusiastic endorsement of twenty-six consultants.

But the Washington editors treated it as though it were a keg of dynamite and returned it with a letter criticizing its lack of objectivity. The WPA administrator in Illinois protested: he was convinced that the manuscript should be published as it was written; he trusted the judgment of the consultants who had reviewed it.* To solve this impasse, Newsom journeyed to Chicago and assured the sponsor and Miss Knoblauch that the manuscript could easily be made acceptable by toning down certain passages and editing others.

Shortly afterwards Miss Knoblauch, who had been employed on the Illinois Writers' Project for three and a half years, was dismissed, ostensibly because of a general reduction in WPA nonrelief personnel. In July 1941, Sterling North in his Chicago *Daily News* column asked: "What happened to *The Pursuit of Freedom,* a history of civil liberties in Illinois, which was promised for publication in January?" Curtis D. MacDougall, state supervisor of the Illinois Writers' Program, replied that "the Washington office had withheld approval of the manuscript until considerable revisions were made," but that the revisions "should be completed soon."

When more than another year passed and it became obvious to the Illinois Civil Liberties Union that the Washington office was stalling, its publication committee asked Newsom to send them the manuscript. Newsom promptly replied that his office would release the manuscript only if he were given written assurance that the published volume would make no reference to the Writers' Program's connection with it. It appeared that

* One of the consultants was Arthur J. Goldberg, who later became Associate Justice of the United States Supreme Court.

either the Washington office or its WPA administrators were suffering from an acute case of funk.

The manuscript continued to engender hard feelings. Marion Knoblauch became miffed when the Civil Liberties Union, ignoring her contribution to the book, asked Harvey O'Connor to make whatever final revisions he considered helpful. O'Connor updated some of the information and deleted chunks of documentary material. When *The Pursuit of Freedom* was published in November 1942, the sponsor gave no credit to Miss Knoblauch and the staff of Project employees who had assisted her. The preface, however, included this enigmatic reference to the Writers' Program: "The compilation of research data which has provided the basis for this book was done for the committee by a public agency which has asked that no credit for this assistance be given either to the two score of research workers or to the agency."

The statement irked some of the reviewers. "What kind of fenagling is this?" asked Lawrence Martin in the Chicago *Sunday Times*. "Is it sheer modesty or sheer timidity? Is the 'public agency' afraid that the Dies Committee will pickle it for doing a democratic job of writing the history of how the Bill of Rights worked and failed to work in Illinois?" Martin then proceeded to identify the "public agency" as well as the Project workers mainly responsible for the book. "It's a pity that the federal government, in its WPA uniform," he concluded, "hadn't the courage to stand back of its own job, and it's a pity that the Chicago Civil Liberties Committee had, in order to get the manuscript, agreed to play this wishy-washy game."

The Chicago *Sun Book Week* attributed the statement in the preface to "the fear of the beleaguered WPA that there would be reactionary charges of radicalism which are usually heaped upon any work that tells the truth about the use and abuse of civil liberties." Although the writer went on to praise the book, he criticized its editors for omitting the documentation and index present in the original manuscript. In Chicago, at least, the contribution made to the work by Marion Knoblauch and her staff received full credit, despite the intentions of the Washington office.

Miss Knoblauch was also the central figure in the publication story of another Writers' Project book which was published despite all the odds against it. This was the 288-page Du Page County Guide, which was prepared by Miss Knoblauch and two of her Project colleagues, Ethel Eyre and Oril Brown, with the help of a dozen research workers. The guide was in page proof form in 1940 when its sponsor, the County Board of Supervisors, decided by a vote of fifteen to five to have nothing more to do with it. They said that it presented a false and insulting view of Du Page County; and that it was finished too late to serve its original purpose, which was to help commemorate the county's 1939 centennial celebration.

The board called the book "scurrilous." One of its members described it as "a story of adultery, rape, and kidnapping, written for nothing except guttersnipes," and said he would not have it in his house "for fear the children would get hold of it." The board's horrified attitude seemed to put an end to any hope of publishing the book.

But eight years later, Miss Knoblauch, who had never lost faith in the value of the project, published the Du Page County Guide on her own initiative, and persuaded Irwin A. Ruby, an Elmhurst, Illinois, businessman, to become its distributor. Miss Knoblauch made so few changes in the contents that it was possible for the printer to utilize the same page proofs that had been prepared in 1940. The published book also salvaged the original illustrations and photographs prepared by members of the Federal Art Project.

The only notable addition was a nicely written preface by Henry Alsberg, who presented the guide as "the latest brushstroke in the portrait of America that the Federal Writers' Project set out to paint." He expressed the opinion that local WPA guides like the Du Page County Guide would prove "most valuable" to future historians since they were "the living flesh and blood of American history." When the book was reviewed, no one found any of the contents "scurrilous" or "insulting." The Chicago *Tribune*, which was one of the newspapers that considered the county guide a worthwhile addition to the American Guide Series, observed: "Now that it has been published at last, one wonders what all the rumpus was all about."

Sponsors had always been useful in the life of the Writers' Project, but after July 1939 they became indispensable since, according to the law, no state office of the Writers' Program could exist without a sponsor's contribution of money, services, or materials. Inevitably, this new state of affairs gave the sponsors more power than was healthy for the general welfare of the Writers' Program. More and more sponsors tended to use the writing staffs for their own purposes — purposes that had little or no relationship to what the Writers' Project had set out to do. In Washington, as well as in the states, supervisors found it expedient to pay close attention to the demands of the sponsors. Survival rather than quality of work became the chief consideration, and they were unhappy about it. A typical complaint was that of Muriel E. Hawks, head of the Massachusetts Writers' Program, whose main sponsor was the State Department of Education: "They were well-meaning," she wrote, "but oh, so bureaucratic, and as hard for us to understand as we were for them." The main difficulty, she added, was the sponsor's insistence on saddling her staff with assignments that the writers found boring.

The fear of displeasing sponsors, coupled with that of provoking the Dies Committee, contributed to the debilitation of the Writers' Program. Substantial book projects, such as social-ethnic studies and collections of living lore, which would have added excitement and dimension to the Program's activity, were soon abandoned in favor of projects which offered no risk of controversy, such as "Factbooks" and recreation guides for each of the states.

The Factbooks, which were inspired by Vardis Fisher's *Encyclopedia of Idaho* (1939), became a pet project of Newsom. In 1940 he announced that with the state guidebook series almost completed, the Writers' Program would concentrate on a series of books that would contain "concrete and succinct data" about any locality that might wish to sponsor a Factbook project. The books were to be published with removable covers in order that new facts could be added annually. He expected the Factbooks to be more popular than the state guides since they would sell for only one dollar, and he hoped the series could be completed within eighteen months. However, when the Writers' Program came to an end more than two years later, not a single Factbook had been published.

The Writers' Program fared better with the state recreational handbooks. By the end of 1941, nearly every state with a Writers' Program had published one. Sponsored usually by the state Conservation Commission, the handbooks were between twenty-four and forty pages long, and contained a map of the state. They sold for twenty cents.

The recreational handbooks were typical of the hack work that became the mainstay of the Program. Laid aside was the dream of exploring the people and places of America to make the portrait of the nation as full and vivid as possible. There were a few token efforts to keep the dream alive by continuing some of the special projects that had been initiated in Alsberg's time; but with only two thousand workers left on the Writers' Program to perform the numerous journalistic chores assigned to them by sponsors, almost none of the books that had been announced optimistically as "forthcoming publications" materialized.

Among the unborn books were six regional guides with the general title of *Hands that Built the Nation,* which were to be a collaborative work by the Art and Writers' Program based on the Index of American Design; *America Eats,* a regional treatment of custom and tradition for serving and preparing food; *The Western Range: the Story of the Grasslands,* which was to tell the story of the vast open-range country of the West in terms of its Indians, Spanish *rancheros* and *vaqueros,* American frontiersmen, cattle barons, sheep men, and modern ranchers; and *Indians of the United States,* a contemporary picture and historical account of what happened to the first Americans under the rule of the white man.

A few major books, other than state and city guides, were produced in the closing years of the Writers' Program, but for the most part the writers spent their time grinding out leaflets, pamphlets, articles, and booklets ordered by the sponsors. In effect, they became a service group at the beck and call of civic and governmental agencies that had no writing staffs of their own. The Writers' Project had occasionally pandered to such groups; on the Writers' Program it became a regular and accepted practice to comply with their requests.

A list of materials reviewed by Stella Hanau in the Washington office suggested the miscellaneous nature of the writing assignments that befell the workers on the Program. The list included a leaflet from the Massachusetts office on "America's Greatest Fish Market," a radio script from Mississippi discussing the subject of diphtheria, leaflets from Alabama on "Rats," "Rabies," "Smallpox," and "Syphilis," a pamphlet from Florida on "Smuggling Aliens into Florida," an article from Kentucky on "War on the Fly," a book from Texas called *Safeguarding the Public Health in Dallas.*

The direction which the Writers' Program was taking was obviously downhill, but none of its members protested. A law passed by Congress in 1940, which forbade government employment of Communists, fascists and Nazis, had either silenced or expelled those Project workers who once felt no restraint in voicing their opinions. The only sharp complaints heard about the decline of the Writers' Program were at two Library of Congress conferences of cultural leaders, which were held late in 1941 at the instigation of WPA Commissioner Howard Hunter for the purpose of evaluating the administration's arts program.*

Bernard De Voto, who had championed the Writers' Project almost from the start, did not like what had developed. He complained that the shift of power from the Washington staff to the state offices was resulting in a great deal of "unimportant" and "trivial" work. Warning that the Writers' Program activity might become "little more than antiquarian leaf raking," he urged the WPA administration to restore to the Washington office the powers it once had.

John Steinbeck, one of the participants in the discussions, raised the more fundamental issue of the administration's intention in maintaining the arts projects. He asked: "Is it the purpose of the arts projects to employ people — to keep from starving to death inexpert people — or is it to increase the expertness of the work . . . Are we feeding artists or creating artistic expression?"

None of the answers to the question met with general agreement. Toward the end of the discussions, Archibald MacLeish, somewhat exasperated by the long-winded and inconclusive talk, lashed out at the WPA administrators with this accusation: "What you people did in WPA was completely hypocritical . . . You kept telling yourself you were actually giving people a job, but you were really more interested in your program."

To this, Florence Kerr responded with one of the brighter utterances of the parley. "You must admit," she told MacLeish, "it was one of the higher forms of hypocrisy."

But all the talk and complaints proved to be academic. The explosion at Pearl Harbor came less than a month later, and its detonations at once became the dominating force of the immediate future. Newsom quickly dispatched a memorandum to all the state offices which began with the ominous words: "The present crisis will undoubtedly mean laying aside many current activities of the Writers' Program and many activities planned for the immediate future."

A few months later the Writers' Program officially became the Writers'

---

* George F. Willison, an executive editor of the Writers' Project who had helped to organize the conferences, reported that when Florence Kerr, Howard Hunter's assistant, opened the first meeting by saying how "kind" the WPA had been to writers and other members of the arts projects, Bernard De Voto objected, declaring that the members of the conference had come to talk about the quality of the Federal Writers' Project, which everyone considered high. "This has nothing to do with being *kind* to people," he said.

Unit of the War Services Subdivision of the WPA, and began to devote most of its effort to such war services as writing sixty-four "Servicemen's Recreational Guides" to the areas surrounding various army camps. In commenting on the changeover, the *New Republic* sighed: "The Project no longer has literary ambitions and no longer writes books on American life for the general public."

The conversion took effect May 1, 1942. In describing its particulars to the field offices, Newsom provided a dour epitaph for the Writers' Program, one which partly answered the question John Steinbeck had raised a few months before:

> Most people on the Writers' Projects today are women of middle age and men well above the age of military and industrial fitness. Usually they are heads of families. Few of them have ever been professional writers . . . The Writers' Projects do not attempt to create literature nor to develop talent. They employ and train needy people who are not absorbed by the Nation's armed or industrial forces on tasks officially requested by local units of the Army, Navy, or civilian defense organizations.

Shortly after these words reached the forty state offices that were left of the Writers' Program, Newsom resigned and joined the army. The project he left behind lasted only another year. The Writers' Program had begun to die months before the war came; the war simply administered the coup de grace.

He [Alsberg] conceived of the Guide not as a revised Baedeker but as a discovery of the roots from which America had grown and a signpost of America's potentialities for the future.

— William F. McDonald, *Federal Relief Administration and the Arts,* 1969

I doubt that he [President Roosevelt] expected the projects to produce paintings or plays or books or records of the first importance. Certainly it was with no such purpose in mind that the projects were established. What was intended was a declaration — the first in modern history of the federal government — that those who follow learning and the arts are as important to the Republic as those who follow other callings . . .

— Archibald MacLeish, *New Republic,* April 15, 1946

Given its day, the cooperative emphasis was inevitable. But I think we have learned, partly from the Project, that scholarship cannot be cooperative to that degree, particularly in history. The sharp edges are blunted by too much interchange of ideas. And sharp edges have their place in all writing.

— Ray A. Billington, historian and former director of the Massachusetts Federal Writers' Project, in a letter to the author, January 28, 1969

If there had been room in Rocinante I would have packed the WPA Guides to all the States, all forty-eight volumes of them. I have all of them . . . The complete set comprises the most comprehensive account of the United States ever got together and nothing since has approached it.

— John Steinbeck, *Travels With Charley,* 1961

Ten.

The Legacy

Just a month before the attack on Pearl Harbor the Writers' Program announced the publication of the last state guidebook in the American Guide Series, *Oklahoma: The Sooner State.** To celebrate the event, the White House proclaimed the week of November 10–16 as "American Guide Week." Most of the fifteen commercial publishers, who had issued the state guides, and the American Booksellers' Association joined forces with the Writers' Program to focus the attention of the American public on the series and its portrayal of the "social, economic, industrial, and historical background of this country."

It had taken the Writers' Project six years to complete and publish the fifty-one major volumes in the American Guide Series, but President Roosevelt evidently did not regard this as an unduly long period. In a letter endorsing "American Guide Week," addressed to assistant WPA commissioner Florence Kerr, he wrote: "It is a tribute to American energy and resourcefulness that the WPA Writers' Program, with the aid of private citizens and public bodies, and the use of skills of unemployed writers and research workers, could have planned and brought to early completion a

---

* Actually, the announcement was premature as the publisher (the University of Oklahoma Press) was a month late delivering finished copies of the guidebook. In order not to put a crimp into "American Guide Week," the publishers provided dummies of the book and sample pages that could be used for display purposes. Lewis Gannett, literary critic of the New York *Herald-Tribune,* considered *Oklahoma* "one of the best of the series, partly because the state's peculiar history gives it special character, perhaps partly because the distinguished historian of the American Indian, Angie Debo, was one of the editors."

guide to each state, principal city, and major region, including the far-flung territories of Alaska and Puerto Rico."

In the euphoria of the occasion no one bothered to point out to the President that none of the six regional guides originally planned had been published; nor was it exactly true that Project guidebooks to "each principal city" were now available. There were no guides for such principal cities as Chicago, Boston, and Detroit. Nevertheless, no one could dispute the surprising profusion of the Writers' Project's achievement. To this day no one knows exactly how many published items it produced. A National Archives report indicates that up until April 1942 the collection consisted of 276 volumes, 701 pamphlets, and 340 issuances (leaflets, articles, radio scripts). An undetermined number of additional volumes were published in the remaining years of the decade. The 1942 total of approximately a thousand books and pamphlets, which filled seven twelve-foot library shelves, included guidebooks for each of the forty-eight states, Washington, D.C., Puerto Rico and Alaska; about thirty guides to cities such as New York, New Orleans, San Francisco, Los Angeles; more than a score of other book-length guides such as *U.S. One, The Ocean Highway, The Oregon Trail, Skiing in the East, Here's New England, Death Valley Guide;* and approximately one hundred and fifty volumes in the Project's highly varied Life in America Series, which ranged in titles from *Hands that Built New Hampshire* to *The Albanian Struggle in the Old World and New.*

Among the most "regional" of the books in the American Guide Series were the three volumes which describe mile by mile historic roadways that traverse a number of states: *U.S. One* covers the distance from Maine to Florida; *The Ocean Highway,* from New Jersey to northern Florida; *The Oregon Trail,* the most fascinating of the three, takes the reader from the Missouri River to the Pacific Ocean. It is laced with excerpts from diaries of early pioneers, and covers a half dozen states where covered wagons once journeyed.

The least known (and the most numerous) publications in the American Guide Series were the books and pamphlets dealing with small-town America. They seldom circulated outside the localities they described. Although they were largely by-products of the mass of material collected for each state guidebook, many of them succeeded in having a character of their own and contributed substantially to the Writers' Project's reputation as the nation's foremost explorer of Americana.

For Robert Cantwell, a discerning critic of that era, the guides to the small towns, counties, and cities seemed potentially far more valuable in their revelation of American social history than the state guidebooks. Writing in the *New Republic* in 1939, he pointed out that the local guidebooks represented the first effort to write American history in terms of its communities. In the past, he said, it had been written in terms of its "leading actors and its dominant economic movements but never in terms of the ups and downs of the towns from which the actors emerged and in which the economic movements had their play." He added that "it is one kind of experience to read, in Beard or Turner, about the opening of the West, but it is another kind of experience to read about the rise and fall of Chillicothe in relation to the railroads, or of Galena in relation to the world of lead." *

Henry Alsberg shared Cantwell's high regard for the local guides. Eight years after his departure from the Project he wrote: "The State books deal in broad generalities of a great community's history, culture, politics, and economy and, of necessity, cannot give a close-up of the local scene such as the local guides, which view the city, county, or village through the magnifying lens of a historic microscope, are about to do. To me these local books always had the sharp flavor of the particular territory which they covered, and most vividly illustrated the flowing pattern of American civilization."

Alsberg was particularly charmed by the large number of local characters recorded in the small-town guides, recalling among them the pyromaniacal drunk who kept the volunteer fire department busy and who, on being imprisoned, burned down the jail in which he was lodged; also, the veteran husband who insisted on being buried among his six wives, with a stone over his grave proudly recording the fact that he had outlived all of them. Alsberg considered especially valuable "the infinite variety of details" in each community guide which spelled out its ups and downs.

While there is some merit to his and Cantwell's appraisal of the local guides, they do not approach the state guides in literary stature. Being uneven in quality, they cannot be taken seriously as a group. Few of the local guides were prepared by the Project's top writers, nor were they

---

* Robert Cantwell was especially impressed by the guide to Galena, which had been produced by the Illinois Project. "You can read a dozen biographies of Grant," he wrote, "and get less insight into his early career than is supplied by a history of Galena."

subjected to the same careful editorial scrutiny applied to the state guide manuscripts. Alsberg's statement that "the state guides deal in broad generalities" was misleading. Some of the essays in the state guides express generalities, but the essays usually constitute only about one third of a state guide's total content. The remaining two sections, one dealing with a state's leading cities and the other with tours, contain an "infinite variety of details" and are heavily populated with local characters.

Most of the critics agreed that the state guidebook series was the Project's most valuable contribution. Considering the large number of persons engaged in the collective effort of producing a state guide, the miracle to some of the reviewers was that, despite their encyclopedic content, a good many of them projected a distinctive and intimate image of the state. The indigenous atmosphere, it was generally agreed, was somehow created by an amalgam of historical and contemporary data, geographic detail, and juicy anecdote. The style was usually straightforward, seldom intruding. Only occasionally were the critics aware of an iconoclastic point of view; at its worst, they found it blatantly New Deal in ideology; at its best, agreeably ironic.

In hundreds of articles the state guides were favorably appraised individually and collectively, but few of the reviewers could begin to suggest the richness and the flavor of their contents. A critic in the *Nation,* commenting on the state guides published by the end of 1938, wrote: "No one of the books is dull, although some are much more sprightly and incisive than others . . . There is a happy want of adjectives and few purple passages. For the most part the writing is firmly knit, effective and workmanlike; in certain volumes, notably in the Idaho and Massachusetts guides, it is brilliant." Four years later, a *New Republic* reviewer, examining the whole series, decided that although the guides were seldom extraordinary as individual volumes, their scope and content as a group struck him with "awe and admiration."

With the exception of the Idaho Guide, which Vardis Fisher wrote according to his own rules, all the state guides followed Washington's uniform format, which consists of three major segments. Part One contains essays on the history, setting, people, commerce, art, literature, recreation, and educational facilities of the state. The second part deals with a state's cities in terms of general information, history, and major points of interest. The longest section, part three, which often takes up half the volume, consists of tours that follow the highways into every corner of the state, illuminating each mile of the way with historical information and Americana which is often amusing. In addition to the three major segments, each state guide is prefaced by information useful to travelers (no names of hotels or restaurants are mentioned, however, unless they are of historic interest) and a calendar of annual events. A historical chronology of significant developments, a bibliography, as many as one hundred photographs, and about a dozen maps (one of them a map of the entire state in color) complete the contents. The longest of the state guides is New York, with 782 pages; the shortest North Dakota, with 371 pages.

Robert Cantwell, though of the opinion that the state guidebooks would "revolutionize the writing of American history and enormously influence the direction and character of our imaginative literature," found their format "cumbersome and unattractive." His chief complaint was that information about a particular person or place was too often too scattered throughout the three sections of a state guide. "A man's life may appear in the historical section, some in connection with his birthplace, some when tours pass scenes of his exploits." He did not like the sharp divisions between the essay section and the other two sections. The organization of the material contributed to his impression that the state guides were "too comprehensive for tourists and too superficial for scholars."

With this objection, Cantwell put his finger on an editorial problem which, from the beginning, had split the ranks of the Washington staff. Apart from drastic differences in their temperaments, the question of how much emphasis should be given to the essay section became the main issue of contention between Henry Alsberg and Katharine Kellock, who was in charge of the tour copy. Alsberg, with his literary propensity, had insisted that a group of essays dealing comprehensively with the major aspects of a state were to be a basic part of every state guide. Mrs. Kellock was equally convinced that the essays should be in the nature of brief preliminary sketches that would provide information the tourist could quickly absorb. She contended that the chief function of the guidebooks, like that of the Baedekers, was to assist the traveler. Alsberg had broader aspirations for the books.

The battle was never resolved, except perhaps in the case of the New York City Guide which was published in two volumes when it was found that the essays and the guide materal were too much for a single volume. The introductory volume of 526 pages, *New York Panorama,* contains a group of twenty-six essays, including Vincent McHugh's brilliant opener

"Metropolis and Her Children," which sets forth the contemporary scene. The second volume, New York City Guide, 680 pages long, presents a detailed description of the communities and points of interest in all the five boroughs of the city, along with maps, photographs, and all the other informational features of the state guidebooks. Had publishers been willing to publish two such volumes for every state, both the scholar and the traveler might have been satisfied. As it was, however, the state guides became a compromise born of two conflicting concepts of what their function should be. Alsberg got his essays, and Katharine Kellock her tours, and the general public got books that were more like encyclopedias than guides.

Mrs. Kellock's dedication to her point of view won her no less an ally than Bernard De Voto, who in the early years of the Project did not hesitate to speak his mind about its deficiencies and those of the guidebooks. Later on, as his respect for the value of the state guidebook series grew, he became one of the Project's staunchest supporters. In 1937, however, he was lambasting the Project for devoting so much space to essays. "We'd trade fifty pages of interpretation for one page of pertinent information," he wrote in the *Saturday Review of Literature*. His principal objection to the WPA guides so far, he said, was that "they are all cluttered up with our cultural heritage." He accused the Project of not publishing "a real guidebook" to date — "try touring Washington, D.C., carrying seven pounds of text." *

Reviewing all of the New England guides the following year, he began by attacking the paucity of writing talent on the Project, saying that 70 percent of its employees were writers by aspiration or appointment; he gleefully recorded the rumor that in one state office a toilet overflowed one day and four journeyman plumbers on the editorial staff volunteered to repair it. But his main complaint concerned the format of the state guides. "The guides suffer," he wrote, "because Washington never quite made up its mind what kind of books it wanted." He declared that the essays were "the conspicuous weakness" of the guides, and cited Vermont as "the most satisfying of the New England guides" because of the brevity of its introductory essays." He had no use for any "subjective interpretation," such as he found in the essays, and was of the opinion that any specific information contained in the essays should be placed in the tours. Only the Washington editors fared well in the article; he attributed the excellent quality

---

* Actually, *Washington: City and Capital* weighed five and one half pounds.

of the books to their expert editing and had special praise for the tour sections. "A guidebook," he declared, "must stand or fall on its tours and here, where the difficulties were greatest, these books score an unquestionable triumph."

Although Alsberg was depressed by De Voto's criticism of the essays, his faith in their value remained intact. It was a faith strongly motivated by his innate love of belles lettres, but there were other reasons for it which were as pragmatic as Mrs. Kellock's reasons for favoring the tours. His ambition was not to have the Project emulate Baedeker, none of whose books had ever won any literary honors, but to build a giant mirror for America that would reflect interpretative as well as factual materials, one that would show the general outlines of the country as well as its myriads of small features.

It was an idealistic ambition but also one that had strong elements of shrewdness. He believed, for example, that if the state guides were broad enough in scope, they could become "new and valuable textbooks for use in the schools and colleges of the nation." Early in the history of the Project Alsberg had discussed this possibility in the *Journal of the National Educational Association,* pointing out that "at present there is no handy reference guide to life in America. The American Guide can be used in schools to acquaint pupils with the unique customs of various parts of the community, as well as with the industrial, agricultural, scientific, artistic, historical, geographical, and scenic features of the United States." Apart from any use that the schools might make of the guides, he considered the support of the educational world indispensable to the success of the Writers' Project.

Alsberg perceived that the most effective way of involving members of the academic world in the Project was through the preparation of the essays, which required checking and sometimes rewriting by experts in the fields they covered. The cities and tour sections of the state guides could be prepared without the expertise of educators, but not the essays. It was with this in mind that Alsberg and his aides enlisted the services of some twelve thousand consultants, most of them educators, who voluntarily reviewed, revised, and sometimes even wrote the essays. Their involvement provided the Project with its most prestigious and politically valuable corps of supporters.

There were also literary considerations for defending the essays. If the guides were to project life in America with any sense of historical perspective, the tours and cities sections, with their emphasis on geographic detail, needed to be prefaced by interpretative material which could impart a sense of historical continuity and development. However, De Voto and Mrs. Kellock could argue with reason that although the essay section was the smallest of the three guidebook sections, it took up so much space as to make the term "guidebook" an obvious misnomer.*

Alsberg realized this but he could not afford to use any other designation for the books. "Guidebook" was easily grasped by the reading public as well as by those politicians who had originally supported the Writers' Project because it had promised to produce guides for travelers which were badly needed. The term also appealed to the publishers who at first regarded the twenty-six million motorists of that era as their most promising potential market. (Later, however, when the initial sales results were in, they realized how few motorists made pleasure trips during the Depression; that, for those who did, the average WPA state guide seemed far more bulky than a guidebook should be.)

The essays were a stumbling block from several points of view. Without them, the guides could have been produced much more rapidly. Their preparation created more editorial and policy problems than either of the other two sections in the guides. Before they could be written to the satisfaction of the Washington editors, the essays had to make frequent trips between the national office and the field staffs. After that the essays had to be approved by the consultants and sponsors; this often meant extended discussions with the Washington editors since a certain degree of subjective interpretation was bound to be part of any essay. Resolving all the controversial points in a single manuscript sometimes took months.

Despite Washington's attempt at uniformity, the essay topics differed in many of the state guides. Daniel M. Fox, a Harvard historian, complained that a large number of the guides do not include a chapter on religion (Massachusetts and New York among them) and that none of the state guides discuss the history of banking and finance. There was also criticism that states with large groups of foreign-born residents often failed to devote an essay to the subject; and that although there are essays on the Negro in most of the southern state guides, a number of northern states, where the black population is substantial, have guidebooks that ignore his presence.

Notwithstanding all the difficulties of including the essays in the state

---

* In the Virginia Guide the essay on history alone runs to forty printed pages.

guides, they contributed substantially to the literary success of the series. It is a tribute to their general excellence that even experts found it hard to tell which of the essays were the result of a collective effort and which ones represented the work of one person. Daniel M. Fox, who was one of those to admit that he could not tell, found the essays "the best expressions of the intellectual and social ideas of the Project writers."

The best of the guidebook essays were often those that dealt with a state's literature and architecture. Roderick Seidenberg, the architectural editor on the Washington staff, was largely responsible for the general excellence of the architectural material in the guides. After his departure in 1939, Harold Rosenberg assumed his duties along with those he had been performing as art editor. The question of what in American art was worthy of historical treatment puzzled Rosenberg at first. The essays from the states that reached his desk were gossipy in nature, and frequently emphasized European painters with easily identifiable names, who happened to pass through a certain locality or who had come there to paint Indians. Rosenberg resolved the problem by eliminating the distinction between folk art and fine art, and by promoting the concept of treating art history as social history. As a result, a midwestern merry-go-round factory, from which the King of Siam had once ordered wooden horses for his wives, became as legitimate a point of interest as the life and work of a state's best-known painters.

As might be expected, the best of the guidebook essays were those produced in the states which had the largest concentration of experienced writers: New York, New Jersey, Illinois, California, Louisiana, and Massachusetts. In New York City the fear that the twenty-six essays in *New York Panorama* might suggest a hodgepodge of personal expression led the editors to disclaim the opinions expressed as representing those of the WPA, the consultants, or the sponsors. Yet Robert M. Coates found these essays "remarkably uniform" and "coherent;" in spite of the diversity of talents represented, he felt that one of the charms of the book was "the constant play of its really graceful commentary." *

* "Portrait of Harlem," one of the essays in *New York Panorama*, is attributed to Richard Wright. In accordance with the Writers' Project policy of anonymity, none of the contributors to that book was permitted to sign his work. The few signed essays in the American Guide Series were those prepared by volunteer consultants with well-established literary reputations, such as Dorothy Canfield Fisher, who contributed an essay titled "Vermonters" to the Vermont Guide; Jonathan Daniels, who wrote the introductory essay for the North Carolina Guide, and Douglas Southall Freeman, who performed the same service for the Virginia Guide.

Frederick Gutheim, writing of the completed state guidebook series in the *Saturday Review of Literature*, praised the essays as "invaluable introductions to the state," but found that in some cases expertise "runs away with an essay," and in other cases the sense of the whole is sacrificed "in the multiplicity of its parts." He was most impressed by the writers of the essays on geology and archaeology, whom he considered "sensationally fine," and noted that "much remarkable and original writing has been done in the difficult pioneering aspects of local culture and folklore."

What astonished the critics most, however, was not so much the generally high quality of the essays but the total impression made by each of the guides. Never before had any single volume presented such a detailed yet comprehensive picture of a state's past and present. "When I think of the number of times an event has been buttoned to a specific place for the first time," wrote Gutheim, "it makes my editorial head reel." Gutheim asserted that "these books are guides to the real America, not the tourist America," then hastened to explain that the "tourist America" had been thrown in for good measure.

In his final appraisal of the American Guide Series, Bernard De Voto saw the books as an "educational force and even a patriotic force, an honorable addition to our awareness of ourselves and our country," echoing in part Lewis Mumford's earlier statement that the guides represented "the finest contribution made to American patriotism" in his generation. Even before the series was completed, Robert Cantwell proclaimed that the guides were shedding a new and unexpected light on America, revealing it as "a land to be taken seriously." He added that nothing quite like it had appeared in our literature. "None of the common generalizations about America and the American temperament seem to fit it, least of all those attributing to Americans qualities of thrift, sobriety, calculation or commercial acumen. On the contrary, it is doubtful if there has ever been assembled anywhere such a portrait, so laboriously and carefully documented, of such a fanciful, impulsive, childlike, absent-minded, capricious and ingenious people . . ."

Behind the enthusiasm of such appreciations was the impact of a multitude of minuscule particulars which, in a manner defying analysis, are fashioned into a gigantic and vivid portrayal. Marveling at the wealth of information he found in the cities and tour sections of the guides, Gutheim observed: "This is not the well selected, carefully sculptured mosaic of formal history or geographical description; it is the profuse disorder of nature and life, the dadaist jumble of the daily newspaper. It gets in your blood and sends you crowing from oddity to anecdote, from curiosity to dazzling illumination of single fact."

For Gutheim, the guides had "the haphazard charm" of an encyclopedia. "You read, for example, about the town of Oberlin, that awoke one morning in February 1909 to find itself buried in Russian thistles, one house twenty feet deep before the wind shifted. Or you learn that the highest postoffice in the United States distinguishes Climax, Colorado (11,320 feet)." For Cantwell the guides exposed strange quirks of the American temperament — the penchant of our New England ancestors, for example, for secret rooms, invisible closets, hidden stairways, sliding panels and false walls, all once considered essential to a well-planned house. He was also surprised to find that Americans were prolific builders of spite fences, spite churches, spite towns — and even spite railroads. On the other hand, these antisocial attitudes, he learned, were counterbalanced by a lunatic sense of humor, as reflected in irreverent jingles on tombstones, jocular names for villages and farms, and the reckless custom of flipping a coin to determine boundary lines and locations of county seats.

For De Voto, who considered the tour section the heartland of the guide, every tour offered "a rich, various and rewarding spectacle." To prove his point, he thrust a finger into the Massachusetts Guide and turned up part of a tour which described a Devil's Den (one of the ten thousand in the country) said to have contained Captain Kidd's treasure, guarded by the ghost of a murdered black. On the next page he found an extinct watering place frequented by nineteenth-century Americans suffering from dyspepsia, and a couple of pages later the figure of Agnes Surriage, a beautiful sinner, who began her career as a scrubwoman, then became the mistress of a rich Tory, then his wife, then his widow, and finally wound up as a titled noblewoman.

The great number of factual tidbits in each state guide presented a problem to every reviewer, for no matter how many were cited they could not possibly suggest their variety and fascination. Hamilton Basso, despairing of trying to do justice to a half dozen state guides the *New Republic* had asked him to review, praised the books for "binding a million stray facts and figures in one handy sheaf," then quoted six facts picked out at random from each of the guidebooks. What made the guidebook facts so frequently engrossing was the writers' seemingly relentless adherence to the truth combined with their determination to pry open the doors of every closet with skeletons in them. There was a beguiling disregard for sacred cows of all description. Yet tempering the revelations of human quirks and eccentric behavior was a genuine regard for any interesting evidence suggesting the magnanimity and ingenuity of Americans in hard-pressed circumstances.

The candor in the guidebooks is often expressed most tellingly in the epic album of major and minor figures that is interlaced throughout the pages of the cities and tour sections. The portraitures are often entertaining and sometimes brash. Writing of John D. Rockefeller, the oil millionaire who used to winter in Florida, the Florida guidebook describes his addiction to golf as he bicycled "from stroke to stroke, followed by two valets, one with milk and crackers, the other with a blanket to be spread on the ground when he wishes to rest. For golf, as for church and ordinary wear, he wore a special wig . . . and a straw hat, held securely in place by a large shawl-like handkerchief tied under his chin." The portrait, which took up two pages, recalled the millionaire's habit of giving new dimes to each of his guests, sometimes with a printed card bearing some of his own verse:

> *I was early taught to work as well as play;*
> *My life has been one long, happy holiday —*
> *Full of work, and full of play —*
> *I dropped the worry on the way —*
> *And God was good to me every day.*

The Delaware Guide resurrected the memory of a happy homicidal vixen who made Lucrezia Borgia seem abnormally inhibited. She was Patty Cannon, a tavern keeper whose bloody deeds take up as much space as that given to Rockefeller. "Murder, by all accounts," reads the guidebook, "came as natural to Patty Cannon as her back-slapping hospitality, her wit and her love of showing her great strength in 'side-hold' wrestling bouts with all comers. She was believed to have killed more than one slave dealer for his money, using impartially a gun, a knife, or a club while the victim ate, drank, or slept. Her victims, black and white, male and female, murdered for various reasons, were supposed to number a score or more . . . She died in jail in 1829, and was buried in the jail yard. Nothing marks her grave, in what is now a parking lot."

Browsing through the guidebook portraits, D. W. Brogan, a British critic, was not surprised to find in the Massachusetts Guide several references to Thoreau and his life, but he did not expect to encounter in the New Orleans Guide a frank account of one Edward Burke, who "was said to have persuaded President Hayes to withdraw federal troops from Louisiana," but who was indicted while State Treasurer for fraudulently negotiating state bonds, and escaped to Honduras to become a banana planter. Reflecting on the Project writers' readiness to record irreverent information, Brogan feared that if England were to produce a series of government-written guides, "we should hear about the withdrawal of Mr. Thoreau to Walden but not of the withdrawal of Mr. Burke to Honduras."

The Project's proclivity for dealing with human foibles must have come as a relief to the reviewers who had expected to be bored by standard tourist boosterism; but it failed to arouse the enthusiasm of some academicians. As a historian writing from a twenty-year perspective, Daniel M. Fox complained that the federal writers often had "a somewhat blurred perspective of history," and he was disturbed by the premise he found implicit in the guidebooks "that the tour technique is an adequate presentation of history." He noted the writers' "impatience with the past, or antiquarian-like fascination with certain aspects of it," which he believed distorted the "relative importance of historical events." Yet at the same time, he admitted that the same fault could be found in most of the poems in Whitman's *Leaves of Grass,* in the early books of Van Wyck Brooks and in the essays of H. L. Mencken; and he acknowledged that, for all their lack of interpretative depth, the mile-by-mile descriptions of the countryside succeeded in emphasizing "in panorama fashion, the unity and diversity of the American landscape."

There were also many instances of adverse criticism. Even while praising the guides, reviewers would often complain about factual errors, glaring omissions, and bad indexing. Some of the reviews were openly hostile, especially in communities that had been ignored in the guides or had not received as much space as they felt their community merited. An editorial in the *Citizen Patriot* of Jackson, Michigan, was entitled "A Misguided Guide" and declared that "so far as factual information is concerned it [the Michigan Guide] belongs properly in the wastebasket." The chief complaint was that there was "no special chapter for Jackson, no map of Jackson, and no pictures of Jackson."

Sometimes the guidebooks were criticized for expressing opinions which offended the sensibilities of the reviewer. Although R. H. Fletcher, a Montana engineer, praised the Montana Guide in the New York *Herald-Tribune* for allowing "the plain unvarnished type of truth to predominate," Florence W. Stephens, reviewing the same guide for the *Saturday Review of Literature,* claimed that the personal opinions of the writers on labor and religion were all too evident, and charged that the accounts of the state's labor difficulties "bordered on propaganda." Jared Putnam, in the *Nation,* was nettled by "three highly objectionable anti-Negro passages" in the Mississippi Guide.

Harry Hansen, the New York *World-Telegram* book critic, had a high opinion of the guides but felt impelled to chastize the editors of *New York Panorama* for the scant attention given to the Jews and Italians, New York City's two largest ethnic groups, which then had a total population of two million persons. Lewis Mumford was puzzled by the failure of the Massachusetts Guide to note the existence of H. H. Richardson's "magnificently indigenous cottage architecture," though gently conceding that specialists can always find fault with any comprehensive work. Friendly and unfriendly critics — the friendly ones by far outnumbered the unfriendly ones and included contributors to rabidly Republican newspapers — found similar faults with many of the guides, but on the whole the growls of fault-finding were easily drowned out by the sounds of applause.

Most of the guides were reviewed individually by reviewers who often had little or no knowledge of what the other published guides were like. But occasionally, particularly in the New York press, a reviewer would speak of all the guidebooks that had come to his attention and discuss their total impact. The novelist Louis Bromfield, while reviewing the Ohio Guide for the New York *Herald-Tribune,* could not resist commenting on the entire series. "The appearance of this series, able and even noble in conception, is an event in our national life which has not been sufficiently appreciated," he wrote. "I can recommend them as the best of reading. I mean to see everyone of the forty-eight on my own library shelves, for the benefit of myself, my children, and grandchildren."

More than one literary critic was impressed by the epic nature of the series and by its potential effect on the national spirit. Writing of the guides in *On Native Grounds,* which was published just as the Writers' Program was coming to an end, Alfred Kazin welcomed the series in exultant language. In a paragraph that could serve as a fitting eulogy for the Project he wrote:

So the WPA state guides, seemingly only a makeshift, a stratagem of administrative relief policy to tide a few thousand people along and keep them working, a business of assigning individuals of assorted skills and interests to map the country, mile by mile, resulted in an extraordinary contemporary epic. Out of the need to find something to say about every community and the country around it, out of the vast storehouse of facts behind the guides — geological, geographic, meteorological, ethnological, historical, political, sociological, economic — there emerged an America unexampled in density and regional diversity.

More than any other literary effort of the thirties, Kazin continued, the Writers' Project set the tone of the period by demonstrating what collective skills could do "to uncover the collective history of the period." He concluded with the assertion that the guidebooks were not merely "super Baedekers" but that they became both a repository and a symbol of the "reawakened American sense of its own history."

A group of the state guidebooks in the American Guide Series

Writing in a similar vein, H. G. Nichols in the British periodical *The Contemporary Review*, regarded the Writers' Project as an effective means of "priming the pump" to national self-awareness. He was confident that with its explorations of America there would result "a kind of second birth of the national consciousness comparable in quality if not in degree with the awakening to nationhood that attended the War of Independence."

Unfortunately, the reawakening was indefinitely postponed by the nation's immersion in World War II; the guidebooks were virtually forgotten as a symbol and largely ignored for their practical value. Perhaps, if by some miracle of publishing or of congressional paternalism, the state guides could have been issued as low-priced sets, easily available to homes and schools, the books might have fulfilled the great expectations of their champions, war or no war. But with fifteen different publishers issuing the forty-eight guides, there was little likelihood that they could be marketed as a group. The possibility of Congress' subsidizing such an enterprise was even more remote. By 1943, when the Writers' Program was officially interred, most of the legislators were relieved to have nothing more to do with it.

The postwar period, with its McCarthy Committee nightmare, drove the memory of the Writers' Project deep into the shade; the significance of the American Guide Series gradually faded. Yet the state guides continued to have a small but steady sale among travelers, libraries, writers, editors, and cognoscenti of Americana.* Some of the publishers kept reprinting the guides in small editions; some allowed theirs to go out of print. A few eventually brought out superficially "revised editions" and some acquired title to state guides which the original publishers no longer wanted.† In recent years several publishers have begun to issue thoroughly revised, updated editions.

Although most of the guides in print were outdated to a certain extent, readers who continued to acquire them found the books extremely useful and illuminating. Writers and editors especially learned how valuable they could be for developing locales in the writing of fiction; for amplifying their knowledge of American towns, rivers, lakes, ports; for gleaning anecdotes and juicy bits of folklore to give extra interest to their own material; and, always, for providing inspiration.

A Project achievement more quickly forgotten than the American Guide Series was its "Life in America" series — some one hundred and fifty volumes dealing with a great diversity of subject matter. Some of the books in

---

* It is estimated that approximately 700,000 copies of the state guides have been sold to date. About twenty-five of the titles in the state series were in print in 1972. See checklist of selected Writers' Project publications, page 375.

† The original copyrights on the state guides, which had been held by local and state government officials in their capacity as sponsors, had all expired by 1971. Inasmuch as the books were produced under federal sponsorship, some observers maintain that they are now in the public domain.

In accordance with this opinion, in 1970 the Maine League of Historical Societies and Museums issued an updated version of the Maine Guide, notwithstanding the fact that Houghton Mifflin, the original publishers of the book, had issued a new edition with the copyright in their own name. Remarkably enough, the Maine League edition was edited by Mrs. Dorris A. Isaacson, formerly Dorris May Westall, who was the state director of the Maine Writers' Project when it produced the Maine Guide in 1937. The new version, which is copyright in her name, follows the original format closely; the revised Houghton Mifflin edition does not.

this series were among the Project's best; one of them, *These Are Our Lives*, probably received stronger praise than any other single Project publication. In several instances, the "Life in America" books outsold any of the state guides.

The New England Hurricane, a 220-page book of text and pictures, not only became a best seller but also made publishing history for having been produced with hurricane speed. Hours after the big blow of 1938 had subsided, a staff of four editors in the Boston office began gathering information and photographs from Massachusetts and the rest of the New England states.* The rapidity with which the state offices acted suggested that the Writers' Project, when it chose, could function as the fastest fact-gathering agency in the country. Marveling at the quality of *The New England Hurricane, Newsweek* commented: "The text to each picture and the short account of the hurricane are superb, the full tragic drama brought home to us with all its force and meaning, without any cheap tricks of writing. There is not a phrase, a sentence in the text that is not of an artist in prose who is conscientious about and proud of his work."

Some of the Project publications designated as part of the American Guide Series were actually accounts of life in America in bygone times. One of these was *Entertaining a Nation: The Career of Long Branch,* produced by the New Jersey Writers' Project, which describes the 19th century cavortings of the affluent and the mighty at this formerly fashionable resort. *The Saturday Review of Literature* found it "a grand anecdotal history of a seashore watering place that saw great railroad, patent medicine, and gambling fortunes at play when the fortunes were making their mightiest experiments in ostentation . . . A gorgeous record of it all."

Drawn in part from memoirs and unpublished papers, the book was largely the work of Reynolds A. Sweetland and Joseph Sugarman, Jr., whose style was anything but saccharine. Their string of peppery anecdotes included one about Ulysses S. Grant's first visit to Long Branch and his encounter with a one-legged collector of tolls. When the old man saw that the President's coachman had driven past the tollhouse without stopping, he hobbled out and demanded his fee. Grant, who was in a sour mood, exclaimed, "Maybe you don't know who I am. I'm President of the

---

* The Boston Project editors chiefly responsible for the preparation of *New England Hurricane* were Frank E. Manuel, the Writers' Project New England regional director; Muriel E. Hawks, director of the Massachusetts Project; Alban Peterson, and William FitzGerald.

United States." To this the toll collector shot back: "I don't care who you are. If you're President of Hell it's your business to pay two cents toll and my business to collect it." The President paid.

The art of telling stories came naturally to many Project writers. Some of the brightest of their anecdotes are found in a half dozen Project books that trace the origins of names for towns, counties, mountains, valleys, rivers, and so on. The most ambitious of these was *South Dakota Place Names,* a 689-page work issued by the University of South Dakota. All the place-name books were designated as part of the American Guide Series, but they are as useful to students of American life as they are to the tourists.

With the exception of the Project's black studies, its books about ethnic groups, and its collections of folklore and ex-slave narratives, the books in the Life in America series were not part of Washington's original plans. Most of them were proliferated in the field offices, usually conceived by chance, for the purpose of making use of surplus materials which had been gathered for the state guides, or to please some sponsor. That accounts for the seemingly senseless diversity of their subject matter.*

Considering how many crises beset the Writers' Project, it had a surprisingly long life-span. Not until the newly created Office of War Information emerged as the all-embracing writing agency for the armed forces did the WPA administrators decide to liquidate it. In February 1943 they summoned to Washington Lyle Saxon, the novelist and long-time director of the Louisiana Writers' Project, to preside over the funeral arrangements.

Only seven members of the Washington staff remained to partake in the wake. Saxon, an appealing wit and raconteur, did his best to dispel their gloom as he went about his business; but it was all too pervasive. The knowledge that their days in the crumbling Old Auditorium (the Project's first and final headquarters) were numbered made it hard to be cheerful. The big silent pipe organ around them became a painfully obvious symbol. The bleakness of those days was accentuated by letters from state

---

* Some of the subjects: volunteer fire departments, state calendars of annual events (some lavishly illustrated by the Federal Art Project), elementary science, whaling fishermen, housing, aviation, conservation, songs, civil liberties, tobacco workers, pioneer settlers, pheasants, floods; histories of newspapers, ports, military groups; mushrooms, pageants, baseball, registered nurses, a celibate society, universities, hospitals, private burial grounds, social hygiene, printing, plants, winter sports, hiking, fairs, churches, agriculture, fish.

supervisors that kept begging the WPA not to shut down the Writers' Program during the cold winter months because the few staff workers left were too old to find other jobs.

Perhaps because of the letters the burial preparations stretched into April. By that time "The Remainders," as the seven Washington editors began to call themselves, had received their termination notices. Several of them had tried to have an audience with Florence Kerr, in the hope of finding work in some other government agency, but Mrs. Kerr would not see anyone. "She's so soft-hearted; she can hardly bear to say farewell," one of her underlings told them.

Two weeks before they were to go their separate ways, "The Remainders" had a final cocktail party at which Merle Colby, the last chief of the Washington staff, jocularly suggested that they gather for cocktails periodically and invite distinguished guests to be present at each session, so as to remind people that once upon a time the United States Government had actually hired writers to be writers.

The final day in the Old Auditorium came on April 27, when, according to Katharine Kellock's diary, "We dribbled out without anyone even saying goodbye . . ."

In its seven and a half years of activity, the Writers' Project had cost approximately $27,000,000, a sum which represented one fifth of one percent of all WPA appropriations.* In its obituary story, *Time* pointed out that, since the Project writers had produced about one thousand published books and pamphlets, it meant that each item had cost approximately $27,000 — admittedly a large sum to pay for the hundreds of pamphlets that were only a few pages long. But such arithmetic was short-sighted, of course, as it did not take into account the millions of dollars that community and state agencies would have been obliged to pay out in welfare funds if destitute writers had not been provided with jobs. It also failed to take into account the vast amount of unpublished source material and manuscripts which the Project left behind, much of it of potential value to scholars.

The leftover material included dozens of manuscripts that might have

---

* Total WPA expenditures for the Writers' Project (1935–1943) amounted to $25,685,756, and were chiefly for relief wages and administrative salaries. Sponsors contributed an additional $1,365,157 for other costs. Total expenditures for all WPA projects came to almost $3 billion.

been published had sponsors and publishers been found for them in time.*
It was not the fault of the Writers' Project that this great legacy has been
virtually ignored. As early as October 1940, Newsom and his associates
foresaw the importance of preserving whatever materials the state offices
had developed which were not in published form. All state supervisors
were directed to supply the Washington office with two copies of all notes,
interviews, records, charts, and unpublished manuscripts.

The enormous quantity of material that came in from the states was
deposited with the Library of Congress. But only a small fraction of it
(such as the ex-slave narratives and some of the folklore manuscripts) was
ever processed and made available. To this day, "due to more pressing
priorities" (the official explanation of the Library), the bulk of the material, which included information for a nationwide study of architecture
and several manuscripts on ethnic studies, has not been systematized. For
eight years the material from the states, which occupied some 325 cubic
feet of space, was moved from one storage place to another, then for many
years allowed to languish in a fourth-floor storeroom. Nowadays it reposes
in a building that is separate from the Library, unavailable to scholars.†

Bernard De Voto, who considered the unpublished data of the Project
no less important than the guidebooks themselves, had a premonition that
it would be wasted. A year before the Writers' Program shut down he complained in *Harper's* that although the mass of data collected by the Project
represented a storehouse of facts such as had never before existed in the
United States, it had not been digested "or even adequately organized."
He warned that the material was in danger of being destroyed as waste
paper and urged that it be organized and indexed so as to be easily available to students, writers, and historians.

Perhaps as a result of his warning, and also because the Library of Congress did not have room for all the material from the state offices, the Writers' Program, early in 1942, began to look for depositories in as many

---

* "At the time of my resignation," wrote Vardis Fisher thirty-one years later, "I had
three more books in manuscript, two large and one small . . . I have no idea where
these manuscripts are — buried somewhere, I assume, under the monstrous bureauc-
racy in Washington." Fisher resigned as director of the Idaho Federal Writers' Project
in 1939.

† A 1949 Library of Congress survey of the Project material, commenting on the
unprocessed folklore material alone, noted: "Because of the bulk of this material and
its present condition, it appears unlikely that the Library will ever have the time,
money, or personnel to finish the processing of this material for the folklore collection
unless another WPA project is established."

states as possible, utilizing such institutions as state historical societies, universities, and public libraries. Depositories for the materials were found for most of the states, but only a few of them took the trouble to systematize what they received.

The general indifference to the Project's unpublished materials constituted a shocking waste of a precious national resource. Apart from the work done by the writers' unit of the Library of Congress under the supervision of Benjamin A. Botkin, the only government agency that did what it could to preserve the last effects of the Project was the National Archives. A singularly alive burial ground, by 1953 it had finished indexing a tremendous mass of records and correspondence that reflected the operations of the projects in the states and in the Washington office; it also published an inventory showing exactly what it had.* Thanks to the National Archives collection and to what Project materials are accessible at the Library of Congress, students of history can resurrect the story of the Writers' Project operation in its general outlines.

During the war years there was a concerted attempt by a team of scholars, headed by Professor William F. McDonald (a specialist in ancient history) to prepare a study dealing with the origins and administrative history of all the arts projects and the Historical Records Survey. Their effort, sponsored by the American Council of Learned Societies and financed by the Rockefeller Foundation, produced a huge manuscript whose publication was held up for twenty years by a former official of the arts program who objected to some of its passages.†

In November 1956 the New England American Studies Association gathered at the Amherst College campus to discuss the WPA arts program, and in a superficial paper that mentioned only one Project book, *American Stuff*, heard Professor Barry Marks say that "the most impressive single feature of the WPA Arts Program was its lack of respect for creativity." In his summary of the conference discussions Professor Daniel Aaron concluded there was general agreement that WPA projects stimulated an interest in the American past which might be considered "a manifestation of a cultural nationalism that complemented the economic nationalism of the New Deal." He also pointed out that there was great

---

* *Records of the Federal Writers' Project* (1935–1944), compiled by Katherine H. Davidson (National Archives Publication No. 54–2) was prefaced by a succinct summary of the Writers' Project's career.

† *Federal Relief Administration and the Arts,* by William F. McDonald, Ohio State University Press, 1969.

disagreement on the value of the WPA arts program and on the question of whether or not the government ought to sponsor programs "for the cultivation of the arts."

Apart from such isolated occurrences, the academic world ignored the Writers' Project and its achievements. No college or university ever saw fit to honor Henry Alsberg, John Newsom or Katharine Kellock — the Project's three main dynamos. And for twenty years not a single scholarly journal paid any attention to the American Guide Series. This was no conspiracy of silence. It was simply a matter of academic fashions and neglect — a neglect which ironically (as I have indicated in an earlier chapter) was abetted by many of the same writers who had once been associated with the Project.

Yet the situation is changing; the memory of the Writers' Project is gradually coming to the fore. Possibly because it was such an innate part of the thirties, a decade which of late has been vigorously promoted in academic circles, the fog which has long obscured its accomplishments has begun to lift. More and more, the Writers' Project, along with the other arts projects, is being discussed at scholarly conferences and in classrooms dealing with American studies. Lately, a number of graduate students have chosen some aspect of the subject as the theme for their dissertations and have been digging into its story with the eagerness of gold rush prospectors. At the same time an increasing number of Project books are being revised and reissued.

What all this will lead to is hard to predict. But this much is clear: while there has been a general failure to make maximum use of the Project's published and unpublished writings, the effect that the Project had on its employees was, on the whole, psychically and economically beneficial. There were, of course, the Project cynics, the incompetents, the drunks, and the workers who did as little work as possible; but they were far outnumbered by the men and women who became deeply involved in the job of recording the America around them. At the center of their effort was the excitement of doing what they knew had never been done before, and the gratification of acquiring knowledge and insights which they would never find in any other books except those they were helping to produce. Some of the more discerning Project workers also realized that the work to which they were contributing would be valuable for a long time to come.*

* In his New York *Times* book column of September 14, 1938, Ralph Thompson

For the great majority of Americans the years of the Depression were a waiting period, a time for marking time until things got better. For most of the Project workers the sense of waiting was not as acute. They were too busy to succumb to the futility overwhelming many of their friends and neighbors. At the same time the experienced writers could have the satisfaction of maintaining their skills while earning their living; the inexperienced writers, who were in the majority, could try to become writers without going hungry.

In addition to what they could do for themselves, the Project members, without realizing it, provided a powerful antithesis to the widespread obsession with proletarian writing that dominated the literary atmosphere of the thirties — the obsession which produced an outpouring of didactic writing that told and retold what was wrong with the country and what Marxist-Leninist solutions could save it from the evils of capitalism. The Project writers, during this same period, simply told their countrymen what their country was like. As Louis Filler put it, ". . . the Communist-minded writers could only talk about the bad time here and the good time coming, but the Federal writers could write about *their* country, *their* government: its present sorrows, weaknesses and promise."

With their publications, the Project workers established a sturdy launching pad for future American writers; and contributed to their own literary development by absorbing, in the course of their work, genetic information about their country and its people that could destroy false myths, dethrone phony heroes, eliminate racial barriers, and promote assistance for disadvantaged Americans.

The experience of the Federal Writers' Project offers no clearly defined lessons for those who champion the cause of governmental subsidy of the arts. Like the other WPA arts projects, it was a freak enterprise, a strange creature of the Depression created by a special breed of men and women known as New Dealers whose motive was more political than cultural. The hope that a writers' project could somehow enhance the nation's culture was a fragile one in the minds of those who fathered it. Before the

---

predicted: "For when we of this generation are all dust and ashes and forgotten — sturdy individualists and collectivists alike, dirty radicals and true Americans, Hooverites and dangerous New Dealers, crackpots, spendthrifts, embattled suburban dames and craven takers of relief — the American Guide Series will be still very much in evidence. And not only in evidence but in use: our children will be thankful for it, and their children, and their children's children. It is certainly one of the most valuable series of books ever issued in the United States."

Project began to show what it could do, Harry Hopkins considered it "fantastic" for the government to dare play the role of author. And fantastic it was; but the writers and the nonwriters on the Project somehow managed to play their role well, so that in spite of all the administrative blunders, the political imbroglios, and the congressional salvos, they produced more good books than anyone dreamed they could.

It was unfortunate for the country that the Writers' Project was not appreciated by the general public. Partly out of philistinism, and partly because of the antagonism generated in the press toward any agency bearing the WPA label, most Americans who were aware of its existence considered it another New Deal boondoggle that should be obliterated. The Project had its advocates, but their voices were neither numerous enough nor loud enough to be heard beyond the tall walls that separate the American intellectual community from the rest of the country.

Selected Publications of the WPA Federal Writers' Project and the Writers' Program

by Arthur Scharf[*]

This list attempts to include the main publications of the Federal Writers' Project (FWP) and after mid-1939, its successor, the Writers' Program (WP), of the various states. The titles are listed by states, followed by regional and administrative publications. Within each state, the titles are listed alphabetically with the letters FWP or WP indicating authorship. Publishers and pagination are given for later editions only if they differ from the original. Items in print, as of 1972, are marked with an asterisk. The following are not included:

1. Publications which were in process but apparently were never published or completed.

2. Publications which were later completed and/or published by an ex-WPA writer under his own name, even though there is an acknowledgment of the WPA contribution.

3. Publications by other WPA groups, such as the Historical Records Survey, Federal Art Project.

4. Issuances such as radio manuscripts, which were not intended for distribution in written form. (Mimeographed items intended for distribution are included.)

5. Minor publications of a narrow technical nature, such as the series of agricultural bulletins in Florida, recreational activities in Chicago, elementary science books in Pennsylvania.

The selection is conservative in not listing some possible publications which

[*] Arthur Scharf, a Pittsburgh engineer and bookseller, has long been a student and collector of Federal Writers' Project publications. His introduction to the American Guide Series came in 1947, when he began to use the books in his travels. His favorite appraisal of the series: "Travel without the guidebooks would seem like dentistry without the X-ray." Since 1967 he has been the writer, printer, and distributor of an irregularly published bulletin, *WPA Writers Notes,* which discusses the Project books in his collection.

may have been issued but which cannot be verified. The September 1941 catalogue of the WPA Writers' publications appears to include a number of items which were not yet published but were close to publication. While many of these did finally come out, the fate of the remainder is not clear. In general the objective is to be selective rather than exhaustive.

The more than four hundred titles in the following checklist form the body of work on which the WPA Writers' Project can be judged. With more vigorous pruning a number of these would be dropped, but surely at least three hundred publications are substantial contributions to the recorded history of the United States. Some of them are contributions to our literature as well.

Alabama

Alabama: A Guide to the Deep South. (WP) New York: R. R. Smith, 1941. New York: Hastings House, 1949. Cloth, 442 pp.

Alabama. (WP) Northport, N.Y.: Bacon & Wieck, 1941. Wrappers, 32 pp. (American Recreation Series)

Alabama Health Almanac. (WP) [Birmingham?]: Alabama Tuberculosis Association, 1941. Wrappers, 36 pp.

Alabama Hunter. (WP) Wetumpka: Wetumpka Printing Co., 1941. Wrappers, 42 pp.

Fish Are Fighters in Alabama. (WP) Wetumpka: Wetumpka Printing Co., 1941. Wrappers, 38 pp.

Alaska

A Guide to Alaska, Last American Frontier, by Merle Colby. (FWP) New York: Macmillan, 1939. Cloth, 427 pp.

Arizona

*Arizona: A State Guide. (WP) New York: Hastings House, 1940. Cloth, 530 pp. The 4th and most recent ed.: Arizona, the Grand Canyon State: A State Guide. Revised by Joseph Miller; edited by Henry G. Alsberg and Harry Hansen. New York: Hastings House, 1966. Cloth, 532 pp.

Arizona. (WP) Northport, N.Y.: Bacon & Wieck, 1940. Wrappers, 44 pp. (American Recreation Series)

The Havasupai and the Hualapai. (WP) Flagstaff: State Teachers College, 1940. Wrappers, 35 pp.

Mission San Xavier del Bac, Arizona: A Descriptive and Historical Guide. (WP) New York: Hastings House, 1940. Cloth, 57 pp.

Arkansas

Arkansas: A Guide to the State. (WP) New York: Hastings House, 1941. Cloth, 447 pp.

Survey of Negroes in Little Rock and North Little Rock. (WP) Little Rock: Urban League of Greater Little Rock, 1941. Wrappers, 101 pp.

California

Almanac for Thirty-niners. (FWP) Palo Alto: J. L. Delkin, 1938. Wrappers, 127 pp.

An Anthology of Music Criticism. (WP) San Francisco, 1942. 479 pp. Mimeographed. (Vol. 7 of History of Music in San Francisco Series)

Balboa Park, San Diego, California: A Comprehensive Guide to the City's Cultural and Recreational Center. (WP) San Diego: Neyenesch Printers. 1941. Wrappers, 83 pp.

Berkeley: The First Seventy-five Years. (WP) Berkeley: Gillick Press, 1941. Cloth, 159 pp.

*California: A Guide to the Golden State. (FWP) New York: Hastings House, 1939. Cloth, 713 pp. The 3rd and most recent ed.: edited by Harry Hansen. 1967. Cloth, 733 pp.

California. (WP) Northport, N.Y.: Bacon & Wieck, 1941. Wrappers, 44 pp. (American Recreation Series)

California's State Capitol. (WP) Sacramento: State Printing Office, 1942. Wrappers, 94 pp.

The Central Valley Project. (WP) Sacramento: State Printing Office, 1942. Cloth, 165 pp.

Death Valley: A Guide. (FWP) Boston: Houghton Mifflin, 1939. Cloth and wrappers, 75 pp. plus. 48 pp. of plates.

Festivals in San Francisco. (WP) Palo Alto: J. L. Delkin, 1939. Boards, 67 pp. with color plates.

History of Journalism in San Francisco. (WP) 7 vols. 1939–1940. Mimeographed.

A History of the Ranchos: the Spanish, Mexican, and American occupation of San Diego . . . (FWP) San Diego: Union Title Insurance & Trust Co., 1939. Wrappers, 86 pp.

Los Angeles: A Guide to the City and Its Environs. (WP) New York: Hastings House, 1941. Cloth, 433 pp. Rev. ed.: 1951. Cloth, 441 pp.

Monterey Peninsula. (WP) Palo Alto: J. L. Delkin, 1941. Cloth, 207 pp. American Centennial ed., 1946. Cloth, 208 pp.

The Old West: Pioneer Tales of San Bernardino County. (WP) San Bernardino: Sun Printing and Publishing House, 1940. Wrappers, 53 pp.

San Diego: A California City. (FWP) San Diego: San Diego Historical Society, 1937. Wrappers, 138 pp.

San Francisco: The Bay and Its Cities. (WP) New York: Hastings House, 1940. Cloth, 531 pp.

Santa Barbara: A Guide to the Channel City and Its Environs. (WP) New York: Hastings House, 1941. Cloth, 206 pp.

Colorado

*Colorado: A Guide to the Highest State. (WP) New York: Hastings House, 1941. Cloth, 511 pp. Rev. ed.: Harry Hansen, ed. 1970. Cloth, 504 pp.

Colorado. (WP) Northport, N.Y.: Bacon & Wieck, 1940. Wrappers, 40 pp. (American Recreation Series)

Ghost Towns of Colorado. (WP) New York: Hastings House, 1947. Cloth, 114 pp.
A Short History of Denver. (WP) Denver: Denver Public Schools, 1940. 83 pp. (Part I, Life in Denver Series)

Connecticut

Connecticut: A Guide to Its Roads, Lore, and People. (FWP) Boston: Houghton Mifflin, 1938. Cloth, 593 pp.
Connecticut. (WP) Northport, N.Y.: Bacon & Wieck, 1940. Wrappers, 36 pp. (American Recreation Series)
A Guide to Summer Recreation in New Haven. (WP) New Haven: 1941. Wrappers, 45 pp.
History of Milford, Connecticut, 1639–1939. (FWP) Bridgeport: Braunworth, 1939. Cloth, 204 pp.
Immigrant Settlements in Connecticut: Their Growth and Characteristics, by Samuel Koenig. (FWP) Hartford: State Department of Education, 1938. Wrappers, 67 pp.
History of West Haven, 1648–1940. (WP) West Haven: Board of Selectmen, 1940. Wrappers, 93 pp.

Delaware

Delaware: A Guide to the First State. (FWP) New York: Viking, 1938. Cloth, 549 pp. Rev. ed.: Jeannette Eckman and Henry G. Alsberg, eds. New York: Hastings House, 1955. Cloth, 562 pp.
Delaware. (WP) Northport, N.Y.: Bacon & Wieck, 1941. Wrappers, 36 pp. (American Recreation Series)
New Castle on the Delaware. (FWP) New Castle: New Castle Historical Society, 1936. Cloth and Wrappers, 142 pp.

Florida

Birds in Florida. (WP) Tallahassee: Florida Dept. of Agriculture, [1942?]. Wrappers, 213 pp.
*Florida: A Guide to the Southern-most State. (FWP) New York: Oxford University Press, 1939. Cloth, 600 pp.
Florida. (WP) Northport, N.Y.: Bacon & Wieck, 1941. Wrappers, 28 pp. (American Recreation Series)
A Guide to Key West. (WP) New York: Hastings House, 1941. Cloth, 122 pp. Rev. ed., 1949.
Planning Your Vacation in Florida: Miami and Dade County, Including Miami Beach and Coral Gables. (WP) Northport, N.Y.: Bacon, Percy & Daggett, 1941. Cloth, 202 pp.
Seeing Fernandina: A Guide to the City and Its Industries. (WP) Fernandina, 1940. Wrappers, 84 pp.
Seeing St. Augustine. (FWP) St. Augustine: Record Co., 1937. Wrappers, 73 pp.

Seminole Indians in Florida. (WP) Tallahassee: Florida Dept. of Agriculture, 1941. Wrappers, 87 pp.
The Spanish Missions of Florida. (WP) St. Augustine: 1940. Wrappers, 51 pp.

Georgia

Atlanta: A City of the Modern South. (WP) New York: Smith & Durrell, 1942. Cloth, 266 pp. Rev. ed.: Atlanta: Capital of the South. Paul W. Miller, ed. New York: Durrell, 1949. Cloth, 318 pp.
Augusta. (FWP) Augusta: Tidwell Printing Supply Co., 1938. Cloth, 218 pp.
Chatham County Map Portfolio. (WP) Athens: University of Georgia Press, 1942. 40 large maps.
Drums and Shadows: Survival Studies among the Georgia Coastal Negroes. (WP) Athens: University of Georgia Press, 1940. Cloth, 274 pp.
Georgia: A Guide to Its Towns and Countryside. (WP) Athens: University of Georgia Press, 1940. Cloth, 559 pp. Rev. ed.: George G. Leckie, ed. Atlanta: Tupper & Love, 1954. Cloth, 457 pp.
Georgia. (WP) Northport, N.Y.: Bacon & Wieck, 1940. Wrappers, 32 pp. (American Recreation Series)
The Macon Guide and Ocmulgee National Monument. (WP) Macon: J. W. Burke Co., 1939. Cloth, 127 pp.
Savannah. (FWP) Savannah: Review Printing Co., 1937. Cloth, 208 pp.
Savannah River Plantations. Mary Granger, ed. (WP) Savannah: Georgia Historical Society, 1947. Wrappers, 475 pp. Limited to 300 copies.
The Story of Washington-Wilkes. (WP) Athens: University of Georgia Press, 1941. Wrappers, 136 pp.

Idaho

*Idaho: A Guide in Word and Picture. (FWP) Caldwell: Caxton Printers, 1937. Cloth, 431 pp. Rev. ed.: New York: Oxford, 1950. Cloth, 300 pp.
The Idaho Encyclopedia. Vardis Fisher, ed. (FWP) Caldwell: Caxton Printers, 1938. Cloth, 452 pp.
Idaho Lore. (FWP) Caldwell: Caxton Printers, 1939. Cloth, 256 pp.
Tours in Eastern Idaho. (FWP) n.p., 1936. Wrappers, 36 pp.

Illinois

Annals of Labor and Industry in Illinois. (WP) 2 vols. Chicago, 1939–1940. Mimeographed. Wrappers, 252 pp.
Baseball in Old Chicago. (FWP) Chicago: McClurg, 1939. Wrappers, 64 pp.
Cairo Guide. (FWP) Nappanee, Ind.: E. V. Publishing House, 1938. Wrappers, 62 pp.
Cavalcade of the American Negro. (WP) Chicago: Diamond Jubilee Exposition Authority, 1940. Wrappers, 95 pp.
Delavan, 1837–1937: A Chronicle of 100 Years. (FWP) Delavan, 1937. Wrappers, 78 pp.
Du Page County: A Descriptive and Historical Guide, 1831–1939. (FWP)

Marion Knoblauch, ed. Elmhurst: I. A. Ruby, 1948. Cloth, 253 pp. Rev. ed.:
Marion Knoblauch, ed. Wheaton: Du Page Title Co., 1951.

Galena Guide. (FWP) Chicago: Fred Klein Co., 1937. Wrappers, 79 pp.

Hillsboro Guide. (WP) Hillsboro: Montgomery News, 1940. 92 pp.

A History of the First Presbyterian Church of Chicago, 1833–1941. (WP)
Chicago: Vittu Print Shop, 1941. 75 pp.

*Illinois: A Descriptive and Historical Guide. (FWP) Chicago: McClurg, 1939.
Cloth, 687 pp. Rev. ed.: Harold L. Hitchens, ed. 1947. 707 pp. Reprint ed.:
New York: Reprint House International, 1970.

Illinois. (WP) Northport, N.Y.: Bacon & Wieck, 1941. Wrappers, 32 pp.
(American Recreation Series)

Illinois Historical Anecdotes. (WP) Chicago: Chicago Library Club, 1940.
Mimeographed. Wrappers, 93 pp.

Nauvoo Guide. (FWP) Chicago: McClurg, 1939. Wrappers, 49 pp.

Pioneer Days in Illinois. (WP) Chicago: 1940. Mimeographed. Wrappers,
78 pp.

Princeton Guide. (FWP) Princeton, Ill.: Republican Printing Co., 1939. Wrappers, 48 pp.

Public Forums in Chicago. (WP) Chicago: 1940. Mimeographed. 102 pp.

Rockford. (WP) Rockford: Graphic Arts Corp., 1941. Wrappers, 144 pp.

Stories from Illinois History. (WP) Chicago: 1941. Mimeographed. 92 pp.

Who's Who in Aviation: A directory of Living Men and Women Who Have
Contributed to the Growth of Aviation in the United States, 1942–1943.
(WP) Chicago: Ziff-Davis Co., 1942. Cloth, 486 pp.

Indiana

The Calumet Region Historical Guide. (WP) East Chicago, Ind.: Garman
Printing Co., 1939. Cloth, 271 pp.

*Indiana: A Guide to the Hoosier State. (WP) New York: Oxford University
Press, 1941. Cloth, 564 pp.

Indiana. (WP) Northport, N.Y.: Bacon & Wieck, 1941. Wrappers, 28 pp.
(American Recreation Series)

Iowa

Bentonsport Memories. (WP) Bentonsport, 1940. Mimeographed. Wrappers,
38 pp.

Buena Vista County History, Iowa. (WP) Storm Lake, 1942. Mimeographed.
87 pp.

Cherokee County, Iowa. (WP) Cherokee, 1940. Mimeographed. 58 pp.

Crawford County History, Iowa. (WP) Denison, 1941. Mimeographed. 88 pp.

Dubuque County History, Iowa. (WP) Dubuque, 1942. Mimeographed. 99 pp.

Franklin County History, Iowa. (WP) Hampton, 1941. Mimeographed. Wrappers, 73 pp.

A Guide to Burlington, Iowa. (FWP) Burlington: Acres-Blackmar Co., 1938.
Wrappers, 72 pp.

Guide to Cedar Rapids and Northeast Iowa. (FWP) Cedar Rapids: Laurance
Press, 1937. Wrappers, 79 pp.

A Guide to Dubuque. (FWP) Dubuque: Hoermann Press, 1937. Wrappers, 32 pp.

A Guide to Estherville, Iowa, Emmet County, and Iowa Great Lakes Region. (FWP) Estherville: Estherville Enterprise Print, 1939. Wrappers, 36 pp.

Iowa: A Guide to the Hawkeye State. (FWP) New York: Viking, 1938. Cloth, 583 pp. Reprint ed.: New York: Hastings House, 1949.

Iowa. (WP) Northport, N.Y.: Bacon & Wieck, 1941. Wrappers, 28 pp. (American Recreation Series)

Jackson County History, Iowa. (WP) Maquoketa, 1942. Mimeographed. 111 pp.

Johnson County History, Iowa. (WP) Iowa City, 1941. Mimeographed. 100 pp.

Lee County History. (WP) Ft. Madison, 1942. Mimeographed. 99 pp.

Monroe County History, Iowa. (WP) Albia, 1940. Mimeographed. 87 pp.

Osceola County History, Iowa. (WP) Sibley, 1942. Mimeographed. 56 pp.

Page County History, Iowa. (WP) Clarinda, 1942. Mimeographed. 99 pp.

Ringgold County History. (WP) Mt. Ayr, 1942. Mimeographed. 65 pp.

Scott County History, Iowa. (WP) Davenport, 1942. Mimeographed. 135 pp.

Southwestern Iowa Guide: Geology, Points of Interest, History. (FWP) Des Moines [1936?]. Mimeographed. Cloth, 325 pp.

Van Buren County. (WP) Farmington: Thomas L. Keith, 1940. Cloth and wrappers, 148 pp.

Woodbury County History, Iowa. (WP) Sioux City, 1942. Mimeographed. 174 pp.

Kansas

A Guide to Hillsboro, Kansas. (WP) Hillsboro: Mennonite Brethren Publishing House, 1940. Wrappers, 91 pp.

A Guide to Leavenworth, Kansas. (WP) Leavenworth: Leavenworth Chronicle, 1940. 67 pp.

A Guide to Salina, Kansas. (FWP) Salina: Advertiser-Sun, 1939. Wrappers, 55 pp.

Kansas: A Guide to the Sunflower State. (FWP) New York: Viking, 1939. Cloth, 538 pp. Reprint ed.: New York: Hastings House, 1949.

Kansas. (WP) Northport, N.Y.: Bacon & Wieck, 1941. Wrappers, 28 pp. (American Recreation Series)

Lamps on the Prairie: A History of Nursing in Kansas. (WP) Emporia: Emporia Gazette Press, 1942. Cloth, 292 pp. Reprint ed.: Topeka: Ives, 1962.

The Larned City Guide. (FWP) Larned: Tiller and Toiler Press, 1938. Wrappers, 34 pp.

Kentucky

A Centennial History of the University of Louisville. (FWP) Louisville: Standard Printing Co., 1939. Cloth, 301 pp.

Fairs and Fairmakers of Kentucky. (WP) 2 vols. Frankfort: Kentucky Dept. of Agriculture, 1942. Mimeographed. 282 pp.

Henderson: A Guide to Audubon's Home Town in Kentucky. (WP) Northport, N.Y.: Bacon, Percy & Daggett, 1941. Cloth, 120 pp.

In the Land of Breathitt. (WP) Northport, N.Y.: Bacon, Percy & Daggett, 1941. Cloth, 165 pp.

Kentucky: A Guide to the Bluegrass State. (FWP) New York: Harcourt, Brace, 1939. Cloth, 489 pp. Rev. ed.: New York: Hastings House, 1954. Cloth, 492 pp.

Kentucky. (WP) Northport, N.Y.: Bacon & Wieck, 1941. Wrappers, 32 pp. (American Recreation Series)

Lexington and the Bluegrass Country. (FWP) Lexington: Commercial Printing Co., 1938. Cloth and Wrappers, 149 pp.

Libraries and Lotteries: A History of the Louisville Free Public Library. (WP) Cynthiana: Hobson Book Press, 1944. Cloth, 300 pp.

Louisville: A Guide to the Falls City. (WP) New York: Barrows, 1940. Cloth, 112 pp.

Military History of Kentucky, Chronologically Arranged. (FWP) Frankfort: State Journal, 1939. Cloth, 493 pp.

Old Capitol and Frankfort Guide. (FWP) Frankfort: Harry McChesney, 1939. Wrappers, 98 pp.

Union County, Past and Present. (WP) Louisville: Schuhmann Printing, 1941. Cloth, 245 pp.

Louisiana

*Gumbo Ya-ya: A Collection of Louisiana Folk Tales. Compiled by Lyle Saxon, Edward Dreyer and Robert Tallant. Boston: Houghton Mifflin, 1945. Cloth, 581 pp. Reprint ed.: New York: Johnson Reprint, 1971.

*Louisiana: A Guide to the State. (WP) New York: Hastings House, 1941. Cloth, 746 pp. Rev. ed.: 1971. 768 pp.

New Orleans City Guide. (FWP) Boston: Houghton Mifflin, 1938. Cloth, 430 pp. Rev. ed. by Robert Tallant, 1952. Cloth, 416 pp.

A Tour of the French Quarter for Service Men. (WP) New Orleans, 1941. Wrappers, 32 pp.

Maine

Augusta-Hallowell on the Kennebec. (WP) Augusta: Kennebec Journal Print Shop, 1940. Wrappers, 123 pp.

*Maine: A Guide 'Down East'. (FWP) Boston: Houghton Mifflin, 1937. Cloth, 476 pp. Rev. eds.: (1) Dorris A. Isaacson, ed. Rockland: Courier-Gazette, 1970. Cloth, 510 pp. (2) Maine: A Guide to the Vacation State. Ray Bearse, ed. Boston: Houghton Mifflin, 1969. Cloth, 460 pp.

Maine. (WP) Northport, N. Y.: Bacon & Wieck, 1941. Wrappers, 32 pp. (American Recreation Series)

Maine's Capitol. (FWP) Augusta: Kennebec Journal Print Shop, 1939. Wrappers, 60 pp.

Portland City Guide. (WP) Portland: Forest City Printing Co., 1940. Cloth, 337 pp.

Maryland

A Guide to the United States Naval Academy. (WP) New York: Devin-Adair, 1941. Cloth, 158 pp.

Maryland: A Guide to the Old Line State. (WP) New York: Oxford University Press, 1940. Cloth, 561 pp.

Maryland. (WP) Northport, N.Y.: Bacon & Wieck, 1941. Wrappers, 28 pp. (American Recreation Series)

Massachusetts

The Albanian Struggle in the Old World and New. (FWP) Boston: Writer, Inc., 1939. Cloth, 168 pp.

An Almanack for Bostonians: 1939. (FWP) New York: Barrows, 1938. Boards, 120 pp.

The Armenians in Massachusetts. (FWP) Boston: Armenian Historical Society, 1937. Cloth, 148 pp.

The Berkshire Hills. (FWP) New York: Funk & Wagnalls, 1939. Cloth, 368 pp. New York: Duell, Sloan and Pearce, 1939. Cloth.

Boston Looks Seaward: The Story of the Port, 1630–1940. (WP) Boston: Bruce Humphries, 1941. Cloth, 316 pp.

A Brief History of the Towne of Sudbury in Massachusetts . . . (FWP) Sudbury, 1939. Wrappers, 64 pp. Rev. ed., 1968.

*Cape Cod Pilot, by Jeremiah Digges [pseud. of Josef Berger]. (FWP) Provincetown: Modern Pilgrim Press, 1937. Cloth, 403 pp. Rev. eds.: (1) New York: Viking, 1937. (2) Cambridge: M.I.T. Press, 1969. Wrappers, 401 pp.

Fairhaven, Massachusetts. (FWP) Fairhaven: Board of Selectmen, 1939. Cloth, 60 pp.

A Historical Sketch of Auburn, Massachusetts. (FWP) Worcester: Charles D. Cady, 1937. Wrappers, 63 pp.

*Massachusetts: A Guide to its Places and People. (FWP) Boston: Houghton Mifflin, 1937. Cloth, 675 pp. Rev. ed.: Massachusetts: A Guide to the Pilgrim State. Ray Bearse, ed. 1971. 525 pp.

Massachusetts. (FWP) New York: American Travels Press, 1939. Wrappers, 32 pp. (American Recreation Series)

Motor Tours in the Berkshire Hills. (FWP) Pittsfield: Berkshire Hills Conf., Inc., 1938. Wrappers, 68 pp.

Old Newbury Tales: An Historical Reader for Children. (FWP) Newburyport: Historical Society of Old Newbury, 1937. Wrappers, 69 pp.

The Origin of Massachusetts Place Names of the State, Counties, Cities, and Towns. (WP) New York: Harian, 1941. Wrappers, 55 pp.

Selective and Critical Bibliography of Horace Mann. (FWP) Roxbury, 1937. Cloth and wrappers, 54 pp.

Springfield, Massachusetts. (WP) Springfield, 1941. Wrappers, 84 pp.

State Forests and Parks of Massachusetts: A Recreation Guide. (WP) Boston, 1941. Wrappers, 58 pp.

The State Teachers College at Westfield. (WP) Boston, 1941. Cloth, 114 pp.

Whaling Masters. (FWP) New Bedford: Old Dartmouth Historical Society, 1938. Cloth, 314 pp.

Michigan

Cosmopolitan Education: A History of Hamtramck High School. (WP) Detroit: Inland Press, 1940. Wrappers, 74 pp.

Knowing the Thunder Bay Region. (WP) Alpena, Mich., 1941. Wrappers, 106 pp.

°Michigan: A Guide to the Wolverine State. (WP) New York: Oxford University Press, 1941. Cloth, 696 pp.

Michigan Log Marks, Their Function and Use During the Great Michigan Pine Harvest. (WP) East Lansing: Michigan State College, 1941. Wrappers, 89 pp.

Northwestern High School, 1914–1939: A History. (FWP) Detroit: Goodwill Printing Co., 1939. Wrappers, 109 pp.

Minnesota

Blue Earth County. (FWP) St. Paul, 1938. Mimeographed. Wrappers, 60 pp. (Minnesota County Histories Series)

The Bohemian Flats. (WP) Minneapolis: University of Minnesota Press, 1941. Cloth, 52 pp. 1,000 numbered copies.

Kittson County (a School History). (WP) 1940. Mimeographed. Wrappers, 69 pp.

Logging Town: The Story of Grand Rapids, Minnesota. (WP) Grand Rapids: Village Council, 1941. Wrappers, 77 pp.

The Mayors of St. Paul, 1850–1940, Including the First Three Town Presidents. (WP) St. Paul: St. Paul Vocational School, 1940. Wrappers, 73 pp.

Minneapolis: The Story of a City. (WP) Minneapolis, 1940. Wrappers, 94 pp.

Minnesota: A State Guide. (FWP) New York: Viking, 1938. Cloth, 523 pp. Rev. ed.: New York: Hastings House, 1954. 545 pp.

Minnesota. (WP) Northport, N.Y.: Bacon & Wieck, 1941. Wrappers, 48 pp. (American Recreation Series)

The Minnesota Arrowhead Country. (WP) Chicago: A. Whitman, 1941. Cloth, 231 pp.

St. Cloud, Minnesota: The Granite City. (FWP) St. Cloud: Chamber of Commerce, 1936. Wrappers, 63 pp.

Mississippi

Mississippi: A Guide to the Magnolia State. (FWP) New York: Viking, 1938. Cloth, 545 pp. Reprint ed.: New York: Hastings House, 1949.

Mississippi Gulf Coast: Yesterday and Today, 1699–1939. (FWP) Gulfport: Gulfport Printing Co., 1939. Wrappers, 162 pp.

Missouri

Missouri: A Guide to the "Show Me" State. (WP) New York: Duell, Sloan & Pearce, 1941. Cloth, 652 pp. Rev. ed.: New York: Hastings House, 1954. Cloth, 654 pp.

Montana

Copper Camp: Stories of the World's Greatest Mining Town, Butte, Montana. (WP) New York: Hastings House, 1943. Cloth, 308 pp.

Land of Nakoda: The Story of the Assiniboine Indians . . . (WP) Helena: State Publishing Co., 1942. Cloth, 296 pp. Reprint ed.: The Assiniboines: From the Accounts of the Old Ones . . . Michael S. Kennedy, ed. Norman, Okla.: University of Oklahoma Press, 1961. 209 pp.

Montana: A State Guide Book. (FWP) New York: Viking, 1939. Cloth, 430 pp. Rev. ed.: New York: Hastings House, 1955.

Montana. (WP) Northport, N.Y.: Bacon & Wieck, 1941. Wrappers, 32 pp. (American Recreation Series)

Montana: A Profile in Pictures. (WP) New York: Fleming Publishing Co., 1941. Cloth, 64 pp.

Montana's Golden Anniversary: Humorous History, Handbook, and 1940 Almanac. (WP) Helena: State Publishing Co., Wrappers, 127 pp.

Nebraska

Almanac for Nebraskans: 1939. (FWP) Lincoln: Woodruff Printing Co., 1938. Wrappers, 112 pp.

The Italians of Omaha. (WP) Omaha: Independent Printing Co., 1941. Cloth, 111 pp.

History of Nebraska Orthopedic Hospital. (WP) Lincoln, 1941. Mimeographed. Wrappers, 62 pp.

Lincoln City Guide. (FWP) Lincoln: Woodruff Printing Co., 1937. Wrappers, 87 pp.

A Military History of Nebraska. (FWP) Lincoln: National Guard of Nebraska, 1939. Mimeographed. Wrappers, 109 pp.

Nebraska: A Guide to the Cornhusker State. (FWP) New York: Viking, 1939. Cloth, 424 pp. Reprint ed.: New York: Hastings House, 1947.

Nebraska. (WP) Northport, N.Y.: Bacon & Wieck, 1941. Wrappers, 28 pp. (American Recreation Series)

Nebraska Folklore. Pamphlets 1–30. (FWP, WP) Sponsored by the State Supt. of Public Instruction, 1937–40. Mimeographed. 15–20 pp. Books 1–3 (printed excerpts from same pamphlet series): Lincoln: Woodruff Printing Co., 1939–1941. Wrappers, 32 pp. each.

The Negroes of Nebraska. (WP) Lincoln: Woodruff Printing Co., 1940. Wrappers, 48 pp.

Old Bellevue. (FWP) Papillion, Neb.: Papillion Times, 1937. Wrappers, 32 pp. 650 numbered copies.

Origin of Nebraska Place Names. (FWP) Lincoln: Woodruff Printing Co., 1938. Wrappers, 28 pp.
Printing Comes to Lincoln. (WP) Lincoln: Woodruff Printing Co., 1940. Wrappers, 80 pp.
The Search for Oil in Nebraska. (WP) Lincoln, 1942. Wrappers, 107 pp.

Nevada

Calendar of Annual Events in Nevada. (FWP) Reno: A. Carlisle, 1939. Wrappers, 32 pp.
*Nevada: A Guide to the Silver State. (WP) Portland, Ore.: Binfords & Mort, 1940, Cloth, 315 pp.

New Hampshire

Festal Days: Songs and Games of the Franco-Americans of New Hampshire. (WP) Manchester: Granite State Press, 1941. Cloth, 49 pp.
Hands That Built New Hampshire: The Story of Granite State Craftsmen Past and Present. (WP) Brattleboro, Vt.: Stephen Daye Press, 1940. Cloth, 288 pp.
New Hampshire: A Guide to the Granite State. (FWP) Boston: Houghton Mifflin, 1938. Cloth, 559 pp.
New Hampshire. (WP) Northport, N.Y.: Bacon & Wieck, 1941. Wrappers, 32 pp. (American Recreation Series)

New Jersey

Bergen County Panorama. (WP) Hackensack, 1941. Cloth, 356 pp.
Entertaining a Nation: The Career of Long Branch. (WP) Bayonne: Jersey Printing Co., 1940. Cloth, 211 pp.
Livingston: The Story of a Community. (WP) Caldwell, 1939. Cloth, 166 pp.
Matawan, 1686–1936. (FWP) Matawan: Matawan Journal, 1936. Boards, 95 pp.
Monroe Township, Middlesex County, New Jersey, 1838–1938. (FWP) New Brunswick, 1938. Wrappers, 140 pp.
New Jersey: A Guide to its Present and Past. (FWP) New York: Viking, 1939. Cloth, 735 pp. Rev. ed.: New York: Hastings House, 1959.
New Jersey. (WP) Northport, N.Y.: Bacon & Wieck, 1941. Wrappers, 36 pp. (American Recreation Series)
New Jersey: A Profile in Pictures. (FWP) New York: Barrows, 1939. Cloth, 59 pp.
Old Princeton's Neighbors. (FWP) Princeton: Graphic Arts Press, 1939. Wrappers, 108 pp.
Princeton's Fire Fighters, 1788–1938. (FWP) Princeton: Herald Press, 1938. Wrappers, 62 pp.
Proceedings of the New Jersey State Constitutional Convention of 1844. (WP) [Trenton, 1942?]. Cloth, 655 pp.
The Records of the Swedish Lutheran Churches at Raccoon and Penns Neck, 1713–1786. (FWP) Elizabeth, 1938. Cloth, 387 pp.

Ridgefield Park Fire Department. (FWP) Ridgefield: Overpeck Press, 1939.
  64 pp.
Stories of New Jersey: Its Significant Places, People and Activities. (FWP)
  New York: Barrows, 1938. Cloth, 422 pp.
The Story of Dunellen, 1887–1937. (FWP) Dunellen: Art Color Printing Co.,
  1937. Wrappers, 111 pp.
The Story of Wyckoff. (FWP) Wyckoff: Wyckoff News, 1939. Wrappers, 47 pp.
The Swedes and Finns in New Jersey. (FWP) Bayonne: Jersey Printing Co.,
  1938. Cloth, 165 pp.

New Mexico

Calendar of Events. (FWP) Santa Fe: Rydall Press, 1937. Wrappers, 32 pp.
  Illustrated by Federal Art Project.
New Mexico: A Guide to the Colorful State. (WP) New York: Hastings House,
  1940. Cloth, 458 pp. Rev. ed.: Joseph Miller and Henry G. Alsberg, eds.
  1962. 472 pp.
New Mexico. (WP) Northport, N.Y.: Bacon & Wieck, 1941. Wrappers, 32 pp.
  (American Recreation Series)
The Spanish-American Song and Game Book. (WP) New York: Barnes, 1942.
  Cloth, 87 pp.

New York City

Almanac for New Yorkers: 1937. (FWP) New York: Simon and Schuster, 1937.
  Wrappers, 128 pp.
Almanac for New Yorkers: 1938. (FWP) New York: Modern Age, 1937. Wrap-
  pers, 118 pp.
Almanac for New Yorkers: 1939. (FWP) New York: Modern Age, 1938. Wrap-
  pers, 153 pp.
American Wild Life, Illustrated. (WP) New York, Wise, 1940. Cloth, 749 pp.
  Reissued in different format, 1954. 625 pp.
*Birds of the World: An Illustrated Natural History. (FWP) Chicago: A. Whit-
  man, 1938. Cloth, 205 pp.
*The Film Index: A Bibliography. Vol. I: The Film as Art. (WP) New York:
  Wilson, 1941. Cloth, 780 pp. Reprint ed.: New York: Arno, 1969.
*The Italians of New York: A Survey . . . (FWP) New York: Random House,
  1938. Cloth, 241 pp. Reprinted: New York: Arno, 1969.
Gli Italiani di New York. (FWP) New York: Labor Press, 1939. Cloth, 242 pp.
  In Italian.
Jewish Families and Family Circles of New York. (FWP) New York, 1939.
  Cloth, 206 pp. In Yiddish.
The Jewish Landsmanschaften of New York. (FWP) New York: I. L. Peretz
  Yiddish Writers' Union, 1938. Cloth, 397 pp. In Yiddish.
A Maritime History of New York. (WP) Garden City, N.Y.: Doubleday, 1941.
  Cloth, 341 pp.
*The Negro in New York: An Informal Social History. Roi Ottley and W. J.
  Weatherby, ed. (FWP) New York: New York Public Library and Oceana,

1967. Cloth, 328 pp. Originally prepared under working title, Harlem: The Negroes of New York.

*New York City Guide: A Comprehensive Guide to the Five Boroughs of the Metropolis . . . (FWP) New York: Random House, 1939. Cloth. 708 pp. Reprint eds.: New York: Reprint House International; Octagon, 1970.

New York City Guide: A Comprehensive Guide to the Five Boroughs of the Metropolis . . . (FWP) London: Constable, 1939. Cloth, 708 pp.

New York City. (WP) New York: America Travels Press, 1939. Wrappers, 32 pp. (American Recreation Series)

New York Learns: A Guide to the Educational Facilities of the Metropolis. (FWP) New York: Barrows, 1939. Cloth, 302 pp.

New York Panorama: A Comprehensive View of the Metropolis . . . (FWP) New York: Random House, 1938. Cloth, 526 pp.

New York Panorama: A Comprehensive View of the Metropolis . . . (FWP) London: Constable, 1939. Cloth, 526 pp.

*Reptiles and Amphibians: An Illustrated Natural History. (FWP) Chicago: A. Whitman, 1939. Cloth, 253 pp.

*Who's Who in the Zoo: Natural History of Mammals. (FWP) New York: Halycon, 1937. Cloth, 211 pp. Reprint ed.: Chicago: A. Whitman, 1969.

New York State

Dutchess County. (FWP) Philadelphia: William Penn Association, 1937. Cloth, 166 pp.

Hick's Neck: The Story of Baldwin, Long Island. (WP) Baldwin: Baldwin Citizen Press, 1939. Wrappers, 61 pp.

Johnstown in New York State's Mohawk Valley . . . (WP) Johnstown, 1941. Wrappers, 89 pp.

*New York: A Guide to the Empire State. (WP) New York: Oxford University Press, 1940. Cloth, 782 pp.

New York State. (WP) Northport, N.Y.: Bacon & Wieck, 1941. Wrappers, 48 pp. (American Recreation Series)

Rochester and Monroe County. (FWP) Rochester: Scrantom's, 1937. Cloth, 460 pp.

The Story of Five Towns: Inwood, Lawrence, Cedarhurst, Woodmere, and Hewlett, Nassau County, Long Island. (WP) Rockville Centre: 1941. Cloth, 70 pp.

Warren County: A History and Guide. (WP) Glen Falls: Glen Falls Post Co., 1942. Cloth, 275 pp.

North Carolina

Bundle of Troubles, and Other Tarheel Tales. W. C. Hendricks, ed. (WP) Durham: Duke University Press, 1943. Cloth, 206 pp.

Charlotte: A Guide to the Queen City of North Carolina. (WP) Charlotte, 1939. Wrappers, 74 pp.

How North Carolina Grew. (WP) Raleigh: News and Observer, 1941. Wrappers, 98 pp.

How They Began — The Story of North Carolina County, Town and Other Place Names. (WP) New York: Harian, 1941. Wrappers, 73 pp.

North Carolina: A Guide to the Old North State. (FWP) Chapel Hill: University of North Carolina Press, 1939. Cloth, 601 pp. Rev. ed.: The North Carolina Guide. Blackwell P. Robinson, ed. 1955. Cloth, 649 pp.

North Carolina. (WP) Northport, N.Y.: Bacon & Wieck, 1941. Wrappers, 32 pp. (American Recreation Series)

Raleigh: Capital of North Carolina. (WP) New Bern: Owen G. Dunn Co., 1942. Wrappers, 170 pp.

North Dakota

*North Dakota: A Guide to the Northern Prairie State. (FWP) Fargo: Knight Printing Co., 1938. Cloth, 371 pp. Rev. ed.: New York: Oxford University Press, 1950. 352 pp.

Ohio

The Army & Navy Union, U.S.A.: A History of the Union and its Auxiliary. (WP) Flint [Mich.?]: 1942. Cloth, 239 pp.

Ashland's Eternity Acres: A Guide to Ashland County Memorials. (WP) Columbus: 1942. Wrappers, 95 pp.

The Beautiful River. (WP) Cincinnati: Wiesen-Hart Press, 1940. Wrappers, 40 pp.

Bryan and Williams County. (WP) Gallipolis: 1941. Wrappers, 117 pp.

Chillicothe and Ross County. (FWP) Columbus: F. J. Heer Printing Co., 1938. Wrappers, 91 pp.

Cincinnati: A Guide to the Queen City and Its Neighbors. (WP) Cincinnati: Wiesen-Hart Press, 1943. Cloth, 570 pp.

City Hall: The Story of Government in Cincinnati. (WP) Cincinnati: Wiesen-Hart Press, 1940. Wrappers, 64 pp.

Findlay and Hancock County Centennial, 1937. (FWP) Findlay: Findlay College, 1937. Wrappers, 52 pp.

Fremont and Sandusky County. (WP) Fremont, 1940. Wrappers, 115 pp.

Gallipolis: Being an account of the French Five Hundred . . . (WP) Gallipolis: Downtain Printing Co., 1940. Wrappers, 47 pp.

Guide Book: The Cincinnati Zoo. (WP) Cincinnati: Wiesen-Hart Press, 1942. Wrappers, 109 pp.

A Guide to Lima and Allen County, Ohio. (FWP) Lima, 1938. Wrappers, 64 pp.

Guide to Tuscarawas County. (FWP) New Philadelphia, Ohio: Tucker Printing Co., 1939. Wrappers, 119 pp.

Lake County History. (WP) Mentor, Ohio: Western Reserve Historical Society, 1941. Wrappers, 100 pp.

Lake Erie, Vacationland in Ohio: A guide to the Sandusky Bay Region. (WP) Sandusky: Stephens Printing Co., 1941. Wrappers, 129 pp.

Models for the Blind. (WP) Columbus: Ohio State School for the Blind, 1941. Wrappers, 198 pp.

The National Road in Song and Story. (WP) Columbus: Stoneman Press, 1940. Wrappers, 48 pp.
*The Ohio Guide. (WP) New York, Oxford University Press, 1940. Cloth, 634 pp.
Ohio. (WP) Northport, N.Y.: Bacon & Wieck, 1941. Wrappers, 36 pp. (American Recreation Series)
Play Spots: Akron and Summit County. (WP) Akron, 1941. Wrappers, 59 pp.
Springfield and Clark County, Ohio. (WP) Springfield: Springfield Tribune Printing, 1941. Cloth, 136 pp.
They Built a City: 150 years of Industrial Cincinnati. (FWP) Cincinnati: Cincinnati Post, 1938. Cloth, 402 pp.
Urbana and Champaign County. (WP) Urbana, Ohio: Gaumer Publishing Co., 1942. Cloth, 147 pp.
Warren and Trumbull County. (FWP) Warren, Ohio, 1938. Wrappers, 60 pp.
Westerville in the American Tradition. (WP) Columbus, 1940. Cloth and wrappers, 119 pp.
Zanesville and Muskingum County. (FWP) Zanesville, 1937. Wrappers, 38 pp.

Oklahoma

Calendar of Annual Events in Oklahoma. (FWP) Oklahoma City: Tribune Publishing Co., 1938. Wrappers, 34 pp.
Labor History of Oklahoma. (FWP) Oklahoma City: A. M. Van Horn, 1939. Cloth, 120 pp.
* Oklahoma: A Guide to the Sooner State. (WP) Norman: University of Oklahoma Press, 1942. Cloth, 442 pp. Rev. ed.: Kent Ruth, ed. 1957. Cloth, 532 pp.
Tulsa: A Guide to the Oil Capital. (FWP) Tulsa: Mid-West Printing Co., 1938. Wrappers, 79 pp.

Oregon

History of Linn County. (WP) Albany, Ore., 1941. Wrappers, 174 pp. Mimeographed.
Mount Hood: A Guide. (WP) New York: Duell, Sloan & Pearce, Hastings House (corr. pub.), 1940. Cloth and wrappers, 132 pp.
*Oregon, End of the Trail. (WP) Portland: Binfords & Mort, 1940. Cloth, 549 pp. Rev. ed.: Howard McKinley Corning, ed. 1951. Cloth.
An Oregon Almanac for 1940. (WP) [Salem ?], 1939. Wrappers, 85 pp.

Pennsylvania

A Bid for Liberty. (FWP) Philadelphia: William Penn Association, 1937. Wrappers, 48 pp.
Erie: A Guide to the City and County. (FWP) Philadelphia: William Penn Association, 1938. Cloth, 134 pp.
The Floods of Johnstown. (FWP) Johnstown: Mayor's Committee, 1939. Wrappers, 36 pp.

The Harmony Society in Pennsylvania. (FWP) Philadelphia: William Penn Association, 1937. Wrappers, 38 pp.

Hikes in Berks. (FWP) Philadelphia: William Penn Association, 1937. Wrappers, 47 pp.

The Horse-shoe Trail. (FWP) Philadelphia: William Penn Association, 1938. Wrappers, 32 pp.

The Making of America: Land of the Free. (WP) New York: Smith & Durrell, 1942. Cloth, 324 pp.

Northampton County Guide. (FWP) Bethlehem: Times Publishing Co., 1939. Cloth, 246 pp.

*Pennsylvania: A Guide to the Keystone State. (WP) New York: Oxford University Press, 1940. Cloth, 660 pp.

Pennsylvania. (WP) Northport, N.Y.: Bacon & Wieck, 1941. Wrappers, 40 pp. (American Recreation Series)

Pennsylvania Cavalcade. (WP) Philadelphia: University of Pennsylvania Press, 1942. Cloth, 462 pp.

Philadelphia: A Guide to the Nation's Birthplace. (FWP) Philadelphia: William Penn Association, 1937. Cloth, 704 pp.

A Picture of Clinton County. (WP) Williamsport, Pa.: Commissioners of Clinton County, 1942. Cloth, 195 pp.

A Picture of Lycoming County. (FWP) Williamsport, Pa.: Commissioners of Lycoming, 1939. Cloth, 223 pp.

Reading's Volunteer Fire Department: Its History and Traditions. (FWP) Philadelphia: William Penn Association, 1938. Cloth, 263 pp.

Story of Old Allegheny City. (WP) Pittsburgh: Allegheny Centennial Committee, 1941. Cloth, 236 pp.

Puerto Rico

Puerto Rico: A Guide to the Island of Boriquén. (WP) New York: University Society, 1940. Cloth, 409 pp.

Rhode Island

Rhode Island: A Guide to the Smallest State. (FWP) Boston: Houghton Mifflin, 1937. Cloth, 500 pp.

Rhode Island. (WP) Northport, N.Y.: Bacon & Wieck, 1941. Wrappers, 28 pp. (American Recreation Series)

South Carolina

Beaufort and the Sea Islands. (FWP) Savannah, Ga.: Clover Club, 1938. Wrappers, 47 pp.

A History of Spartanburg County. (WP) Spartanburg: American Association of University Women, 1940. Cloth, 304 pp.

Palmetto Pioneers: Six Stories of Early South Carolinians. (FWP) Columbia: R. L. Bryan, 1938. Boards, 81 pp.

Palmetto Place Names. (WP) Columbia: South Carolina Education Association, 1941. Boards, 158 pp.

Our South Carolina: Today from Yesterday. (WP) Clinton: P C Press, 1942. Cloth, 436 pp.

*South Carolina: A Guide to the Palmetto State. (WP) New York: Oxford University Press, 1941. Cloth, 514 pp.

South Carolina. (WP) Northport, N.Y.: Bacon & Wieck, 1941. Wrappers, 32 pp. (American Recreation Series)

South Carolina Folk Tales: Stories of Animals and Supernatural Beings. (WP) Columbia: University of South Carolina, 1941. Wrappers, 122 pp.

South Carolina State Parks. (WP) Columbia: South Carolina State Forest Service, 1940. 43 pp.

South Dakota

Aberdeen: A Middle Border City. (WP) Vermillion: University of South Dakota, 1940. Wrappers, 94 pp.

Hamlin Garland Memorial. (WP) Mitchell: South Dakota Writers' League, 1939. Wrappers, 33 pp.

Homesteaders of McPherson County. (WP) Pierre: 1941. Wrappers, 86 pp.

Legends of the Mighty Sioux. (WP) Chicago, Ill.: A. Whitman, 1941. Cloth, 158 pp. Sioux Falls: Fantab, 1960. Wrappers.

Mitchell, South Dakota: An Industrial and Recreational Guide. (FWP) Mitchell, 1938. Wrappers, 32 pp.

"Our Landlady," by L. Frank Baum. (WP) Mitchell: Prairie Workshop, 1941. Wrappers, 46 pp.

Prairie Tamers of Miner County. (FWP) Mitchell, 1939. Wrappers, 35 pp.

Sodbusters: Tales of Southeastern South Dakota. (FWP) Alexandria: South Dakota Writers' League, 1938. Wrappers, 27 pp.

A South Dakota Guide. (FWP) Pierre: State Publishing Co., 1938. Cloth, 441 pp. Rev. ed.: South Dakota: A Guide to the State. M. Lisle Reese, ed. New York: Hastings House, 1952. Cloth, 421 pp.

South Dakota. Northport, N.Y.: Bacon & Wieck, 1940. Wrappers, 32 pp. (American Recreation Series)

South Dakota Place Names. (WP) Vermillion: University of South Dakota, 1940. (In six parts). Wrappers, 418 pp. Mimeographed. Rev. ed., 1941. 690 pp.

Unfinished Histories: Tales of Aberdeen and Brown County. (FWP) Mitchell: South Dakota Writers' League, 1938. Wrappers, 58 pp.

A Vacation Guide to Custer State Park in the Black Hills of South Dakota. (FWP) Pierre: State Pub. Co., 1938. 32 pp.

Tennessee

God Bless the Devil! Liars' Bench Tales. (WP) Chapel Hill: University of North Carolina Press, 1940. Cloth, 254 pp.

Tennessee: A Guide to the State. (FWP) New York: Viking, 1939. Cloth, 558 pp. Rev. ed.: New York: Hastings House, 1949. Cloth.

Tennessee. (WP) Northport, N.Y.: Bacon & Wieck, 1941. Wrappers, 28 pp. (American Recreation Series)

Texas

Along the San Antonio River. (WP) San Antonio: Clegg Co., 1941. Wrappers, 36 pp.

Beaumont: A Guide to the City and its Environs. (FWP) Houston: Anson Jones, 1939. Boards, 167 pp.

Corpus Christi: A History and Guide. (WP) Corpus Christi: Caller-Times, 1942. Cloth, 245 pp.

Houston: A History and Guide. (WP) Houston: Anson Jones, 1942. Cloth, 363 pp.

Port Arthur. (WP) Houston: Anson Jones, 1940. Cloth, 164 pp.

Randolph Field: A History and Guide. (WP) New York: Devin-Adair, 1942. Cloth, 156 pp.

San Antonio: An Authoritative Guide to the City and its Environs. (FWP) San Antonio: Clegg Co., 1938. Wrappers, 106 pp. Rev. ed.: San Antonio: A History and Guide, 1941. Wrappers, 111 pp.

St. David's Through the Years. (WP) Austin: St. David's Guild, St. David's Episcopal Church, 1942. Wrappers, 94 pp.

*Texas: A Guide to the Lone Star State. (WP) New York: Hastings House, 1940. Cloth, 718 pp. Rev. ed.: Harry Hansen, ed. 1969. Cloth, 717 pp.

Texas. (WP) Northport, N.Y.: Bacon & Wieck, 1941. Wrappers, 36 pp. (American Recreation Series)

Utah

Origins of Utah Place Names. (FWP) Salt Lake City: State Dept. of Public Instruction, 1938. Wrappers, 29 pp. Mimeographed. 3rd ed., 1940.

Provo: Pioneer Mormon City. (WP) Portland, Ore.: Binfords & Mort, 1942. Cloth, 223 pp.

Utah: A Guide to the State. (WP) New York: Hastings House, 1941. Cloth, 595 pp.

Utah's Story. (WP) Salt Lake City, 1942. Wrappers, 90 pp.

Vermont

*Vermont: A Guide to the Green Mountain State. (FWP) Boston: Houghton Mifflin, 1937. Cloth, 392 pp. Rev. ed.: Ray Bearse, ed. 1968. Cloth, 452 pp.

Vermont. (WP) Northport, N.Y.: Bacon & Wieck, 1941. Wrappers, 32 pp. (American Recreation Series)

Vermont: A Profile of the Green Mountain State. (WP) New York: Fleming, 1941. Cloth, 57 pp.

Virginia

Dinwiddie County: "The Countrey of the Apamatica." (WP) Richmond: Whittet & Shepperson Printers, 1942. Cloth, 302 pp.

A Guide to Hopewell and Prince George County. Hopewell: Hopewell News, 1939. Wrappers, 68 pp.

Jefferson's Albermarle: A Guide to Albermarle County and the City of Charlottesville, Virginia. (WP) Charlottesville: Jarman's, 1941. Wrappers, 157 pp.

°The Negro in Virginia. (WP) New York: Hastings House, 1940. Cloth, 380 pp. Reprint ed.: New York: Arno, 1969. (American Negro: His History and Literature Series)

Prince William: The Story of its People and its Places. (WP) Richmond: Whittet & Shepperson Printers, 1941. Cloth, 261 pp.

Roanoke: Story of County and City. (WP) Roanoke: Stone Printing & Manufacturing, 1942. Cloth, 390 pp.

Sussex County: A Tale of Three Centuries. (WP) Richmond. Whittet & Shepperson Printers, 1942. Cloth, 324 pp.

°Virginia: A Guide to the Old Dominion. (WP) New York: Oxford University Press, 1940. Cloth, 699 pp. Reissued in 1952. 710 pp.

Virginia. (WP) Northport, N.Y.: Bacon & Wieck, 1941. Wrappers, 35 pp. (American Recreation Series)

Virginia: The Old Dominion in Pictures. (WP) New York: Fleming, 1941. Cloth, 58 pp.

Washington State

°Washington: A Guide to the Evergreen State. (WP) Portland, Ore.: Binfords & Mort, 1941. Cloth, 687 pp. Rev. ed.: New Washington: A Guide to the Evergreen State. Howard McKinley Corning, ed. 1950. Cloth, 688 pp.

Washington. (WP) Northport, N. Y.: Bacon & Wieck, 1941. Wrappers, 36 pp. (American Recreation Series)

West Virginia

The First Census of Hampshire County. (FWP) Romney: West Virginia Schools for the Deaf and Blind, 1937. Wrappers, 68 pp.

Historic Romney, 1762–1937. (FWP) Romney: Town Council of Romney, 1937. Wrappers, 67 pp.

°West Virginia: A Guide to the Mountain State. (WP) New York: Oxford University Press, 1941. Cloth, 559 pp.

West Virginia. (WP) Northport, N.Y.: Bacon & Wieck, 1941. Wrappers, 24 pp. (American Recreation Series)

Wisconsin

Portage. (FWP) Portage: Portage Chamber of Commerce, 1938. Wrappers, 85 pp.

Shorewood. (FWP) Shorewood: Village Board of Shorewood, 1939. Wrappers, 109 pp.

Wisconsin: A Guide to the Badger State. (WP) New York: Duell, Sloan & Pearce, 1941. Cloth, 651 pp. Rev. ed.: New York: Hastings House, 1954.

Wisconsin. (WP) Northport, N.Y.: Bacon & Wieck, 1941. Wrappers, 32 pp. (American Recreation Series)

Wisconsin Circus Lore. (FWP) Madison, 1937. Mimeographed. Cloth, 58 pp.

Wisconsin Indian Place Legends. (FWP) Madison, 1936. Mimeographed. Cloth, 50 pp. Rev. ed.: Wisconsin Indian Place-Name Legends. Dorothy M. Brown, ed. 1948. 30 pp. (Wisconsin Centennial Issue, Wisconsin Folklore Publications)

Wyoming

*Wyoming: A Guide to Its History, Highways, and People. (WP) New York: Oxford University Press, 1941. Cloth, 490 pp.

Washington, D.C.

The Angler's Guide for Washington and Vicinity . . . (WP) Northport, N.Y.: Bacon, Percy & Daggett, 1941. Wrappers, 61 pp.

Credo de Libertad: La Constitución y otros Documentos Históricos de los Estados Unidos. (WP) Washington: Government Printing Office, 1942. Wrappers, 47 pp. In Spanish.

District of Columbia. (WP) Northport, N.Y.: Bacon & Wieck, 1940. Wrappers, 40 pp. (American Recreation Series)

Estampas de una Democracia: Los Estados Unidos de América. (WP) Washington: Government Printing Office [1942?]. Cloth, 181 pp. Quarto. In Spanish.

Our Federal Government and How It Functions. (FWP) Joseph Gaer, ed. New York: Hastings House, 1939. Cloth, 234 pp. Rev. ed., 1941, 272 pp.

Our Washington: A Comprehensive Album of the Nation's Capital in Words and Pictures. (FWP) Chicago: McClurg, 1939. Cloth, 178 pp.

*Washington: City and Capital. (FWP) Washington: Government Printing Office, 1937. Cloth, 1140 pp. Rev. ed.: Washington, D.C.: A Guide to the Nation's Capital. R. B. Truett, ed. New York: Hastings House, 1968. 528 pp.

Regional

Here's New England! A Guide to Vacationland. (FWP) Boston: Houghton Mifflin, 1939. Cloth and wrappers, 122 pp.

The Intracoastal Waterway: Norfolk to Key West. (FWP) Washington, D.C.: Government Printing Office, 1937. Wrappers, 143 pp.

New England Hurricane: A Factual, Pictorial Record. (FWP) Boston: Hale, Cushman & Flint, 1938. Cloth 220 pp.

The Ocean Highway: New Brunswick, New Jersey, to Jacksonville, Florida. (FWP) New York: Modern Age, 1938. Cloth, 244 pp.

*The Oregon Trail: The Missouri River to the Pacific Ocean. (FWP) New York: Hastings House, 1939. Cloth, 244 pp. Reprint ed.: New York: Reprint House International, 1970.

Skiing in the East: The Best Trails and How to Get There. (FWP) New York: Barrows, 1939. Cloth, 334 pp.

*These Are Our Lives, As Told by the People. (FWP) Chapel Hill: University of North Carolina Press, 1939. Cloth, 421 pp. Reprint eds.: New York: Reprint House International; Arno, 1969.

U.S. One: Maine to Florida. (FWP) New York: Modern Age, 1938. Cloth, 344 pp.

After Hours Writings

American Stuff: An Anthology of Prose and Verse by Members of the Federal Writers' Project. New York: Viking, 1937. Cloth, 301 pp.

American Stuff: by Workers of Federal Writers' Project. Darien, Conn.: 1938. Wrappers, 128 pp. Special issue of *Direction*, Vol. 1, No. 3.

Administrative

The American Guide Manual. (FWP) Washington, D.C., 1935. Mimeographed. 86 pp.

Catalog of Publications. (FWP) Washington, D.C., [1937?] Wrappers, 40 pp. The first printed catalog, illustrated.

Catalog, American Guide Series. (FWP) Washington, D.C.: Government Printing Office, 1938. Wrappers, 31 pp., illustrated.

List of Major Books Issued by Federal Writers' Project (supplementary to catalog published Fall 1938). (FWP) Washington, D.C., 1939. Mimeographed. 4 pp.

Supplementary List of Publications Following the Fall 1938 Catalog. (WP) Washington, D.C., 1939. Mimeographed. 8 pp.

Catalogue, WPA Writers' Program Publications. (The American Guide Series, the American Life Series) (WP) Washington, D.C.: Government Printing Office, 1942. Wrappers, 54 pp.

Final Report on Disposition of Unpublished Materials of WPA Writers' Program, April 8, 1943, by Merle Colby. Washington, D.C., 1943. 12 pp.

Sources Consulted

Government Documents

Frances T. Bourne. "Report and Recommendation for the Disposition of Records of the Federal Writers' Project." Library of Congress, July 29, 1949.

Katharine H. Davidson. *Preliminary Inventory of the Records of the Federal Writers' Project, Work Projects Administration, 1935–44.* National Archives, Record Group 69. Washington, D.C., 1953. National Archives Publication No. 54–2.

U.S. House of Representatives. Special Committee on Un-American Activities. *Investigation of Un-American Propaganda Activities in the United States.* Hearings on H. Res. 282, Vols. 1–4, 75th Cong., 3rd Sess., 1938.

———. *Report of the Special Committee on Un-American Activities — Pursuant to H. Res. 282, 75th Cong., 4th Sess., 1939.*

———. Sub-Committee of the Committee on Appropriations. *Further Additional Appropriations for Work Relief and Relief, Fiscal Year 1939.* Hearings on H. J. Res. 209 and 246, 76th Cong., 1st Sess., 1939.

———. Sub-Committee of the Committee on Appropriations. *Investigation and Study of the Works Progress Administration.* Hearings on H. Res. 130, Pt. 1, 76th Cong., 1st Sess. 1939–40.

———. Sub-Committee of the Committee on Appropriations. *Work Relief and Relief for Fiscal Year 1940.* Hearings on H. J. Res. 326, 76th Cong., 1st Sess., 1939.

U.S. Senate. Committee on Appropriations. *Work Relief and Public Works Appropriation Act of 1939.* Hearings on H. J. Res. 326, 76th Cong., 1st Sess., 1939.

———. Senate Armed Forces Committee. Hearings on Nomination of Anna M. Rosenberg to be Assistant Secretary of Defense. 81st Cong., 2nd Sess., 1950.

Works Progress Administration. Federal Writers' Project. Brief containing detailed answers to charges concerning the Federal Writers' Project made by witnesses who appeared before the Special Committee to Investigate Un-American Activities, House of Representatives. Washington, D.C., 1939.

————. Henry G. Alsberg's statement refuting charges made by witnesses testi-fying before House Sub-Committee of the Committee on Appropriations on the Works Progress Administration. May 1, 1939.

Articles

Aaron, Daniel, moderator. "Thirty Years Later: Memories of the First American Writers' Congress." *American Scholar*, XXXV (Summer 1935), 495. A sym-posium with Kenneth Burke, Malcolm Cowley, Granville Hicks, and William Phillips.

Alsberg, Henry G. "Federal Writers' Project and Education." *Journal of the National Education Association*, XXV (March 1936), 86.

————. "Writers and the Government: Federal Writers' Projects." *Saturday Review of Literature*, XIII (January 4, 1936), 13.

Bendiner, Robert. "When Culture Came to Main Street." *Saturday Review*, L (April 1, 1967), 19.

Benét, Stephen Vincent. "Patchwork Quilt of These United States." New York Herald-Tribune *Books*, XVIII (December 28, 1941), 1.

Billington, Ray Allen. "Government and the Arts: The WPA Experience." *American Quarterly*, XIII (Winter 1961), 466.

Bolles, Blair. "The Federal Writers' Project." *Saturday Review of Literature*, XVIII (July 9, 1938), 3.

Botkin, Benjamin A. "Living Lore on the New York City Writers' Project," *New York Folklore Quarterly*, II (November 1946), 252.

————. "Regionalism: Cult or Culture?" *English Journal*, XXV (March 1936), 181.

————. "We Called it 'Living Lore.'" *New York Folklore Quarterly*, XIV (Autumn 1958), 189.

————. "WPA and Folklore Research: 'Bread and Song.'" *Southern Folklore Quarterly*, III (March 1939), 7.

Brandt, R. P. "The Dies Committee: An Appraisal." *Atlantic Monthly*, CLXV (February 1940), 232.

Brogan, D. W. "Uncle Sam's Guides." *The Spectator* (London), CLXI (August 5, 1938), 226.

Brown, Sterling A. "A Century of Negro Portraiture in American Literature." *The Massachusetts Review*, VII (Winter 1966), 73.

Cantwell, Robert. "America and the Writers' Project." *New Republic*, LXXXX-VIII (April 26, 1939), 323.

Colby, Merle. "Presenting America to All Americans." *Publishers' Weekly*, CXXXIX (May 3, 1941), 1815.

"Completion of American Guide Series." *Publishers' Weekly*, CXXXIX (May 3, 1941), 1815.

Conroy, Jack. "Writers Disturbing the Peace," *New Masses*, XXI (November 17, 1936), 13.

————. "American Stuff: An Anthology of WPA Creative Writing," *New Masses*, XXIV (September 14, 1937), 24.

Cowley, Malcolm. "While They Waited for Lefty," *Saturday Review*, XLVIII (June 6, 1941), 16.

———. "The 1930's Were an Age of Faith." *New York Times Book Review*, LXIX (December 13, 1964), 16.

Current-Garcia, E. "Writers in the 'Sticks.'" *Prairie Schooner*, XII (Winter 1938), 294.

De Voto, Bernard. "The First WPA Guide." *Saturday Review of Literature*, XV (February 27, 1937), 8.

———. "New England Via WPA." *Saturday Review of Literature*, XVIII (May 14, 1938), 3.

———. "The Writers' Project." *Harper's Magazine*, CLXXXIV (January 1942), 221.

"Distributing the Guides." *Publishers' Weekly*, CXXXVII (May 11, 1940), 1836.

Drennen, Marguerite. "New Deal's Huge Cultural Program Launched With $27,000,000 Fund." *Washington Sunday Post*, September 8, 1935.

"'Federal Art.'" *The Times* (London), July 21, 1939.

"Federal Guide Disturbs Massachusetts Officials." *Publishers' Weekly*, CXXXII (August 28, 1937), 713.

Fox, Daniel M. "Archives of the Federal Writers." *American Quarterly*, XIII (Spring 1961), 3.

Gutheim, Frederick. "America in Guide Books." *Saturday Review of Literature*, XXIV (June 14, 1941), 3.

Horlings, Albert. "Guidebooks to America." *New Republic*, CVI (April 3, 1942), 501.

Kellock, Katharine. "The WPA Writers: Portraitists of the United States." *American Scholar*, IX (October 1940), 473.

Kernan, Michael, "Memories of Slave Days." *Washington Post*, November 7, 1969.

"Killing the Writers' Project." *New Republic*, C (August 23, 1969), 62.

Leighton, George R. "And If the Revolution Comes . . . ?" *Harper's Magazine*, CLXIV (March 1932), 446.

MacLeish, Archibald. "He [Franklin D. Roosevelt] Cherished American Culture." *New Republic*, CXIV (April 15, 1946), 540.

Mangione, Jerre. "Federal Writers' Project." *New York Times Book Review*, LXXIV (May 18, 1969), 2.

"Mirror of America." *Time*, XXXI (January 3, 1938), 55.

Mumford, Lewis. "A Letter to the President." *New Republic*, LXXXIX (December 30, 1936), 263.

———. "Writers' Project." *New Republic*, LXXXXII (October 20, 1937), 306.

Nichols, H. G. "Writer and the State: American Guide." *Contemporary Review*, CLV (January 1939), 89.

Osofsky, Gilbert. "The Negro in New York: An Informal Social History." *New York Times Book Review*, LXXII (June 25, 1967), 7.

"Pen Project — America, the WPA, and 20,000,000 Words." *The Pathfinder* (December 17, 1938).

Peter, Emmett. "Library of Folklore?" [recounting Zora Neale Hurston's unpublished tale, "Diddy-Wah-Diddy"]. Orlando (Fla.) *Sentinel*, February 22, 1970.

"Publishers' Letter on Federal Writers' Project." *Publishers' Weekly,* CXXXV (May 27, 1939), 1919.

"Publishers Praise Federal Writers' Projects." *Publishers' Weekly,* CXXXV (May 20, 1939), 1817.

Putnam, Jared. "Guides to America." *The Nation,* CIIIL (December 24, 1938), 694.

Soule, George. "Are We Going to Have a Revolution?" *Harper's Magazine,* CLXV (August 1932), 277.

Taber, Ronald W. "Vardis Fisher and the 'Idaho Guide.'" *Pacific Northwest Quarterly,* LIX (April 1968), 68.

————. "Vardis Fisher of Idaho, March 31, 1895–July 9, 1968." *Idaho Yesterdays,* XII (Fall 1968), 2.

"The 1930's." *The Carleton Miscellany* (special issue), VI (Winter 1965).

"Their Own Baedeker" [Henry G. Alsberg]. *New Yorker,* XXV (August 20, 1949), 17.

Touhey, Eleanor. "The American Baedekers." *Library Journal,* LXVI (April 15, 1941), 339.

Ulrich, Mabel S. "Salvaging Culture for the WPA." *Harper's Magazine,* CLXXVIII (May 1939), 653.

Umland, Rudolph. "On Editing WPA Guide Books." *Prairie Schooner,* XIII (Fall 1939), 160.

Walton, Eda Lou. "A Federal Writers' Anthology" [*American Stuff*], *New York Times Book Review* (August 29, 1937), 2.

Wechsler, James. "Record of the Boondogglers" (Part II). *The Nation,* CXXXXV (December 25, 1937), 715.

West, Hollie I. "The Teacher" [Sterling A. Brown]. *Washington Post,* November 16, 1969.

"What the Writers Wrote." *New Republic,* LXXXXII (September 1, 1937), 89.

"Work of the Federal Writers' Project of WPA." *Publishers' Weekly,* CXXXV (March 18, 1939), 1130.

"WPAccounting." *Time,* XXXXI (February 15, 1943), 96.

"WPAchievement." *Time,* XXXV (August 12, 1940), 64.

"WPA Writers to Gather Municipal Data in 191 Cities." *American City,* LII (January 1937), 75.

Yetman, Norman R. "Background of the Slave Narrative Collection." *American Quarterly,* XIX (Fall 1967), 534.

Magazine Compilations of Prose and Poetry Written by Members of the Federal Writers' Project

American Stuff (special issue of *Direction,* Vol. 1, No. 3), 1938.

Coast. "An unofficial co-operative publication of writers on the San Francisco Project." Spring 1937.

Frontier and Midland, Winter 1938.

"Material Gathered." Federal Writers' Project in San Francisco. 1936. Mimeographed.

New Masses, XXVII, May 10, 1938.

New Republic. "Federal Poets: An Anthology." XCV, May 11, 1938.

Poetry. "Federal Poets Number." LII, July 1938. With supplementary articles by Malcolm Cowley, Alfred Kreymborg, *et. al.*

"Shucks." Nebraska Federal Writers' Project. October 1936. Mimeographed.

Books

For the American Guide Series and other volumes produced by the Federal Writers' Project and Writers' Program, see list of selected publications, pages 375–396.

Aaron, Daniel. *Writers on the Left: Episodes in American Literary Communism.* New York: Harcourt Brace and World, 1961.

Alsberg, Henry G., ed. *The American Guide.* New York: Hastings, 1949.

Baedeker, Karl, ed. *United States.* (J. F. Muirhead, writer.) London: Dulau, 1893.

Bendiner, Robert. *Just Around the Corner: A Highly Selective History of the Thirties.* New York: Dutton, 1968.

Bird, Caroline. *The Invisible Scar.* New York: McKay, 1966.

Bontemps, Arna, and Jack Conroy. *Anyplace but Here.* New York: Hill & Wang, 1966.

Botkin, Benjamin A., ed. *Lay My Burden Down: A Folk History of Slavery.* Chicago: University of Chicago Press, 1945.

———. *Treasury of American Folklore.* New York: Crown, 1944.

Boyden, Polly. *The Pink Egg.* Truro, Mass.: Pamet, 1942.

Cayton, Horace. *Long Old Road.* New York: Trident, 1965.

Charles, Searle F. *Minister of Relief: Harry Hopkins and the Depression.* Syracuse, N.Y.: Syracuse University Press, 1963.

Congdon, Don, ed. *The Thirties: A Time to Remember.* New York: Simon & Schuster, 1962.

Conrad, Earl. *Jim Crow America.* New York: Duell, Sloan and Pearce, 1947.

Conroy, Jack. *The Disinherited.* New York: Covici-Friede, 1933.

Cowley, Malcolm. *Exile's Return: A Literary Odyssey of the 1920's.* New York: Viking, 1951.

———. *Think Back on Us: A Contemporary Chronicle of the 1930's.* Ed. by Henry Dan Piper. Carbondale, Ill.: Southern Illinois University Press, 1967.

Crossman, Richard, ed. *The God That Failed.* Contributors: Richard Wright, André Gide, Ignazio Silone, *et al.* New York: Harper, 1950.

Dies, Martin. *Martin Dies' Story.* New York: Bookmailer, 1963.

Donohue, H. E. F. *Conversations with Nelson Algren.* New York: Hill & Wang, 1964.

Drinnon, Richard. *Rebel in Paradise: A Biography of Emma Goldman.* New York: Doubleday, Page, 1923.

Ellison, Ralph. *Shadow and Act.* New York: Random House, 1964.

Emanuel, James, ed. *Dark Symphony: Negro Literature in America.* New York: Free Press, 1968. (Contains Ralph Ellison's "King of the Bingo Game.")

Filler, Louis, ed. *The Anxious Years: America in the Nineteen Thirties.* New York: Putnam's, 1963.

Flanagan, Hallie. *Arena.* New York: Duell, Sloan and Pearce, 1940.

Freidel, Frank, ed. *The New Deal and the American People.* Englewood Cliffs, N.J.: Prentice-Hall, 1964.

Gibson, William. *A Mass for the Dead.* New York: Atheneum, 1968.

Gilbert, James Burkhardt. *Writers and Partisans: A History of American Radicalism in America.* New York, Wiley, 1968.

Goodman, Walter. *The Committee: The Extraordinary Career of the House Committee on Un-American Activities.* New York: Farrar, Straus & Giroux, 1968.

Harevan, Tamara K. *Eleanor Roosevelt: An American Conscience.* Chicago: Quadrangle, 1968.

Hart, Henry, ed. *American Writers' Congress, 1st.* New York: International Publishers, 1935.

————. *The Writer in a Changing World.* Report on the second American Writers' Congress. New York: Equinox Cooperative Press, 1937.

Howard, Donald S. *The WPA and Federal Relief Policy.* New York: Russell Sage Foundation, 1943.

Ickes, Harold L. *The Secret Diary of Harold L. Ickes.* 3 vols. New York: Simon and Schuster, 1954. II: *The Inside Struggle, 1936–1939.*

Josephson, Matthew. *Infidel in the Temple.* New York: Knopf, 1967.

Kazin, Alfred. *On Native Grounds: An Interpretation of Modern American Prose Literature.* New York: Reynal and Hitchcock, 1942.

————. *Starting Out in the Thirties.* Boston: Little, Brown, 1965.

Leuchtenburg, William E. *Franklin D. Roosevelt and the New Deal, 1932–1940.* New York: Harper, 1963.

Lomax, John. *Adventures of a Ballad Hunter.* New York: Macmillan, 1947.

Madden, David. *Proletarian Writers of the Thirties.* Carbondale, Ill.: Southern Illinois University Press, 1967.

Mathews, Jane De Hart. *The Federal Theater, 1935–1939: Plays, Relief, and Politics.* Princeton, N.J.: Princeton University Press, 1967.

McDonald, William F. *Federal Relief Administration and the Arts.* Columbus, Ohio: Ohio State University Press, 1969.

McKinzie, Kathleen O'Connor. "Writers on Relief: 1935–1942." Unpublished Ph.D. thesis, Department of History, Indiana University, 1970.

O'Connor, Francis V. *Federal Support for the Visual Arts: The New Deal and Now.* Greenwich, Conn.: New York Graphic Society, 1969.

Ottley, Roi. *New World A-Coming.* Boston: Houghton Mifflin, 1943.

Overmyer, Grace. *Government and the Arts.* New York: Norton, 1939.

Rideout, Walter B. *The Radical Novel in the United States, 1900–1954.* Cambridge, Mass.: Harvard University Press, 1956.

Rosenman, Samuel, ed. *The Public Papers and Addresses of Franklin D. Roosevelt.* 13 vols. New York: Random House, 1938–1950.

Salzman, Jack, ed. *Years of Protest: A Collection of American Writing of the 1930's.* New York: Pegasus, 1967.

Schlesinger, Arthur M., Jr. *The Age of Roosevelt.* 3 vols. Boston: Houghton Mifflin, 1957–1960.

Shannon, David A., ed. *The Great Depression.* Englewood Cliffs, N.J.: Prentice-Hall, 1960.

Sherwood, Robert E. *Roosevelt and Hopkins.* New York: Harper, 1948.

Stearns, Harold E., ed. *Civilization in the United States: An Inquiry by Thirty Americans,* New York: Harcourt, 1922.

————. *A Re-Appraisal.* New York: Hillman-Curl, 1937.

Steinbeck, John. *Travels with Charley*. New York: Viking, 1962.

Swados, Harvey, ed. *The American Writer and the Great Depression*. Indianapolis: Bobbs-Merrill, 1966.

Taber, Ronald Warren. "The Federal Writers' Project in the Pacific Northwest: A Case Study." Unpublished Ph.D. thesis, Program in American Studies, Washington State University, 1969.

Webb, Constance. *Richard Wright, a Biography*. New York: Putnam's, 1968.

Wecter, Dixon. *The Age of the Great Depression*. New York: Macmillan, 1948.

Wright, Richard. *Uncle Tom's Children*. New York: Harper, 1940.

Novels and Memoirs Dealing with the Federal Writers' Project, by Former Project Members

Balch, Jack. *Lamps at High Noon*. New York: Modern Age, 1941.

Fisher, Vardis. *Orphans in Gethsemane: A Novel of the Past in the Present*. Denver: Alan Swallow, 1960.

Johns, Orrick. *Time of Our Lives: The Story of My Father and Myself*. New York: Stackpole, 1937.

Macleod, Norman. *You Get What You Ask For*. New York: Harrison-Hilton, 1939.

Roskolenko, Harry. *When I Was Last on Cherry Street*. New York: Stein and Day, 1965.

Yezierska, Anzia. *Red Ribbon on a White Horse*. New York: Scribner's, 1950.

Taped Interviews with Former Members of the Federal Writers' Project

Henry G. Alsberg. May 23 and 24, 1968.

Jack Balch. February 11, 1968.

Josef Berger (Jeremiah Digges). July 24, 1968.

Jack Conroy. June 14, 1968.

Leon (Bill) Dorais. May 28, 1968.

Ralph Ellison. June 30, 1969.

Samuel Epstein. July 25, 1968.

Vardis Fisher. June 4 and 5, 1968.

Reed Harris. January 11, 1968.

James McGraw. December 15, 1967; May 16, 1968.

Vincent McHugh. May 29, 1968.

Lawrence Morris. May 17, 1968.

Harold Rosenberg. August 20, 1968.

Morton W. Royse. June 8, 1970.

Studs Terkel. January 5, 1969.

Donald Thompson. November 17, 1968.

Basil Vaerlen. July 5, 1968.

George F. Willison. November 24, 1967.

Other Interviews, 1967–70

Salvatore Attanasio
Allan Angoff
*Mildred Baker
 (Mrs. Jacob Baker)
Aubrey Baldwin
*Robert Bendiner

Leonard Bidwell
Benjamin A. Botkin
*Millen Brand
Kay Britton
Sterling A. Brown
*Kenneth Burke

Robert Carlson
*Horace R. Cayton
John Cheever
Fred Christensen
Merle Colby
Earl Conrad

* Not a member of the FWP.

SOURCES CONSULTED

Paul Corey
*Julius Davidson
Miriam Allen deFord
Arnold de Mille
Loren Eiseley
Lawrence Estavan
*Thomas Hornsby
  Ferrill
Marion Knoblauch
  Franc
Lawrence Gellert
Margaret Gleason
*Arthur Goldschmidt
*Elizabeth Goldschmidt
Stella B. Hanau
Leon Srabian Herald
*Josephine Herbst
Dora Thea Hettwer

Eugene Holmes
Robert West Howard
Irving Ignatin
David Ignatow
*Alfred Kazin
Katharine Kellock
Angelica Kinkead
Robin Kinkead
*Walter Krimont
Saul Levitt
Mary Lloyd
Bert James Loewenberg
Curtis D. MacDougall
Carl Malmberg
Frank E. Manuel
Frank Mead
Henry Lee Moon
Dale Morgan

Nathan Morris
Gorham Munson
*Harvey O'Connor
Ethel Schlasinger
  Overby
Ed Radenzel
Kenneth Rexroth
Roderick Seidenberg
Harry L. Shaw, Jr.
Agnes Wright Spring
Walter Storey
Ellen Tarry
Paul Ellsworth Triem
Rudolph Umland
Charles van
  Ravenswaay
Margaret Walker
Nicholas Wirth

* Not a member of the FWP.

Illustration Credits

For permission to include the illustrations in this book the author is grateful to the following individuals, companies and institutions:

Dora Thea Hettwer: *pages 7, 25, 67, 82, 219, 233*
Leon Srabian Herald: *35*
The New York *Daily Mirror: 38*
Mrs. Jacob Baker: *41*
The Library of Congress: *64, 67, 71, 332*
World Wide Photos: *85, 295, 311*
Mrs. Dorris Westall Isaacson: *90*
Cartoon by Lloyd Coe. Copyright 1936 by the Saturday Review Company, Inc.;
    Copyright © renewed 1963 by Saturday Review, Inc.: *107*
Maurice Johnson: *110*
Rudolph Umland: *114*
Sam Ross: *118*
Nelson Algren: *120*
Saul Bellow: *122*
Jack Conroy: *126, 274*
Dial Press: *129*
Studs Terkel: *130*
Katherine Dunham: *130*
Kenneth Rexroth (photograph by John Ferren): *133*
Miriam Allen deFord: *139*

ILLUSTRATION CREDITS

Alice Neel: *142, 179, 183*
Aubrey Baldwin: *145*
Paul Corey: *151*
The New York *Daily News: 162*
Vincent McHugh: *171*
Ralph Ellison: *171*
Harry Roskolenko: *174*
Norman Macleod: *180*
James McGraw: *185*
Mrs. Vardis Fisher: *202*
Joseph Berger: *214*
Dora Thea Hettwer (photographs by Katharine Kellock): *82, 231, 233, 271*
Reed Harris: *234*
Lisle Reese: *236*
Morton Royse: *279*

Index

407